Fabrics in Celebration from the Collection

Fabrics in Celebration from the Collection

Peggy Stoltz Gilfoy

Technical Analysis by Katherine Dolk-Ellis

Indianapolis Museum of Art
1983

3

Editor: Jean Kane

Designer: Marcia K. Hadley

Photographer: Robert Wallace

Typesetting and Composition: Weimer Typesetting Company, Inc., Indianapolis

Color Separations: Loxley Color Separations, Inc., Dayton, Ohio

Printing: Design Printing Company, Inc., Indianapolis

Distributed in cooperation with Indiana University Press, Bloomington

This catalogue and the exhibition on which it is based would not have been possible without the generous support of several agencies, which we gratefully acknowledge here:

Research and editorial costs have been funded, in part, by a generous grant from the Andrew W. Mellon Foundation. Support for the exhibition has been provided by a grant from the National Endowment for the Arts, a federal agency, Washington, D.C.

Additional funding for the exhibition and this catalogue has been provided by the Indiana Arts Commission and the Institute of Museum Services, a federal agency that offers general operating and program support to the nation's museums.

ISBN: 0–936260–09–2   cloth

ISBN: 0–936260–10–6   paper

Library of Congress Catalog Card Number: 82–084075

On the cover: Detail, Fez, Morocco, *Häiti*

Acknowledgements

This catalogue and exhibition would never have been realized if not for the generous aid of a large number of my friends. Even after a lifetime of research, an individual could not accurately describe the wide range of textile traditions without such assistance. My own research has focused on Southeast Asian, European, and some aspects of American and African textile arts. A number of people unstintingly provided information on the rest of the material. John Vollmer and Louise Mackie of the Textiles Department of the Royal Ontario Museum, Toronto, supervised the Far Eastern and Middle Eastern entries by supplying primary information and reading the final copy for errors. John must also be credited for naming the exhibition. Mattiebelle Gittinger of The Textile Museum, Washington, D.C., assisted me with some vexing problems related to Indonesian and Indian textiles; Ann Rowe, also of The Textile Museum, helped me with the Nasca and Chimu entries; and Christa Thurman of the Department of Textiles at the Art Institute of Chicago advised me on some particularly difficult European examples. Maria Luisa Herrera of the Museo Nacional del Pueblo Español in Madrid and Natalie Rothstein and Santina Levey from the Victoria and Albert Museum in London graciously answered my written pleas for assistance, as did Alan Sawyer of the University of Vancouver and James Fox of the Australian National University, Canberra.

Two sections of the catalogue would never have appeared in their present form without the aid of some extremely devoted volunteers. Janet Welliver set herself to the task of researching the fascinating Niblack family. Barbara Frank, a graduate student in African art history at Indiana University, did research on our Moroccan Berber woven textiles for her master's thesis. Elizabeth Lantz, a former graduate student in art history at Ohio University, Athens, worked with Barbara on Moroccan embroideries. Dorit Paul, a longtime docent at the Museum, took on the complicated iconography of our German embroidered apron (cat. 123), as well as several other difficult problems. Sue Claycomb and Alice Berkowitz, also Museum docents, have helped with the research and proofreading of the catalogue and with other tasks. Raj Bavanati and Muhammed Zafrulla Khan helped me with Persian and Arabic translations. Anthony Janson, Senior Curator at the Indianapolis Museum, gave advice when all other sources seemed unproductive. Without this extraordinary research effort, the catalogue would have been greatly diminished.

Katherine Dolk-Ellis did the technical research and analysis of each piece and coordinated the activity of two of my most devoted volunteers, Gene Wright and Miriam Taylor. These two women, who have been helping me for many years on projects especially related to embroidery, analyzed the various stitches used in the pieces and attempted the difficult task of developing a terminology that would be both comprehensible to the generalist and specific enough for the specialist. I also extend my thanks to Michael Ellis for translating technical descriptions from French and German texts and to Leon Stodulski and his assistant, Mary Kennedy, for analyzing all of the metallic threads in the textiles. The results of their work are evident. Ms. Dolk-Ellis prepared and assembled all these data in a logical and consistent catalogue form.

The basis for our analyses is Irene Emery's landmark publication, *The Primary Structure of Fabrics*. Much of our terminology is derived from her book, and I refer the reader to it for further explanations of technique. Through this effort I hope we have set a standard that others will follow and further develop.

Harold Mailand, Associate Conservator for Textiles, supervised conservation of the textiles presented here with the aid of assistants Judy Ozone and Dorothy Stites. Not only did they prepare the pieces for exhibition, but they also made important contributions to our technical analysis. I am deeply indebted to them for their help and advice on a wide range of issues. Further details on their procedures can be found in the Conservator's Report.

Countless hours of sympathetic help were given by friends who read the manuscript for clarity and by editor Jean Kane, who made my technical language comprehensible. Her editorial assistants, Carol Haywood and Jeanne Hill, exhibited diligence and grace under pressure.

Photographer Robert Wallace overcame the numerous difficulties inherent in reproducing textiles to present the stunning plates.

As always, Marcia Hadley arranged the presentation of the material and illustrations into a beautifully designed whole.

Of course, the catalogue is only one facet of the preparation of such an exhibition. It must be arranged in a way that will make sense visually and show each piece at its best. For this Herculean task—with such a diversity of material—I commend chief preparator Sherman O'Hara for planning the installation and his able crew for executing it. His sensitivity to the presentation of the textile arts is always a wonder to me.

Finally I owe a debt to the donors; to the trustees, who supported my purchases; to the Museum itself; and to director Robert Yassin, all of whom allowed me the opportunity to execute such a monumental yet pleasurable task.

The effort was arduous and fraught with frustration, but in the end it is my honor to present the best of our textile collection in this, our centennial year.

Formation of the Collection

Though the first textiles in the collection were acquired in 1888, a serious acquisition effort began with the purchase of over one hundred Chinese textiles and costumes in 1906—a very early date to collect such objects. A number of generous donors added to our European collections until 1915, and the Museum itself purchased European, Indian, and Iranian textiles during that time. In 1916 the Museum acquired a group of 130 Japanese textiles, more Middle Eastern and European items, and the first of the many generous gifts that form the nucleus of our present collection. Eliza M. Niblack's donation of over six hundred pieces contained more Japanese fabrics, and it was probably her guidance that led the Museum to purchase pieces from Asia and the Middle East. From 1917 through 1925 various groups of European, Asian, and Middle Eastern pieces were added, among them a group of carpets donated by the Delavan Smith Bequest in 1925, to establish the rug collection. In 1930 Miss Niblack gave another four hundred textiles to the Museum, and after her death in 1933, the remaining two thousand examples in her collection were donated. These two groups form the core of the present collection, which contains a number of masterpieces, as the exhibition and catalogue reveal.

Recent research has unveiled the truly remarkable character of the Niblack family, especially of Eliza and her brother Albert. William Ellis Niblack (1822–1893) and Eliza Ann Sherman, William's second wife, had three children: Albert Parker, born in 1859; Eliza Marie, in 1864; and Sarah Lydia, in 1868. William had an illustrious political career as an Indiana state legislator, a United States Representative, and later, an Indiana Supreme Court judge. Although the children were born in Vincennes, the family moved to Indianapolis in 1889.

Albert was graduated from the Naval Academy at Annapolis in 1880. His first assignments were to the South Pacific and the North Atlantic commands. In 1884 he was relocated to Alaska, where he must have developed an intense interest in its native peoples, for in 1887 he published *Coast Indians of Southern Alaska and Northern British Columbia*, an early ethnographic study of these peoples that is still recognized today. From 1898 through 1907, Albert was stationed in various areas of the Pacific. He also spent two years at the Naval Academy before receiving later assignments, to Buenos Aires, in 1910, and Berlin, in 1913. After leaving Berlin, he spent three years with the Atlantic Fleet and in 1917 began his command of U.S. naval forces based in Gibraltar. He was placed in command of the U.S. naval forces in European waters in 1921 and retired as a vice admiral in July, 1923.

Albert died in 1929 and is buried in Arlington Cemetery.

Throughout his life, Albert apparently sustained the early interest in cultural anthropology he demonstrated in his first publication. Relatives' accounts and newspaper articles confirm that he was a collector of some note. If the gifts of Northwest Coast Indian art donated to the Museum at his death are any indication, he also had a highly developed aesthetic sense. His posts in the Pacific, Europe, and Gibraltar partially explain the unusual strength of the fabric collections from those areas among the Niblack gifts.

Albert's younger sister Eliza was involved with the fledgling John Herron Art Museum from its beginning in 1906. She apparently made her first trip to Europe in 1907, and during the next few years she lectured on Iranian shawls and Chinese art at the Museum. She traveled to Japan in 1909 and presented material on that culture at the Museum in 1912; in 1915 she arranged a large loan exhibition of oriental art and gave an associated series of lectures. Several accounts mention that although she was offered the curatorship of textiles at the Brooklyn Museum of Art in 1916, war conditions prevented the creation of the position. At that time, Vice Admiral Niblack apparently brought her a number of Moroccan embroideries. Eliza herself may have travelled to Morocco in 1920, but the records are unclear about this. It is definitely known that by 1924 Eliza was living in Brooklyn; whether she had moved there before that year is not documented, however. In 1924 and 1928 loan exhibitions from her textile collection were presented at the Herron Museum. Eliza's death occurred in 1930, when she was killed in the streets of New York by an automobile. Her collection was left to her sister Sarah.

Sarah Lydia, who remained in Indianapolis, belonged to the Propylaeum, the Indiana Historical Society, the Daughters of the American Revolution, and the Episcopal church. She was apparently respected and well liked. She loaned furniture to the Museum for an exhibition in 1930, and the textiles she donated that autumn probably came from her recently deceased sister's collection. In 1932 and 1933 Sarah lent textiles to the Herron Museum for a large exhibition. At Sarah's death in 1933, her nieces inherited the collection. Then living in Chicago, Narcissa Thorne and Lydia Swift were the daughters of William Caldwell Niblack, Sarah and Eliza's oldest brother. Soon after Sarah's death they donated the pieces designated as the Eliza M. and Sarah L. Niblack Collection to the Art Association of Indianapolis. As has been previously outlined, Vice Admiral Albert Niblack and his sister Eliza acquired the bulk of this outstanding collection. Apparently their behavior was not unusual at the time, for several large textile collections that form the nucleus of important museum collections in this country were built during the decades surrounding the beginning of the twentieth century. We in Indianapolis are indeed fortunate to have had individuals of such taste and foresight directing their generosity to a public collection that generations of residents would enjoy.

During the rest of the 1930s, the Museum made a number of purchases, from a fund established by the Niblack Bequest. In 1936 Mrs. Charles Crosley made an important gift of fine nineteenth-century laces. From the 1940s to the 1960s, a number of noteworthy additions were made to the collection. In 1966 Mr. and Mrs. Herman C. Krannert donated an important set of seventeenth-century Belgian tapestries.

Since 1970 there have been several significant donations: one group of over one hundred pieces came from the Robert Morse House, an Art Deco building in Chicago. In 1973 the estate of the late Norman Norell gave the collection five pieces that established the Indiana Fashion Design Collection. In 1976 Mrs. William Garrigues gave the Museum many costumes and accessories from the estate of her mother, Caroline Burford Danner; and Mrs. Gerrish Thurber donated a group of quilts made by her mother-in-law, Marie Webster.

From the late 1970s into the 1980s, the Museum has been enriched by a number of gifts of contemporary costume, especially from designers born in Indiana—Norman Norell, Bill Blass, and Halston. Stanley Weaver and David Campbell have been responsible for arranging many of these donations, which enrich our collection of Indiana-designer fashion, as well as those from other designers working in the United States and Europe.

The significance of this collection is the result of the generosity of donors cited and other, unnamed individuals, as well as benefactors who established purchase funds for the acquisition of important pieces.

The largest single group, European textiles and costumes, forms nearly one-half of the collection. Of the nearly three thousand pieces, about six hundred are costumes and accessories. There are over a thousand examples of Far Eastern textiles and costume, three-quarters of which are from China. Approximately two-thirds of the seven hundred Southeast Asian pieces are from India and the rest from Indonesia. There are about one thousand Middle Eastern examples in the collection, among them a large group of Mediterranean embroideries and about seventy-five rugs. Two hundred Coptic pieces and an important group of over seven hundred textiles from the Islamic cultures of North Africa are also included. Pieces from the Americas compose the smallest group in the collection: among the approximately five hundred North American pieces are costumes, quilts, and coverlets, and the two hundred and fifty Central and South American examples include about fifty pieces from ancient Peru. Finally, there are about one hundred pieces from Subsaharan Africa and Oceania.

Both in quality and in depth, the real strengths of the collection are the European, North African, and Indonesian groups, a status that doubtless largely reflects the interests of the Niblacks, who formed these areas of the collection at the turn of this century.

History of the Department

In the fall of 1973, the Museum established the Textiles Department to maintain and exhibit about seven thousand pieces, including costumes, carpets, tapestries, and other fabrics. Most of the collection had not been previously exhibited or published. Although part of it was briefly shown in 1933, the holdings had been stored for forty years in cardboard boxes, in the basement of the former John Herron Art Institute. In 1974 the Museum began to receive grants to train a conservator in the proper storage and treatment of the collection. By 1980 the majority of the collection was safely stored in the third floor ballroom of the Lilly Pavilion of Decorative Arts, on the grounds of the Indianapolis Museum.

Soon after its founding, the Department launched an active exhibition program to acquaint the public with its extensive holdings. One part of the public education program was realized when the Textile Study Group was established in 1980, and another when students from Indiana and Purdue Universities were accepted as interns. Since then, students and professors alike have worked on specific projects in conservation, collection management, special exhibition, and research. In accordance with this educational mission, the collection is also available to researchers. Part of the collection has, in fact, been specifically designed for study: the Museum's docents and staff use it for educational programs that require pieces that can be handled. In summary, the goal of this department is to introduce its important collection to the general public as well as to the scholar.

Textiles Exhibition List

Eighteenth-Century European Textiles	October, 1973
Lace	February, 1974
American Costumes from 1850–1950	August, 1974
Indiana Coverlets	November, 1974
Embroidery	March, 1975 Indianapolis Museum of Art at Columbus (IMAC), 1975
Old, New, Borrowed, Blue	June, 1975
Printed European Textiles	November, 1975
Chinese Textiles	December, 1975
Beadwork on Costumes	April, 1976
A Stitch for all Seasons: American Quilts from the Collection	1976
African Decorative Arts	March, 1976
Buttons from the Collection of Mrs. R. Norris Shreve	December, 1976
Indiana Coverlets	July, 1977
A Loomful of Animals	August, 1977
Quilts from the Collection	December, 1977 IMAC, 1978
The Fabric of Jewish Life	February, 1978
Indonesian Textiles: Ikat and Batik	March, 1978
Eighteenth- and Nineteenth-Century Printed and Dyed European Textiles	Purdue University, April, 1978
Guatemalan Textiles	July, 1978
Masterpieces from the Textile Collection	September, 1978
A Rustle of Silk: Costumes from the Caroline Burford Danner Estate	October, 1979 IMAC, 1980 Campbell House, St. Louis, 1981
A Decorative Arts Potpourri: Recent Accessions	January, 1980
Ikat	July, 1980
Key Acquisitions since 1970	September, 1980
Birds and Flowers on Porcelain and Textiles	September, 1980
Masterpieces of Embroidery from the Collection	January, 1981 IMAC, 1981
Quilts and Coverlets from the Collection	December, 1981
Fashion Technology: A Tribute to the Modiste	August, 1982
Chinese Sleevebands	December, 1982

Conservator's Report

Though conservation is often thought synonymous with preservation treatments, this work includes an equal share of scientific analysis. In addition to prolonging the life of an object, the Museum's conservation department works with the curator to determine the piece's construction, materials, condition, and authenticity. This centennial exhibition has given the staff a unique chance to further technical understanding of 180 of the 7,000 textiles and costumes in the permanent collection.

Scientific examination reveals not only the present condition of an object, but also the stages of its construction and later alteration, whether by time or man. In a museum this evidence is an invaluable guide to the curator in charting the history of a piece, and to the conservator in treating it. To aid their research, they may put a particular object through a series of optical examinations, chemical tests, and photographic procedures.

For this exhibit, data were recorded on worksheets kept for each piece. Black-and-white photographs or color slides were taken to document selected tests. The Museum will keep this documentation in a permanent file for future research. An immediate benefit from our intensive efforts to examine and analyze can be seen, however, in the body of the catalogue itself. The didactic and technical information that accompanies each entry directly results from the research and data compiled over the past year. The expanded and detailed description of each piece is unusual in a major textile exhibition catalogue. This considerably updated information is intended to provide—for the scholar and interested lay person alike—a workable reference for future research as well as comparisons of similar textiles and costumes.

Here, then, is a brief explanation of the various, and often innovative, applications of examination techniques used to research this exhibition.

I. *Examination of Textiles with the Unaided Eye*
The first step in analyzing a textile is viewing the object with the unaided eye, under natural, incandescent, and/or fluorescent light. This procedure immediately supplies information about the object's fabrication and construction, as well as its current state of repair. During this phase the examiner measures the height, width, and depth of the piece. S/he then sketches it to indicate its overall shape, orientation, fabrication, and construction, and records its design motifs, pattern repeat, finish, dye color, and surface embellishment.

The examiner also assesses the object's condition without using instruments. During the condition report stage, s/he notes the piece's strength or fragility and looks for irregularities and damage. Signs of distortion, abrasion, fiber loss, tears, cuts, soil, stains, yellowing, fading, dye bleeding, insect damage, mildew, previous repair, finishes, marks or labels, support structures, linings, and backing material can then help the conservator select the appropriate treatments.

II. *Examination of Textiles with the Microscope*
With controlled light sources, specialized lenses can greatly enhance the eye's ability to examine the techniques, material, and condition of a piece. The examiner's tools may range from low-power lenses that can enlarge the image of an area up to five times (5X), to high-power ones that can enlarge it up to ten thousand times (10,000X). The great advantage to examining a textile with a microscope is that no part of the textile is removed, altered, or damaged in any way, and can even be viewed *in situ*.

In micro-sampling, another means of analysis, the examiner carefully removes a minute fiber sample (less than ½ in., or 1.2 cm long), mounts it on a glass slide, and views it under a microscope. The advantages of this method are twofold: testing is completed away from the piece—so it is not handled excessively—and the samples can be collected, retained, and easily re-examined.

Microscopic examinations provide the primary data needed to identify and understand the materials and techniques of each piece. Each technical entry in this catalogue is based on the following consistent and duplicable procedures.

A. **Structure Analysis.** The examiner used a Bausch & Lomb stereomicroscope with a 10X to 20X magnification and directed light, as well as the unaided eye, to analyze the object's weave structure and embroidery stitches and the twist and ply of the individual yarns.

B. **Thread Count.** To determine the accurate thread, mesh, or knot count of each piece, a Sutter Pick Counter was used under the available light. With this instrument, a monocular device with an interchangeable 7X or 14X broad field lens, the examiner registered each successive thread with a finger touch control counter.

C. **Fiber Identification.** Fibers were identified through micro-sampling. The examiner took a sample from each different component of construction—that is, from the warp, weft, and surface embellishment—mounted it on a glass slide, and separated the individual fibers. By transmitted light, the examiner then observed the sample under a Zeiss polarizing microscope, using 156.25X to 390X magnification. By manipulating the light and magnifications, the examiner could readily identify the textile fibers by comparing their physical characteristics to known controls.

III. *Examination and Photo-Documentation of Textiles Using Visible and Invisible Radiation.*

A. **Visible Light.** Along with written records, photographs are indispensable aids in surveying the physical components and condition of a textile. They not only document what the eye can see under normal light, but with appropriate filtration can also record the effects of invisible radiation. Most of these photographs are taken under normal light—that is, daylight or incandescent or fluorescent light. Conservators most often use 35 mm color slides to record the piece before, during, and after treatment, and may supplement these with 4 x 5 in., 35 mm, or Polaroid 52 black-and-white photographs.

In controlled photography situations, the examiner uses tungsten lighting (3200° K). The lamps stand either at an angle or perpendicular to the piece as the object's surface is photographed. When the fragility or size of the piece prevent the use of controlled light, it is photographed with existing—that is, overhead fluorescent or incandescent—light, with the appropriate camera filters for color balance.

The examiner may employ photomicrography when s/he needs a more detailed record of a particular construction or documentation of a particular condition. By using a camera and various kinds of microscopes, s/he can enlarge an area from 10X magnification, with an ordinary microscope, to 10,000X magnification, with an electron microscope. This form of documentation is particularly helpful in isolating, identifying, and recording the specific physical components and conditions of a piece. Additionally, this type of photodocumentation precludes re-examining the piece, and consequently, the conservator and curator limit their handling of the object.

B. **Ultra-Violet Fluorescence.** Ultra-violet rays, found in sunlight and various forms of artificial light, occur in the invisible range of the spectrum. Ordinarily, one of the conservator's primary concerns is the elimination of ultra-violet rays since they can considerably damage dye stuffs and organic material, but under controlled situations ultra-violet light can be a valuable diagnostic tool. The degree to which various substances absorb ultra-violet, as well as the amount of visible fluorescence they produce, is of interest to the conservator. By examining a textile under ultra-violet light, s/he can discern certain irregularities in the surface, such as various types of dyes, fabric finishes, and repairs. Notably, the examiner can also discern previous treatments such as bleaching, over dyeing, or cleaning with contemporary commercial washing aids, which contain optical whiteners or brighteners. These techniques not only aid understanding of the textile's previous treatments, but may help the monitoring of subsequent ones as well.

A common source of ultra-violet rays are the fluorescent tubes that contain mercury vapor in a partial vac-

Figure 1. Black-and-white photograph, using tungsten lighting of Swiss Gothic embroidery, cat. 100 (¼ sec. at f/11)

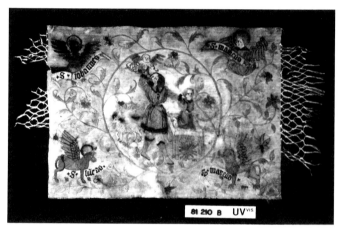

Figure 2. Ultra-violet light photograph of Swiss Gothic embroidery, cat. 100 (1 min. at f/6.3 with #8 filter)

uum, "black light." Film can record visible fluorescence produced by ultra-violet radiation if the camera is fitted with a filter that absorbs other wavelengths.

When the Gothic embroidery (cat. 100) was examined under ultra-violet light, considerable information about its condition and previous treatment was discovered. This examination revealed the locations of prior spot-bleaching with a modern agent, enhanced a large stain in the textile's lower center portion, and showed a radiating discoloration around the eagle in its upper left hand corner (figs. 1 and 2).

During the treatment the conservator found a faint image on a linen panel behind the rear orphrey of the chasuble (cat. 96). Under the ultra-violet light the image was enhanced. This examination procedure facilitated further curatorial research in the dating and provenance of this interestingly married chasuble (figs. 3 and 4).

C. **X-Radiography.** X-rays are often capable of penetrating substances that appear opaque to the unaided eye. Exposing film to x-rays as they pass through an object produces a radiograph. The different densities of the substances, their atomic weight, and their ability to

Figure 3. Black-and-white photograph, using tungsten lighting, of the linen panel found behind the rear orphrey of chasuble, cat. 96 (⅛ sec. at f/30)

Figure 4. Ultra-violet light photograph of the linen panel found behind the rear orphrey of chasuble, cat. 96 (1 min. at f/6.3 with #8 filter)

absorb or inhibit the x-rays produce the contrast, or image, on the film. Radiographs have been extremely important to painting and object conservators in determining the condition, techniques, and alterations in a variety of art objects. Here, conservators experimented with x-ray of textiles with multiple layers or metallic threads to see what information it might reveal. For these experiments, the examiners used black-and-white Polaroid film, which produced a positive image of the object.

X-raying the lower panel of the rear orphrey of the chasuble (cat. 96) produced startling clarity and delineation. The radiographs could delineate the different diameters of the metal strips and the difference in the wrapping of the metal threads around the various cores in the embroidery, trim, and brocade of the chasuble. The examiner could also discern intricate detail about the weave structure, embellishments, and construction methods. S/he could read both silk and linen weaves along with the selvedges and seam allowances. The radiograph was sensitive enough to pick up even the dyed silk embroidery thread that formed the saint's eye. In addition, the radiograph showed continuation of the embroidered gold work under the saint's appliquéd head scarf and an earlier attempt to stabilize the abraded bottom trim of the orphrey (figs. 5 and 6). These radiographs, which were helpful in distinguishing different

layers of construction and various fabrication techniques, should therefore prove useful in examining multi-layered textiles that would otherwise require physically separating and removing original material for analysis and thus disrupt the historical integrity of the piece.

IV. *Examination of Textiles with Chemical Tests*
A. **Dye Solubility Test.** The conservation staff routinely checks the dye solubility of the textiles and costumes it receives for examination and treatment. When a wet or dry cleaning method is being considered, solubility testing is necessary to determine whether dyes are fast. This information is also important to have in the permanent record in case the textile's fragile condition or exhibition device later precludes testing and handling.

In this test a drop of deionized water and a solution of deionized water with an anionic detergent and/or a dry cleaning solvent are sequentially placed on selected dye areas of the textile. After the droplet has soaked in, the fibers are pressed with white blotter paper to determine if the dye is fugitive, that is, capable of bleeding into other design areas.

B. **Chemical Dye Tests.** When a textile's age or authenticity is in question, testing to determine its dye group may prove helpful; in this procedure micro-samples of dyed fibers are boiled in a series of different reagents. Different dye groups respond differently to the

Figure 5. Black-and-white photograph, using tungsten lighting, of the lower panel of the rear orphrey of chasuble, cat. 96 (2 sec. at f/22)

Figure 6. Composite Polaroid 52 radiograph of the lower panel of the rear orphrey of chasuble, cat. 96 (16 kilovolts, 3 milliamperes, 3 min.)

reagents, so if a dye responds in a certain manner when tested, its group can be extrapolated. The history and development of synthetic dyes has been well documented. Synthetic dyes were not in commercial use before 1860, so if a positive reaction to the reagents denotes a synthetic class of dyes, a probable date can be ascribed. *Green's Tables* were followed in these tests. Other tests that are more sophisticated, such as thin-layer chromatography and emission spectroscopy, might have been more conclusive, but were not yet feasible.

V. *Specialized Methods of Examining Textiles*
The previous examinations were conducted either on site in the textile and costume study area or in the conservation laboratory of the Indianapolis Museum of Art. What follows is a brief description of a special research project undertaken at Indiana University-Purdue University at Indianapolis and Western Electric of Indianapolis. This study, designed to analyze the individual metallic threads of each textile in this catalogue, has provided invaluable information about the technology associated with the use of precious metals in textiles.

A. **Atomic Emission Spectrographic Analysis.** This analysis was performed through micro-sampling. The examiner inspected each sample under a Nikon optical microscope, using 40X or 100X magnification under reflected light, a process that sometimes revealed how the metal had been fashioned into a thread and how much the metal had been corroded. A 3 mm length of this sample was then removed, placed in a graphite electrode, packed with pure graphite, and subjected to Atomic Emission Spectrographic analysis (see Technical Appendix). The examiners determined the elements present spectrographically and estimated the relative amounts of

gold, silver, copper, and other elements in each strip by comparing spectral line intensities with a known standard and with the appropriate values, given in the tables. Each element could, therefore, be identified as a major, minor, or trace amount.

B. **Scanning Electron Microscopy (SEM).** The examiners studied selected samples with a scanning electron microscope, a process that involved examining a cross-section of the metallic thread. Mounted in epoxy resin, the sample was sectioned by cutting it perpendicular to its length with an Ultramicrotome, using a diamond knife. This specimen was then placed in the vacuum chamber of the microscope and scanned with a narrow beam of high energy electrons. Using an x-ray energy analyzer, the examiners could then determine the identity and estimate the relative amounts of the metallic elements present throughout the strip. A series of photographs, at magnifications of up to 10,000X, were taken for measurement and study of the specimens. The SEM studies revealed the shape and dimensions of the thread as seen in cross-section, the width and thickness of the metal strip, the thickness of the gold layer on its surface, its relative metallic composition (except for trace amounts), an estimate of the distribution of the major and minor elements within it from the top to the back surface, and an idea of the extent of its corrosion.

Acknowledgements
The research and examination activities undertaken this past year would not have been possible without the close cooperation of Indianapolis Museum of Art staff and volunteers in the curatorial and conservation departments, as well as research specialists and scientists in Indianapolis. This author would like to thank the

20

individuals who gave their time, enthusiasm, and expertise to advance the study and care of these textiles and costumes.

I would like to thank Katherine Dolk-Ellis for selecting micro-samples and examining and coordinating all the information about structure analysis, thread count, and fiber identification for each piece in the catalogue.

Special thanks must be given to Leon P. Stodulski, Assistant Professor of Analytical Chemistry, Indiana University-Purdue University at Indianapolis, Mary M. Kennedy, his graduate assistant, and Delbert Nauman, Senior Development Engineer at Western Electric of Indianapolis, for their combined efforts to advance the understanding of the technology associated with precious metals in textiles. This study should prove to be an invaluable reference for the application of scientific examinations for works of art.

Judy Ozone, Assistant Conservator of Textiles, and Dorothy Stites, Textile Technician, have worked diligently to write numerous condition reports and treatment proposals. They also cleaned, treated, and mounted textiles for this exhibition. Without their dedication to conservation and their penchant for detail and scheduling, this exhibition could not have been prepared.

Mae Danneman and Beulah Cobb, long-term textile conservation volunteers, have given considerable time and done exquisite handwork for this exhibition. Their perspective, enthusiasm, and good humor have cheered us all. I am also grateful to the Indiana State Historical Society Library for allowing Ramona Duncan, Assistant Conservator, to assist us with treatments during the weeks before the opening.

My thanks to Ken Myers, mannequin designer; Michael Ellis, carpenter for exhibition strainers; Cynthia Kuniej and Charla Adams, volunteers, for preparing exhibition mounts; and Sherman O'Hara, Chief Preparator, and his staff—Sam Smith, Ted Allen, Tom Keesee, Cindy Dunham-Heimbuch, and Laura Marshall—for constructing and preparing the many handsomely crafted exhibition devices and mounts. With their assistance the textiles and costumes in this exhibition have been safely and beautifully presented to the gallery viewer.

Martin J. Radecki, Chief Conservator; David A. Miller, Associate Conservator of Paintings; Rick Sherin, Assistant Conservator of Objects; and E. John Hartmann, Jr., Assistant Conservator of Paintings, have been most generous to share with us their technical training and their knowledge of diagnostic equipment. Their cooperation enabled us to apply sophisticated analytical procedures to the research and documentation of the pieces in this exhibition. Their encouragement and interest in our concerns have been most welcome.

Harold F. Mailand
Associate Conservator of Textiles

Author's Note

This catalogue, written mainly for the Museum's public, presents our collection both for aesthetic enjoyment and educational enlightenment. Many aspects of textile history can be illustrated within the confines of a finite group of objects such as this one. Textiles' manufacturing techniques, materials, cultural use, and importance in international trade are all outlined, as is the infinitely rich design vocabulary. The strengths and weaknesses of the collection, as well as the preferences of the author, determined that some aspects would be dwelt upon and others treated lightly.

In presenting our textile collection for the first time, it seemed most appropriate to outline its history. Generous individuals who contribute to public collections are the Museum's lifeblood; this publication is ultimately a document of appreciation for those donors. Further, the catalogue serves to display the collection to its best advantage both artistically and intellectually, so that the public will be able to gain a greater appreciation for the world's textile arts and the men and women who made them.

Each culture creates art forms that uniquely reflect its heritage. Some of these traits are outlined in the sections introducing each cultural region. Following these general remarks are analyses specifically related to individual examples. In some sections the pieces are arranged by chronology, and in others by function. Because of the importance of the Southeast Asian pieces and the unique world view they exemplify, Indonesia and India are presented first. The next entries describe the Far Eastern cultures of China and Japan. The catalogue then moves from East to West, traversing Asia and the southern Mediterranean, to discuss the Islamic world. Finally, Europe and America are presented, beginning with the interaction between Islamic and European textiles in the fifteenth century. The two are treated as a single unit because they share many technical, design, and historical features. At the end of that section are the textiles produced by the native Americans, both to the north and the south, as well as those made by the peoples living in Subsaharan West Africa. That this arrangement is somewhat arbitrary is understood, but any method of organizing such disparate material would place artificial constraints on it. The geographical presentation is intended, then, to illuminate many facets of the historical relationships these regions have had.

Certain aspects of the catalogue's arrangement should be clarified. The notes located at the end of each section, as well as the publication information section in individual entries, give minimal information and are intended to serve only as a guide to the bibliography. Contained within the bibliography are a number of citations related to Moroccan weaving and embroidery that should aid researchers in the future. Since explanation of most technical terms is located somewhere in the text, the index is arranged to serve as a glossary. It contains references to the techniques, materials, equipment, function, and native names of the pieces in the catalogue. The page that gives an explanation of a term is indicated in italics.

One of the most important aspects of this catalogue is the complete technical analysis, prepared by Katherine Dolk-Ellis. At the beginning of this project it was decided that the catalogue would serve two equally important functions: illustrating the depth of the collection to those unfamiliar with it and providing a complete physical description of each piece for the specialist. Such information is critical to understanding the medium of textile arts and, when combined with historical sources and known examples, serves as an invaluable tool for dating and attribution. Two parts of this process are particularly important. First is an initial attempt to bring order to the description of embroidery stitches. What we have done here is merely a beginning: much further work is necessary. The other innovative procedure is analysis of the chemical components in the metallic threads. In the past, the differences between Chinese and European metal threads, for example, were known in a general way, but precise readings were not prepared. Here, we have given those readings in the Technical Appendix for the reader's edification. Unfortunately, the results were not known in time for cultural analysis to be presented in the text, but the statistics are available for interested individuals. We hope that these results will be used by the scholars of the future as tools for advancing textile research.

P. S. G.

Notes on Technical Analysis

Technical analysis provides the vital statistics of the art work's physical features. Analysis is especially important in documenting a textile because of the wide range of materials and techniques used in fabrics from various cultures and periods. Textile analysis reveals the weave structure; construction and embellishment techniques; the materials' content, such as fiber identification, thread composition, and color; and the dimensions. The curator uses this valuable technical information, along with his or her stylistic analysis, in determining the textile's date and attribution. Style may change rapidly within a culture and designs may be influenced by or borrowed from other cultures, but methods of construction remain relatively constant. They are, therefore, reliable indicators of a piece's origin.

The technical analysis of each textile in the exhibition appears with the catalogue entry and photograph so that the reader may refer to the image while reading the information. Techniques are indexed to aid comparative studies. Each textile is identified in the entry heading by artist, if known; place of manufacture; name and date; a brief technical description; dimensions; and donor and accession number. The artist may be a member of a particular cultural group, or a named individual. The place of manufacture is listed in ascending order, beginning with the smallest area: the town or city, area, region, and country are given, depending upon which are known. A generic term is used for the name of the object, followed by the cultural name, if it is known; the title, if it is given; and the date. The brief technical information describes both the materials and the techniques, and includes the cultural terminology in parentheses. These terms are defined in the glossary. For a complete technical description, the reader should refer to the conclusion of the entry. Dimensions are given in inches and the equivalent centimeters in parentheses; the largest dimension is listed first. The directions of the warp and weft are also indicated. Because a fabric naturally stretches and contracts, the textiles were measured under slight tension. Here, the inches are rounded off to the nearest half-inch and centimeters to the nearest five-tenths of a centimeter. The dimension of the opposite sides of a textile is rarely identical on all four sides, so the largest dimension, including the fringe, is reported.

The technical analysis is divided into three major categories: materials, techniques, and measurements (which includes thread count, pattern repeat, and overall dimensions). This listing begins with the description of the smallest unit of materials and continues in ascending order to the overall description of techniques.

Materials, the first major heading in the technical entry, are listed in outline form for the basic fabric, embroidery, trim, backing, lining, and other fabrics. After the weave structure is determined, each weaving element, such as the warp and weft, and type of embellishment, such as the embroidery and trim, is examined to determine fiber content, composition, and color. A fiber sample of each element was viewed under a polarizing light microscope to determine the fiber content.

The majority of the textiles in this exhibition are constructed of natural fibers; the remaining few are synthetic, or man-made, fibers that are identified if they could be clearly matched with a known sample. The natural fibers fall into five main groups: bast, leaf, cotton (vegetable/cellulosic), wool, and silk (animal/protein). Bast fibers are obtained from the stems of dicotyledonous plants and include flax or linen, hemp, ramie, and paper mulberry. Definite identification of the various bast fibers is difficult; however, many samples can be matched with known materials. Leaf fibers are taken from the leaf and/or leaf stalks of monocotyledonous plants, and include abaca and raffia. Cotton fibers are the seed hair of a cotton plant. In this analysis no distinction is made between the plant varieties or the mercerized and unmercerized fibers. Wool fibers come from animal hair, most often from sheep. The term wool also includes goat hair, and a sample that closely resembles a known sample of common goat hair is noted as such. No distinction is made between different breeds of sheep, such as merino, or between breeds of goats such as mohair or kashmir. When forming the cocoon, a silkworm excretes a continuous filament that is silk. The silkworm is actually the larva of a moth, and the filaments are excreted in pairs in a sticky substance that binds them together. No distinction is made between cultivated or tussah (wild) silk, or gummed and degummed silk.

Metallic threads are a type of natural thread manufactured by wrapping an inorganic metal strip around a natural fiber core thread. The metallic content of the strip was analyzed by a chemist, whose findings are recorded in the Technical Appendix. In the technical entry only the major and minor elements are listed, separated by the word "with." As explained in the appendix, some of the metals were applied to a fibrous backing, which is referred to as "paper" in the entry. The direction of twist around the core thread and the appearance of color are also described. The core threads are presented in the same manner that the other natural fibers are.

The structural composition of a thread describes the number of plies and the direction of twist. Most natural fibers, except silk and some bast, are short lengths that must be twisted or spun together to form a thread. A group of fibers twisted together is a single-ply thread. Two single threads, combined, form a two-ply thread. The direction of twist refers to the angle of thread fibers as they turn around a central axis, as compared to the cross bar of the letter S or Z. One ply (or more) may be twisted so tightly that it tends to turn back on itself, a condition that is labeled "overspun." Silk need not be spun at all because of the long length of the filaments, so it has "no twist" or a "slight twist." Silk may also be broken into short lengths and spun like other fibers.

The color of the threads of each set of elements is described in the most basic names for hues: yellow, orange, red, violet, blue, green, white, tan (because so many of the fibers were not dyed but could not be described as white), gray, and black. These names may be qualified with further description, such as light, medium, or dark, or with a number of shades; they also may be modified by another hue name connected with a hyphen. For example, gold is called brown-yellow. When a fabric of the same structure and material is in different solid colors, the word "or" appears in the listing of colors. "Gold," "silver," and "copper" are reserved for the metallic thread descriptions. By avoiding popular names for colors, the descriptions are less subjective or likely to change.

A precise description of color is impossible because its appearance changes according to the surrounding colors and the character of the light. The determination of color in this analysis was made with natural light, that is, indirect sunlight, in the context of the textile; in other words, the color is not separated from the surrounding ones. Furthermore, the colors are described as they appear today. No attempt was made to try to determine the original color. Most of the textiles are colored with natural dyes, which often change over time. In this analysis the type of dye, whether natural or synthetic, was not determined.

If dyes or pigments were applied after the weaving process, as they may be in printing or painting, the colors are listed under a separate heading from the weaving elements. Dyes are coloring agents that penetrate the fabric and bind to the fibers; in contrast, pigments stay on the surface of the fabric. If no distinction could be made about the coloring agent, the designation "dyes/pigments" appears in the entry.

Technique is the second major heading of the technical entries. It begins with a complete description of weave structure, or other interworking of the elements, of the basic fabric. This examiner used the system developed by Irene Emery for classifying and describing textile structures. The system attempts to identify every single element and/or sets of elements in the textile and to define their relationship to one another. According to this method, the physical characteristics of the construction of the textile are considered, though the kind of tools employed in its manufacture—such as a Jacquard loom or the drawloom—need not be known.

First, the ground weave or combination of weaves is listed, followed by the other weave structures that appear on the front face of the textile in compound weave structures. These weaves may be identified through the terms "figure" and "background" to help define areas of the design, but these descriptive aids should not be confused with technical terms. In a compound weave structure, each set of supplementary warps or wefts is listed. Wefts are described as continuous (selvedge to selvedge), or discontinuous (not selvedge to selvedge; in the pattern area only). Though the same principle applies to the supplementary warp, this technique is seldom used, so the supplementary warps listed here are continuous unless otherwise noted. The definition of continuous/discontinuous also applies to the main warp and weft.

The proportions of the weave structure are the ratios of the supplementary elements to the main elements—information that is reflected in the thread count. Selvedges, headings, finish, fringe, and other features are described when appropriate. Most of the textiles were examined under a stereo-zoom microscope so the examiner could accurately identify the techniques.

Following the description of weave structure, the post-weaving process of coloring and/or fabricating is listed. Patterning the textile with applied color includes the processes of printing, painting, and resist dyeing. The specific techniques of coloring and fabricating are defined in the glossary.

Analysis of the embroidery stitches forms another major part of the description of techniques. Each stitch was examined by an embroiderer who looked for the relationship of the continuous element with itself, with the other elements, and with the ground fabric. The stitches were named according to the terms given in Barbara Snook's book, *Embroidery Stitches*, and they were then grouped into flat, looped, or combination stitches. The stitches not diagrammed in *Embroidery Stitches* were found in other sources.

Finally trim, lining, backing, and other fabrics are analyzed, and the weave structure is given when possible.

The third and fourth headings, thread count and pattern repeat, concern the measurements of the textile. The overall dimensions of the piece are given in the entry heading, so they are not repeated in the technical entry.

The thread count, which is the number of threads or group of threads per unit, is given for each set of weaving elements as an average number of threads per inch (2.533 cm). This number was determined by averaging the measurements of three different areas of the textile with a pick counter. The width and, therefore, the warp thread count may vary along the length of the fabric, particularly in those woven on a body-tensioned loom. The weft thread count may differ if the materials or the density of wefts used are various. Warp or weft threads may be paired so that the group functions as a single element. Thread count, often referred to as ends per inch, describes the number of threads or the group of threads that functions as a single one. To give the most accurate description, the count is given for the number of warp ends or weft picks, and the number of individual threads is given in parentheses.

Three other types of thread counts may be listed. The knots per inch of supplementary weft knotted pile is recorded both warpwise (along the warp) and weftwise (along the weft), figures that may be multiplied to determine the total number of knots per square inch. The mesh, or open background, of bobbin lace is counted vertically and horizontally, as are the threads of the solid areas. The number of buttonhole stitches in needle lace and of looped stitches in knitting is also counted.

The pattern repeat is the smallest unit of design, which, when repeated, constitutes the overall design. It is measured warpwise and weftwise in several places on the textile, and an average number is given. The measurement of a pattern repeat of a printed textile remains constant, but a woven repeat may vary depending upon how compactly the weft is placed. A full width repeat refers to a pattern that does not repeat weftwise, or across the width (selvedge to selvedge), of the textile. A point repeat is a pattern that repeats in a mirror image around a central axis of the design, and in the case of these textiles, the weftwise point repeat is the full width of the fabric.

K. D. E.

Glossary of Technical Terms

Some of these terms are defined according to their relation to the textiles in this catalogue rather than to the entire discipline.

appliqué: the application of one fabric on top of another, usually with stitches

background: a descriptive reference to the field of the design, not necessarily the structural ground

band: a narrow woven trim

batik: a method of resist dyeing in which liquified wax or vegetable paste is applied to the fabric and hardens to protect or reserve an area from dye penetration; the resistant material is removed after the fabric has been dyed

batting: the layer of padding between the top and the backing or lining of a fabric; often it is quilted

binding warp or weft: a descriptive reference to the supplementary warp or weft that secures the pattern warp or weft

block printing: a method of patterning a textile by applying dye or pigment with a block that has a raised surface; this is coated with a coloring agent and stamped onto the fabric

bobbin lace: a set of elements that is twisted, plaited, and interlaced; it is worked with threads wound on bobbins

braid: an obliquely interlaced trim

braiding: an obliquely interlaced set of elements; that is, elements worked over and under one another

brocade: a term with no precise meaning, it is used in this catalogue to describe a fabric of supplementary weft patterning with continuous or discontinuous elements

chenille: a novelty thread composed of a core and pile

chiné: a method of patterning textiles with warp and/or weft threads that are printed before weaving, and thus resemble ikat

combination stitches: a combination of at least two distinct types of stitches; "laid work" is included here

compact countered twining: two rows of adjacent twining worked in opposite directions, which produce a chevron pattern

complementary warp or weft: two sets of warp or weft elements essential to the ground weave

compound weave: a weave structure with more than one set of warps and/or wefts.

copper plate printing: a method of creating textile patterns by applying dye or pigment with a flat copper plate engraved or etched with a pattern

copper roller printing: a method similar to copper plate printing except that the printing surface is cylindrical and the dye or pigment is rolled across the surface of the textile

crepe: a fabric that is woven with overspun warps and/or wefts

cut velvet: a structure in which the pile loops are cut, usually during the weaving process

damask: a term with no precise meaning, it is used in this catalogue to describe a fabric with patterned areas of contrasting weave structures that reverse on the other side of the fabric

double interlocking tapestry join: the meeting of two different wefts at the edge of a color area; at this point, each weft wraps around the other weft and a common warp before continuing its path

double weave: two weave structures woven with complementary warps and wefts; they exchange faces in weaving, and thus connect the two layers

eccentric weft: one that is not at right angles to the warp

embroidery: a single set (or sets) of continuous elements worked in and out of a ground fabric with a needle or other tool; they are decorative stitches

felting: the process of adhering fibers to each other by applying friction and pressure

figure: a descriptive reference to a design's pattern or image rather than to a specific weave structure

flat stitches: ones in which the embroidery element is straight between the exit and entrance into fabric, although the thread may overlap itself

floats: an area of the warp or weft element that is produced when the element travels over or under two or more elements of the opposite set

ground weave: the structure formed by the main warp and the main weft in a fabric that has more than one set of warps and/or wefts; it is the structural foundation of the fabric

heading: a narrow woven area at each warp end of the textile that helps to hold the weft in the weaving; usually a weft-faced plain weave

ikat: a method in which threads are resist dyed before they are woven. Patterns are most commonly created by binding structural threads with a resistant fiber in different combinations for several colors. A textile may be warp ikat, weft ikat, or double ikat (both warp and weft)

katazome: a method of Japanese resist dyeing in which a paste is drawn or stenciled onto the fabric to protect an area from dye; the paste is removed after the fabric has been dyed

kilim: a rug of weft-faced plain weave with discontinuous wefts, also called a tapestry weave, that may be used with techniques such as twining; a flat-weave

knitting: the vertical interlooping of a single, continuous element in successive rows of loops

knotted pile: a supplementary weft wrapping that forms a pile through looping and cutting

k'o-ssu: a Chinese term for weft-faced plain weave with discontinuous wefts; a tapestry weave

laminating: the process of adhering fibers to each other by using a sticky substance such as resin or glue

looped stitches: an embroidery element that is interworked with itself and is pulled from a straight path between the exit and the entrance into the fabric; the thread may be knotted

macramé: the interknotting of one set of elements; elements are worked with adjacent ones

main warp or weft: the principle set of elements essential to the fabric structure

mordant: a chemical used with dye to set the color into the fabric

mordant and resist dyeing: a process that combines two dyeing techniques: the application of mordants by painting, drawing, or stamping, and finally dyeing and the application of a wax resist and then dyeing

needle lace: a single, continuous element that is worked with a needle in buttonhole stitches

organza: a sheer, stiff, silk fabric

painting: liquid dye or pigment applied with a brush

pattern warp or weft: a descriptive reference to the supplementary warp or weft used to create design patterns

piecing: the joining of two fabrics with stitches

pile-on-pile velvet: a weave that has contrasting areas of cut and/or uncut pile of different heights

plain weave: the simple interlacing of two sets of elements, the warp and weft, in an over-one-under-one arrangement

plaiting: the interlinking of one set of elements; elements are twisted around adjacent ones but remain in a row

plangi: a method of resist dyeing in which a resist thread is stitched through or tied around gathered fabric to protect areas from dye

prada: an Indonesian term for the application of gold leaf to the surface of a textile

quilting: the joining of at least two layers of fabric using stitches

resist dyeing: a method of protecting areas of the fabric from dye penetration

satin: a fabric produced by satin weave

satin weave: a type of structure that is based on a unit of at least five warps and wefts, in which one set of elements passes over four or more elements, and then under one element of the opposite set, to form long floats in a random alignment; the number 4/1 refers to the number of elements in each over/under sequence—for example, over-four-under-one

selvedge: the warpwise edge of a textile in which wefts encircle the outer warp ends

shibori: a Japanese method of resist dyeing in which the fabric is folded, stitched, tied, and/or clamped to protect areas from dye

slit tapestry join: the point two different wefts meet at the edge of a color area and each weft wraps around adjacent warps, continuing its path without interlocking with the other weft, to form a slit in the textile

solid velvet: a weave in which the pile is the same all over

soumak: successive supplementary weft wrapping in which the element is worked over a group of warps and back under part of the group, and thus encircles the warps—for example, over-four-back-two

spaced dyeing: a coloring of the warp and/or weft before the fabric is woven, by some process other than binding and dyeing; painting is one such example

stained details: a method of coloring areas of the textile with dye that is daubed on after the weaving process

stenciled resist: a resist material applied through a cut-out design

supplementary warp or weft: the secondary set of elements used to create pattern in the design or to bind the opposite set of elements

taffeta: a fabric of warp-faced or warp-dominant plain weave

tape lace: a structure that imitates bobbin lace in which the figure is made with prewoven strips or tapes

tapestry: weft-faced plain weave, usually with a discontinuous weft

trapunto: the quilting of two layers of fabric into which cord or batting is stuffed

twill weave: a structure that is based on a unit of at least three warps and wefts, in which one set of elements passes over two or more elements, and under one or more elements of the opposite set, to form floats in a diagonal alignment; the figures 2/1 refer to the number of elements in each over/under sequence—for example, over-two-under-one

twining: see weft twining

uncut velvet: a weave in which the pile loops remain looped

velvet rod: a wire-shaped tool used in weaving to lift and hold loops of supplementary warp above the ground weave, and thus form pile

velvet weave: a compound weave structure with supplementary warp pile that is formed through cut or uncut loops above the ground weave

voided velvet: a weave in which areas with supplementary warp pile contrast with those that are free of pile, and thus reveal either the ground weave or supplementary weft patterning; the supplementary warp is woven into the ground

warp: the threads that are put on a loom, which holds them under tension

warp-dominant: warp elements that almost conceal the weft elements

warp-faced: warp elements that completely cover the weft elements

weft: the threads that are interworked or woven into the warp

weft-dominant: weft elements that almost conceal the warp elements

weft-faced: weft elements that completely cover the warp elements

weft twining: two elements worked together by spiraling around each other while encircling successive warps

Catalogue of the Collection

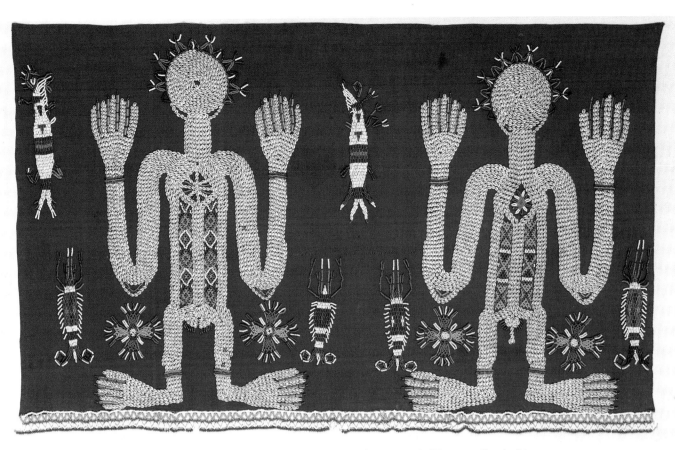

Catalogue Number 14 Sumba, Indonesia, Woman's Wrapper (*lau hada*)

Catalogue Number 12 Sumba, Indonesia, Man's Wrapper (*hinggi kombu*, detail)

Catalogue Number 26 Gujarat, India, Woman's Wrapper (*patolu sari*, detail)

Catalogue Number 28 Gujarat, India, Bed Cover (*palampore*)

Catalogue Number 30 Coromandel Coast, India, Wrapper (*phanung*, detail)

Catalogue Number 36 China, Imperial Bed Valance (detail)

Catalogue Number 38 China, Valance (details)

Catalogue Number 46 Japan, Yardage from a Woman's Coat

Catalogue Number 50 Japan, Gift Wrapper (*fukusa*)

Catalogue Number 67 Uzbekistan, U.S.S.R., Furnishing Fabric

Catalogue Number 68 Uzbekistan, U.S.S.R., Garment Fabric

Catalogue Number 71 Uzbekistan, U.S.S.R., Furnishing Fabric (*suzani*)

44

Catalogue Number 72 Caucasus, U.S.S.R., Rug

Catalogue Number 77 Spain, Fragment of Garment or Furnishing Fabric

Catalogue Number 80 Fez, Morocco, Woman's Belt (*hzūm*)

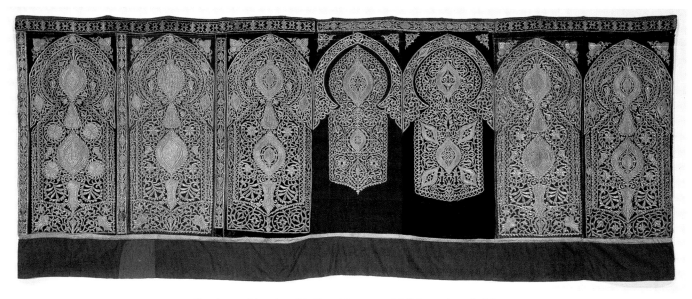

Catalogue Number 81 Fez, Morocco, Wall Hanging (*häiti*)

Catalogue Number 89 Berber People, Morocco, Man's Cape (*akhnif*)

Catalogue Number 94 Italy, Garment or Furnishing Fabric (detail)

Catalogue Number 96 Italy, Chausuble (back)

Catalogue Number 99 Italy, Portugal, or Spain, Garment or Furnishing Fabric

Catalogue Number 100 Switzerland, Furnishing Fabric

Catalogue Number 106 Spain or Portugal, Fragment of Furnishing Fabric

Catalogue Number 114 Lyon, France, Garment or Furnishing Fabric (detail)

Catalogue Number 118 Lyon, France, Statue Cape (?) (detail)

Catalogue Number 123 Germany (?), Woman's Apron

Catalogue Number 124 France, Woman's Dress

Catalogue Number 134 William Morris, England, Furnishing Fabric, *Honeysuckle*

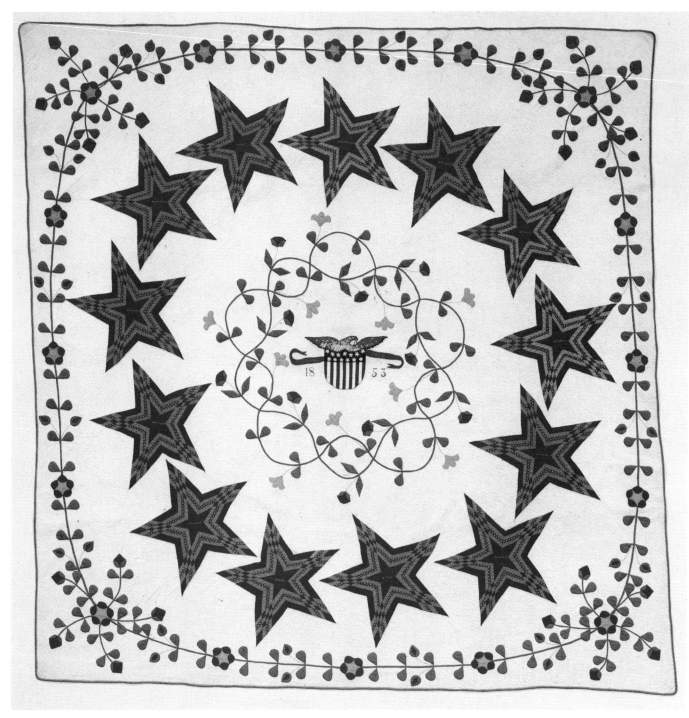

Catalogue Number 143 United States, Bed Cover (quilt)

Catalogue Number 151 Callot Soeurs, France, Evening Dress

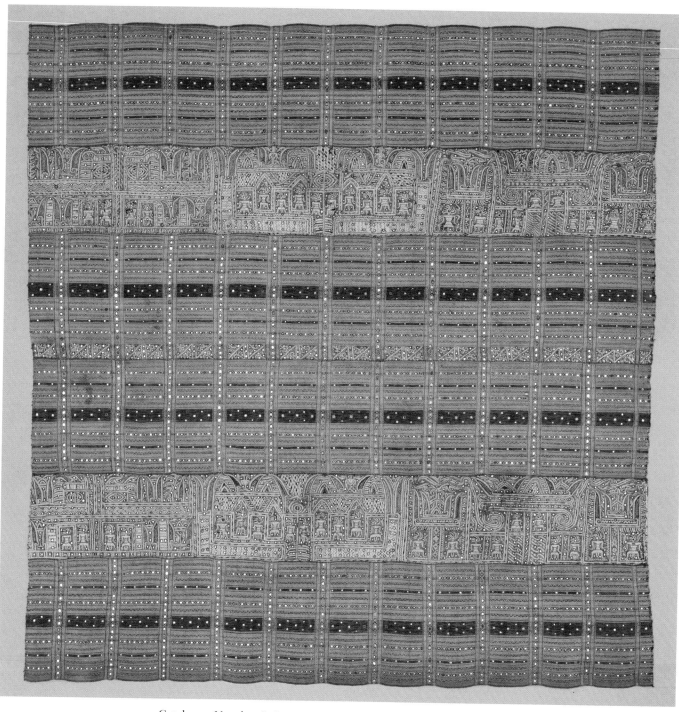

Catalogue Number 5 Sumatra, Indonesia, Woman's Wrapper (*tapis*)

Indonesia

Indonesian textiles hold a corpus of information about life on earth, and beyond, that indicates the paramount importance of fabric to spiritual and personal prestige. In few areas of the world do we know of the richness of material and iconography or the breadth of social usage and trade influences that we find in the archipelago of Indonesia. In many areas textiles play important ritual functions: some, such as Sarawak *pua* (see cat. 16) and Sumatran *tampan* (see cat. 4), are never worn because of their sacredness; others, such as Sumba *hinggi* (see cat. 12 and 13), are used as adornment but also serve as a means of exchange and finally, as wrappings for the dead. Certain Javanese batiks (see cat. 1) and imported Indian silk *patola* (see cat. 26) were restricted to use in the court.

The Indonesian archipelago is composed of thousands of islands that extend 2,500 miles, from Southeast Asia to Western New Guinea. These remarkably diverse peoples were unified in a reverence for cloth that little resembles our own culture's utilitarian view of it. The original inhabitants who migrated from southeastern and central Asia several millenia ago brought with them certain animistic beliefs and pattern systems that still exist in remote regions. This original culture was influenced by centuries of ocean trade, west from the ports of China to India, East Africa, and later, Europe. The supporting evidence indicates that during the trade's earlier phases—especially the one that lasted from the beginning of the Christian Era until the tenth century—Indonesian sailors manned many of the vessels transporting goods between China and the West.[1] Textiles, the most notable of which were Indian *patola* (see cat. 26), were traded among the Indonesian islands as well as with other parts of Asia. The importance of Indonesian spices as commodities in this international commerce led to the archipelago's designation as the "Spice Islands." Control of the vast trade routes brought them wealth and stimulated cultural development. The kingdom of Srivijaya in Sumatra arose during the seventh century and dominated trade in the islands until the tenth century, when the Arabs assumed control. The Arabic hegemony was overthrown by the Portuguese in the sixteenth century, and the Dutch and English quickly followed during the seventeenth century, in order to reap benefits from the important commodities that were available in the islands.

This enormous volume of trade from without and within the archipelago created material excess and promoted the development of court systems like the ones in Java and social prestige structures like the ones in the Lampong region of Sumatra. In such milieus textiles played significant symbolic roles as expressions of prestige, but more important, they expressed the history and ritual life of the people. Textiles thus assumed a life of their own: they put people and spirits in a proper symbiotic relationship that allowed for all facets of existence to interact harmoniously and thus to benefit both realms. Furthermore, textiles became a crucial element when an individual's status in society or the spirit world changed. Birth, puberty, marriage, and death were the most significant transitions and were known as times of life crisis.

Textiles functioned as symbols of stability in the rituals accompanying these changes. If the proper ritual was not performed in certain instances, the gods wreaked havoc on the earthly sphere. In other instances beautifully executed fabrics could lure the gods into amicable participation in rituals, for it was believed that success in this life or the next was impossible without the proper ordering of both the earthly and spiritual realms. Indonesians carried many of these attitudes into daily life. Negotiations between individuals and families could not be executed properly without the correct exchange of fabrics and other materials.

Trade added another dimension to this already complex system of social exchange. Trade goods were prestigious by definition because they were costly and exotic. Some fabrics, for example, Indian *patola* (see cat. 26) in Java and Java batik in Bali, were used in their original state. In other areas, however, foreign patterns were copied and reinterpreted so their prestige would be lent to locally produced objects. Such was the treatment of *patola* patterns in Sumbanese and Rotinese ikats, Chinese porcelain designs in northern Javanese batiks, and later, European motifs, such as heraldic lions from ship flags, on Sumbanese ikats. Europeans purchased many of these exotic fabrics for trade with southeastern and eastern Asia. This practice, in turn, led to a whole corpus of fabric made specifically for export. Often coarsely and quickly made, these textiles were no longer under the control of local patronage and thus the quality of their execution diminished.

These developments resulted in a very complex textile tradition, which expressed local religious values and social status. The accumulation of wealth and external trade influences further altered this tradition, and meeting those very trade requirements changed it. Indonesian culture is particularly complicated because of the archipelago's location in the middle of the Indian Ocean, at the juncture of cultural influences from three continents.

Catalogue Number 1
Central Java
Ceremonial Wrapper (*dodot*), ca. 1900
cotton plain weave, resist dyed (batik)
132 x 85 (334.5 x 215.5) warp x weft
Eliza M. and Sarah L. Niblack Collection 33.647

Batik executed with wax was probably preceded by a form of vegetable paste resist in Indonesia, as in other parts of the world. Drawing with wax required a ground of finely woven cotton,[2] which was imported first from India and then Europe. It has been noted that fourteenth-century sources do not mention batik, and it seems widely accepted that the art did not reach its apogee until the nineteenth century.[3]

This magnificent batik belongs to the type traditionally seen only in the central Javanese courts of Surakarta and Jojakarta, where it was worn by officials, nobles, and occasionally, court dancers. Unlike the more common *kain* or *sarong*, this cloth's generous size added to its worth. It was wrapped so that the pleats and flowing train fell to the side. Underneath it noblemen often wore pants made of Indian *patola* (see cat. 26).

The technique used to produce such a textile has been described as arduous:

The batik process at its apogee evolved into a labor-intensive procedure that involved predyeing processes, repeated starching, and multiple applications of wax resists. The cotton piece was first washed, then rubbed and kneaded in vegetable oil to enable the fibers to accept the red and brown vegetable dyes. Then the oil was removed in alkaline baths, and the cloth beaten with heavy wooden mallets to prepare the surface for the wax. The wax was a combination of resist materials such as beeswax, resins, and paraffin. These gave the substance greater viscosity in the molten state, which allowed finer control in the application and enabled the wax to seal but not penetrate the cloth surface.

The major outlines of a batik design were drawn in wax on the cloth first, then the smaller filling elements were added, and finally the areas to remain white and/or those to be dyed brown or red were filled in. Depending on the final color combination, there might be three applications of wax on both sides of the cloth before any dye was applied. Different colors of wax were used to distinguish the applications, so that they could later be scraped away as needed in the dye sequence. The textile was then dyed blue. Wax from the areas to be dyed brown was scraped away, and the blue areas were covered with wax. The next dye bath was brown or red, which not only gave that color, but also changed exposed areas of blue to violet or black. Additional wax was scraped away or applied for other colors, and extremely fine details achieved by actual brushwork. An alternative to scraping the wax was melting, but this required rewaxing both sides of the entire cloth again. In the final stage the wax was melted off, but a small residue remained. This gave the batik a distinctive texture which would last for many years if the cloth were washed in cold water only. Many of these stages are omitted or have been altered today, although the basic elements of the batik process remain.[4]

Designs on these fabrics allude to the most important symbols of life, death, and man's relation to the universe. The complex interplay of densely drawn pattern units lends visual excitement to spiritual interpretations of the macrocosm and earthly paradise. This textile teems with plant tendrils, leaves, flowers, peacocks, water creatures, and other wild life. In Java the motifs on this cloth are called *semen* (from *semi*, to sprout), leaflike tendrils that symbolize explosive growth and fertility. Tendrils are considered *nunggak semi*, old Javanese for "to sprout up anew from an old trunk or to create new from old."[5] In addition an overall rhythm of wavy forms denotes the sacred mountain, or *meru*, with small shrines on its slopes.

The cosmic symbolism of plant forms in *semen* patterns, which probably derives in part from Indian concepts of creation and the nature of the macrocosm, can be further elaborated.

In some Indian myths of creation, the tree is primary, springing from the navel of a primeval being to become the cosmic tree. There are many variations of the cosmic tree idea: the tree of life, the world tree, the pillar that supports the firmament, the axis of the universe, the lingga as the male creative element, etc. We cannot identify the plant forms on semen specifically, but probably some of the variations can be attributed to the multiple character of these trees.

In other Indian creation myths, the lotus is seen as embodying the vital creative energy of life as it rose from the primeval waters. The particular attributes of the lotus vary according to the myth, but association with the female element and water is consistent. The hanging roots of semen probably belong to the lotus. In nature, the roots of the lotus, and stems with buds and leaves, are put out from nodes along its underwater rhizome. In the batiks, the node or its equivalent is centralized, with the stems, buds and roots symmetrical around it. Some myths require the male element, the creative breath, to enter the waters for creation to occur. Thus in art, the lotus may be combined with its male counterpart, symbolized by the tree. In semen, the lotus buds and leaves are replaced by definite tree forms with their own branches and leaves—a lotus-tree combination.[6]

In this piece an axis, alternately dotted or solid, connects the flowering tree above and complex blossom or root structure beneath.[7] Considered the home of the ancestors and seat of the gods, the mountains that appear here as undulating forms are directly related to those found on Javanese temple sculpture. The pavilions (*candi*) that nest among the mountain forms are used for meditation and self-purification as well as for communion with the spirit world. Birds are also symbolic of heaven and the upper world: Garuda, the sacred eagle of Hindus, is

called golden phoenix (*merek elas*) in Java,[8] and, likewise, the peacocks in this piece may be interpreted as religious symbols. Thus, we have an intensively rich array of cosmic symbols on a garment intended for display at court, where such symbolism linked secular prestige with the spirit world.

Materials
  Basic fabric
    warp: cotton, single-ply Z-twist; white
    weft: cotton, single-ply Z-twist; white
    dyes: tan, dark blue
Techniques
  Balanced plain weave
  Resist dyed with drawn wax resist
  Two panels joined at selvedges with zigzag running stitch
  Finish: raw edges hemmed before waxing and dyeing
  Marker of light red and yellow weft and number 16
    embroidered at one end of fabric
Thread count
  Basic fabric
    warp: 114   weft: 108
Literature
  Gilfoy and Vollmer, *Arts of Asia*, March–April 1981, p. 133.

Catalogue Number 2
Indramaju Region, North Coast of Java
Woman's Wrapper (*sarong*), 19th century
cotton plain weave, resist dyed (batik),
   applied gold leaf (*prada*)
81 x 42½ (205.5 x 108) warp x weft
Eliza M. and Sarah L. Niblack Collection 33.686

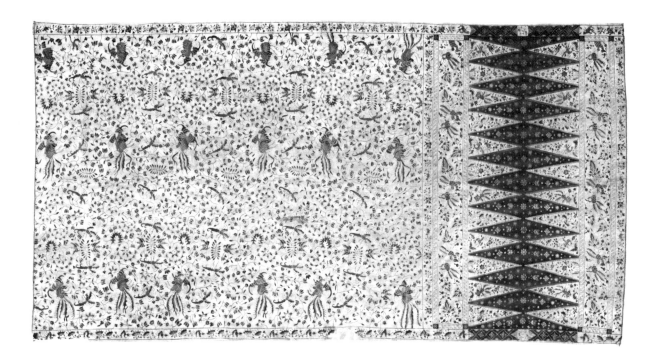

Wax-resist dyeing developed to the highest degree in the two areas of Indonesia with most trade activity: the courts of central Java and along the northern coast, where ocean trade established contacts with Asia, India, the Arab world, East Africa, and ultimately Europe. On the north coast, the influence of this contact appeared in batik floral designs, a number of which were derived from Indian and European motifs (see cat. 27 and 29). Other north coast patterns came from Chinese porcelains imported early enough to have achieved the status of family heirlooms.[9] Spiky phoenixes, called *burung hook*,[10] carried the same auspicious connotation in Java as they had in their native land. While the floral designs seem more Indian in character in this piece, the influence of Chinese blue and white porcelain is obvious in the design and color scheme, especially in the phoenix, butterfly, and broken meander patterns.

Applying gold leaf (*prada*) to the surface of textiles is an old technique that may have been one of the antecedents of wax batik.[11] After batik developed, gold was still used to highlight batik patterns. The gold on this piece is applied over what appears to be a layer of yellow clay. On the gilded side, the textile is also glazed. Along the top edge, a band of the indigo blue pattern was not gilded, because here the garment was folded over and covered by a belt. Along the north coast, *sarong* were commonly sewn into a tube before they were worn. This piece has been cut apart from the middle of the original seam, which is embellished with a pair of couched metal-wrapped threads stitched with red.

The *kapala*, or head of the textile, is here decorated with opposing rows of triangular shapes known as *tumpals*. This pattern also occurs in mainland Southeast Asia, and the form may

be a remnant of the jagged edges of bark cloth garments. This motif occurs widely on Indonesian ikats, *songket* (supplementary weft), and batiks. Here, the very strong geometric statement of the *tumpal* is tempered by curvilinear patterns in the white portions of the cloth and in the delicate gold overlay.

Lighter, more linear designs on white backgrounds are typical of the north coast. The technical expertise needed to resist the background, leaving only the finest lines to absorb the dye, is awe-inspiring.

Materials
   Basic fabric
      warp: cotton, single-ply Z-twist; tan
      weft: cotton, single-ply S-twist; tan
      dyes/pigments: dark blue, gold leaf
Techniques
   Balanced plain weave
   Resist dyed with drawn wax resist
   Applied gold leaf with yellow adhesive, glazed
   Finish: two raw edges sewn together and embroidered with
      couched metallic threads, seam cut through center
Thread count
   Basic fabric
      warp: 118   weft: 105
Literature
   Gilfoy and Vollmer, *Arts of Asia*, March–April 1981, p. 133.
   Kahlenberg, *Textile Traditions of Indonesia*, p. 63.
Exhibition
   Textile Traditions of Indonesia, Los Angeles County Museum
      of Art, 1977

Catalogue Number 3
Town of Pekalongan, North Coast of Java
Woman's Wrapper (*sarong*), ca. 1900
cotton plain weave, resist dyed (batik)
78 x 41¾ (198 x 106) warp x weft
Gift of Hillis L. Howie 77.375

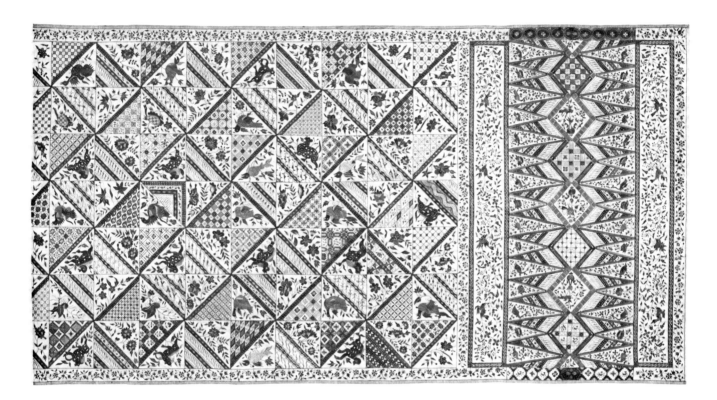

A visual glossary of batik designs, this *sarong* takes its patterns from a variety of sources. The bird and animal forms seem to be based on Chinese motifs, as is common in north coast textiles. In addition, the floral patterns derive from Indian as well as Chinese and European models. Geometric design belongs to the extensive vocabulary established at the central Javanese courts. Most of the patterns on this cloth seem to fall into three of the five categories established for Javanese batiks: small geometric designs (*tjeploken*), circular patterns (*kanung*), and diagonal stripes (*garis miring*).[12] The arrangement of the patterns into divided squares is called *tambal* and is thought to imitate patchwork garments worn by mendicant monks.[13] Along the edges of the cloth is a delicate striped pattern that may allude to fringe found on woven textiles. That it should be imitated in batik in such a delicate manner is certainly anachronistic. This treatment is also evident in the gold-leafed north coast *sarong* (see cat. 2).

The wax resist on this cloth was hand drawn, a procedure called *tulis* in Indonesia. The word, which may have designated batik in early sources, means "writing" or "painting," and it may be that batik had its origins in some form of painting rather than in the textile arts.[14] The colors on this piece, blue and brown, were achieved by dyeing first with indigo and then overdyeing with a red dye (*morinda citrifolia*) obtained from tree roots. Indigo dyeing was frequently done by men, while red dye was produced and the cloth dipped by women. The ex-

traordinary care and skill needed to produce such a cloth are evident in the careful control of the *canting*, or waxing tool, during the waxing procedure, and the very small amount of cracking that occurred during the dye baths.

This particular piece, which originally was joined into a tubular *sarong*, must have been a very expensive, prestigious garment. Women still wear the *sarong* or *kain* (cloth) wrapped and pleated around the waist, so that the *kapala*, or head of the cloth containing the opposing *tumpals*, is conspicuously placed either to the front, back, or side, depending upon local style.[13]

Materials
Basic fabric
    warp: cotton, single-ply Z-twist; yellow-tan
    weft: cotton, single-ply S-twist; yellow-tan
    dyes: blue, dark violet-brown
Techniques
Balanced plain weave
Resist dyed with drawn wax resist
Finish: raw edges sewn together, stitches removed
Thread count
Basic fabric
    warp: 116   weft: 116

Catalogue Number 4
Lampong Region, Southern Sumatra
Ceremonial Cloth (*tampan*), 19th century
cotton plain weave with cotton supplementary weft (brocade)
34½ x 29½ (87.5 x 75) with fringe, warp x weft
Mr. and Mrs. Julius F. Pratt Fund 79.144

The Lampong region of southern Sumatra had great wealth from the pepper trade that was carried on through the Srivijaya court (ca. A.D. 650–1392) in western Java. Srivijaya was able to maintain its dominance through control of mercantile activity in the Malacca Straits, which consisted of exotica from western Asia, Africa, and Europe to the Chinese courts. Although some authors think that Lampong's role in this trade was marginal, it may actually have been a major participant in the Srivijaya court during the height of its power.[16]

The region's material wealth fostered the development of a system of ranks and titles within the society, which were visually realized at great feasts and ceremonies on elaborately woven textiles.[17] These textiles, the famous ship cloths, or *palepai*, also had lesser counterparts, the smaller squares known as *tampan*. Unlike the ship cloths, *tampan* were used by all levels of society and in numerous ceremonies:

> A common use of the tampan was in the ceremonies surrounding marriage. Large numbers were included in the bride's dowry, and they were used in gift exchange for such purposes as wrapping small presents of food which were exchanged between the lineages of a bride and groom. Similar exchanges subsequently occurred at all life-crisis ceremonies involving the same participants who had been initially linked by tampan exchanges at the time of marriage. The exchange of these cloths, which may still occur today in a token capacity, symbolizes the multiple bonds between lineages joined by marriage.
>
> Other uses for the tampan were quite varied. The elder who presided over the yearly law gathering sat on a tampan, and on other ceremonial occasions certain groups of elders gathered around a tampan to eat the festival meal. In the south, the handles of the funeral bier were wrapped with tampan, and in the traditional marriage ceremony the bride sits on one or more tampan at specific times in the ceremony. On the Krui coast, the head of a deceased person rested on one of the small cloths while the body was washed. At house consecration ceremonies, a tampan was tied to the ridgepole and stayed there for the life of the house.[18]

Patterns on these cloths seem less related to function than to size. The creature on this piece is probably an abstracted hornbill. In some areas of Indonesia, the hornbill is the high god, although throughout the archipelago birds are associated with creation myths. The geometric pattern of the background is characteristic of these textiles regardless of their size and is a technical device to hold the weft in place, which in these pieces floats on the top surface rather than underneath.

Tampan have not been made for three-quarters of a century as the skill and impetus for creating them were lost. Their decline may have resulted from the abolition of slavery in 1859, a decline in the pepper trade, and changes in marriage traditions.

Materials
Basic fabric
warp: cotton, single-ply Z-twist; tan
weft: cotton, single-ply Z-twist; tan
supplementary weft: cotton, single-ply Z-twist; brown, dark green, yellow
Techniques
Balanced plain weave and weft-faced floats, with continuous supplementary weft, paired supplementary weft
proportions: one pair supplementary weft per one main weft
Dark green and yellow supplementary weft at top and bottom borders only
Fringe: individual warp ends
Thread count
Basic fabric
warp: 44   weft: 28
supplementary weft: 28 pairs (56 threads)
Literature
Gilfoy and Vollmer, *Arts of Asia*, March–April 1981, p. 136.

Catalogue Number 5 (see color plate, p. 64)
Lampong Region, Southern Sumatra
Woman's Wrapper (*tapis*), 19th century
four panels of silk and cotton plain weave with cotton and
    metallic supplementary weft, resist-dyed warp (ikat);
    embroidered with silk, metallic thread, and mirrors
two panels of cotton plain weave, embroidered with silk and
    mirrors
52¼ x 51½ (132.5 x 131) weft x warp
Martha Delzell Memorial Fund 82.149

Embroidery is not a traditional method for decorating textiles in Indonesia. Only in the southern region of Lampong was the technique truly assimilated from trade goods into the local design vocabulary. The combination is best expressed in the woman's *tapis*. The design is made up of human figures surrounded by rigid compartments that may indicate ships. In addition, rich vegetal forms swirl among the figures. The symbolism of growth, allied with the ship, emblem of passage from one life stage to another, is appropriate for apparel intended for important ceremonial occasions.

The various elements are embroidered in light tan and are surrounded by different colors as if to make the motifs stand out in visual relief. The outlining of the forms suggests that the designs on these textiles originated in painted wood, metal, or bamboo.[19] The organic quality of the embroidered pattern contrasts dramatically with the banded woven cotton and silk ground, which is sprinkled with embroidered bits of silvered-glass mirrors (*cermuk*).

The cloth was joined at each end to make a tubular *sarong*, which was then gathered and held in place with tucks that were folded into the top. It was probably worn with a jacket, elaborate jewelry, and a headpiece—all of which created a dramatic, scintillating effect when the wearer moved. While *tapis* made in the coastal regions of Lampong were important to the system of ranks and titles and were worn during festivals celebrating various aspects of that social order, those made in the highlands, like this piece, were probably less tied to this social system. The amount of time and expensive materials expended on this cloth did, however, make wearing it a statement of tremendous personal prestige.

Materials
Basic fabric panels
    warp: cotton, single-ply Z-twist; light and medium red,
        dark blue-black
            silk, single-ply Z-twist; yellow-orange
    weft: cotton, single-ply Z-twist, red
    supplementary weft:
        cotton, single-ply Z-twist; red
        silk, single-ply Z-twist; yellow-orange
        metallic
            core thread: bast, single-ply Z-twist; tan
            strip: silver with silicon on paper, Z-twist; silver colored
        embroidery:
            silk, single-ply Z-twist; yellow-orange, red, tan
            mirrors, silvered glass

Embroidered fabric panels
    warp: cotton, single-ply Z-twist; dark blue-black
    weft: cotton, single-ply Z-twist; dark blue-black
    embroidery:
        silk, single-ply Z-twist; yellow-orange, red, tan, dark
            blue, black
        mirrors, silvered glass
Techniques
Four panels of warp-faced plain weave and weft-faced
    floats, with continuous supplementary weft
        proportions: one supplementary weft per one
            main weft
Resist-dyed warp
Two panels of balanced plain weave
Embroidery
    flat stitches: couching of doubled elements; herringbone;
        double running; surface satin; stem; straight
    looped stitches: fly; shi sha
    combination flat and looped stitches: fly over surface
        satin; fly over stem
Six panels sewn together at selvedges
Finish: raw edges sewn together, stitches removed
Thread count
Basic fabric panels
    warp: 124   weft: 22   supplementary weft: 22
Embroidered fabric panels
    warp: 63   weft: 54

Catalogue Number 6
Batak People, Sumatra
Ceremonial Cloth (*radigup*), ca. 1900
center panel of cotton plain weave, with warp replacement of
    cotton plain weave with cotton supplementary weft
    (brocade)
side panels of cotton plain weave with cotton supplementary
    warp, cotton twining
85½ x 47 (217 x 119.5) with fringe, warp x weft
Eliza M. and Sarah L. Niblack Collection 33.629

Among traditional Batak, the *radigup* was, and continues to be, one of the most prestigious and sacred cloths. It is wrapped around the groom's mother by the bride's father during a wedding ceremony, and thus symbolizes the union of the two lineages.[20] Presented to the young married woman by her parents when she is six months pregnant with her first child, it becomes her *ulos ni tondi* (soul cloth). A knowledgeable person interprets the patterns on the end bands of the cloth to divine the woman's future.[21] The two ends of the central panel were termed "male"[22] and "female."

If no child is born within a suitable time, the young husband goes to the wife's family with a pig and demands their blessing in the form of a *radigup*.[23] The textile is thus a symbol *par excellence* of fertility and the continuity of life. In the interior mountain region of Sumatra, the Batak still weave these pieces and use them in the traditional way; in the coastal regions, however, long-term trading relationships have altered the execution and use of such textiles.

Technically, these cloths are remarkable. They are formed of three separately woven pieces joined at the selvedges. The central part of the middle panel is woven first, using a continuous warp. When the central part is finished, the unwoven section is laid over the white warps of the end sections. The brown and white warps, lying together, are bound by about four or five passes of the weft; these warps are then cut, leaving the woven brown center with unwoven white warps at each end. The weaver then weaves the patterns on each white end with a black supplementary weft. The reason for this enormously elaborate technique is not understood. In very recent times, the white panel has been separately made and then sewn on rather than woven in.

Materials
  Center panel, center warp
    warp: cotton, single-ply Z-twist; dark brown-red, white,
      black, light blue
    weft: cotton, single-ply Z-twist; black
  Center panel, replacement warp
    warp: cotton, single-ply Z-twist; white
    weft: cotton, single-ply Z-twist; white
    supplementary weft: cotton, single-ply Z-twist; black
  Side panels
    warp: cotton, single-ply Z-twist; dark brown-red, black,
      white, light blue
    weft: cotton, single-ply Z-twist; black
  Finish
    twining: cotton, single-ply Z-twist; dark brown-red
Techniques
  Center panel: warp-faced plain weave; first warp replaced
    by a second warp woven in warp-dominant plain
    weave and weft-faced floats, with continuous
    supplementary weft
      proportions: one supplementary weft per one
        main weft
  Side panels: warp-faced plain weave and warp-faced floats,
    with paired supplementary warp
      proportions: one pair supplementary warp per two
        main warps
  Three panels sewn together at selvedges with whip stitch
  Finish: seven rows of countered compact weft twining
    around fringe and across seam
  Fringe: four-ply Z-twist grouped warps, each ply is one
    warp end
Thread count
  Center panel
    center warp, warp: 104   weft: 42
    replacement warp, warp: 87   weft: 24
    supplementary weft: 24
  Side panels
    warp: 120   weft: 40
    supplementary warp: 60 pairs (120 threads)

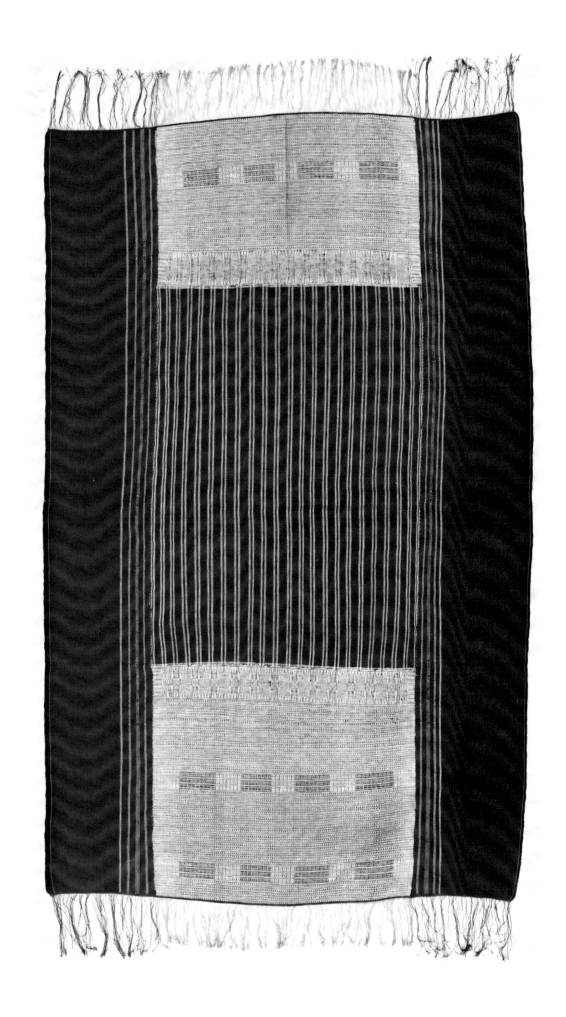

73

Catalogue Number 7
Minangkabau People, Agam District, Western Sumatra
Woman's Headwrapper (*tilakuang*), ca. 1900
silk plain weave with metallic supplementary weft (brocade),
    trimmed with cotton and metallic fringe
109 x 20¼ (276.5 x 51.5) with fringe, warp x weft
Eliza M. and Sarah L. Niblack Collection 76.338

The textiles of Sumatra that are heavily decorated with metal threads seem to fall outside the traditional use of textiles in Indonesia. They are apparently intended to display wealth and are less tied to the traditional bride-giver, bride-taker exchange of goods (see cat. 12). When used in those rituals, however, they are considered primarily metal, or male, commodities instead of cloth, or female, gifts. This is probably because of their high metal content and the fact that they are often purchased objects, not cloths produced by female members of the family. Among the Minangkabau, these gold-bordered textiles are worn for high ceremonial occasions and are folded and wrapped in a variety of styles as a headtie.[24]

In this particular cloth, the red, green, and yellow threads that underlie the supplementary weft metallic threads create subtle color variations in the gold. The geometric patterns may be abstracted from local flora and fauna.[25]

Unfortunately, little has been published on these rich cloths and the stunning objects remain inadequately explained.

Materials
Basic fabric
    warp: silk, single-ply Z-twist; dark red
    weft: silk, single-ply Z-twist; red, yellow, dark green
        cotton, single-ply Z-twist; dark violet
    supplementary weft:
    metallic #1
        core thread: silk, two-ply S-twist; tan
        strip: silver and copper with gold, S-twist; gold colored
Trim 1
    warp: cotton, two-ply S-twist; yellow
    weft: cotton, two-ply S-twist; yellow
    supplementary weft:
    metallic #2
        core thread: cotton, two-ply S-twist; yellow
        strip: copper with silver, S-twist; gold colored
Trim 2
    warp: cotton, three-ply S-twist; yellow
    weft: cotton, three-ply S-twist; yellow
    supplementary weft wrapping:
    metallic #3
        flat strip only: copper; gold colored
Techniques
Balanced plain weave, weft thicker than warp, and weft-
    faced floats, with continuous supplementary weft
        proportions: one supplementary weft per
        one main weft
Trim 1: band of plain weave and weft-faced floats, with
    supplementary weft
Trim 2: band of warp-faced plain weave with wefts
    extended on one side and wrapped with twisted metallic
    strips to form fringe
Thread count
Basic fabric
    warp: 68
    weft: 110 in area of plain weave, 101 in area with
        supplementary weft
    supplementary weft: 101
Literature
Gilfoy and Vollmer, *Arts of Asia*, March–April 1981, p. 134.

Catalogue Number 8
Palembang or Bangka Region, Sumatra
Woman's Wrapper (*sarong* or *kain songket*), ca. 1900
silk plain weave with metallic supplementary weft (brocade),
    resist-dyed weft (ikat)
81 x 35¼ (205.5 x 89.5) warp x weft
Eliza M. and Sarah L. Niblack Collection 33.681

Palembang was the seat of Srivijaya, the first Sumatran king-dom, which grew powerful in the seventh and eighth centuries under the influence of Indian and Chinese traders.[26] The sumptuous glowing red and gold silk *sarong* produced in that region originated in a complicated combination of local tradi-tion and trade influence.

Indian prototypes have heavily influenced the composition, technique, and materials as well as the iconography of these silk *sarong*. This piece has the typical center field, side border, and *tumpal* end borders of Indian *sari* design, executed in silk weft ikat. The *lar* wing motif, which when presented in pairs represents the Hindu god Garuda, is another Indian import. As a material, silk was unknown in Indonesia before its impor-tation from India and China. While sericulture developed suc-cessfully on Sumatra, trade supplied the vast quantities of silk used in the rest of the archipelago. In addition, even though ikat was probably practiced in Indonesia from earliest times, it was usually made of cotton, rather than silk, and traditionally it was the warp that was resisted. Thus, the combination of silk as a material and weft ikat as a decorative device points to In-dian inspiration. The extensive gold dye coloring on the piece implies a Bangka attribution.[27] The extremely delicate render-ing of the *tumpal* decoration and the central field patterning, played against the gold supplementary weft (*songket*), set this piece apart as a superb example of textile design.

Materials
  Basic fabric
    warp: silk, no twist; red
    weft: silk, no twist; red, violet, yellow, green, light blue
    supplementary warp:
      silk, no twist; white
    supplementary weft:
      metallic
        core thread: silk, single-ply Z-twist; white
        strip: gold and silver with copper and silicon on paper,
        Z-twist; gold colored
Techniques
  Weft-dominant plain weave (background) and weft-faced
    floats (figure), with discontinuous supplementary warp
    and continuous supplementary weft
      proportions: one supplementary warp per one main
        warp, one supplementary weft per one main weft
  Resist-dyed weft
  Finish: rolled hem with whip stitch
Thread count
  Basic fabric
    warp: 81
    weft: 93 in area of plain weave, 60 in area of
      supplementary weft
    supplementary weft: 60
Pattern repeat
  warpwise: 7¼ in. (18.5 cm)   weftwise: 7 in. (18.0 cm)
Literature
  Gilfoy and Vollmer, *Arts of Asia*, March–April 1981, p. 134.

Catalogue Number 9
Palembang Region, Sumatra
Man's Headwrapper (*kain kapala*), ca. 1900
silk plain weave, resist-dyed weft (ikat), applied gold leaf
   (*prada*)
34½ x 34 (87.5 x 86.5) weft x warp
Eliza M. and Sarah L. Niblack Collection 33.692

This silk square is ikat dyed in the weft with red, blue, and orange and further decorated with gold overlay (*prada*). The slight irregularity of the gilded pattern suggests that the adhesive used to secure gold leaf or dust to the surface was applied freehand with a brush. This technique of applying gold to the surface may be an imitation of a woven tradition, or it may relate to the *prada*-decorated cloths of Java (see cat. 2). Only the central area carries ikat patterning; the borders, where gold was applied, were left unpatterned, implying that gold overlay was part of the original design. One corner is more heavily decorated, because when the *kapala* is worn, it is folded into a point with one corner showing.[28]

Materials
   Basic fabric
      warp: silk, single-ply slight S-twist; dark red
      weft: silk, no twist; dark red, dark violet, light
         blue-green, light and medium blue, white, orange
      pigment: gold leaf
Techniques
   Weft-dominant plain weave
   Resist-dyed weft
   Applied gold leaf with clear adhesive
   Finish: rolled hem with whip stitch
Thread count
   Basic fabric
      warp: 95   weft: 73
Pattern repeat
   warpwise: 8 in. (20.0 cm)   weftwise: 11 in. (28.0 cm)

Catalogue Number 10
Town of Tenganan Pageringsingan, Bali
Woman's Shoulder Cloth or Breast Wrapper (*geringsing
    wayang kebo*), ca. 1900
cotton plain weave, resist-dyed warp and weft (ikat)
91½ x 19½ (232 x 49.5) with fringe, warp x weft
Mr. and Mrs. Julius F. Pratt Fund 79.143

In Indonesia, many textiles play an important part in the high rituals that mark rites of passage or life crises: birth, coming of age, marriage, and death. Perhaps one of the most sacred of textiles on the archipelago that are used in such rites, the *geringsing*, is subject to the strictest religious law, or *adat*, from the time the yarn is measured until the cloth wears out. *Geringsing* means sick (*gering*) and without (*sing*),[29] and the term implies the cloth has magical control over evil forces. *Geringsing* of this size are used uncut, in the circular form they have when they come from the loom, as presentation pieces, or cut, as women's breast wrappers or shoulder cloths.

Patterns on this cloth come from a number of sources. The three large, starlike shapes in the central field and the bands of smaller, similar forms at the ends clearly derive from Indian *patola* (see cat. 26). Tenganan Pageringsingan is the one place in Indonesia where *patola* motifs and technique merge, but whether *patola* cloths influenced the development of double ikat *geringsing* on Bali is unknown at present. It is notable, however, that in Southeast Asia, only the towns of Gujarat in western India and Tenganan Pageringsingan traditionally produce fine double ikat.

Between the two abstractly patterned areas of starlike forms are figure groups arranged with a dominant and subsidiary figure in mirror image. The larger figure is apparently a priest, wearing typical headdress and seated with one hand on his hip in the "noble ease" position. The smaller figure is a devotee whose hand gesture implies reverence.[30] This iconography may originate in three different sources. Most often mentioned are thirteenth- to fourteenth-century Javanese temple reliefs.[31] The figures, in rich reddish purple against a light background, also suggest analogies with Javanese *wayang kulit*, or shadow puppets. Finally, the flat shapes and classic postures recall the structured meeting scenes of old Javanese *wayang beber*, or narrative scrolls.[32] Whatever the origin of the iconography, these textiles abound with a symbolism meant to reinforce their mystical powers.

The production of a *geringsing* is not a task taken lightly:

The nuances and precision in color are crucial to the ritual value of these ceremonial textiles in the vil-

lage where they were made. The subtle coloration is achieved by an incredibly long and complex dye process. First the yarns are soaked and kneaded in oil and ash solutions for forty-two days, then hung to dry for a similar period. This chemically prepares the yarns for later red dyeing, and also endows them with their rich beige or ecru tones. After careful measuring and tying of the warp and weft designs, the yarns are sent to the neighboring village of Bugbug to be dyed dark blue, because indigo dyeing is forbidden in Tenganan Pageringsingan. When they are returned, more of the resists are cut away and the yarns dyed red. This overdye process gives the reddish-purple colors with their shadowed accents. To obtain the deep tones demanded, however, the dyeing must be repeated in a cycle of immersions in the dye baths and drying, with exposure to the night dew—a process that continues for five to eight years.[33]

When the fabric is finished, only those cloths most perfectly dyed and woven are used in local rituals; the others are sold elsewhere in Bali, where they are considered very important and are used as headrests during tooth filing and to encircle a bride and groom on their wedding day. Fragments of the fabric are even mixed into potions used in ritual curings.

Materials
    Basic fabric
        warp: cotton, single-ply Z-twist; dark brown, tan
        weft: cotton, single-ply Z-twist; dark brown, tan
Techniques
    Balanced plain weave, loosely woven
    Resist-dyed warp and weft
    Selvedge: ¾ in. (2.0 cm) wide, warp-faced plain weave
    Fringe: individual warp ends
Thread count
    Basic fabric
        warp: 43   weft: 24
Pattern repeat
    warpwise: 22¼ in. (56.5 cm)   weftwise: point repeat

Catalogue Number 11
Ndao
Man's Wrapper (*selimut*), ca. 1900
cotton plain weave, resist-dyed warp (ikat), cotton twining
82½ x 37 (209 x 94) with fringe, warp x weft
Eliza M. and Sarah L. Niblack Collection 33.634

European trade greatly affected the islands of Ndao, Roti, and Savu in southeastern Indonesia. The islands' rulers began commerce with Portugal in the early seventeenth century and by mid-century had developed exclusive trade franchises with the Dutch East India Company. In exchange for native wax, foodstuffs, and slaves, the Dutch provided muskets, gin, and royal regalia, consisting most often of Indian *patola* (see cat. 26).[34] *Patola* consequently became synonymous with rank and status. When Dutch trade disintegrated, *patola* patterns came to be imitated in textiles made on the islands, since they were less expensive and more easily obtained symbols of prestige.[35] One such garment was the *selimut*, which men wore in pairs: one as a waist wrapper and the other across the chest or draped over one shoulder.

Dutch trade fostered a lively partnership between the neighboring islands, Roti, Savu, and Ndao, though its relationship with Roti, the largest of the three islands, was the most active. Independent of the Dutch, Roti also had a particularly interesting relationship with Ndao. Since their island had few natural resources, Ndao men developed a gold- and silversmithing industry, which they practiced largely on Roti during the annual dry season. While the men were gone, the Ndao women wove. To increase their island's productivity, Ndao men began to supply Roti with the weavings their female relatives had completed. This trade flourished to such an extent that today most Rotinese women no longer weave.[36] Ironically, according to Rotinese tradition, Ndao first introduced the art of weaving to Roti:

The origin of weaving begins in the Heavens. The first woman to tie and weave is Henge Ne Ledo ma Feo Futu Bulan ('Tying Sun' and 'Binding Moon'). After a while, she descends from the Heavens and gives the shuttle and loom to her counterpart in the sea, Lui Liuk ma Kea Saik ('Seacow of the Ocean' and 'Turtle of the Sea'). Thus both the Heavens and the Seas are able "to throw the shuttle and work the loom . . . to fashion good, bright designs and proper fine patterns." Earth, however, is without the shuttle and loom until the day a woman from Ndao, Haba Ndao ma Lida Fola ('Gold Braid of Ndao' and 'Golden Strand of Fola'), goes to the sea to obtain these implements. One version describes this as follows:

Boe te besak-ka inak-ka Haba Ndao	Now the woman, Haba Ndao
Ma fetok Lida Fola	And the girl, Lida Fola
Ana kosu haba dua langan	She takes off a gold braid with two heads
De haba Ndao dua langan	A gold braid from Ndao with two heads
Ma ana tete lida telu ein	And she cuts off a gold strand of three feet
De lida Fola telu ein	A gold strand from Fola of three feet
De neni fe Kea Saik	She carries it to Turtle of the Sea
Ma neni fe Lui Liuk	And carries it to Seacow of the Ocean
Fo tadi neu ndolo seluk	To gain knowledge of the weaving sword
Ma asa neu nggiti atik.	And to buy the loom beams.

News of these implements spreads to Roti and the myth recounts how the implements and the knowledge of their use is transmitted from domain to domain until "the knowledge of tying and weaving has trunk and roots on Lote of the Outstretched Legs and Kale of the Cradled Arms."[37]

Descended from *patola* prototypes, Rotinese models greatly influenced the patterns on Ndao cloths. The composition of this piece is indebted to the classical Indian *sarong* whose end and side borders are commonly well defined. Indian as well as Indonesian wrappers frequently have ends with *tumpals*, or heads. In this piece, *patola* influence seems most evident in the basic composition and the eight-sided stars in the borders, but other patterns are more related to Ndao tradition. A humanoid figure appears between the *tumpals* and is repeated in a truncated form in the band above. Along the side border is a treelike shape related to banded Ndao ikat *selimut*; the motif in the central field is nontraditional. James Fox said of this piece:

My main problem remains in that I cannot recognize, nor fit with any traditional motif, the main pattern (which looks like a bird in flight). It is quite marvelous and, as I said, intriguing. . . . I think you have a marvelous piece which seems superb in all details including the colouring of the fringe which is also unusual.[38]

The technique of patterning textiles through ikat resist is one of the most exciting and most complicated of all dyeing processes. Its origins are open to conjecture. Warp ikat may have first been used in central Asia, and from there diffused to southeastern Asia. It is certainly equally plausible that this method of dye resist developed independently in places such as India, pre-Columbian Peru, and central Asia, where methods of patterned dyeing were advanced. To produce an ikat-dyed fabric the warp or weft, or both, must be stretched onto a tying frame before the weaving begins. Threads to be patterned identically are bundled, and then wrapped with a dye-resistant fiber. In fact, the term "ikat" derives from the Malayo-Polynesian *mengikat*, "to tie or bind." If the cloth has mirror imagery, as this one does (see also cat. 12, 13, 67, and 68), it can be doubled and both its ends can be tied at once. If the pattern is continuous (see cat. 16, 17, and 18), the whole length of the cloth is tie-resisted. To make a multicolored cloth, one must retie and dye again for each color, a process that requires very careful plan-

Materials
    Basic fabric
        warp: cotton, two-ply S-twist; tan, red, light and
           dark blue
        weft: cotton, two-ply S-twist; dark blue
        dye: brown-yellow
        twining: cotton, two-ply S-twist; red, tan

Techniques
    Warp-faced plain weave
    Resist-dyed warp, stained details
    Two panels sewn together with whip stitch
    Finish: four rows of countered compact weft twining
      around grouped warps
    Fringe: two-ply Z-twist, each ply is six warp ends

Thread count
    Basic fabric
      warp: 84   weft: 14

ning and execution if the pattern is to emerge clearly once the cloth is woven. When dyeing is finished, the dyed warps are strung onto the loom with consummate care so accurate alignment will not be destroyed and the precision of the pattern lost. Slight seepage of dye under some of the ties and variations in stringing the loom produce a feathery effect on some patterns' edges. During the weaving of the warp ikat, the heavier warp threads are manipulated to dominate the weft, another measure that enhances the pattern's clarity. The bottom of this cloth is finished with twining to prevent ravelling.

Catalogue Number 12 (see color plate, p. 34)
East Sumba
Man's Wrapper (*hinggi kombu*), ca. 1900
cotton plain weave, resist-dyed warp (ikat),
   cotton finishing warp
109¼ x 44 (277 x 112) with fringe, warp x weft
Eliza M. and Sarah L. Niblack Collection 33.628

The ritual and symbolic importance of textiles, something Westerners can barely imagine, is manifest in Sumba. The famous ikat *hinggi* testify to the critical role textiles can play in this life and the next. They serve as part of the exchange of goods, as ritual wrapping for the body—both alive and dead—and as visual metaphors for the richness of both the physical and spiritual life in Sumba.

Hinggi appear only during important rituals, especially funerals, where the family of the deceased is expected not only to wrap the body of the dead man with one hundred or more *hinggi*, but also to provide great numbers of them as gifts to those who attend. If the funeral is for an important man, the family may have spent the months or years since his death preparing for the celebration. The Sumba native spends a lifetime collecting wealth to assure proper fittings for the afterlife and a grand display at his own and his relatives' funerals. As the high point of the ceremony, the body is wrapped in the multitudes of textiles, the folds of which are stuffed with foreign coins and jewelry.

After the burial, a great limestone monolith is hauled to the grave to serve as a monument. As it is dragged, the stone bears a *hinggi* on a pole, transforming the construction into a metaphor for the ship of the dead, which transports the soul to the hereafter. It is believed that if a sufficient amount of goods is not provided or if corners are cut during the ceremony, the soul, unable to find the heavenly village, is doomed to wander among the stars. Only lengthy and costly ceremonies can retrieve it and ensure its future aid. The imagery on textiles, reinforced by other ritual acts, aids the soul on its labyrinthine journey to the beyond. The ultimate aim is to convey the soul to its proper place, with the forefathers, and to secure its aid for those who remain on earth.

Hinggi are also part of the bride-giving and bride-taking exchanges that occur in many areas of Indonesia. In Sumba, as in most areas, textiles are considered part of the gift from the bride's family because they are executed largely by women. In exchange for the textiles, the bride-takers offer items symbolic of men: metal, horses, and imported goods. Tradition (*adat*) strictly controls these gifts, each type of which is exchanged at particular times.

In the past, textiles were also traded in the interior for goods unavailable on the coast. In some areas of the interior, weaving was prohibited by *adat*. Thus, through a tightly controlled system of barter and gift-giving, commodities that were necessary for life—food, utensils, and clothing—and for the proper execution of ritual—textiles, gold jewelry, and sacrificial animals—were acquired without using currency.[39]

Hinggi are made in pairs, with one worn by a man as a wrapper around the waist and the other on the shoulder. Each *hinggi* is constructed of two panels sewn along the selvedges. A pair of cloths, constructed of four panels, is resisted at one time. In contrast to the practice in other areas of Indonesia, in Sumba the central field is tied and dyed first. The textile is then folded, and the end borders are all dyed simultaneously. The central

field on this piece carries a dot-within-a-circle pattern that may be associated with the ancient Javanese batik pattern of *gringsing* or may represent plangi or tie-dye. Frequently, *patola* designs (see cat. 26) inspired the motifs on these central panels, although that is not the case here. In the wide border at either end of this *hinggi* are large shrimp with a treelike form between them, which may be either a skull tree or a kapok tree in flower.[40] This motif also appears in the woman's skirt, or *lau* (see cat. 15). The skull tree was part of the headhunting rituals practiced in several places in the archipelago further to empower and protect the people's strength. In Sumba, the skulls of the vanquished were placed on branches of a dead tree, which was set in a pile of rocks in the open area of the ritual village. Located on a hill or rise in the ground (*priang*), this village was occupied only on ritual occasions. In addition to the skull tree, it contained stone monuments to the dead and houses with tall superstructures where family heirlooms were stored.

The rest of the imagery on this cloth comes from living forms familiar to the coastal Sumbanese. The large shrimp with lobsterlike claws that proliferate in the Indian Ocean represent regeneration because they shed and replace the shells they have outgrown. Also present on this *hinggi* are water birds, which symbolize transition in Sumba because they can soar from the water to the heavens.

The oldest and finest of these cloths carry end borders that are woven after the cloth panels have been sewn together. A small belt-loom is placed perpendicular to the warps, which then become the wefts of the new structure. The loose warp ends of the *kabakil*, or end border, were frequently bunched together to form tassels. This finishing was thought to empower or animate the cloth.[41]

This cloth was dyed with indigo to produce the blue, whose two different shades required two different tyings, and with *morinda citrifolia* or *kombu* red, a root dye that often took several dippings to achieve the proper depth of color.[42] In addition, yellow was daubed onto the cloth after it was finished, a practice that may allude to an older tradition of gilding fabric.[43] This extremely fine cloth, with its rich *kombu* red and beautifully finished end border, must have belonged at one time to a wealthy Sumbanese nobleman.

Materials

Basic fabric

    warp: cotton, two-ply S-twist; red, light and dark
      blue, tan

    weft: cotton, two-ply S-twist; dark blue, red

    dye: brown-yellow

    finishing warp: cotton, two-ply S-twist; black, red, tan

Techniques

Warp-faced plain weave

Resist-dyed warp, stained details

Two panels sewn together at selvedges with zigzag running
    stitch

Finish: warp ends grouped, used as weft in second weaving
    for horizontal bands at top and bottom edge; finishing
    warp of warp-faced plain weave with paired warp; warp
    ends wrapped

Fringe: two-ply Z-twist; each ply is ten warp ends

Thread count

Basic fabric

    warp: 99   weft: 28

    finishing warp: 71 pairs (142 threads)

Literature

Gilfoy and Vollmer, *Arts of Asia*, March–April 1981, p. 136.

Indianapolis Museum of Art, *Indiana Collects and Cooks*,
    1980, cover.

Catalogue Number 13
East Sumba
Man's Wrapper (*hinggi kombu*), ca. 1900
cotton plain weave, resist-dyed warp (ikat), cotton
    finishing warp
108 x 39½ (274 x 100.5) with fringe, warp x weft
Eliza M. and Sarah L. Niblack Collection 76.333

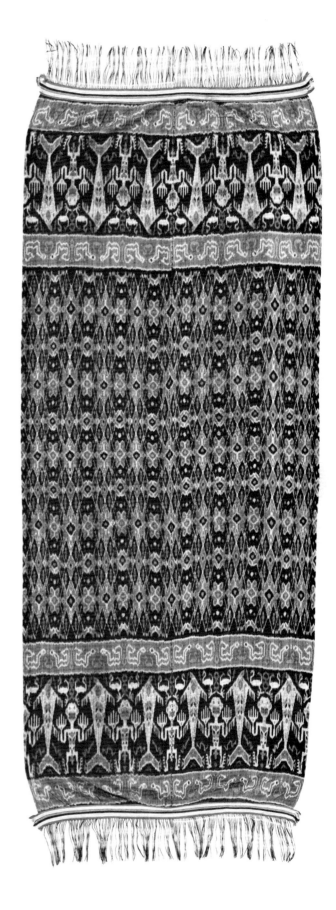

The central field on this piece is patterned after *patola* motifs.
The wide bottom border shows male figures in the orant position, flanked by what appear to be sea mammals; water fowl,
snake forms, and other birds fill the intervals. The orant figure,
an ancient motif many cultures have used, appears frequently
on Sumbanese textiles (see cat. 14 and 15). It has been specu-
lated that the form represents a man raising his hands to im-
plore or worship the gods.

Warp ikats such as this one were woven on the body-
tensioned loom, which was widely used in Indonesia. This type
of loom is represented on the lid of a bronze vessel from a
Chinese site in the Yunnan Province of the Western Han Empire (206 B.C.–A.D. 8).[44] In addition to widespread use in Asia,
the body-tensioned loom was also known in the pre-Columbian
Americas and is still employed today in several Central and
South American traditional cultures. This loom is unusual in
that the weaver controls warp tension with her back: at one end
the warp threads are fastened to a beam held in place by a rigid
support and at the other they are attached to a beam that rests
in the weaver's lap; the strap, fastened to each end of the lap
beam, passes behind her back. The weaver's control of the warp
tension with her body allows her a great deal of flexibility as
she works. The loom's widespread popularity attests to the
desirability of this feature.

Materials
    Basic fabric
        warp: cotton, two-ply S-twist; tan, brown-red, light and
            dark blue
        weft: cotton, two-ply S-twist; dark blue
        dye: brown-yellow
        finishing warp: cotton, two-ply S-twist; red, yellow
            cotton, single-ply Z-twist; medium blue
Techniques
    Warp-faced plain weave, paired wefts
    Resist-dyed warp, stained details
    Two panels sewn together at selvedges with a Z-patterned
        stitch
    Finish: warp ends grouped and used as wefts in second
        weaving for horizontal bands at top and bottom edge;
        finishing warp of warp-faced plain weave with paired
        warp; warp ends left as short fringe
    Fringe: two-ply Z-twist grouped warps; each ply is
        eight warp ends
Thread count
    Basic fabric
        warp: 104   weft: 35 pairs (70 threads)
        finishing warp: 66 pairs (132 threads)

Catalogue Number 14 (see color plate, p. 33)
Sumba
Woman's Wrapper (*lau hada*), 19th century
cotton plain weave, embroidered with shells and beads
46½ x 29 (118 x 74) warp x weft
Eliza M. and Sarah L. Niblack Collection 33.682

The highest nobility owned *lau hada* embroidered with glass trade beads and imported *nassa* shells.[45] They were referred to as *pakiri mbola* or "at the bottom of the basket," which is where the bride placed them when she brought this part of her marriage gift.[46] The skirt was also considered a "screen against the moon and a protection against the sun."[47]

The dominant pattern is striking. It features male and female figures in the orant position, flanked by shrimp, and what appears to be a starlike form just below the figures' elbows. This latter design may derive from Indian *patola* patterns, which were widely used in Sumba. The presence of male and female figures alludes to fertility and the continuity of life, which is fitting for a dowry gift. Thus, the imagery performs the important function of encouraging increase and promoting a good relationship with the spirit world. The shrimp are also important here, as on *hinggi* (see cat. 12), because they are symbols of regeneration.

Since they were such important burial goods, these pieces rarely enter museum collections.

Materials
Basic fabric
warp: cotton, single-ply Z-twist; red
weft: cotton, single-ply Z-twist; red
Embroidery
cotton, four-ply S-twist; white
glass beads; white, blue, red, yellow, green, light red
nassa shells; white
Techniques
Balanced plain weave
Embroidery
flat stitches: straight, detached straight
Fringe: interworked beads at bottom edge
Thread count
Basic fabric
warp: 73   weft: 68
Literature
Gilfoy and Vollmer, *Arts of Asia*, March–April 1981, p. 136.
Kahlenberg, *Textile Traditions of Indonesia*, p. 19.
Exhibition
Textile Traditions of Indonesia, Los Angeles County Museum of Art, 1977

Catalogue Number 15
Sumba
Woman's Wrapper (*lau pahuda*), ca. 1900
cotton plain weave and cotton plain weave with cotton
    supplementary warp and weft
48 x 44½ (122 x 113) warp x weft
Eliza M. and Sarah L. Niblack Collection 33.631

Women's skirts are also part of the important rituals of gift exchange. Their iconography resembles designs found on men's *hinggi*. Executed in white supplementary warp on a black ground, this skirt is patterned with orant male figures who may guide the soul to the other world.[48] The image between the figures may be a kapok tree or a skull tree (see cat. 12). Additionally, two types of birds appear on the narrow red bands flanking the main pattern field. The yellow stained coloring on this piece is also typical of *hinggi*.

Materials
Top panel
    warp:
        cotton, two-ply S-twist; orange, red
        cotton, six-ply Z-twist; yellow
        cotton, single-ply Z-twist; black
    weft:
        cotton, two-ply S-twist; black
Bottom panel
    warp:
        cotton, two-ply S-twist; orange, red
        cotton, six-ply Z-twist; yellow
        cotton, single-ply Z-twist; black
    weft:
        cotton, two-ply S-twist; black
    supplementary warp:
        cotton, two-ply S-twist; white
        cotton, five-ply S-twist, each ply is two-ply S-twist; light
            green-gray
        cotton, six-ply Z-twist; yellow
    supplementary weft:
        cotton, two-ply S-twist
    dye: brown-yellow

Techniques
Top panel: warp-faced plain weave, red warp sometimes
    paired
Bottom panel: warp-faced plain weave (background)
    and warp-faced floats (figure), with continuous
    supplementary warp (pattern) and continuous
    supplementary binding weft
        proportions: one supplementary warp per two main
            warps, one supplementary weft per thirteen main
            wefts
Stained details
Two panels sewn together at selvedges with patterned whip
    stitch
Raw edges sewn together, stitches removed

Thread count
Top panel
    warp: 70   weft: 26
Bottom panel
    warp: 60   weft: 26
    supplementary warp: 30   supplementary weft: 2

Literature
Gilfoy and Vollmer, *Arts of Asia*, March–April 1981, p. 136.

Catalogue Number 16
Iban People, Sarawak
Ceremonial Cloth (*pua*), 19th century
cotton plain weave, resist-dyed warp (ikat)
99 x 32 (251 x 81) with fringe, warp x weft
Eliza M. and Sarah L. Niblack Collection 33.645

A number of scholars consider the patterns on Iban *pua* to be closest to the ancient design vocabulary brought to Indonesia from central and eastern Asia, in the millenia preceding the beginning of the Christian Era. The complex interlacing of forms and *horror vacui*, or the filling of every available space with curling shapes, seems to have ancient prototypes. It is often difficult to identify the motifs in these pieces because of this elaborate embellishment. Iban design may represent objects of nature and spirit worship. The most important motifs are humans, crocodiles (lords of the waters and devourers of evil spirits), birds, deer (omen bearers and intermediaries), rice, creeping vines, rattan, fruit, and flowers.[49] Because of its isolation from the outside world, Sarawak maintained these ancient forms, as well as methods and ceremonies that may have been widespread in Indonesia in early times. The land was so foreboding and the people reputedly so ferocious that no trade relationships were established with Sarawak, unlike other areas of the archipelago, and the region was thus little influenced by external change.

Nowhere else in Indonesia were asymmetrical patterns executed in ikat. This tedious process, which required the whole length of the thread to be tied without doubling, was even more so during the execution of the complicated patterns exhibited on the finest of these cloths.

One would expect such production from a culture in which weaving was a sacred act. Among the Iban, no man was considered an adult before he had taken a head and no woman before she had woven a *pua*.[50] While weaving, women withdrew from the community and observed strict taboos.[51] The inspiration came to a woman from the spirit world during her dreams. She would never have considered weaving a *pua* without receiving such spiritual intervention, or ignored the call once it was received. While most women took their designs from older *pua*, the experienced weaver who invented her own was especially revered by both the earthly and spiritual communities.[52] The process of laying out the threads, called "warpath of women," was considered equal to headhunting[53] and was performed first. At the request of her spiritual helper, a woman then held a special ceremony (*ngar*) to prepare the yarns for accepting the red dye, which was actually a mordanting process. The weaver might take one to two years to finish a piece once these rites were completed. During that time she was in an endangered state and had to observe ritual precautions.[54]

In many traditional cultures the making and wearing of textiles are sanctified in myths that explain the people's history and their relation to the physical and spiritual world. One such myth was recounted in the records of the missionary William Howell in 1909:

> One day an Iban hunter shot a bird and as he went to retrieve it, it became a woman's skirt, the bidang. Concealing the garment in his arrow case, the hunter hurried home. Soon a beautiful girl who was, in reality, the daughter of the major god, Singalang Burong,

appeared to inquire about her skirt. After a time she consented to become the mortal's wife and later bore him a son. But soon she tired of mortals and prepared to return to more amorous affairs in heaven. Before leaving she wove two coats for her husband and son that were called "jackets of the birds" because of their pattern. These were capable of transporting her husband and son to heaven should they wish to join her. Eventually, after the mother had returned to heaven in the form of a bird, the son donned his jacket and followed her. In heaven it was a time of mourning for a deceased warrior, and the son was taught to observe the omen birds, to take heads to avenge the dead, how the newly taken head was to be received into the great blankets, the pua, and the details of the Festival of the Dead. The boy returned to the world and taught these culture traits to all the Iban.[55]

As suggested in the myth, *pua* were in fact used to carry heads taken in war. Headhunting, an important ritual for spiritual protection and empowerment, was only one of the ritual activities in which *pua* were used:

> The large cloths called pua are sometimes used to define a ritual area. At the Feast of the Whetstones, pua are used as an awning over the elder who sits below the eaves of the roof to make sacrifices to the stones, or they are hung about the stones themselves. On other occasions, a pua serves as a blanket for someone sleeping in a "dream house" on the roof of the longhouse, seeking a spirit helper from beyond. The pua may also form a small room or enclosure on the gallery, built to contain the dead and his mourners or a new mother and her child. This cloth is used too in adoption proceedings.[56]

The cloths apparently have only ritual function and, at the time early writers visited the island, were not worn as garments, though this may not always have been the case.[57]

Materials

Basic fabric
    warp: cotton, single-ply Z-twist; tan, brown-red, dark
        violet-black
    weft: cotton, single-ply Z-twist; brown-red, tan
    supplementary weft: cotton, single-ply Z-twist; white
    border warp: cotton, single-ply Z-twist; red, orange-
        yellow, white, tan
    twining: cotton, single-ply Z-twist; red, yellow, violet

Techniques

Warp-faced plain weave and weft-faced floats bound in a
    plain weave alignment (finish), with continuous
    supplementary weft, paired warp and weft
Finish: ten rows of countered compact twining bordered by
    supplementary weft at top and bottom edges
Two panels sewn together at selvedges with zigzag running
    stitch
Fringe: two ply Z-twist; each ply is six warp ends, knotted

Thread count

Basic fabric
    warp: 74 pairs (148 threads)
    weft: 24 pairs (48 threads)

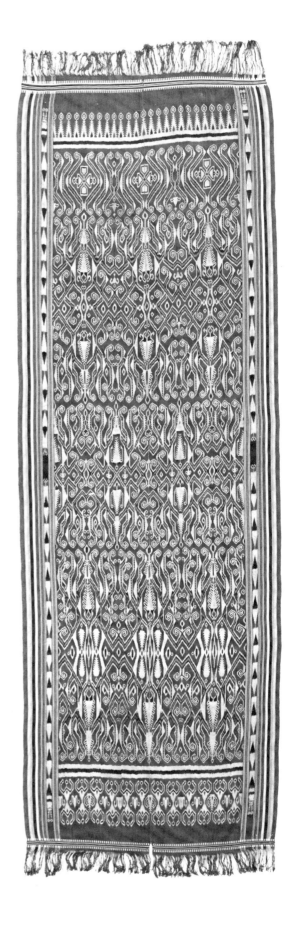

Catalogue Number 17
Iban People, Sarawak
Woman's Wrapper (*bidang*), 19th century
cotton plain weave, resist-dyed warp (ikat)
42 x 19½ (107 x 49.5) warp x weft
Mr. and Mrs. Julius F. Pratt Fund 79.142

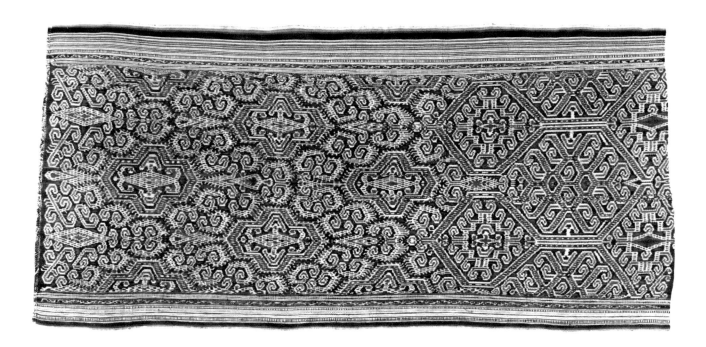

While *pua* were used strictly for ceremonial purposes, Iban women wore *bidang* for everyday as well as ritual garb. This piece still retains the seam at one side and a raw cut edge at the other, indicating that it was sewn into a tube and traditionally worn with a metal belt that held the garment at the waist. At dangerous times a *bidang* was given to the shaman to aid the soul of the dead woman in the journey beyond. The cloths were to "screen her from the dangers of Hades," enabling her soul to escape evil places and thus to aid the living.[58] *Bidang* and *pua* share the same design vocabulary and meticulosity of execution, but since *bidang* are smaller, their patterns are more delicate than the dramatic ones found on *pua*. The clarity of the small-scale pattern was enhanced by careful tying of the threads, which were spun very tightly before they were dyed, and by equally careful control of the dyed warp as it was woven. As with *hinggi* (see cat. 12 and 13), the tied warp threads of the *bidang* were dyed in an indigo bath and then overdyed with red. This created red, dark blue, and, where they overlapped, a brownish purple color. The yellow stain sometimes applied later added to the rich tonality. Such cloths were executed in a culture in which weaving was considered the consummate act of creation for a woman.

Materials
  Basic fabric
    warp: cotton, single-ply Z-twist; tan, blue, brown, black
    weft: cotton, single-ply slight Z-twist; brown
    border warp: two-ply S-twist; yellow, red, tan, light green

Techniques
  Warp-faced plain weave, paired warp
  Resist-dyed warp
  Finish: raw edges sewn together, cut apart later

Thread count
  Basic fabric
    warp: 52 pairs (104 threads)   weft: 23
    selvedge warp: 74 pairs (148 threads)

Catalogue Number 18
Highland Mindanao Region, Philippines
Panel from Woman's Wrapper (*malong*), ca. 1900
abaca plain weave, resist-dyed warp (ikat)
60½ x 14 (153.5 x 35.5) with fringe, warp x weft
Gift in Memory of Dr. and Mrs. E. K. Higdon 80.313

The abstract, interlocking, linear patterns on this cloth resemble those produced on Sarawak (see cat. 16 and 17). These peoples had much less contact with outsiders than those who lived in coastal regions did, so their retention of earlier designs and of bast fiber probably represents traditions that were widespread in Indonesia prior to extensive trade. In these two rather isolated regions of Southeast Asia, there is consequently evidence of an extremely early design vocabulary that probably predates outside influences.

In both Sarawak and Mindanao, the asymmetrical pattern on the cloth was, and is, applied through resist dyeing. The abaca fiber used to produce this cloth came from the mature stalk of a species of wild banana. Long, silken threads were obtained by combing the inner bark. They were later bleached in the sun and, if necessary, tied end to end to produce longer fibers. Rubbing the fibers in dry ashes and polishing them with a shell created the characteristic sheen. To produce such a fabric, dye-resistant fibers were tied around the warp bundles in the desired pattern and, in this case, dipped in red dye (*sikarig*)—one of the most costly and highly prized colors used by the Mindanaoans because of the number of times the threads had to be dipped to obtain the desired rich hue. The warps were stretched on a simple body-tensioned loom (*hablan* or *sekaran*) after they had been dyed. Bells or clappers were attached to the loom to produce a rhythmic sound that was believed to drive away evil spirits and to identify an industrious woman.[59] Loom weaving in this region probably originated at the onset of the Philippine Iron Age, around 200 B.C. Before that time, beaten bark cloth (*tapa*) was used, as was customary thoughout the tropical regions of the Eastern Hemisphere.

Materials
   Basic fabric
      warp: leaf fiber (abaca), no twist; dark tan and red-violet
      weft: leaf fiber (abaca), no twist; dark red-violet
Techniques
      Warp-faced plain weave, paired weft
      Resist-dyed warp
      Fringe: individual warp ends
Thread count
   Basic fabric
      warp: 63   weft: 22 pairs (44 threads)

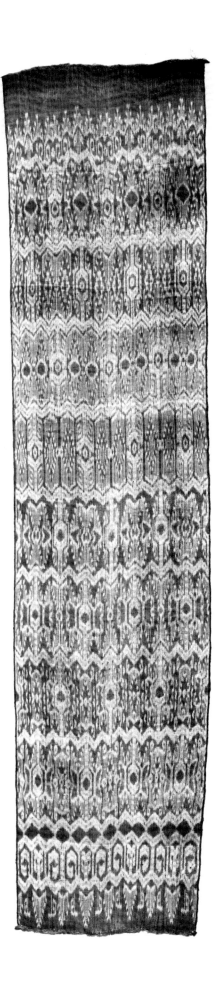

Catalogue Number 19
Toradja People, Celebes
Man's Head Wrapper (*siga*), ca. 1900
bark cloth, painted
51¼ x 42¼ (130 x 107.5) point to point
Eliza M. and Sarah L. Niblack Collection 33.1715

Bark cloth manufacture implies a technology that preceded use of the loom, and at one time it was probably widely practiced in warm climates. While some fabrics of this type are still being made in neighboring Polynesia, the art is virtually extinct in Indonesia. The material was formed by beating the inner bark of the mulberry tree until the individual fibers meshed into a felted sheet, from which various garments and furnishing fabrics were made. As the first step in making bark cloth, the inner bark from a paper mulberry tree was pulled away, beaten, washed, and rinsed. It was then fermented for ten to twelve days before the final beating, which was done on a beating plank (*tutua*) with a beater (*ike*). In Celebes, the beater was made of stone though wooden beaters were far more common in Polynesia and in the rest of Indonesia. The beaten bast strips were joined by felting them together with further beating. The finished pieces were partially dried and while still damp, beaten again with a smooth, ebony stick. At this time, plant juice, or *ula* sap, was added to give further durability.[60]

Curved forms in the decorative panels of this piece represent buffalo horns (*petono*), which in Celebes belief relate to headhunting and the cosmic sphere. A Toradja myth recounts a female buffalo's entering heaven, where the god Pue mPalaburu transformed her into a woman. She then returned to her earthly lover and brought order to natural phenomena.[61] Only experienced headtakers were allowed to wear *siga* that were decorated with buffalo horn motifs.[62] In addition, the division of the compositional field into four triangles is symbolic of the upper world; thus the warrior is equated with the "lord of heavens" and the sun.[63]

After the bark cloth was prepared, it was decorated using a brush made of the softened tip of a bamboo stick. Paints were made of tree bark (yellow), roots (red), and flowers (purple). In the lowlands at this time, women did the painting. In the mountainous regions, decorations were executed not only by women, but also by men who belonged to a special caste. Its members dressed and acted like women and served as shamans, also a female role.[64]

Materials
  Basic fabric
    fiber: bast (paper mulberry); light tan
    dyes: light and dark red, violet-red, violet, light orange, light green, black
Techniques
  Felted fibers
  Painted
Thread count
  not applicable

Catalogue Number 20
Toradja People, Celebes
Woman's Shirt (*lemba* or *karaba*), ca. 1900
bark cloth, appliquéd
23 (58) length
Eliza M. and Sarah L. Niblack Collection 33.641

Bark cloth was commonly used in the original rectangular shape. In Celebes, however, the art reached a high form, and bark cloth (*fuga*) was cut and shaped into women's shirts (*lemba*). A woman probably made the *lemba* shown here as ordinary daily apparel. It was given a coat of protective sap, as is evidenced by its slightly yellowish cast. Dark brown bark cloth appliqué added subtle decoration. If the garment had been intended for ceremonial use, it would have been decorated in a manner similar to the man's headtie (see cat. 19).

Materials
  Basic fabric
    fiber: bast (paper mulberry); light yellow
  Appliquéd fabric
    fiber: bast (paper mulberry); brown and black
Techniques
  Felted fibers
  Appliquéd
  Pieced garment
Thread count
  not applicable
Literature
  Gilfoy and Vollmer, *Arts of Asia*, March–April 1981, p. 135.

Catalogue Number 21
Samoa
Furnishing Fabric, ca. 1900
bark cloth (*tapa*), printed and painted
62¾ x 51 (159 x 129.5)
Gift of Mrs. C. W. Bispham 48.30

The existence of bark cloth in eastern Asia was documented in sixth-century B.C. Chinese sources and was mentioned by Marco Polo in the thirteenth century. The plant and cloth making technology probably passed from eastern Asia into Indochina, to Indonesia, and outward to Polynesia.[65] By the end of the eighteenth century, European whalers working in Polynesian waters collected the decorative cloths and spread the Hawaiian term for bark cloth, *tapa* (*kapa*), throughout the Polynesian islands.[66] In Samoa, the art of making cloth from the inner bark of the paper mulberry tree was retained well after Western contact had replaced other traditional goods with foreign imports.[67]

The manufacture of *siapo* (Samoan for *tapa*) differed somewhat from the procedure in Indonesia (see cat. 19). The inner bark was stripped, rolled, and kept damp. When ready, it was beaten on a wooden anvil (*tutua*), which was hollowed out to enable the women using the wooden beaters (*i'e*) to execute sonorous rhythms. Beating this bark was not a felting process; rather, the fibers in the thin cloth were united by a gluelike material in the bark. Instead of being felted together, as they were in Indonesia and in other parts of Polynesia, the strips were joined with paste.[68] This method of joining was executed on a board patterned with strips of sennet cord or relief woodcarving.

When colored material (here a reddish color probably from an imported earth color) was rubbed over the cloth on top of a patterned board, it created a surface design on the cloth. The glossy dark brown paint on the surface derived from a bark with resinlike qualities that created a waterproof glaze.[69]

Large, rectangular pieces such as this one were used as house screens, curtains, or bed sheets.[70] The amount of decoration on these pieces indicated social status. Their execution was a communal effort, and many were made in factorylike production. Perhaps because their largely social role was devoid of religious connotations, their manufacture was not severely affected by the Western influences that destroyed many Polynesian religious practices.[71]

Materials
Basic fabric
fiber: bast (paper mulberry); tan
dyes: light red-brown, medium brown, dark brown-black
Techniques
Laminated fibers, layered so that fibers in different layers run perpendicular, with overlapping edges
Rubbed and painted designs
Thread count
not applicable

Catalogue Number 21

Notes

1. Gilfoy, 1980, pp. 357-58.

2. The cotton was marked with a pink weft thread and a "16," also embroidered in pink, that was later covered with wax and dyed. This system was used in India to designate export cottons (Gittinger, personal communication).

3. Gittinger, 1979b, p. 115.

4. Gittinger, 1979b, p. 117.

5. Solyom, 1980, p. 255.

6. G. and B. Solyom, 1980, p. 250.

7. Conversely, Adams reads these forms as symbols for the ship of the dead, which denotes the cosmic trip of the soul (Adams, 1970, pp. 25-40).

8. G. and B. Solyom, 1980, pp. 253-54.

9. Gittinger, 1979b, p. 127.

10. Kahlenberg, 1977, essay by B. and G. Solyom, p. 63.

11. Gittinger, 1979b, p. 116.

12. Tirtaamidjaja, 1966.

13. Gittinger, 1979b, p. 123.

14. Gittinger, 1979b, p. 125.

15. Kahlenberg, 1977, essay by B. and G. Solyom, p. 59.

16. Holmgren, 1980, pp. 164-65.

17. Gittinger, 1979b, p. 79.

18. Gittinger, 1979b, p. 88.

19. Kahlenberg, 1977, essay by Gittinger, p. 27.

20. Gittinger, 1979b, p. 95.

21. Gittinger, 1979b, p. 99.

22. The male end is characterized by a wider and more complicated pattern.

23. Gittinger, 1979b, p. 101.

24. Gittinger, 1979b, pp. 112-13.

25. Kartiwa, 1980, p. 59.

26. Gittinger, 1979b, p. 102.

27. Gittinger, 1979b, p. 102.

28. Kahlenberg, 1979, essay by B. and G. Solyom, p. 12.

29. Kahlenberg, 1977, essay by B. and G. Solyom, pp. 74-75.

30. Identical pieces published in Mary Kahlenberg, *Rites of Passage*, Mingei International Museum of World Folk Art, San Diego, 1979, p. 29; Robert von Heine-Geldern, *Indonesian Art: A Loan Exhibition from the Royal Indies Institute, Amsterdam, the Netherlands*, Albright-Knox Gallery, Buffalo, 1949, p. 52.

31. Gittinger, 1979b, p. 148.

32. Larsen, 1976, p. 222.

33. Gittinger, 1979b, p. 147.

34. Kahlenberg, 1977, essay by Fox, p. 98.

35. Gittinger, 1979b, p. 185.

36. Kahlenberg, 1977, essay by Fox, pp. 97-98.

37. Gittinger, 1979b, pp. 44-45.

38. Fox, personal communication.

39. Most of the preceding material is derived from Marie Jean Adams's research on Sumba (Adams, 1965, 1969, and 1970).

40. Gittinger, 1982, p. 158.

41. Kahlenberg, 1977, entry by Leland, p. 82.

42. Bühler, 1941, pp. 1423-26.

43. Kahlenberg, 1977, p. 82.

44. Vollmer, 1979, p. 78.

45. Kahlenberg, 1977, essay by Albert, p. 79.

46. Gittinger, 1979, p. 162.

47. Adams, 1969, p. 166.

48. Kahlenberg, 1977, entry by Leland, p. 85.

49. Kahlenberg, 1977, essay by Spertus and Holmgren, pp. 41-42.

50. Gittinger, 1979b, p. 218.

51. Kahlenberg, 1977, essay by Spertus and Holmgren, p. 41.

52. Vogelsanger, 1980, pp. 116-18.

53. Gittinger, 1979b, p. 219.

54. Vogelsanger, 1980, pp. 117-18.

55. Gittinger, 1979b, p. 218.

56. Gittinger, 1979b, p. 218.

57. Kahlenberg, 1977, essay by Spertus and Holmgren, p. 41.

58. Gittinger, 1979b, p. 218.

59. Casal, 1981, pp. 130-32.

60. Kooijman, 1963, pp. 57-58.

61. Kooijman, 1963, p. 26.

62. Kooijman, 1963, p. 20.

63. Kooijman, 1963, p. 56.

64. Kooijman, 1963, pp. 68-69.

65. Kooijman, 1972, p. 1.

66. Kooijman, 1972, p. 4.

67. Kooijman, 1971, p. 421.

68. Kooijman, 1972, pp. 213-16.

69. Kooijman, 1972, pp. 217-19.

70. Kooijman, 1972, p. 245.

71. Kooijman, 1972, p. 421.

Catalogue Number 22
Khatrie Muslims, Kutch Area, Gujarat State
Woman's Bridal Wrapper (*odhani*), ca. 1900
silk satin weave, resist dyed (plangi), embroidered with silk,
   metallic thread and mirrors
69 x 59 (175 x 150) warp x weft
Gift of Myla Jo Closser 38.63

Especially fine pieces of tie-dye, such as this *odhani*, continue to be made for the Mahajan, who are well-to-do urban merchants, landlords, and higher class craftsmen. The technique of tie-dyeing was mentioned in the seventh-century Indian source *Harshacharita* and is represented in the fifth-century cave paintings at Ajanta.[11] The Indian term for tie resist, *bandhani*, derives from the Sanskrit *bandha*, meaning "to tie."[12] The specific term for tie-dyeing in northwestern India is *chunari*, a Rajasthani word for *bandhani*.[13]

Learning to make ties for *chunari* textiles does not require years of apprenticeship; most are produced by women and girls working in their homes. The cloth trader distributes fabric to workers who are paid for each piece they tie. The cloth is folded into quarters by the colorer (*rangara*), who marks out the pattern on the fabric with woodblocks dipped in a burnt sienna mixture. With the sharpened nail of her little finger, the tier raises a point through all four layers, following the previously stamped pattern; ties it with a dye-resistant thread; and passes to the next point, tying it without breaking the thread. The cloth is then given to the dyer, who immerses it in the dye bath (in this case, indigo). If further colored patterns are desired, the tier reties what is wanted and the piece is redipped. Finally, the textile goes to the washerwoman. When it is ready for sale, a few ties are released to show the pattern, so the patron knows she has purchased a hand-tied cloth, not an imitation. The cloth is pulled sharply to release the remainder of the ties, and the threads fall into a loose mass.[14]

Khatrie Muslims and Hindus often wear tie-dyed wedding clothes adorned with glass and gold-thread embroidery. Professional dyers living in the urban centers of Kutch, Khatrie Muslims wear black *chunari odhanis* at their weddings.[15] These are decorated with medallion patterns and embroidered with gold in the center seam.[16] Since marriage ensures continuity of the community, it is one of the most important rites of passage celebrated throughout Southeast Asia. The cut, material, and ornamentation of garments in India, as in other parts of the world, are important symbols of the status of a woman and reflect her material possessions, marital status, age, occupation, origin, and even the caste to which she belongs. Marriage garments such as the one here are part of a girl's dowry, which, with other household goods and clothing, are intended to provide for her first married years.[17]

Odhanis are worn with one corner tucked into the front waist of a skirt, or *ghaghara* (see cat. 25), draped over the skirt in the back, and pulled up over the head to fall over the shoulders.[18] The tied areas have not been ironed out in this piece, except in the areas that were embroidered. The elasticity this procedure gives to the *odhani* makes it cling easily to the body as well as drape gracefully from the head. The intricate fineness of mica embroidery on this piece is similar to that on the Banni embroidered shirt or *aba* (see cat. 24).

Materials
   Basic fabric
      warp: silk, no twist; red
      weft: silk, no twist; red
      dye: dark blue-black
   Embroidery
      silk, no twist; white, yellow, red, brown, dark green, dark
      brown
      metallic #1
         core thread: silk, two-ply S-twist; yellow
         strip: silver with gold, Z-twist; gold colored
      metallic #2
         core thread: silk, two-ply S-twist; white
         strip: silver, Z-twist; silver colored
Techniques
   Warp-faced 5/1 satin weave
   Resist dyed with tied resists
   Embroidery
      flat stitches: double back stitch; couching of tripled
         elements; cross; Roumanian
      looped stitches: buttonhole; chain, open chain;
         shi sha
      combination of flat and looped stitches: buttonhole
         combined with a variation of long-armed cross
   Finish: raw edges turned under 1 in. (2.5 cm) and stitched
Thread Count
   Basic fabric
      warp: 264   weft: 113
Literature
   Gilfoy and Vollmer, *Arts of Asia*, March–April 1981, p. 131.

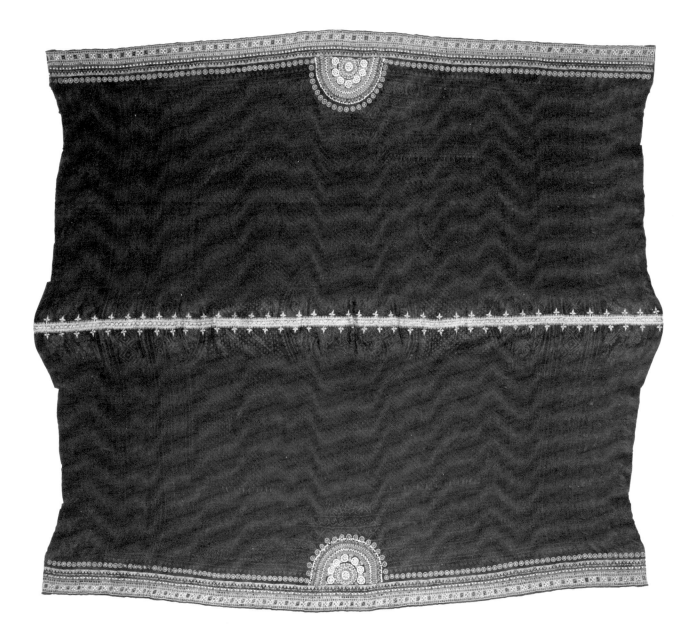

Catalogue Number 23
Khatrie Muslims, Kutch Area, Gujarat State
Woman's Bridal Shirt (*aba*), ca. 1900
silk satin weave, embroidered with silk and metallic thread,
    trimmed with silk and metallic bands
47½ (120.5) length, warp
Eliza M. and Sarah L. Niblack Collection 33.735

Red silk satin shirts like this are an important part of a girl's dowry and are presented to her by the groom's family at the time of her marriage. With the shirt[19] girls typically wear a decorated shawl, or *odhani* (see cat. 22), and embroidered trousers (*ejar*). The color red is associated with marriage and the pattern, here, executed with couched gold threads, has been used by Muslim craftsmen for a long time.[20]

Materials
  Basic fabric
    warp: silk, single-ply slight Z-twist; red
    weft: silk, no twist; red
  Embroidery
    silk, two-ply S-twist; orange, blue, light green
    metallic #1
      core thread: silk, single-ply S-twist; orange
      strip: silver with gold and copper, Z-twist; gold colored
    metallic #2
      core thread: silk, single-ply S-twist; white
      strip: silver with copper, Z-twist; silver colored
  Trim 1
    warp: silk, single-ply S-twist; red, dark violet, light red
    weft: silk, single-ply S-twist; red
    supplementary warp:
     metallic #3
      core thread: cotton, single-ply S-twist; orange
      strip: silver with copper, Z-twist; gold colored
     metallic #4
      core thread: cotton, single-ply S-twist; white
      strip: silver, Z-twist; silver colored
  Trim 2
    warp:
     metallic #5
      core thread: cotton, two-ply S-twist; white
      strip: silver with copper and lead, Z-twist; gold colored
    weft:
     metallic #6
      core thread: cotton, two-ply S-twist; white
      strip: silver with copper and lead, Z-twist; silver
       colored
     metallic #7
      flat strip only: gold and silver with copper, gold
       colored

Techniques
  Warp-faced 7/1 satin weave
  Embroidery
    flat stitches: invisible couching, pattern couching,
      patterned couching, all with tripled elements
  Embroidered area backed with cotton balanced plain weave
    fabric
  Selvedge: ⅛ in. (0.3 cm) wide, warp-faced plain weave of
    light blue and light green silk
  Pieced garment
  Trim 1: warp-faced plain weave with supplementary warp,
    paired supplementary warp
      proportions: one pair supplementary warp per one
        main warp
  Trim 2: warp-faced plain weave
Thread count
  Basic fabric
    warp: 352   weft: 101
  Trim 1
    warp: 61   weft: 45   supplementary warp: 122

Catalogue Number 24
Jat People of Banni, Northern Kutch Area, Gujarat State
Woman's Shirt (*aba*), ca. 1900
silk satin weave, embroidered with silk and mirrors
45 (114.5) length, weft
Eliza M. and Sarah L. Niblack Collection 33.745

Some of the finest embroidery in India was done as a home craft in the Banni region. When the Jats immigrated to Kutch from Baluchistan, they retained the intricate patterning, based on a geometric grid, that was characteristic of their homeland.[21] The fabric used in this garment and in cat. 22, 23, 24, and 25 was probably imported from Bombay, which was famous for its satin weaving.[22]

In northern Kutch, *abas* were worn with ankle-length trousers (*salwar*) embroidered at the lower edges.

Materials

Basic fabric
warp: silk, single-ply slight Z-twist; red
weft: silk, no twist; red
Embroidery
silk, single-ply slight S-twist; dark yellow, light brown, red, dark green, dark blue, white, black
mirrors, mica
Facing
warp: cotton, single-ply Z-twist; tan
weft: cotton, single-ply Z-twist; tan
dyes/pigments: brown, red-brown

Techniques

Warp-faced 7/1 satin weave
Embroidery
flat stitches: cross; dot; closed herringbone; Roumanian; satin; stem
looped stitches: buttonhole; open chain; fly; shi sha
combination flat and looped stitches:
buttonhole in combination with long-armed cross
Selvedge: 1/8 in. (0.3 cm) wide, warp-faced plain weave of red with white stripes
Pieced garment with asymmetrical seams
Neck facing: balanced plain weave, printed

Thread count

Basic fabric
warp: 320   weft: 100
Facing
warp: 57   weft: 51

103

Catalogue Number 25
Mochi Craftsmen of Bhuj, Kutch Area, Gujarat State
Woman's Skirt (*ghaghara*), ca. 1900
silk satin weave, embroidered with silk
38½ (98) length, weft
Gift of Mrs. Tade Hartsuff Kuhns Bequest 38.72

When Marco Polo described embroidered leatherwork in the thirteenth century, Indian embroidery from the northwestern region was reputedly the best in the world. The intrepid traveler Barbosa mentioned that chain stitch embroidery on cotton was being done in Bombay at the beginning of the sixteenth century, and according to the English East India Company's records, "patania quilts" of Gujarat embroidery entered European trade in the early seventeenth century.[23] Motifs of peacocks and flowering plants are highly characteristic of the professional Mochi embroiderers who supplied the court of Bhuj.[24] The Mochis were traditionally members of the shoemakers' community[25] that reportedly learned embroidery from Muslim craftsmen. They may have done so in the sixteenth and seventeenth centuries, when embroidery flourished under Mughal court sponsorship.[26]

The fine tambour or chain stitch embroidery in this piece, in multicolored silk threads on dark red silk satin, is executed with an *aar* or *ari*, a fine awl with a small notch above the point. When imported to Europe, embroidery such as this had a profound influence on the art, especially in England, where local imitations in wool on linen became known as crewel work. The ladies of the landed aristocracy at the northwest Indian court of Bhuj wore a *ghaghara* such as this one with a blouse (*choli*) and headcover (*odhani*, see cat. 22).

Materials
Basic fabric
  warp: silk, single-ply slight Z-twist; red
  weft: silk, no twist; red
Embroidery
  silk, no twist; light and medium red, white, light green, yellow, blue, blue-green, black
Appliquéd fabric
  warp: silk, single-ply slight Z-twist; dark blue, light blue, yellow, or red
  weft: silk, no twist; dark blue, light blue, yellow, or red
Lining
  warp: cotton, single-ply Z-twist; red-brown
  weft: cotton, single-ply Z-twist; red-brown

Techniques
Warp-faced 7/1 satin weave
Embroidery
  flat stitches: back
  looped stitches: chain stitch worked with tambour hook
  smocking stitches: stem; trellis
Selvedge: ⅛ in. (0.3 cm) wide, warp-faced plain weave of red with white stripes
Appliquéd with warp-faced 7/1 satin weave fabric strips
Pieced garment
Waist band lining: balanced plain weave
Finish: selvedge at bottom edge with no hem

Thread count
Basic fabric
  warp: 324   weft: 116
Lining
  warp: 60   weft: 48

Catalogue Number 26 (see color plate, p. 35)
Town of Patan, Kutch Area, Gujarat State
Woman's Wrapper (*patolu sari*), ca. 1900
silk plain weave, resist-dyed warp and weft (ikat)
213 x 39¾ (540 x 101) with fringe, warp x weft
Emma Harter Sweetser Fund 82.12

The earliest evidence for *patola* patterns is in fresco painting in temples and palaces of southern India from the sixteenth to the eighteenth century. While the term *patolu* (singular; *patola*, plural) appears first in tenth-century Indian literature, it was not until the eighteenth century that it became definitely associated with silk textiles. The technique of warp ikat dyeing (see cat. 11) probably originated in eastern Asia and passed from there to central Asia and India, where the much more complicated technique of double ikat developed. In India this type of cloth may have originated in Gujarat.[27] Established in A.D. 746, Patan, the historic center of *patola* weaving, was the seat of the Gujarati court until Muslim domination in 1306.[28] The weavers, mainly of the *Salvi* caste (*sal*, loom; *vi*, sword), occupied a quarter of the city where long, straight streets gave them room to stretch out warp threads.[29]

A single *patolu* usually measures five to six feet in length (warpwise) and generally, enough thread for three *saris* was put on the warping frame.[30] After the bundles of threads were wrapped with a cotton thread to resist the dye, they were dipped in red, then yellow, blue, and black dyes.[31] Patterns on *patola* fall into three categories: botanic; zoomorphic and anthropomorphic; and abstract or geometric.[32] The design on this piece is in this last category and has the Gujarati name *chhabadi* (basket) *bhat* (design).[33] Although cloths in this particular pattern are traditional in India, they were also frequently exported to Indonesia, especially to Java and Sumba (see cat. 13).[34] This *patolu* is composed in much the same way as all Indian *saris*, with side borders and decorative end panels (*pallav*). Frequently, as here, gold threads embellish the end border, which is draped over the shoulder when worn.

In western India the color red is closely associated with weddings, and *patola* were used in that context. Interestingly though, they were not worn as bridal garb but by mothers and other female relatives of Hindu brides. Additionally, *patola* were used as temple hangings, clothing for idols, elephant blankets, and gifts by princes.[35] These multiple functions indicate that the cloths had ritual significance and associated prestige on several levels.

Generally, *patola* were considered auspicious. Their imagery of gems, leaves, and blossoms and the protective colors of red and green were ritually important.[36] In fact, the basket pattern of this *patola* relates to the basket with vegetable sprouts in it that the Naga Brahmans worshipped as a symbol of the mother goddess. Pieces of *patola* were even burned and the ashes mixed with other materials to create a protective salve.[37]

Export of *patola* to Indonesia began early as the amount of ceremonial significance attached to the cloths in Java and elsewhere demonstrates. In the Javanese courts of Jojakarta and Surakarta, *patola* were wrapped and worn as *dodots* (see cat. 1) or cut into trousers. They were also used during weddings and to cover the altar of *Devi Shri*, the mother deity. As in India, the cloths were thought to have magical powers and, hence, were used for medicinal purposes.[38] *Patola* were prime articles of exchange in the trade for the spices and aromatic woods of

Indonesia, and as a result the eight-point star pattern on this piece can be found from Sumatra in the west to Mindanao in the east.[39] The north coast Java batik pattern called *djelamprang* may have come from *patola*,[40] and the famous double ikats of Tenganan, Bali (see cat. 10), frequently employ *patola* patterns derived from ones similar to this.

Diffused by the sandalwood trade, *patola* affected patterns on Sumba and Roti fairly early. In Roti, the Dutch established a clearly defined social hierarchy based on favors (which were *patola*) that were granted to particular rulers in exchange for local goods. In Sumba, only the highest classes used the pattern called *patola ratu* (see cat. 13), which the star motif seen here influenced. In fact, in Sumba the term *Hunda Rangga Ru Patola* means nobleman.[41]

Materials
Basic fabric
  warp: silk, single-ply slight Z-twist; red, tan, light yellow, brown-violet, blue, green
  weft: silk, single-ply slight Z-twist; red, tan, light yellow, brown-violet, blue, green
  side border warp:
    silk, single-ply Z-twist; green, violet, yellow, red
  end border weft:
    metallic
      core thread: silk, single-ply S-twist; light yellow
      strip: gold, silver and copper with calcium, Z-twist; gold colored, core exposed

Techniques
Balanced plain weave, loosely woven; side borders with thicker warp
Resist-dyed warp and weft
Finish: end borders have narrow area of metallic weft and narrow area of no weft, small metal weight attached to fringe at one end
Fringe: individual warp ends

Thread count
Basic fabric
  warp: 54   weft: 53   side border warp: 40

Pattern Repeat
warpwise: 8¼ in. (21.0 cm)   weftwise: 7 in. (18.0 cm)

Catalogue Number 27
Coromandel Coast Area (for export to England)
Bed Cover (*palampore*), ca. 1770
cotton plain weave, mordant and resist dyed
129 x 92 (327 x 233) warp x weft
Eliza M. and Sarah L. Niblack Collection 33.1324

Fragments of Indian dyed cottons from the thirteenth to the fifteenth centuries have been excavated at the important trading center of Fustat, Egypt. These low-quality fabrics were obviously not intended for the prestige market.[42] In addition to the northwest trade, India was in the same period participating in the active East-West trade centered in the Indian Ocean. The ancient kingdom of Srivijaya in Sumatra dominated this activity until the tenth century, when Arabs assumed control of it.[43] The major items for export from India were cloth, opium, and minerals, which were traded for Chinese raw silk, silk textiles, and porcelains and Indonesian spices, aromatic woods, and gums. Each of these Eastern markets made special demands on the Indian traders, so particular types of cloth were produced to satisfy each one (see cat. 30).[44]

When the Europeans arrived in Southeast Asia in the late fifteenth century, they immediately saw the financial benefits of participating in this trade. By the early seventeenth century, the English and Dutch had established trading companies to reap the wealth of the Eastern trade, especially in spices. While the Dutch controlled trade to the East, the English dominated the European market. By the end of the seventeenth century, the "Indian craze" had hit Europe and vast quantities of mordant-dyed cloth were being shipped to England, France, and other parts of northern Europe.

The first fabrics to become fashionable in the early part of the seventeenth century were the furnishing cloths used to redecorate interiors. Bed hangings had been elaborately decorated since before Elizabethan times (see cat. 101), for the bed had enormous importance in dwellings of the period, and much effort and expense were lavished on its decoration.[45] It was one of the few large, freestanding pieces of furniture in the home; and to make it comfortable for sleeping, it was surrounded by curtains to mitigate drafts and to create the only privacy possible in the dwelling's open spaces. Although dyed *palampores* (from the Hindi-Persian *palang posh*, or bed cover[46]) are cited in import lists in the first decades of the seventeenth century, they did not surpass the exportation of Indian quilts until late in the century.

The use of the flowering tree as a decorative motif on these bed accoutrements has a long and complicated history. In antiquity the "tree of life" was used in Assyrian relief sculpture, in which the tree was a symbol of fertility and renewal because of its apparent death in the fall and regeneration in the spring. In addition, the tree might have had a symbolic function as the polar unifier between heaven and earth. Thus it may be that tree cults were more widely distributed than has previously been realized, a hypothesis that is supported by motifs of trees enshrined within buildings from ancient Scandinavian and Indian relief sculpture as well as by the Elizabethan practice of installing living trees in halls of grand homes.[47] The symbolic function of the large, painted image of a flowering tree being placed on the bed is, therefore, apparent.

At the beginning of the Indian trade to Europe, complaints in correspondence note the unsuitability of the dreary colors and foreign designs to European tastes. At first, some suggestions were acted upon—once the background color of *palampores* was changed to white, their bright colors became clearer—but soon the Europeans were supplying Indian producers with patterns. Their sources were probably embroidery and lace patterns and contemporary illustrated botanical books. In textiles, these influences were combined with the European chinoiserie style, which was an eccentric mix of European-influenced Chinese and Turkish motifs. In addition, patterns were derived from Chinese wares that had been made for the European market, such as porcelain, textiles, and wallpaper (see cat. 42). Persian designs from paintings and other media, which had already reached India through the Mughal courts, were also influential.

Many of these influences can be seen in this *palampore*. The dominant motif of the central tree possibly evolved from Persian miniature painting, which frequently depicted trees with sinuous branches and partially exposed roots and placed them on a rocky outcropping. The interlacing of bamboo branches with tree limbs evolved from Chinese sources, and the flowering vines in the borders probably originated in Chinese export wallpaper (see cat. 42) and in European embroidery, lace, and silk patterns. This amalgam of design sources created a new, highly desirable image that in itself had enormous impact on subsequent design in Europe and elsewhere.

Perhaps the single most important impetus for the popularity of Indian dyed cottons was the coloring, which retained its brilliance even after numerous washings. As reported by many travelers since the sixteenth century, several specialists had to execute a number of steps during the complicated dyeing process. Europeans preferred red and indigo, each of which required a different and complex dyeing procedure. Cotton fiber, unlike animal fibers such as silk and wool, rejects the permanent union of fiber and dye. The dye—except for indigo, which is not water soluble—must therefore be combined with a mordant or chemical solution to make it colorfast. Indian mastery of the complicated mordant-dyeing techniques and manufacture of superbly woven cottons allowed the country to dominate cotton production until European industrialization in the nineteenth century.

Producing a *palampore* started with preparation of the cloth in a fatty astringent solution. The pattern was then pounced on the fabric with charcoal dust, and the mordants for red and black were painted onto the surface with a pen made of split bamboo. After the piece was dipped into a vat of madder red dye, the two different mordants produced the design in red and black. The white background areas were then sun-bleached and immersed in a dung bath to heighten the color. The next step was to apply wax over all the surface that was not to receive indigo dye. Since indigo does not require a mordant, the portions of the cloth to be blue were placed directly into the dye bath. More mordants were applied to achieve other colors on the cloth, which was waxed and dipped further until it was ready for the final bleaching. After that was accomplished,

109

yellow dye was manually applied to the surface, both by itself and, to produce green, over indigo. Only such painstaking labor created the brilliant, colorfast hues that amazed Europe. They were not successfully imitated in the West until late in the eighteenth century.

The design, and particularly delicate floral border of this piece, place it in the second half of the eighteenth century.[48]

Materials
Basic fabric
warp: cotton, single-ply Z-twist; tan
weft: cotton, single-ply Z-twist; tan
dyes: medium and dark blue, medium and dark red, light and dark brown, black

Techniques
Balanced plain weave
Painted mordant and wax-resist dyed
Finish: rolled hem with whip stitch
Marker of light red discontinuous wefts near top

Thread count
warp : 80   weft: 72

Literature
Gilfoy and Vollmer, *Arts of Asia*, March–April 1981, p. 132.

Catalogue Number 28 (see color plate, p. 36)
Gujarat State (?) (for export to Europe)
Bed Cover (*palampore*), ca. 1850 (?)
silk plain weave, embroidered with silk and metallic thread
111½ x 82½ (282.5 x 209) warp x weft
Eliza M. and Sarah L. Niblack Collection 33.748

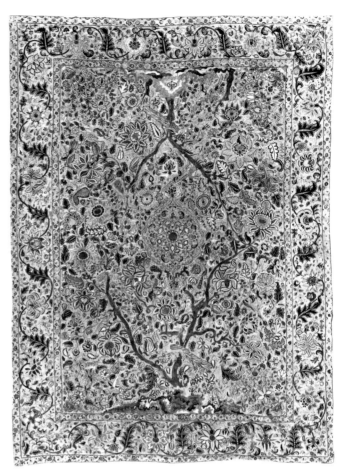

Determining where this extravagantly embroidered bed cover was made has been a bit difficult. The design and drawing certainly owe a great deal to printed and dyed Indian *palampores;* however, examples using the double tree and medallion center seem to be far less common than those with single trees.[49] Though most embroidered Indian spreads are executed in silk stitches on a cotton ground, the piece illustrated here is on a silk ground. A British order from 1682 for Indian silk quilts mentions embroidered quilts:

Wee intend not any of the embrodered white Quilts of Silke needleworke but beside the mixtures and flowers of the Silke Quilts you may send Us 20 plaine Silke ones of every good colour. . . .[50]

The stitches used here are stem and satin rather than the chain or tambour stitches more common on Indian export embroidery. Whatever the point of origin, this magnificent spread must have been an object of immense admiration in its luxurious European setting.

Materials
Basic fabric
warp: silk, no twist; tan
weft: silk, no twist; tan
Embroidery
silk, no twist; white, two yellows, two light greens, medium and dark green, light, medium, and dark blue, light, medium, and dark red, light and dark violet, light brown, dark blue-green
metallic
core thread: silk, no twist; white
strip: silver, Z-twist; gray colored
Lining
warp: cotton, single-ply Z-twist; tan
weft: cotton, single-ply Z-twist; tan
Backing
warp: silk, no twist; light orange
weft: silk, no twist; light orange
Techniques
Weft-dominant plain weave, weft thicker than warp
Embroidery
flat stitches: couching, pattern couching, patterned couching; satin, encroaching satin, long and short satin, padded satin; split; stem; straight
combination flat stitches: arrowhead over satin; cross and couching over surface satin; trellis couching over surface satin; trellis couching and upright cross over surface satin; couching and straight over surface satin; straight over satin; fern over long and short satin; running over long and short satin; stem over long and short satin; straight over long and short satin; burden over surface satin; burden and Bokhara couching over surface satin; burden and running over surface satin; upright cross and dot over surface satin; upright cross and split over surface satin; running over surface satin combination flat and looped stitches: split and variation of fly over surface satin
Lining: balanced plain weave, embroidered through top fabric and lining
Backing: weft-dominant plain weave, weft thicker than warp
Thread count
Basic fabric
warp: 94   weft: 74
Lining
warp: 39   weft: 37
Backing
warp: 124   weft: 108
Literature
Gilfoy and Vollmer, *Arts of Asia*, March–April 1981, p. 132.

Catalogue Number 29
Coromandel Coast Area (for export to Holland?)
Fragment of Garment Fabric, 18th century
cotton plain weave, mordant and resist dyed
37 x 24 (94 x 61) warp x weft (?)
Eliza M. and Sarah L. Niblack Collection 33.1247

A wide variety of Indian cottons were exported to the West. This piece, which was seamed and then quilted, probably belonged to a petticoat. Although the alteration is not easily seen in the photograph, the quilting pattern changes at one end to undulating lines that define a bottom edge. The length from top to bottom is appropriate for the kind of petticoat an eighteenth-century woman would have worn under an open robe (see cat. 124 and 125).

To make this fabric, the chintz painter first stencilled the floral pattern with charcoal. After removing the stencil, he used the pounced charcoal pattern to draw in the design, often changing or adding variants on the original.[51] As with the *palampore* (see cat. 27), the pattern was drawn with a mordant and the same procedures of resisting, dyeing, and bleaching were followed. The design's origins are undoubtedly in European textiles. Many patterns and textiles were sent from Europe to India, where Indian artists copied and reinterpreted the designs before exporting them.

One reason for the increased demand for imports was European acceptance of Indian chintz as a clothing fabric:

> The growth of this fashion was described in vivid terms by the English writer Daniel Defoe, who started his career in the clothing trade and was a critic of the East India trade: ". . . Chints and Painted Callicoes, which before were only made use of for Carpets, Quilts, etc., and to cloth children or ordinary people, became now the Dress of our Ladies, and such is the Power of a Mode; we saw our Persons of Quality dressed in Indian Carpets, which but a few Years before their Chamber-Maids would have thought too ordinary for them; the Chints were advanced from lying on their Floors to their Backs, from the Foot-cloth to the Petticoat . . ."[52]

The great volume of chintz imports in the late seventeenth century alarmed European wool and silk weavers, who pressed for bans on cotton. France enacted bans in 1681 and England in 1700; Holland, however, never imposed sumptuary laws because Dutch importers also controlled domestic cloth production.[53] Cottons, therefore, flowed more freely through Dutch ports.

Materials
Basic fabric
warp: cotton, single-ply Z-twist; white
weft: cotton, single-ply Z-twist; white
dyes: light, medium, and dark red, yellow, tan, brown-yellow, light violet, light blue, green, black
Batting
cotton
Quilting thread
cotton, two-ply S-twist; white
Techniques
Balanced plain weave
Painted mordant and wax-resist dyed; painted details
Pieced and quilted
Initialed in light red cross-stitch embroidery
Thread count
warp: 65   weft: 77
Pattern repeat
warpwise: 16½ in. (42.0 cm)
Literature
Gittinger, *Master Dyers to the World*, p. 179.
Exhibition
Master Dyers to the World, The Textile Museum, Washington, D.C., 1982; The Field Museum, Chicago, 1983; Asia House, New York, 1983

Catalogue Number 30 (see color plate, p. 37)
Coromandel Coast Area (for export to Thailand)
Wrapper (*phanung*), 18th century
cotton plain weave, mordant and resist dyed
133 x 45 (337 x 114) warp x weft
Jacob Metzger Fund 47.184

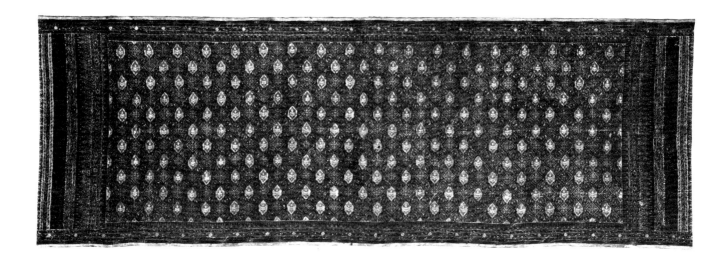

India's trade network also extended eastward to Indonesia, Thailand, and Japan. The Thai preferred Indian cloths made on the Coromandel Coast.[54] As with the beginnings of the Indonesian-European trade, various types of goods passed through several transactions before reaching the market. Europeans supplied Thailand with Indian textiles in exchange for skins, and sappenwood for dye, which was then traded to Japan for silver and copper.[55] While the Dutch were important in the Indian-Thai trade throughout the seventeenth century, they never dominated it because the Japanese, Thai, English, and Muslims were all vying for their share.[56]

Textiles such as these are illustrated in Thai manuscripts as seating or reclining cloths.[57] They were probably also used as wrappers, for the composition of their designs is drawn from that of Indian *sari*. The broad side and end borders and the central field are filled with intricate filigree tracery, a type of design especially preferred by the Thai that also occurs in lacquer work; gold appliqué; carving in wood and stone; and late period ceramic tiles. There is an enormous amount of delicate resist patterning in the double triangle (*tumpal*) border and central area, which consists of latticework surrounding the torsos of the heavenly beings (*apsaras*), who make gestures of adoration.[58]

Materials

Basic fabric

warp: cotton, single-ply S-twist; white

weft: cotton, single-ply S-twist; white

dyes: light and dark red, tan, blue, violet-red, brown-yellow

Techniques

Balanced plain weave

Painted mordant and wax-resist dyed, glazed

Finish: selvedge edges embroidered in buttonhole stitch

Thread count

Basic fabric

warp: 85   weft: 81

Pattern repeat

warpwise: 5¾ in. (14.5 cm)   weftwise: 6¼ in. (16 cm)

Literature

Gilfoy and Vollmer, *Arts of Asia*, March–April 1981, p. 130.

Gittinger, *Master Dyers to the World*, p. 157, color detail, p. 158.

Exhibition

Master Dyers to the World, The Textile Museum, Washington, D.C., 1982; The Field Museum, Chicago, 1983; Asia House, New York, 1983

Catalogue Number 31
Kashmir Area (for export to Europe)
Woman's Wrapper (*amlikar*), ca. 1850
wool twill weave, pieced, appliquéd, embroidered with wool
79½ x 79½ (201.5 x 201.5) warp x weft
Gift of Mr. R. M. Bowen in memory of Grace M. Bowen
   45.191

Local Kashmiri tradition relates that patterned shawl weaving began during the Mughal reign of Zain-ul-'Abden (A.D. 1420-70). Sixteenth-century documents from Emperor Akbar's reign, however, imply that the origins of this art were pre-Mughal.[59] The earliest surviving seventeenth-century examples have a large, plain central field. Their ends or heads carry the motif of flowering plants (*buta*) that came from Iranian influenced Mughal design. By the mid-eighteenth century this pattern was circumscribed by a cone-shaped outline, which had antecedents in regions to the north and west of India. Great numbers of shawls with this motif were being exported to Europe by the third quarter of the eighteenth century.[60]

Because producing a handwoven shawl in Kashmir was a laborious and costly task, the needleworked shawl evolved in nineteenth-century India as a faster and cheaper way to meet European demand. Khiwaja Yusef, an Armenian agent for a trading firm in Constantinople, supposedly first used the method, and by 1820, shawl producers employed about five thousand needleworkers.

After polishing the plain cloth—which was woven in a variety of colors—and pouncing a pattern onto the ground with powder or charcoal, the needleworker (*rafugar*) embroidered the shawl, mostly in stem and satin stitches. Seen from a distance, the shawl appeared to be a more expensive woven garment because these stitches lay flat on the surface.[61] Several *rafugar* executed the shawl illustrated here as piecework and then assembled it like a giant jigsaw puzzle, a procedure that decreased the time lapse between the order's placement and the product's completion. These more moderately priced shawls were enormously popular and, like this example, many were extremely well executed and designed.

Materials
   Basic and appliquéd fabrics
      warp: wool, single-ply S-twist; red, black, light green, light and medium red-violet, light blue, yellow-green, white, or brown-yellow
      weft: wool, single-ply S-twist; red, black, light green, light and medium red-violet, light blue, yellow-green, white, or brown-yellow
   Embroidery
      wool, two-ply S-twist; black, red, white, dark green, light blue, brown-yellow, light and medium red-violet, tan
Techniques
   Warp- or weft-faced 3/1 diagonal twill weave
   Embroidery
      flat stitches: couching; Roumanian; seeding; stem; straight
      looped stitches: buttonhole; chain, open chain; fly
   Pieced; appliquéd (small areas) with fabric of warp- or weft-faced 3/1 diagonal twill weave
   Fringe: unraveled fabric on all four sides
   Signed in white chain stitch and numbered in white stem stitch
Thread count
   Basic fabric
      warp: 80   weft: 80

Catalogue Number 31

Notes

[1] Gittinger, 1982, p. 16.

[2] Peebles, 1981, pp. 9-10.

[3] Bühler, 1979, p. 1.

[4] Calico Museum, 1980, p. 42.

[5] Peebles, 1981, p. 10.

[6] Gittinger, 1982, pp. 31-57.

[7] Calico Museum, 1980, p. 79.

[8] Gittinger, 1982, p. 137.

[9] The intricacies and intrigue that came to characterize the Indo-European trade can only be outlined here. Further discussion is found in individual entries.

[10] Beer, 1970, p. 15.

[11] Calico Museum, 1980, p. 107.

[12] Bühler, 1980, p. 103.

[13] Gittinger, 1979b, p. 197.

[14] Bühler, 1980, pp. 107-8.

[15] Ellson, 1979, p. 112.

[16] Ellson, 1979, p. 116.

[17] Ellson, 1979, pp. 18-19.

[18] Irwin, 1973a, p. 73.

[19] This particular aba is very similar to one illustrated in Ellson (Ellson, 1979, p. 114, fig. 123).

[20] Ellson, 1979, pp. 113-14.

[21] Irwin, 1973a, p. 80.

[22] Irwin, 1973a, p. 74.

[23] Irwin, 1973a, p. 29.

[24] Peebles, 1981, p. 23.

[25] Nanavati, 1966, p. 11.

[26] Irwin, 1973a, p. 197.

[27] Bühler, 1979, pp. 340-41.

[28] Bühler, 1979, p. 326.

[29] Bühler, 1979, p. 250.

[30] Bühler, 1979, p. 227.

[31] Bühler, 1979, p. 234.

[32] Bühler, 1979, p. 338.

[33] Bühler, 1979, p. 214.

[34] Bühler, 1979, p. 68.

[35] Bühler, 1979, p. 340.

[36] Bühler, 1979, p. 269.

[37] Bühler, 1979, p. 270.

[38] Bühler, 1979, pp. 288-90.

[39] Bühler, 1979, p. 286.

[40] Bühler, 1979, p. 281.

[41] Adams, 1969, p. 145.

[42] Gittinger, 1982, pp. 31-33.

[43] Gilfoy, 1980, p. 357.

[44] Gittinger, 1982, p. 137.

[45] Irwin, 1971, p. 37.

[46] Gittinger, 1982, p. 186.

[47] Irwin, personal communication.

[48] This piece is very similar to one dated to 1770 that is illustrated in Irwin (Irwin, 1971, pl. 15).

[49] A dyed cotton palampore of this type is illustrated in Beer (Beer, 1970, cat. 6).

[50] Irwin, 1971, pp. 148-49.

[51] Gittinger, 1982, p. 179.

[52] Irwin, 1971, p. 37.

[53] Gittinger, 1982, pp. 187-90.

[54] Gittinger, 1982, p. 161.

[55] Gittinger, 1982, p. 165.

[56] Gittinger, 1982, p. 163.

[57] Gittinger, 1982, fig. 135, p. 156.

[58] Gittinger, personal communication.

[59] Karpinski, 1963, p. 119.

[60] Irwin, 1955, p. 12.

[61] Irwin, 1955, pp. 3-4.

China

Silk and China have been synonymous in many parts of the world since trade began. From the fifth century B.C. until the time of the Roman Empire in the first century A.D.[1], woven silks came to be used extensively in commerce to the West and as prestigious diplomatic gifts. In fact, the ancient Greeks refer to the world of the *Seres* (people who make silk) though they have no idea of its location. By the time of the founding of the Roman Empire, the Chinese were called *Serika*, from which our word silk derives.[2]

Silk is known to have been manufactured in China since the second millenium B.C. Producing a continuous filament of that lustrous fiber initially involved a slow, tedious process of raising a domesticated variety of silkworm on mulberry leaves. The secrets of making silk of this type remained with the Chinese until the Middle Ages. Sir Aurel Stein discovered the earliest Chinese silks thus found, along the old Silk Route from China to the West: these figured fragments date from the Han dynasty (206 B.C.-A.D., 220). By the fifth century A.D., great quantities of woven silk from both China and the Middle East were flowing westward to Byzantium, which eventually also developed its own sericulture. Its output was never great enough to satisfy the demand, however, and China has consequently remained the primary producer of silk until today.

China became an international power during the period of consolidation in the Ch'in dynasty (256-206 B.C.). During the Han dynasty, China began to expand beyond its frontiers to assume an active role in the trade rapidly developing throughout the Eastern Hemisphere. A well-structured political system and long experience with a highly desirable luxury product put the Chinese in an excellent position to benefit economically as exchanges of commodities increased. These activities further strengthened the already systematized social order by infusing it with added wealth and increased the gap between the central agrarian religio-political state and the "barbarian" nomads to the north and east.

In addition to the Han fragments Stein discovered, a number of Chinese silks from the T'ang dynasty (A.D. 618-906) also survive in the Japanese imperial Shosoin repository, which was assembled during the eighth-century reign of Emperor Shōmu.[3] In spite of the export of silk technology to the Byzantine Empire early in the sixth century, the Chinese Silk Route continued to be the most active one until the rise of Islam in the seventh century. The trade, primarily in silks from the Far East and spices from Southeast Asia, traversed central Asia and the Indian Ocean. The increasing importance of the Sasanians in Iran in the sixth century and the Islamic thrust in the seventh and eighth centuries limited East-West trade,[4] but Mongol control of central Asia in the early thirteenth century allowed for the Silk Route's past strength to be reestablished.[5] Though the amount of activity varied, the commerce continued until the ocean routes dominated by European sea powers eliminated the need for overland trade.

By the second millenium B.C., China had developed a stratified social order, established large urban centers, and based a complicated material culture on a settled agrarian way of life. This system included the concept that the emperor's right to rule was based on the moral imperatives of heaven and a reverence for the past that became pivotal in the culture.[6] By the third century A.D., native Taoism as well as Indian Buddhism had contributed a huge symbolic vocabulary to the imperial state. Chinese literacy promoted the development of a complex and sophisticated symbolism built on verbal puns called rebus. Punning is a feature unique to spoken Chinese because many of its thousands of characters share the same sound. A wealth of pictorial images increased the elegance and flexibility of Chinese writing: decoration that could be read like a poem—or an edict—could be created. Thus, in a way unfamiliar to Westerners, Chinese costume and furnishing fabrics embodied visual and literary references that put their wearers in harmony with the social order and the universe.

In the Ch'ing dynasty (A.D. 1644-1911), Manchu tribal warriors from the north seized the imperial throne. Their active lifestyle starkly contrasted with the effete, luxurious one of the preceding urban Ming court. In an attempt to glorify their heritage yet still claim the imperial mandate, the Manchu combined their typical form of dress with Chinese imperial symbols. By 1759 the shape, color, decoration, and even the accessories of each type of court garment were codified in an imperial edict. This development further enriched costume vocabulary.

As Manchu power diminished toward the end of the nineteenth century, both the vigor of the symbolism and the quality of workmanship declined. Because the greatest number of surviving costumes and textiles come from this period, our view of Chinese achievements has been distorted. It is unfortunate that more of the early garments have not survived, for they would give us a truer picture of the visual splendor of the ancient Chinese textiles, among the oldest and most highly developed in the world.

Catalogue Number 32
China
Taoist Priest's Coat, ca. 1900
silk satin weave, embroidered with silk and metallic thread
50½ (128) length, warp
Eliza M. and Sarah L. Niblack Collection 33.365

Taoism, one of the most ancient Chinese belief systems, probably dates from the fourth century B.C. A fundamental precept of Taoist belief is the complementary polarity existing in the *yin* and *yang*, or negative and positive. Balance between the various attributes of these two forces is the goal of Taoism and underlies its most important principle, that of eternal change. The number five, representing the elements wood, fire, earth, metal, and water, is also significant in Taoist symbolism.[7] All substance, composed of various combinations of the five basic elements, expresses this fundamental duality.

Many of these ideas are visually realized on this coat. The symbols for the sun and moon (*yang* and *yin*) appear at the top. On a dark blue satin field at the center is the heavenly pagoda surrounded by twenty-four balls that probably represent stars. The combination evokes the notion of heavenly paradise. Flanked by cranes, emblems of longevity, the pagoda becomes associated with the home of the immortals, the mythical Isle of the Blest in the Eastern Sea.[8] Five four-clawed dragons swirl in the sky, each in quest of the flaming pearl. The dragon is a *yang* force, and the depiction of five of them on this robe accords with Taoist numerology. The whole design, with its astral symbols of sun, moon, and stars and with four earthly gates and five mystic peaks centered around the Isle of the Blest, becomes a diagram of the unseen universe to which the Taoists aspire in their quest for immortality.[9]

Materials
Basic fabric
warp: silk, single-ply Z-twist; dark blue
weft: silk, no twist; brown
Embroidery
silk, no twist; white, light and medium orange, two light greens, light blue-green, light, medium, and dark blue, yellow-brown
silk, two-ply Z-twist; white, light orange
metallic #1
core thread: cotton, two-ply Z-twist; white
strip: copper with gold, on paper Z-twist; gold colored
metallic #2
core thread: cotton, two-ply Z-twist; white
strip: copper with silver on paper, Z-twist; copper colored
Trim fabric
warp: silk, single-ply Z-twist; blue
weft: silk, no twist; gray
Lining
warp: bast (ramie), no twist; tan
weft: bast (ramie), no twist; tan
Techniques
Warp-faced 7/1 satin weave
Embroidery
flat stitches: couching of single, doubled, and tripled elements; satin, encroaching satin, long and short satin, padded satin; stem; split
looped stitches: Chinese knot
combination flat stitches: couching over couching; counching over satin; straight over couching; straight over satin
Pieced garment with sleeve openings and neck band stiffened with paper
Trim: 7/1 satin weave
Lining: balanced plain weave
Thread count
Basic fabric
warp: 288   weft: 112
Trim fabric
warp: 288   weft: 112
Lining
warp: 24   weft: 24

Catalogue Number 32, Back

Catalogue Number 33
China
Taoist Priest's Coat, ca. 1870
silk plain and twill weaves; embroidered with silk, metallic
    thread and discs; trimmed with silk interknotted fringe
    (macramé)
54 (137) length, warp
Gift of the Doris Meltzer Gallery TR 9024

The rich designs on this coat are derived from both Buddhist and Taoist images that were employed as auspicious symbols during the Ch'ing dynasty (A.D. 1644-1911). The symbols of the eight Taoist immortals embellish the wide bands at each sleeve edge. On one sleeve, from top to bottom, are the fan of Chung-li Chuan, the lotus pod of Ho Hsien Ku, the flute of Han Hsiang-tzu, and the pilgrim's gourd and iron crutch of Li T'ieh-kuai. On the other sleeve are the sword of Lu Tung-pin, the bamboo tube and rods of Chuang Kuo Lao, the castenets of Ts'ao Kuo-ch'iu, and the basket of peaches of Lan Ts'ai-ho. Each of these motifs is interspersed with bats, punning devices for prosperity (*fu*).

The main symbol is the Taoist pagoda. It is surrounded by dragons pursuing flaming pearls (see cat. 32); in the field are four four-clawed dragons in rondels in a cloud-filled sky. Between these motifs on the back are the eight Buddhist symbols in couched gold embroidery. On top from left to right are the umbrella, canopy, and vase; and on the bottom are the fish, wheel, knot, and conch shell; beneath is the lotus. On the very bottom panel is a pair of dragons flanking the earth mountain that rises from the universal sea. The two lower bands of the front contain wheels as well as lions with peonies. The neck band displays the character *shou* (longevity) among the cranes of longevity and clouds; and on the loose lower flaps of the front are flowers, a lion on one side, and an elephant on the other. All of this imagery is embroidered on green- and red-figured silk with woven patterns of phoenixes in a cloud-filled sky, perhaps a reference to the Empress as a balance for the Emperor's dragon.

While the shape of this garment is not that of a classic Taoist priest's coat (see cat. 32), the inscription on the inside of the garment says it was respectfully submitted to a religious building in the eighth lunar month, the fifteenth day in 1873, with wishes for everlasting prosperity (see detail, p. 123).[10] The coat does not appear to have been altered from a liturgical garment, for the embroidery is designed to fill its spaces and is interrupted only in the side bands, where the coat appears to have been cut and then shortened through the addition of inside loops and buttons. The dramatic design and color and the flashy fringe added to the back suggest the coat was a theatrical costume. However, it might also be a secondary vestment that the head priest wore for less important occasions or the lesser priest wore when the head priest had taken the more common garment (see cat. 32).[11]

Materials
Basic fabric
    warp: silk, no twist; red, green, yellow or light blue-green
    weft: silk, no twist; red, green, yellow or light blue-green
Embroidery
    silk, no twist; dark brown, yellow-green, white, light,
        medium, and dark orange-red, brown-yellow, light,
        medium, and dark blue, light violet, dark blue-green,
        light and medium yellow
    silk, two-ply S-twist; light and dark blue, black
    metallic #1
        core thread: silk, two-ply Z-twist; white
        strip: silver with gold and copper on paper,
            Z-twist; copper colored
    metallic #2
        core thread: silk, single-ply Z-twist; yellow
        strip: silver with gold and copper on paper,
            Z-twist; gold colored
Trim
    knotting: silk, two-ply S-twist; black
    tassels: silk, two-ply Z-twist; white
Lining
    warp: bast (ramie), no twist: light red-orange
    weft: bast (ramie), no twist: light red-orange
Techniques
Warp-dominant plain weave (background) and warp-faced
    3/1 diagonal twill weave (figure)
Embroidery
    flat stitches: couching of single and doubled elements;
        pattern couching; satin, encroaching satin, long and
        short satin, padded satin; stem; split; straight
    combination flat stitches: couching over couching;
        couching over satin; herringbone over surface satin;
        satin over satin; split over satin; straight over couching;
        straight over satin
Pieced garment with two pieces
Trim: narrow strips of black or white silk satin,
    interknotted fringe, tassels, and metal discs
Lining: balanced plain weave
Inscription on inside at center back
Thread count
Basic fabric
    warp: 126   weft: 71
Lining
    warp: 43   weft: 43
Pattern repeat
warpwise: 6¼ in. (16.0 cm)   weftwise: 3 in. (7.5 cm)

Catalogue Number 33, Back

Catalogue Number 33, Front

Catalogue Number 33, Detail

同治十二年八月十五日訃洋洋世元人信
永福東院仰明如

Catalogue Number 34
China
Informal Imperial Coat (*ch'i-fu*), 1775-1825
silk and metallic plain weave (*k'o-ssu*)
64½ (163.5) length, warp
Gift of Sonia and Joseph M. Lesser 76.541

The development of the *ch'i-fu* is intimately connected with Manchu dominance in China beginning in A.D. 1644. A symbol central to Manchu power, the *ch'i-fu* mixed ancient Chinese imperial iconography with a nomadic cut to assert Manchu tribal heritage and form a solid bond with the Chinese imperial past.

The *ch'i-fu* as a form of costume did not fully evolve until the Manchu Ch'ing dynasty (A.D. 1644-1911). It has been suggested[12] that the *ch'i-fu* depended upon an animal-skin model for its form. The double-layered front and the slits in the front and back of the piece have antecedents in nomadic skin garments, which were designed to be comfortable during the active life of a horse-riding nomad. Those coats afforded protection from the wind because of their double layer in front and their long sleeves and cuffs, which were shaped to fit over the hand. Additionally, the garment had open flaps in front and back to allow for comfortable seating on horseback. Earlier Chinese court costume was based on the use of luxurious, woven, rectangular fabric that was joined without tailoring, much in the way a Japanese kimono was, and is, assembled (see cat. 47 and 48). This method of construction maintained the integrity of the woven structure while it served as prestige clothing for sedentary court life.

Decoration of the *ch'i-fu* was linked to ancient Chinese imperial tradition. Dragons on imperial coats were used at least as early as the T'ang dynasty (A.D. 618-906).[13] The change in their size and position on the Manchu coat became formally codified in A.D. 1759 with the issuance of the *Huang-ch'ao li-ch'i t'u shih* or *Illustrated Catalogue of Ritual Paraphernalia of the Ch'ing Dynasty*.[14] That document established for the *ch'i-fu* the placement of dragons, the use of clouds in five colors, yellow as the symbol of the Manchu dynasty, the establishment of twelve ancient imperial symbols, and other details.[15]

The coat expresses the basic unity of man, heaven, and earth. In the heavens, filled with rain-giving clouds, nine imperial dragons twist: four on the chest, back, and shoulders; four near the lower border; and one hidden from view, under the flap. According to ancient Taoist symbolism, nine is an auspicious number. The flaming orb near the dragon's head has been called the pearl of wisdom, and the dragon's attempt to seize it represents the Emperor's quest for virtue as he guides his empire.[16] This symbol has also been interpreted as the morning star in the eastern quarter, or vernal equinox.[17] At the bottom of the coat swirls the universal ocean, which surrounds the earth mountain, here represented by four angular rock formations in the front and back and at the hem, symbolizing the four cardinal points of the compass. Thus when the Emperor wears the coat, he becomes the world axis and the neck opening serves as the gate of heaven.[18]

The twelve ancient Chinese imperial symbols added to the coat of the Emperor in 1759 visualized his authority. Dating from at least the second century B.C., the twelve symbols are placed on the *ch'i-fu* in descending concentric rings according to their importance. The sun and moon on the shoulders and the constellations and mountain on the chest and back allude to the Emperor's yearly state sacrifices. At waist level, the judgment sign (*fu*) and the axe on the front extol temporal power; the paired dragons and pheasant on the back connote dominance over the natural world. At knee level are representations of four of the five elements: a water weed (water), a pair of ceremonial cups (metal), a flame (fire), and a plate of millet (wood). The mountain on the center back represents the fifth element, earth.[19]

In addition, Eight Precious Things are tucked into the waves of the universal ocean: pearls, coral, gold circular and rectangular ornaments, rhinoceros horn, ingot, *ju-i* scepter, and bolts or rolls of tribute silk. These were considered auspicious and were thought to bring good luck. At another level are red bats forming the rebus for happiness. Other symbols include peaches and the written character *shou*, both of which symbolize longevity.

This coat is woven of silk and gold threads in *k'o-ssu* technique (see cat. 35). Here small alterations have replaced the sleeve extensions and lining with yellow damask, and seamed the original front and back vents. The cuffs and collar were embroidered separately and applied to the garment.[20]

Materials
Basic fabric
warp: silk, single-ply Z-twist; white
weft: silk, no twist; yellow, white, seven shades of gray, blue, green-blue, red-orange, yellow-brown
metallic
core thread: silk single-ply Z-twist; white, orange or yellow
strip: gold with silicon on paper, Z-twist; gold colored
dyes/pigments: green, dark blue, black, orange

Techniques
Weft-faced plain weave with eccentric and discontinuous wefts, slit tapestry joins
Painted details
Pieced garment with replacement lining and sleeve extensions
Appliquéd collar and cuffs with details embroidered in: flat stitches: padded satin; stem

Thread count
Basic fabric
warp: 54   weft: silk, 109   metallic, 57

Literature
Gilfoy and Vollmer, *Arts of Asia*, March–April 1981, p. 127.

Catalogue Number 35
China
Pair of Imperial Throne Cushion Covers, ca. 1820
silk and metallic plain weave (k'o-ssu)
seat: 54 x 42¼ (137 x 107.5) weft x warp
back: 25½ x 25½ (65 x 65) warp x weft
Gift of Mrs. Louis Wolf 62.203 and 62.204

These elegantly patterned cushion covers were intended for the Emperor's throne. The hard, flat seat was made more comfortable by the addition of a large, rectangular seat pad; a shaped back cushion; and two bolsters for the arms. These covers display a number of imperial symbols: nine five-clawed dragons writhe in a cloud-filled sky in the larger cover and three on the smaller one. Yellow background color was strictly limited to Manchu imperial use, as were five-colored clouds. In addition, there are white peonies, which are symbolic of summer and which also carry the attribute of riches and honor.[21] Bats bearing the reversed swastika, or *wan*, form a rebus expressing wishes for great fortune.[22] The *shou* character prominent on the top of the smaller cover also denotes longevity.[23]

K'o-ssu tapestry weave developed fairly late in the history of Chinese silk weaving. The first evidence of the use of this technique is from the fourth century A.D. after the Han Emperor Wu-ti opened the famed Silk Route to the West. This method of weaving is both time-consuming and costly, and it was probably used mainly for prestige cloth that only the wealthy Chinese could afford.[24] By the Sung dynasty (A.D. 960-1279) *k'o-ssu* was used to copy famous paintings (see cat. 40).[25] Metal-wrapped threads were introduced during the Yuan dynasty (A.D. 1279-1368) and in the eighteenth century pigment, seen here, was first applied for fine detail. The court largely controlled *k'o-ssu* production, so Westerners were seldom exposed to it before the twentieth century.[26]

Seat
Materials
  Basic fabric
    warp: silk, single-ply Z-twist; white
    weft: silk, no twist; white, yellow, light, medium, and
      dark blue, light and medium orange, light and
      medium blue-green, gray
        metallic
          core thread: silk, single-ply Z-twist; white
          strip: copper with gold and silver on paper,
            Z-twist; gold colored
    dyes/pigments: orange, blue, black, brown
Techniques
  Weft-faced plain weave with eccentric and discontinuous
    wefts, slit tapestry joins
  Painted areas and details
Thread count
  Basic fabric
    warp: 56   weft: silk, 105   metallic, 50
Back
Materials
  Basic fabric
    warp: silk, single-ply Z-twist; white
    weft: silk, no twist; white, yellow, light and medium
      orange, light and medium blue, gray
        metallic
          core thread: silk, single-ply Z-twist; white
          strip: gold on paper, Z-twist; gold colored
    dyes/pigments: orange, blue, black
  Lining
    warp: silk, no twist; yellow
    weft: silk, no twist; yellow
Techniques
  Weft-faced plain weave with eccentric and discontinuous
    wefts, slit tapestry joins
  Painted areas and details
  Lining: weft-faced 2/1 diagonal twill weave
Thread count
  Basic fabric
    warp: 56   weft: silk, 88   metallic, 47
  Lining
    warp: 70   weft: 138

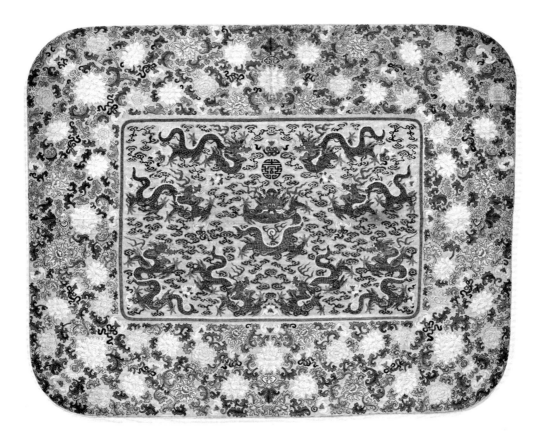

Catalogue Number 36 (see color plate, p. 38)
China
Imperial Bed Valance, ca. 1880
silk satin weave, embroidered with silk and metallic thread
131¼ x 39½ (332.5 x 100.5) weft x warp
Gift of Mrs. J. D. Gould 69.69.2

From the beginning of silk cultivation, embroidery was used to exploit its lustrous quality. A bronze axe that survives from the Shang dynasty (1766-1122 B.C.) carries the imprint of its embroidered silk wrapper. In China as in Europe (see cat. 27 and 101), the bed was an important piece of furniture that, for comfort and prestige, was decorated with valances and curtains (see cat. 37). The function of the valance was to cover the curtain railing. Embroidered on the silk, whose yellow color was especially favored by the Manchu rulers, are a number of imperial symbols. Five-clawed dragons swirl in a cloud-filled sky above the eternal sea and the rocky outcroppings of the earth mountain. In the sea as well are the eight auspicious symbols (see cat. 34). There are six large dragons on the main field, which is covered by six flaps also embroidered with dragons.

Materials
Basic fabric
warp: silk, single-ply slight Z-twist; yellow
weft: silk, no twist; yellow
Embroidery: silk, no twist; five shades yellow-brown, four shades orange-red, four shades blue, four shades green-blue, four shades of violet, white
silk, two-ply tight S-twist; dark brown
metallic #1
core thread: single-ply Z-twist; red
strip: gold with silver and copper on paper, Z-twist; gold colored
metallic #2
core thread: silk, single-ply Z-twist; yellow
strip: silver with gold and copper on paper, Z-twist; gold colored
metallic #3
core thread: silk, single-ply Z-twist; white
strip: silver on paper, Z-twist; silver colored
metallic #4
core thread: silk, single-ply Z-twist; white
strip: silver with copper on paper, Z-twist; gray-silver colored

Backing
warp: silk, no twist; yellow
weft: silk, no twist; yellow
Techniques
Warp-faced 7/1 satin weave
Embroidery
flat stitches: couching of doubled elements; pattern couching; satin, encroaching satin, padded satin; stem
Pieced fabric, pleated fabric at top with free-hanging flaps
Backing: weft-dominant plain weave, weft thicker than warp
Thread count
Basic fabric
warp: 397   weft: 91
Backing
warp: 82   weft: 38
Literature
Gilfoy and Vollmer, *Arts of Asia*, March–April 1981, p. 126.

Catalogue Number 37
China
Pair of Bridal Bed Curtains, ca. 1820
silk satin weave, embroidered with silk
each panel 77¾ x 70 (197 x 177.5) warp x weft
Gift of the Oriental Art Society of the
  Indianapolis Museum of Art 80.43 a-b

During the Manchu period it was appropriate for a bride to wear imperial symbols on the garments and other textiles associated with her wedding. She literally became "Empress for a Day," and her union with her husband duplicated that of the parents of the state, the Emperor and his consort. The presence here of the Emperor's five-clawed dragon and the Empress's phoenix represents the duality of the royal pair as well as the balance between male and female and the Taoist *yin* and *yang*.[27] The five-colored clouds and the flaming pearl, as well as the universal sea and rocky earth, are also part of the imperial iconography found on coats and other furnishings (see cat. 34). The Eight Precious Things, connoting wealth and good luck, are displayed here, as are the double fish (*yu*). On this piece the symbol probably indicates the rebus for abundance, also called *yu*.[28] The fish hang from a pair of musical stones, and the combination reads, "May you have double abundance."[29] On either side of the central opening are the peaches of immortality and the flowers of riches and honor, peonies.[30]

A woman finally achieved social status on her wedding day, for men had appropriated the economic place of Chinese women as the country's wealth increased. The decline in women's status can be traced to the eleventh and twelfth centuries, when the custom of binding women's feet was introduced as a display of a husband's ability to support the entire family. Because the state was based on family relationships, the one place of honor women could achieve was to become, through marriage, the progenitor of the future state.

Tied to imperial symbolism was the Confucian belief in familial reverence. Many Confucian symbols connote longevity, and the Taoist system was associated with the quest for immortality. A number of these attributes were combined with official symbols to create a filial vocabulary.[31] These curtains serve, then, as statements of the crucial role of marriage in the continuity of the state.

Materials
  Basic fabric
    warp: silk, single-ply slight Z-twist, dark blue
    weft: silk, no twist; gray
  Embroidery
    silk, no twist; four shades blue, four shades green-blue,
      three shades brown, brown-yellow, three shades gray,
      three shades orange-red, yellow-green, white
  Backing
    warp: silk, no twist; light blue-gray
    weft: silk, no twist; light blue-gray
Techniques
  Warp-faced 7/1 satin weave
  Embroidery
    flat stitches: trellis couching, invisible couching; satin,
      encroaching satin, long and short satin, padded satin,
      surface satin; stem; split; straight
    looped stitches: chain; Chinese knot; fly
    combination flat stitches: couching over satin; stem over
      surface satin
    combination flat and looped stitches: fly over
      surface satin
  Pieced with seam at center of each panel, two panels
  Backing: balanced plain weave
Thread count
  Basic fabric
    warp: 356   weft: 98
  Backing
    warp: 118   weft: 94
Literature
  Gilfoy and Vollmer, *Arts of Asia*, March–April 1981, p. 128.

Catalogue Number 37

Catalogue Number 38 (see color plate, p. 39)
China
Valance, ca. 1820
silk satin weave, embroidered with silk and metallic thread
139 x 20 (253 x 51) warp x weft
Gift of the Oriental Art Society of the
 Indianapolis Museum of Art 80.43c

This long valance may have served as a stage set or a dedicatory panel for the opening of a new business. The central inscription, *hang-tien*, roughly translates to mean a hostel or traveler's rest area. Imagery on the panel is in keeping with good wishes for success. On the left side is a peach tree, representing immortality, and on the right a pine, symbolizing steadfastness and longevity. The creatures—probably lions—bear coral, horns, and pearls, each of which is one of the Eight Precious Things. Dressed in nomadic short coats, trousers, and boots, the figures carry containers of precious jewels, pearls, horns, coral, and peacock feathers, all of which are symbols of wealth. These tribute-bearers to the imperial court belong to an iconography developed during the T'ang dynasty (A.D. 618-90) but rarely encountered in embroidery of the nineteenth century.[32] Bats (*fu*), which are symbols of prosperity, fly in the field. The drawing and the interplay between multicolored satin stitches and delicate couched threads, all on a black ground, give this piece vitality.

Materials
Basic fabric
 warp: silk, single-ply slight Z-twist; black
 weft: silk, no twist; black
 dye/pigment: black
Embroidery
 silk, no twist; four shades blue, four shades green, three shades orange, three shades yellow, two shades brown, white
 silk, two-ply S-twist with one ply wrapped tightly around the other; white, blue, orange
 silk, two-ply slight Z-twist; white, light blue-green
 silk, two-ply slight Z-twist with plies of different colors; light blue-green and yellow, light blue-green and white
 metallic #1
 core thread: silk, single-ply Z-twist; light blue-green
 strip: copper on paper, Z-twist; copper colored
 metallic #2
 core thread: silk, two-ply Z-twist; white
 strip: silver with silicon on paper, Z-twist; gold colored
Backing
 warp: silk, no twist; light blue-gray
 weft: silk, no twist; light blue-gray

Techniques
Warp-faced 7/1 satin weave
Embroidery
 flat stitches: couching; Roumanian; satin, encroaching satin, long and short satin, padded satin, surface satin; stem; straight
 looped stitches: Chinese knot
 combination flat stitches: couching over long and short satin; satin over long and short satin; stem over long and short satin; straight over long and short satin; trellis couching over surface satin
 combination flat and looped stitches: cross and Chinese knot over long and short satin
Painted details in trees
Backing: balanced plain weave
Thread count
Basic fabric
 warp: 344   weft: 130
Backing
 warp: 112   weft: 90
Literature
Gilfoy and Vollmer, *Arts of Asia*, March–April 1981, p. 129.

Catalogue Number 39
China
Collar (*yün chien*) for Woman's Informal Coat, ca. 1860
silk satin weave, embroidered with silk
20¼ x 19¾ (51.5 x 50) front to back x side to side,
    warp runs diagonally
John Herron Fund 06.89

This delicately embroidered collar was part of the first major acquisition for the textiles collection. Over one hundred Chinese textiles and costumes were purchased in 1906, before the fall of the Ch'ing dynasty in 1911 and the subsequent dispersal of Chinese artifacts. It is remarkable that the fledgling John Herron Art Institute was purchasing such material at so early a date.

This *yün chien* was originally stitched to the neck edge of a woman's informal coat that had a side closure. The four-lobed collar, which represents the universe by marking the sky gate and the points of the compass, has had a history in Chinese costume since the twelfth century.[33]

Combinations of birds and plant life enliven the four lobes of the collar and may relate to the four seasons, which are especially appropriate to the cardinal symbolism of the collar. The front lobe contains a pair of mandarin ducks, which were thought to mate for life and thus came to symbolize enduring marriage (see cat. 40). Surrounding them are water flowers and willow branches, perhaps alluding to summer. On the back lobe is the *ch'i-lin*, or unicorn, a composite beast with a scaly coat; a long, flowing tail; horns; and hooves. Above him are branches of pine, which may allude to winter. On one side panel is a crane and on the other a silver pheasant or fly catcher.

These animals, part of the symbolic vocabulary of ranks,[34] appear on badges awarded to men who attain certain levels within the army and the civil service. Also represented here is the rebus symbol of the bat (*fu*), which characterizes prosperity.[35]

Materials
Basic fabric
    warp: silk, single-ply slight Z-twist; brown
    weft: silk, no twist; brown
Embroidery
    silk, no twist; light, medium, and dark blue, light,
        medium, and dark blue-green, green, yellow-green,
        white, light and dark orange
    silk, two-ply Z-twist; blue-green, white and orange plied
        together
Trim 1
    warp: silk, single-ply Z-twist; white
    weft: silk, single-ply Z-twist; white
    supplementary warp: silk, single-ply Z-twist; blue, orange
Trim 2
    warp: silk, single-ply Z-twist; tan
    weft: gilt paper Z-twist around a white Z-twist silk core
    supplementary warp: silk, single-ply Z-twist; black,
        orange, yellow
Lining
    warp: silk, single-ply Z-twist; light blue
    weft: silk, no twist; light blue

Techniques
Warp-faced 7/1 satin weave
Embroidery
    flat stitches: couching; dot; satin, encroaching satin, long
        and short satin, padded satin; stem; straight
    looped stitches: Chinese knot
    combination flat stitches: straight over satin; straight over
        long and short satin
    combination flat and looped stitches: fly over
        encroaching satin
Trim 1 and 2: narrow bands of warp-faced plain weave
    with supplementary warp
        proportions: one supplementary warp per one
            main warp
Interlining: paper adhered to fabric
Neck lining: balanced plain weave (background) and warp-
    faced 5/1 satin weave (figure), paired warp
Finish: edges bound in black silk satin

Thread count
Basic fabric
    warp: 336   weft: 100
Lining
    warp: 156 pairs (312 threads)   weft: 69

Catalogue Number 40
China
Wall Hanging (hanging scroll), ca. 1750
silk plain weave (*k'o-ssu*)
woven center: 32 x 17½ (81 x 44.5) warp x weft
Gift of Mr. Robert J. Shula 75.775

Weavings that imitate paintings are known from Sung period (A.D. 960–1279) writings that describe woven pictures. The blunt, flat, abstract form of this particular picture owes allegiance to Ming (A.D. 1368-1644) painting style. Typical of that style is the placement of floral forms in the foreground plane, which opens onto a more distant vista. In this example a pair of mandarin ducks seen in the mid-distance distorts the illusion of receding space, since their tail feathers cover the foreground plant forms. Because this is a later copy of a previous style, the original artistic intention may have been misunderstood and reinterpreted.

Mandarin ducks were a popular subject in Chinese art: thought to mate for life, they came to symbolize marital fidelity. This belief, in fact, has a scientific basis since the ducks' number of chromosomes is incompatible with that of other species.

All details in this picture were woven, including the outlines and feather markings. *K'o-ssu*, or slit tapestry weave, was used with the application of an eccentric weft, probably inserted from a single bobbin to weave details.

Materials
   Basic fabric
      warp: silk, single-ply slight Z-twist; light brown
      weft: silk, no twist; black, light brown, tan, gray, light and
         medium green, light orange, light violet
Techniques
   Weft-faced plain weave with discontinuous wefts; slit
      tapestry joins, some eccentric outlining wefts
   No selvedge
Thread count
   Basic fabric
      warp: 78   weft: 100

Catalogue Number 41
China (for export to Europe)
Woman's Wrapper (shawl), ca. 1900
silk plain weave (crepe), embroidered with silk, trimmed with
    silk interknotted fringe (macramé)
94 x 91 (238.5 x 231) with fringe, weft x warp
Gift of Mrs. Tade Hartsuff Kuhns 38.83

Europe was ripe for the exotic in the seventeenth and especially the eighteenth century, when the cult of chinoiserie became an overriding expression of taste. The desire for exotic shawls (see cat. 31) in the Victorian period extended beyond India to embroidered Chinese silks. As they had in India (see cat. 27), European entrepreneurs exploited the insatiable appetite for exotica by sending patterns to China to be produced for Europeans. While the multicolored floral vocabulary, embroidery techniques, and certain aspects of design are part of Chinese interpretation of European models, the composition of the shawl, with its long, luxurious, black silk fringe, was strictly in the nineteenth-century European taste. These shawls are variously ascribed to the Philippines (Manila shawls) and to Spain because of their continued use in those places long after the fashion for shawls waned in the mid-1860s, but at present it seems most reasonable to assume a Chinese origin for this piece.

Materials
Basic fabric
    warp: silk, no twist; black
    weft: silk, two-ply Z-twist with both plies overspun; black
Embroidery
    silk, two-ply Z-twist; four shades orange-red, three
        shades gray, three shades green, two shades yellow,
        yellow-green, white, violet-red, light, medium, and dark
        green-blue
    silk, three-ply Z-twist; yellow, green-blue, orange-red
    silk, no twist; yellow
Trim
    fringe: silk, two-ply Z-twist; black
Techniques
Warp-dominant plain weave, with overspun weft
Embroidery
    flat stitches: pattern couching; variation of cross; satin,
        encroaching satin, long and short satin; stem; straight
        combination flat stitches: straight over satin; spaced satin
        over couching
Finish: rolled hem
Trim: attached interknotted fringe
Thread count
Basic fabric
    warp: 126   weft: 79

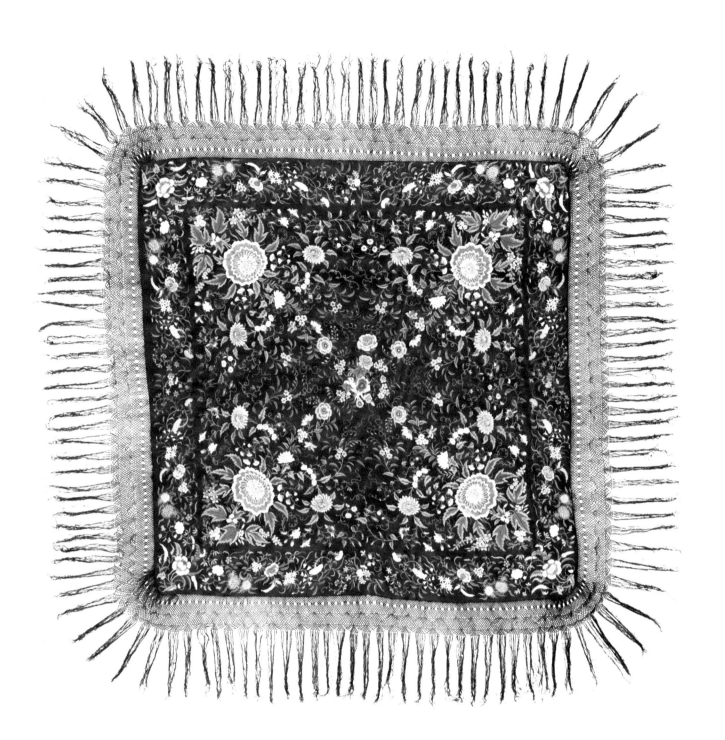

Catalogue Number 42
China (for export to Europe)
Fabric for Wall Covering, ca. 1770
silk plain weave, painted
82 x 30½ (208 x 77.5) warp x weft
Delavan Smith Fund 76.162

In wealthy European homes decorative fabrics were used for wall covering as well as furniture embellishment. This Chinese silk is painted with trailing floral vines that are greatly indebted to Indian dyed cottons (see cat. 27 and 29). To supply the insatiable eighteenth-century trade market, the enterprising Chinese adapted European conceptions of exotic Asian taste.

Materials
  Basic fabric
    warp: silk, single-ply slight Z-twist; light brown
    weft: silk, no twist; light brown
    dyes/pigments: light, medium, and dark green, dark
      brown, light and medium red, light and medium violet,
      medium and dark blue, light and medium orange,
      yellow, white
Techniques
  Balanced plain weave, paired warps
  Painted
  Two overlapping panels
  No selvedges
  Double-faced metal seal attached to edge with doubled red
    thread
Thread count
  Basic fabric
    warp: 108 pairs (216 threads)   weft: 80
Literature
  Gilfoy and Vollmer, *Arts of Asia*, March–April 1981, p. 132.

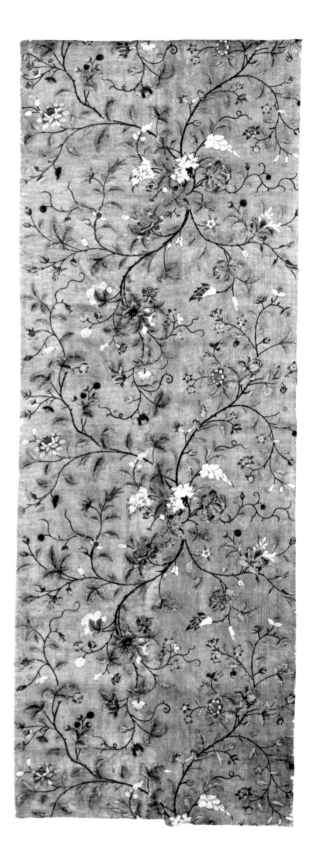

Notes

[1] Vollmer, 1977, p. 16.

[2] Priest, 1934, p. 4.

[3] Priest, 1934, p. 9.

[4] Impey, 1977, pp. 20-21.

[5] Simmons, 1948, p. 21.

[6] Vollmer, 1978, p. 42.

[7] Legenza, 1977, pp. 23-24.

[8] Vollmer, personal communication.

[9] Vollmer, 1983.

[10] The Chinese inscription is as follows: *t'ung-chih shih-erh nien* (year), *pa-yüeh shih-wu-jih* (date).

[11] de Groot, 1910, p. 1265.

[12] Vollmer, 1977, p. 21.

[13] Vollmer, 1977, p. 40.

[14] Vollmer, 1977, p. 30.

[15] Vollmer, 1977, pp. 53-54.

[16] Vollmer, 1980, p. 18.

[17] Vollmer, personal communication.

[18] Vollmer, 1980, pp. 18-19.

[19] Vollmer, 1980, pp. 22-23.

[20] The coat is very similar to one in the collection of the Victoria and Albert Museum, London (number 1643.1901), in its construction, blue fretwork background, and overall spatial and decorative organization.

[21] Vollmer, 1980, p. 42.

[22] Vollmer, 1980. p. 67.

[23] Vollmer, 1980. p. 36.

[24] Vollmer, 1980, p. 36.

[25] Vollmer, 1980, p. 39.

[26] Vollmer, 1982, p. 41.

[27] Vollmer, 1980, p. 36.

[28] Vollmer, 1980, p. 63.

[29] Vollmer, personal communication.

[30] Vollmer, 1980, p. 42.

[31] Vollmer, 1980, pp. 37-39.

[32] Vollmer, personal communication.

[33] Camman, 1962, p. 4.

[34] Vollmer, 1977, pp. 71-73.

[35] Vollmer, 1980, p. 49.

Japan

Japan's official acceptance of Buddhism in A.D. 552 marks the beginning of Japanese recorded history with the Asuka period (A.D. 552-710). T'ang China (A.D. 618-906) strongly influenced Japan in the following Nara period (A.D. 710-794).[1] Draped with flowing sleeves, a costume found in both Japan and China was constructed much like a modern kimono, with rectangular lengths of cloth. As the T'ang faded and the Heian period (A.D. 794-1185) began, so did the Chinese influence. The Japanese court moved to Kyoto and established a standard of refinement and luxury new to the country.

It was in this period that Japanese costume first asserted its independence from Chinese models, both in daily wear and in costume for the Noh theater.[2] The *juni hitoe*, or twelve unlined robes, constituted female attire.[3] Stiff, wide-sleeved, solid-colored silk robes were piled upon one another in a specified order that corresponded with seasonal and social demands.[4]

The following Kamakura period (A.D. 1185-1392) witnessed a major political shift as power passed from the reigning nobility to the shōgun and his warrior class. The burdensome, luxurious habits of the nobility were ill-suited to the more active and ascetic warriors, who rejected court costume as a breach of practicality and a symbol of past decadence. The outer layers of the unlined robes were discarded and one of the undergarments, the *kosode*, became the top garment.

That only one basic garment was available for decorative expression indeed affected the history of Japanese costume, for the uniformity of design regenerated a host of artistic methods that had languished since the eighth century. Artists fully exploited the greater freedom of expression dye resist and embroidery allowed them. The soft, flowing *kosode* gave birth to the great period of patterned dyeing, an art in which the Japanese excelled.

The Muromachi period (A.D. 1192-1568) shogunate intensified trade with Ming China and, toward its end, with Portugal. The many foreign materials entering the country whetted a taste for the exotic, especially for metallic brocades from China and later from Europe, and even for Indian dyed cottons. The Nishijin sector of Kyoto was established to develop the woven silks the Japanese so admired. The weaving industry developed large patterned silks for daily wear and denser, stiffer fabrics for the Noh theater. Large, dramatic patterns executed in dyed techniques became paramount, however, in the Momoyama period (A.D. 1568-1615). With a new freedom to display their growing wealth, women at many social levels wore colorful *kosode* on the streets. Embroidery was added to accent established patterns and to give

them luster and a depth of surface during this truly creative period in textile design.

The following Edo or Tokugawa period (A.D. 1615-1867) reacted to these freedoms with constraints. The country entered a feudal period and closed itself off from the outer world. In reaction to supposed excesses of the earlier period, the Tokugawa issued many sumptuary laws to a now rigidly stratified society.[5] These changes created an aura of refinement and simplicity in garments. The display of process became important during this period; coats were covered with thousands of tiny tie-dyed patterns with intricate resist-dyed and delicately hand-painted designs.[6]

Catalogue Number 43
Japan
Monk's Wrapper (*kesa*), ca. 1775
silk twill weave with silk supplementary weft (brocade),
    pieced, appliquéd
68 x 41 (173 x 104) weft x warp
Eliza M. and Sarah L. Niblack Collection 33.488

The scintillating silk surface of this *kesa* is enhanced in large part by the use of long floats in diagonal twill brocade (*nishiki*). Brocaded fabric (*kara-ori*) from China was probably first brought to Japan by Buddhist monks returning from study on the mainland during the Kamakura period (A.D. 1185-1392).[7] Such silks became highly prized articles of trade and were imported in great quantities especially for use in coats for the Noh drama. The original period of brocade production in Japan probably occurred from the Nara period (A.D. 710-794) to the Muromachi (A.D. 1192-1568),[8] but the greatest stimulation came in the latter part of the sixteenth century, when Chinese weavers fled the mainland after the collapse of the Ming dynasty. They settled near Kyoto[9] and furthered production already established in the Nishijin sector of that city.

Japanese silk weaving probably reached its zenith in the seventeenth century during the early Edo period, under the tutelage of the flourishing Noh drama. Noh enjoyed considerable patronage from the shogunate as early as the fifteenth century. Samurai supported this art form and lavished expensive imported silks on the performers.[10]

Each Noh role came to have certain forms and textiles associated with it; the red-grounded silk shown here was probably originally made into a coat for a female Noh character.[11] The patterns of phoenix (*hō-ō*) and pawlonia (*kiri*) used here derive from the Chinese *feng huang*, which was believed to live only in the pawlonia tree. The combination of the Chinese imperial symbol for the Empress (phoenix) and the auspicious pawlonia tree was considered very favorable.[12] *Ukimon-ori*, the "floating design weave" used in the fabric for this *kesa*, may have originated as an attempt to emulate embroidery.[13] Certainly the long, glossy silk threads would have presented a dramatic effect as the Noh actor moved on stage.

Such magnificent silks were frequently donated to religious orders and were used to make vestments. The construction of this garment derives from patchwork mantles worn by mendicant Buddhist monks, which were themselves based on patched shawl garments of southern Asia. The *kesa* was worn over a coat, draped under the right arm, with the ends fastened by a cord on the left shoulder.[14] Over the right arm a narrow stole (*ohi*, see cat. 44 and 45) of matching fabric was worn.[15]

The four patches, one in each corner, represent the four Deva kings, guardians of the cardinal points and protectors of Buddhist law (*dharma*). The two larger patches (*botatsu*) are symbolic of Fugan and Monju (Samantahhadra and Manjusri), the principal attendants of the historic Buddha Shaku. Amulets or relics might be placed under these patches, which in this garment are probably made from domestic silk.[16]

Materials
  Basic fabric
    warp: silk, no twist; orange
    weft: silk, no twist; orange
    supplementary weft: silk, no twist; light and dark orange,
      light, medium, and dark blue, light and dark green,
      violet, dark yellow, white
  Appliquéd fabric
    warp: silk, single-ply slight S-twist; dark blue
    weft: silk, no twist; dark blue
    supplementary warp:
      silk, single-ply slight S-twist; tan
    supplementary weft:
      silk, no twist; white, light orange, light green
      metallic (visual identification)
        flat strip only: gold colored, on paper
  Lining
    warp: silk, no twist; dark blue
    weft: silk, no twist; gray
Techniques
  Balanced 3/1 diagonal twill weave (background) and weft-
    faced floats bound in a diagonal twill alignment (figure),
    with discontinuous supplementary weft, thicker than warp
      proportions: one supplementary weft per two main
        wefts
  Pieced
  Appliquéd with fabric of warp-faced 7/1 satin weave
    (background) and weft-faced floats bound in a diagonal
    twill alignment (figure), with supplementary binding warp
    and continuous supplementary weft
      proportions: one supplementary warp per four main
        warps, one supplementary weft per one main weft
  Lining: balanced plain weave
Thread count
  Basic fabric
    warp: 153   weft: 86   supplementary weft: 43
  Appliquéd fabric
    warp: 200   weft: 38   supplementary warp: 50
    supplementary weft: 38

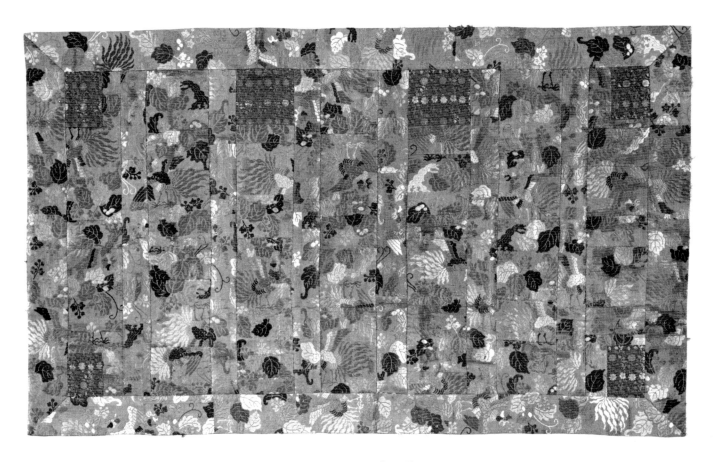

Catalogue Number 43

Catalogue Number 44
Japan
Monk's Stole (*ohi*), 17th century, 16th century fabric
silk twill weave with silk supplementary warp and metallic
   supplementary weft (brocade), pieced, appliquéd
62¼ x 12 (157.5 x 30.5) warp x weft
Eliza M. and Sarah L. Niblack Collection 33.498

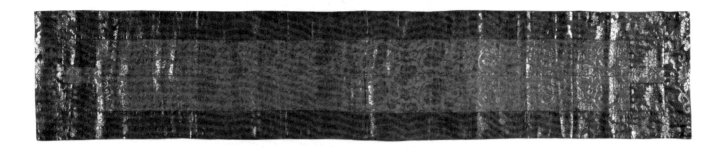

The technique of producing patterns with supplementary weft metallic threads was not part of Japanese weaving technology until the seventeenth century, when Chinese weavers emigrated in great numbers from the mainland during the collapse of the Ming dynasty. Prior to that time gold brocade (*kinran*) was imported from China,[17] as was the fabric for this piece. Its metallic fibers are made of a flat tough paper overlaid with silver and then gilded. Executed in gold on green, the pattern on the outside border represents the tree peony (*botan*), which was originally a Chinese symbol of wealth and nobility. The central field design on red silk represents the pawlonia, an auspicious tree for the Chinese (see cat. 43).[18] These fabrics were probably used domestically before being donated to a temple by a pious Buddhist laity.

Materials
   Center fabric
      warp: silk, single-ply slight S-twist; light brown
      weft: silk, no twist; light brown
      supplementary warp:
       silk, no twist; white
      supplementary weft:
       metallic
       flat strip only: gold with silver on paper; gold colored
   Border fabric
      warp: silk, single-ply slight S-twist; blue-green
      weft: silk, no twist; blue-green
      supplementary warp:
       silk, no twist; white
      supplementary weft:
       metallic
       flat strip only: gold with silver on paper; gold colored
   Lining
      warp: silk, no twist; yellow
      weft: silk, no twist, yellow
Techniques
   Center fabric: warp-faced 3/1 diagonal twill weave
      (background) and weft-faced floats bound in a diagonal
      twill alignment (figure), with supplementary binding warp
      and continuous supplementary weft
         proportions: one supplementary warp per eight main
            warps, one supplementary weft per two main wefts

Border fabric: same structure as center fabric with
   different design
Pieced, appliquéd with fabric same as border
Lining: balanced plain weave
Thread count
   Center fabric
      warp: 208   weft: 64
      supplementary warp: 26
      supplementary weft: 32
   Border fabric
      warp: 208   weft: 74
      supplementary warp: 26
      supplementary weft: 37
   Lining
      warp: 112   weft: 112
Pattern repeat
   Center fabric
      warpwise: 5¾ in. (14.5 cm)   weftwise: not discernible
   Border fabric
      warpwise: 9¼ in. (23.5 cm)   weftwise: not discernible
Literature
Gilfoy and Vollmer, *Arts of Asia*, March–April 1981, p. 128.

Catalogue Number 45
Japan
Monk's Stole (*ohi*), 17th–18th century
silk twill weave with silk supplementary warp and metallic
    supplementary weft (brocade), resist-dyed warp (ikat),
    pieced, appliquéd
59½ x 11¼ (151 x 28.5) warp x weft
Eliza M. and Sarah L. Niblack Collection 33.504

An *ohi* is worn over the right arm, which is left uncovered by
the mantle (*kesa*, see cat. 43). The fabric in this piece is of the
type that would have originally been used for a Noh coat. Its
characteristic dense twill structure, ikat change from red to
green in the background, and "floating design weave" (*ukimon-
ori*) were common in theatrical costumes.[19] The decorative pattern of chrysanthemum (*kiku*) and pawlonia (*kiri*) both derive
from Chinese motifs and are meant to convey good fortune.
The ancient Chinese pawlonia housed the mythical *feng huang*,
or phoenix; and the chrysanthemum was prized as a symbol of
longevity and was one of The Four Worthies (*Shi Kunshi*).[20]
Their presence together was reserved for Japanese imperial
costume.

Materials
  Basic fabric
      warp: silk, no twist; light green, brown-yellow
      weft: silk, no twist; white, light yellow
  Appliquéd fabric
      warp: silk, two-ply slight S-twist; orange
      weft: silk, no twist; orange
      supplementary warp:
        silk, no twist; white
      supplementary weft:
        metallic
          flat strip only: silver with gold and copper on paper;
            gold colored
  Lining
      warp: bast (ramie), single-ply slight S-twist; light blue
      weft: bast (ramie), single-ply slight S-twist; light blue
Techniques
  Warp-faced 5/1 diagonal twill weave (background) and
      weft-faced floats bound in a diagonal twill alignment
      (figure)
  Resist-dyed warp
  Pieced
  Appliquéd with fabric of warp-faced 2/1 diagonal twill
      weave (background) and weft-faced floats bound in a
      diagonal twill alignment (figure), with supplementary
      binding warp and continuous supplementary weft
        proportions: one supplementary warp per six main
            warps, one supplementary weft per two main wefts
  Lining: balanced plain weave
Thread count
  Basic fabric
      warp: 139   weft: 75
  Appliquéd fabric
      warp: 159   weft: 110
      supplementary warp: 26
      supplementary weft: 55
  Lining
      warp: 45   weft: 60
Pattern repeat
  warpwise: 3¾ in. (9.5 cm)   weftwise: 3¾ in. (9.5 cm)

Catalogue Number 46 (see color plate, p. 40)
Japan
Yardage from a Woman's Coat, 1675-1700
silk satin and twill weaves (damask or *rinzu*), resist dyed
  (*katazome*), embroidered with silk and metallic thread
68 x 64 (172 x 162) weft x warp
Museum Accession 4893.83.1

The dramatic pattern of pine, plum, and bamboo on this yardage from a woman's *kosode* or *furisode* is typical of the early Edo period (A.D. 1615-1868), when bold designs swept from hem to shoulder. The panels are shown in the way they were joined, as a dedicatory gift to a temple.[21] Cut along the shoulder fold, the two central panels at the back of the garment and those from either front side have been seamed flat; the sleeves (short for the *kosode* or long for the *furisode*) are now missing.

Pine, plum, and bamboo (*sho-chiku-bai*), The Three Wintry Comrades, form the decoration. This theme actually comes from Chinese sources. Evergreen pine (*matsu*), the most revered of the auspicious plants, represents strength and longevity. Regarded as noble and virtuous, bamboo (*take*) produces the only fruit consumed by the *feng huang* (*hō-ō* or phoenix). The plum, or prunus (*ume*), is first to bloom in early spring and therefore symbolizes strength. Together they refer to the attributes of the Confucian gentlemen and form one of the oldest and most frequent patterns in Japanese textile design.[22]

During the Empo period (A.D. 1673-1681), many stories were written that illustrate the importance of coats to the lives of those who owned them. A number of the stories describe the display of coats as works of art, either on special racks built for the purpose or during cherry blossom time, when owners exhibited them in the park draped on the walls of their outdoor pavilions. In 1683 one of many sumptuary edicts was issued to control the costly display of prestige costume. Overall tie-dye (*kokeche*) and the inclusion of gold were among the techniques that were limited.[23] As a result, the use of imitation tie-dye (*surihitta*)—seen here executed with a stencil and starch resist (*somenuke*)—and other resist techniques increased. This piece seems to have been produced under some of these influences. They are illustrated by the greater use of broad, simply produced resist areas in a bold, gold-enhanced design that is reminiscent of earlier large, sweeping patterns.

For centuries, dyeing methods were enormously important to the Japanese. In fact, they exhibited their independence from early Chinese influence through their exquisite innovations in dyeing methods. The Chinese had become highly sophisticated in manipulating silk through patterning on the loom or with the needle, while the Japanese expanded coloring devices in their work with dyes and resist techniques.

The softer *kosode* form of coat, which had been fully adopted by the Momoyama period (A.D. 1568-1615),[24] allowed for greater ease of dyeing. *Rinzu*, the soft, patterned damask weave seen here, often had a geometric ground that made it ideal for dye-resist patterning. This particular piece shows the synthesis of many influences: the Chinese contribution is apparent in the background silk, which was widely imported from China in the Momoyama period and into the early Edo,[25] and in the use of gold-couched threads and satin stitch embroidery. However, the combination of these elements, used to enhance a large, sweeping design in resist techniques, is typically Japanese.

Materials
Basic fabric
  warp: silk, no twist; white
  weft: silk, no twist; white
  dyes: blue, brown .
Embroidery
  silk, no twist; orange, green
  metallic
    core thread: cotton, three-ply Z-twist; white
    strip: gold on paper, Z-twist; gold colored

Techniques
Warp-faced 4/1 satin weave (background) and
  weft-dominant 2/1 diagonal twill weave (figure)
Resist dyed with stenciled starch resist
Embroidery
  flat stitches: couching of doubled elements; satin, surface
    satin; satin over paper
  combination flat stitches: couching over satin
Selvedge to selvedge width: 17 in. (43.0 cm)

Thread count
Basic fabric
  warp: 195   weft: 86

Pattern repeat
  warpwise: 2¾ in. (7.0 cm)   weftwise: 2¼ in. (5.5 cm)

Literature
Gilfoy and Vollmer, *Arts of Asia*, March–April 1981, p. 128.

Catalogue Number 47
Japan
Woman's Coat (*uchikake*), 1775-1850
silk plain weave (crepe), resist dyed (*shibori*),
   embroidered with silk and metallic thread
65 (165) length, warp
Museum Accession 13.47

The *uchikake* is a coat worn over the *kosode* on formal occasions. It is held together in front with the hands, and the padded hem is allowed to trail elegantly behind.[26] Both the *kosode* and *uchikake* emerged as dominant forms of dress during the Kamakura period (A.D. 1185-1392) in reaction to the heavier multi-layered dress of the previous Heian period (A.D. 794-1185). In this *uchikake*, the design of trailing mandarin orange flowers (*tachibana*) is in white on a red ground, and is created in a combination of hand-painted details and sew dye resist or *boshi-shibori*—so named because of the small "hat" of bamboo (*boshi*) placed on top of the stitched section to prevent the dye from penetrating. In addition, some flowers and the trailing branches are patterned with tie-dye (*kokeche* or the modern *shibori*). For greater definition, some blossoms are worked over with satin stitch embroidery. Over all this coat are decorative motifs in gold-wrapped thread couched to the surface. Using these multiple media seems extravagant, but this garment was actually made under laws to curb excess labor on women's garments. The pattern of mandarin oranges was popular in Japan from early times. Its fragrant flowers and beautiful fruit, combined with the evergreen qualities of the tree, made it an auspicious symbol.[27]

Materials
  Basic fabric
    warp: silk, no twist; white
    weft: silk, single-ply tight Z-twist; white
    dye: red-orange
  Embroidery
    silk, no twist; orange, light and medium green
    metallic
      core thread: cotton, three-ply Z-twist; white
      strip: gold with silver on paper, Z-twist; gold colored
  Batting
    silk
  Lining
    warp: silk, no twist; red-orange
    weft: silk, no twist; red-orange

Techniques
  Balanced plain weave, loosely woven with overspun weft
  Resist dyed with tied and stitched resists
  Painted details
  Embroidery
    flat stitches: couching of single and doubled elements;
      satin; stem
    combination flat stitches: spaced satin over satin; satin
      over couching
  Selvedge: ⅛ in. (0.4 cm) of warp-dominant plain weave
  Selvedge to selvedge width: 13 in. (33.0 cm)
  Pieced garment with batting and padded hem
  Lining: balanced plain weave

Thread count
  Basic fabric
    warp: 148   weft: 83
  Lining
    warp: 136   weft: 108

Literature
  Gilfoy and Vollmer, *Arts of Asia*, March–April 1981, p. 128.

145

Catalogue Number 48
Japan
Woman's Coat (*uchikake*), 1800-50
silk satin and twill weaves (damask or *rinzu*), resist dyed
  (*shibori*), embroidered with silk and metallic thread
65 (165) length, warp
Museum Accession 13.48

This *furisode*, or long-sleeved coat, was probably worn as an outer garment (*uchikake*), as is indicated by its long, padded hem (see cat. 47). The pine pattern is here executed on *rinzu* with tie-dye (*kokeche*) resist, which blocked out the white areas while dyeing the blue, red, and brown. In addition, there are details hand-drawn in ink with a brush. The small scale of this pattern and its scattered composition suggest that it was probably made rather late in the Edo period.

The resist patterning on this garment was probably achieved through the technique of "bucket resist." The areas to receive the dye were gathered up with sewn stitches and placed on the outside rim of a special wooden bucket; the part of the yardage to remain undyed sat inside the bucket. A tight-fitting lid was clamped on top of the bucket, which was then immersed in the dye bath. When removed from the dye, the cloth was dried and the lid removed.[28] This method was not only much faster than resisting each area, but also allowed for large areas of undyed background.

The separation between "fine arts" such as painting and decorative arts like clothing and household goods was significantly blurred at the upper levels. Many famous Japanese painters designed garments as well as other domestic goods.[29] Beauty was appreciated regardless of medium or source, whether natural or exquisitely handmade.

Materials
  Basic fabric
    warp: silk, no twist; white
    weft: silk, no twist; white
    dyes: orange, blue, dark brown, black
  Embroidery
    silk, no twist; green
    metallic
      core thread: cotton, two-ply Z-twist; white
      strip: gold with silver on paper, Z-twist; gold colored
  Batting
    silk
  Lining
    warp: silk, no twist; red-orange
    weft: silk, no twist; red-orange
Techniques
  Warp-faced 4/1 satin weave (background) and 2/1 diagonal
    twill weave (figure)
  Resist dyed with tied, stitched, and clamped resists
  Embroidery
    flat stitches: couching of doubled elements; satin
  Pieced garment with batting and padded hem
  Selvedge to selvedge width: 12½ in. (32.0 cm)
  Lining: balanced plain weave
Thread count
  Basic fabric
    warp: 204   weft: 80
  Lining
    warp: 120   weft: 120
Pattern repeat
  warpwise: 3¾ in. (9.5 cm)   weftwise: 2¼ in. (5.5 cm)

Catalogue Number 49
Japan
Coat for Noh Theater (?) (*osode* or *choken*), 1775-1800
silk plain weave (crepe), resist dyed (*katazome*), embroidered
  with silk and metallic thread
62 (157) length, warp
Eliza M. and Sarah L. Niblack Collection 33.514

Dramatic presentation of the theme of phoenix and pawlonia on this garment plus the large, rectangular, open sleeves suggest a theatrical origin. At present this piece is unlined, but the creases along its edges may have been lining seams which, if the coat was worn in Noh theater, would have been of a stiff fabric. Many of the most dramatic and creative Japanese coat designs originated in the theater district because it was not controlled by the sumptuary laws that circumscribed daily domestic wear (see cat. 43). If this piece were not intended for the stage, it was probably—as its shape indicates—an outside garment (*osode*) that was held together rather than constricted by an *obi* or sash, which would have visually destroyed the dramatic sweep of the pattern. Whatever the use, the huge multicolored phoenix and pawlonia (see cat. 43), on a green ground, totally dominate the garment with the bird's dramatic wings and head on the back and the long, sweeping tail falling down the front. A Noh coat with a very similar design in the Tokugawa collection is described as representing the tale of the coat of feathers a fisherman found on the beach; he returned the garment to the angel who had lost it. In the play *Hagoromo*, the feathers shimmered as the angel danced, rejoicing in the return of the coat.[30]

Suri-hitta, or resist dyeing, is done here with a stencil, an imitation of tie-dye, and with ink overdrawing for many of the finer details of leaf veins. As a result of sumptuary legislation controlling the amount of time spent on execution of a garment—and therefore its cost—this quicker and cheaper method evolved. The pattern is further enhanced with silk embroidery and gold thread couching.

Thread count
  Basic fabric
    warp: 139   weft: 78

Literature
  Gilfoy and Vollmer, *Arts of Asia*, March–April 1981, p. 130.

Materials
  Basic fabric
    warp: silk, no twist; white
    weft: silk, single-ply tight S-twist; white
        silk, single-ply tight Z-twist; white
    dyes: light green, light brown, black
  Embroidery
    silk, no twist; green, yellow-green, light and dark orange,
      light yellow-brown, white
    metallic
      core thread: cotton, four-ply Z-twist; light tan
      strip: gold with silver on paper, Z-twist; gold colored
Techniques
  Weft-dominant plain weave, overspun weft
  Resist dyed with stenciled starch resist
  Painted details
  Embroidery
    flat stitches: couching of doubled elements, pattern
      couching; satin, spaced satin; stem
    combination flat stitches: couching over surface satin;
      satin over couching; straight and couching over surface
      satin; straight and satin over surface satin
  Pieced garment, unlined

149

Catalogue Number 50 (see color plate, p. 41)
Japan
Gift Wrapper (*fukusa*), 19th century
silk plain weave (crepe), painted, embroidered with silk and
  metallic thread
28 x 25½ (71 x 65) warp x weft
Gift of Eliza M. Niblack 16.881

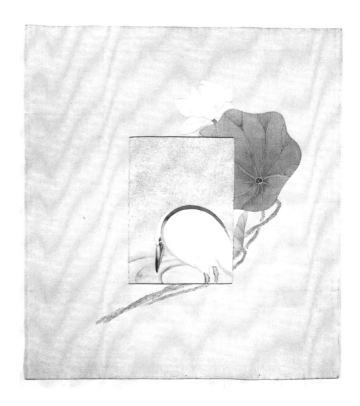

The decorative style on this *fukusa* is reminiscent of the Rimpa
school of Japanese painting begun in the late seventeenth century. The gold-spattered background and the simplified, flat,
planar treatment of the bird and flower are similar to Rimpa
designs, as is the device of cutting the picture field and over-
laying it with another cropped image.[31]
   The egret and lotus motifs derive from Chinese iconography.
The lotus (*hasu*) is a flower sacred to Buddhists,[32] and the egret
carries seasonal connotations. The combination of these two
motifs on a square used to wrap gifts is noteworthy. The *fukusa*
itself would then carry an additional message of the donor's
seasonal good wishes to the recipient.

Materials
  Basic fabric
    warp: silk, no twist; white
    weft: silk, two-ply Z-twist, one-ply tight S-twist, and the
      other no twist; white
    dyes/pigments: light green, orange, white, gray, light
      blue, gold leaf
  Embroidery
    silk, no twist; light gray, white, red, light green
    metallic (visual identification)
      core thread: silk, no twist, white
      strip: gold color on paper, Z-twist
  Backing
    warp: silk, no twist; white
    weft: silk, no twist; white
Techniques
  Weft-dominant plain weave, loosely woven with
    overspun weft
  Painted with dyes, pigments and gold leaf
  Embroidery
    flat stitches: couching of doubled elements; satin
    looped stitches: Chinese knot
  Backing: warp-dominant plain weave (background) and
    warp-dominant 3/1 diagonal twill weave (figure)
Thread count
  Basic fabric
    warp: 125   weft: 49
  Backing
    warp: 130   weft: 52
Pattern repeat
  Backing
    warpwise: 12⅛ in. (31.0 cm)
    weftwise: 6¼ in. (16.0 cm)

Notes

1 Minnich, 1963, p. 28.

2 Noma, 1974, pp. 9-10.

3 Noma, 1974, p. 14.

4 Minnich, 1963, p. 30.

5 Noma, 1974, p. 89.

6 Noma, 1974, pp. 91-92.

7 Seni, vol. II, 1962, p. 35.

8 Noma, 1974, p. 150.

9 Vollmer, 1972, p. 140.

10 Noma, 1974, pp. 54-56.

11 Vollmer, personal communication.

12 Seni, vol. I, 1962, p. 31.

13 Noma, 1974, pp. 151-53.

14 Vollmer, 1972, p. 28.

15 Minnich, 1963, p. 197.

16 Vollmer, 1972, p. 28.

17 Vollmer, personal communication.

18 Seni, vol. I, 1962, p. 3.

19 Noma, 1974, p. 150.

20 Seni, vol. I, pp. 31-32.

21 The inscription notes that the panel was given to a religious building (yin-lin yüan) by a reverent Buddhist disciple (tsung-fan wei-hsin) on the first of the lunar month in the fourteenth year of the Ch'ing reign, August 11, 1809.

22 Seni, vol. I, p. 35.

23 Hyōbu, 1976, p. 14.

24 Hyōbu, 1976, p. 113.

25 Hyōbu, 1976, p. 116.

26 Hyōbu, 1976, p. 120.

27 Seni, vol. II, 1962, p. 34.

28 Larsen, 1976, p. 38.

29 Noma, 1974, p. 94.

30 Tokugawa, 1977, p. 64.

31 Link, 1980, Cat. 46.

32 Seni, vol. I, 1962, p. 32.

Catalogue Number 51
Town of Rayy, Iran
Fragment of Garment Fabric, 10th century
silk twill weaves with silk supplementary warp and weft
12¾ x 10¼ (32.5 x 26) weft x warp
Delavan Smith Fund 76.159

In 1925, a number of textiles were found in ruined tomb towers outside the ancient capital of Rayy. Rayy was a major weaving center and producer of technically intricate cloth before the Mongol invasion of 1227, which destroyed both the city and this site. The piece illustrated here uses a secondary warp that binds the pattern wefts, a technique that had been known in many areas of Iran since the fifth to sixth centuries A.D. The use of an inner, unseen warp in these textiles increases luster of the patterning wefts by allowing longer floats without endangering the overall structural strength.[11] That surface quality was further enhanced here by the use of larger silk threads for the brown floats and of much smaller tan binding warps. Such technical virtuosity and delicacy of patterning are in fact characteristic of the period. The design on this piece is unlike many known "Buyid" pieces, which are decorated with intricate interlacings and elaborate inscriptions.

Since few miniature painters of great quality designed for textiles during this period, weavers looked to earlier silver and pottery for their inspiration.[12] The Sasanian king in this piece, though appropriated from another medium, is typically portrayed in a crown with flying ribbons, rendered in brown. The brown and tan pattern of the mounted ruler engaged in a lion hunt is surrounded by a "pearl" border, another common device in earlier Iranian Sasanian silks. As seen in the photograph, the motif is repeated three times across the width of the fabric.

These silks survived because they were used as burial garments and shrouds. Like other peoples, Iranians dressed the body for burial in expensive textiles. Since the tombs in this area were intended for royalty, it is logical that they should contain rich stuffs. Construction of the coat this fabric came from is unusual: other known Rayy burial garments from this period were woven to shape on the loom, but this piece was constructed from lengths of silk that wrapped around the body, with the selvedges seamed at hip level. The Museum's fragment apparently came from the area beneath the bottom of the hem, which grave robbers may have torn and trimmed off to make the coat more appealing to buyers.

Rayy silks have been the subject of a great deal of controversy. They were originally found and excavated under uncontrolled circumstances—by grave robbers, searching for marketable antiquities. The largest holdings of these fragments, many of which are now in public collections, are in the Cleveland Museum of Art and The Textile Museum in Washington, D.C. Scholars have questioned the authenticity of some of these pieces, including this one, pictured with the full coat from which it must have been taken.[13] Further technical research remains to be done before all doubts about its origin can be erased.

Iran, Buyid Period
CAFTAN, 10th century
55⅛ (140) length, weft
The Cleveland Museum of Art, Purchase from the J. H. Wade Fund 82.43

Materials
  Basic fabric
    warp: silk, single-ply Z-twist; light tan
    weft: silk, no twist; white
    supplementary warp: silk, single-ply Z-twist; light tan
    supplementary weft: silk, no twist; dark brown
Techniques
  Warp-dominant 3/1 diagonal twill weave (background) and
    weft-faced floats bound in a diagonal twill alignment
    (figure), with supplementary binding warp and
    continuous supplementary weft
      proportions: one supplementary warp per two main
        warps, one supplementary weft per one main weft
  No selvedge
Thread count
  Basic fabric
    warp: 124   weft: 60
    supplementary warp: 62
    supplementary weft: 60

Catalogue Number 52
Iran
Man's or Woman's Jacket, 18th or 19th century
silk twill weaves with silk and metallic complementary weft
20¼ (51.5) length, warp
John Herron Fund 18.139

Jackets cut in this shape are known from the seventeenth through the nineteenth centuries. The long, narrow sleeves with points that fall over the back of the hand originated in the Asian steppes. The owner of this jacket, like the owner of cat. 53, apparently found the sleeve extensions awkward, for soil marks show that they were folded back into a cuff. The jacket's flanged hip was probably inspired by the padded hips of European women's costume during the seventeenth century. Continental influence was transmitted through the ambassadors, painters, and engravers who came to the court at Isfahan and by the Christian Armenian traders living just outside the city who dealt with European textile merchants. Iranians thus had ample opportunity to see the exotic features of European costume.[14]

Silk jackets were more prestigious and expensive than cotton ones, and silk clothing was more popular in the winter than in the summer. The floral pattern in staggered rows, here worked in twill weave with five differently colored complementary wefts, was popular from the seventeenth through the nineteenth centuries.

Materials
  Basic fabric
    warp: silk, single-ply Z-twist; light orange
    complementary weft:
      silk, no twist: orange, light green, white, tan
      metallic
        core thread: silk, no twist; yellow
        strip: silver with copper, S-twist; gold colored
  Lining
    warp: cotton, single-ply Z-twist; light tan
    weft: cotton, single-ply Z-twist; light tan
    dyes: red, black
Techniques
  Weft-dominant 5/1 diagonal twill weave, with continuous complementary weft, grouped wefts
  Pieced garment
  Quilted
  Trim: silk braid, narrow woven band, and fabric of warp-faced twill weave
  Lining: balanced plain weave, printed
Thread count
  Basic fabric
    warp: 100   complementary weft: 105 groups
  Lining
    warp: 60   weft: 45
Pattern repeat
  warpwise: 1½ in. (4.0 cm)   weftwise: 2⅝ in. (6.5 cm)

Catalogue Number 53
Iran
Man's or Woman's Jacket, ca. 1800
cotton plain weave, mordant and resist dyed
19¼ (49) length, warp
Eliza M. and Sarah L. Niblack Collection 33.882

During the seventeenth century, a number of Iranian centers produced patterned cottons. The design on this piece was applied through a combination of dyeing methods. The blues were dyed by applying a resistant material to the cloth, which was then dipped in an indigo dye bath. The red and black were achieved by hand painting different mordants before dyeing, and the yellow dye was hand applied, both alone and over blue to produce green. This method was carried to sophisticated heights in India (see cat. 27).

This jacket was made of inexpensive material and was probably worn in summer. The sleeve extensions were folded back on this garment, as well as on cat. 52.

Materials
  Basic fabric
    warp: cotton, single-ply Z-twist; white
    weft: cotton, single-ply Z-twist; white
    dyes: black, red, blue, brown-yellow, green
  Lining
    warp: cotton, single-ply Z-twist; white
    weft: cotton, single-ply Z-twist; white
Techniques
  Balanced plain weave
  Painted mordant and wax-resist dyed, with painted details, glazed
  Pieced garment
  Quilted
  Trim: silk braid, metal buttons, and bias-cut basic fabric
  Lining: balanced plain weave, glazed
Thread count
  Basic fabric
    warp: 105   weft: 99
  Lining
    warp: 76   weft: 72
Pattern repeat
  warpwise: 3⅛ in. (8.0 cm)   weftwise: 2⅛ in. (5.5 cm)

Catalogue Number 54
Iran or Northern India
Pair of Socks, 19th century
wool vertical interlooping (knitting), trimmed with silk band
30½ (77.5) length
Gift of Mrs. Henry Schurmann 16.1117 a & b

Patterned socks are knitted in many areas of the Islamic world. One of the earliest known surviving examples, from around A.D. 750 to 1050, was found in Fustat, near Cairo. Men and women wear patterned socks in Iranian paintings that date from the seventeenth century on.[15]

Floral sprigs, rendered here in multicolored wool yarns on a dark blue ground, are typical of Iranian design. A significant Indian Moghul motif, the *buta* pattern was especially popular in wool shawls produced in northern India (see cat. 31). Since the *buta* represents a flowering spray, its importance in Iranian design is unsurprising: the Iranians loved flowers and cultivated exotic gardens; contemplation of flowers was in fact a pastime in the courts and gardens of the wealthy.

Materials
  Basic fabric
    wool, three-ply S-twist; light and dark blue, yellow, light
    and medium red, white, black, dark brown, light blue-
    green
  Trim
    silk, single-ply S-twist; yellow, light red, light green
  Lining
    wool, three-ply S-twist; dark brown, black
Techniques
  Vertical interlooping (plain knitting), with complementary
    elements
    stocking stitch with floats of complementary elements on
    the inside, worked in the round
  Trim: narrow band of two sets of elements interworked,
    tassels
  Lining: vertical interlooping (plain knitting), stocking stitch
Thread count
  Basic fabric
    stitches: 21   rows: 19
Pattern repeat
  Basic fabric
    horizontal: 1¼ in. (3.0 cm)   vertical: 3¾ in. (9.5 cm)

Catalogue Number 55
Zoroastrian People, Iran
Woman's Shirt, Pants, and Wrapper (*macna-eh*),
   ca. 1900 (?)
shirt of silk plain weave and cotton plain weave,
   embroidered with silk
pants of silk plain weaves and printed cotton plain weave,
   embroidered with silk
wrapper of silk plain weave, embroidered with silk
shirt: 40¼ (102) length, warp
pants: 30½ (77.5) length, warp
wrapper: 123½ (313.5) with fringe, warp
Eliza M. and Sarah L. Niblack Collection 33.790, 33.814, and
   33.815

The cult of Zoroastrianism developed in and around Yazd, a
city in central Iran. A Zoroastrian girl was expected to be a
skilled needlewoman by the time she married and to provide
numerous articles for her dowry. This is the type of long shawl
that was draped over the bride's shoulders; here, the black
background is embroidered in brightly colored silk threads.[16]
A typical Middle and Near Eastern shape, the full black and
red pants are gathered at the waist with a drawstring and caught
around the ankles. The attenuated forms of the birds and
cut-out quality of the design are characteristic of Zoroastrian
embroidery.

Wrapper
Materials
Basic fabric
   warp: silk, single-ply Z-twist; black
   weft: silk, single-ply Z-twist; black
Embroidery
   silk, two-ply Z-twist; white, tan, light and medium red,
     light, medium, and dark blue, three light greens, light,
     medium, and dark orange, yellow
Techniques
Balanced plain weave
Embroidery
   flat stitches: arrowhead; couching; satin; stem; variation
     of double running
   looped stitches: Chinese knot
Finish: countered compact weft twining at ends around
   paired warps
Fringe: three-ply S-twist, grouped warp ends, knotted
Thread count
Basic fabric
   warp: 61   weft: 58

Shirt
Materials
Fabric 1 (solid)
   warp: silk, single-ply Z-twist; red or black
   weft: silk, single-ply Z-twist; red or black
Fabric 2 (striped)
   warp: cotton, single-ply Z-twist; white
   weft: cotton, single-ply Z-twist; white, red, dark blue,
     brown-yellow
Embroidery
   silk, two-ply Z-twist; two light greens, blue-green, green,
     brown, yellow, light and medium red, medium and dark
     blue, orange, white

Catalogue Number 55

Techniques
   Fabric 1: balanced plain weave
   Fabric 2: weft-dominant plain weave
   Embroidery
     flat stitches: arrowhead; pattern couching; cross; dot;
      satin; stem; straight
     looped stitches: variation of buttonhole insertion
   Pieced garment
Thread count
   Fabric 1
     warp: 39   weft: 39
   Fabric 2
     warp: 44   weft: 46

Pants
Materials
   Fabric 1 (printed)
     warp: cotton, single-ply Z-twist; tan
     weft: cotton, single-ply Z-twist; tan
     dyes/pigments: light orange-brown, brown, black
   Fabric 2 (solid)
     warp: silk, single-ply Z-twist; red or black
     weft: silk, single-ply Z-twist; red or black
   Fabric 3 (striped)
     warp: silk, single-ply Z-twist; red
     weft: silk, single-ply Z-twist; red, yellow, black, white
   Embroidery
     silk, two-ply Z-twist; black, yellow, white, red, orange,
      green, blue
Techniques
   Fabric 1: balanced plain weave, printed
   Fabric 2: balanced plain weave
   Fabric 3: weft-dominant plain weave
   Embroidery
     flat stitches: arrowhead; pattern couching; dot; satin;
      stem; straight
   Pieced garment, pieced then embroidered
Thread count
   Fabric 1
     warp: 45   weft: 49
   Fabric 2
     warp: 48   weft: 67
   Fabric 3
     warp: 45   weft: 56

Catalogue Number 56
Iran
Dervish Hat, ca. 1875
wool plain weave, embroidered with silk and metallic thread
5 x 7 (12.5 x 18) height x diameter
Eliza M. and Sarah L. Niblack Collection 33.834

This finely embroidered wool hat was worn by a dervish from the Muslim Shi'ite sect established by Ali, the Prophet Muhammed's son-in-law. The hat is inscribed in Arabic and Persian and the appeal, "Ali, be my help," is repeated around the bottom tier. Embroidered in black, the larger medallions above it contain Chapter 3, verses 26-27, of the Quran:

O Allah, Lord of Sovereignty, Thou bestoweth sovereignty upon whomsoever Thou pleaseth and Thou taketh away sovereignty from whomsoever Thou pleaseth. Thou exalteth whomsoever Thou pleaseth. Thou abaseth whomsoever Thou pleaseth.

In Thy hand is all good.

Thou surely hath power to do all that Thou doth will.

Thou maketh the night pass into day, and maketh the day pass into night. Thou bringeth forth the living from the dead, and bringeth forth the dead from the living. Thou bestoweth upon whomsoever Thou pleaseth without measure.*

Above that are Persian poetic verses:

Monarchs of the world who own crowns, throne and wealth
And are busy taking from the needy
If they think wisely, they will realize
That they are the needy to have to resort to taking from the poor to exist.
Oh Almighty God at whose court rich and poor are needy alike
You give everyone what he deserves.†

The top tier could not be translated.

Dervishes have been known to embroider caps with God's attributes in a ritual called the *zikr*, which promotes the attainment of salvation.[17] Dervishes wear such hats in other ritual performances, and these hats are also found under Hazrat Ali's portrait in tea houses, where men often meet.[18]

*Trans. Zafrulla Khan
†Trans. Raj. Bavanati

Materials
  Basic fabric
    warp: wool, single-ply S-twist; white
    weft: wool, single-ply S-twist; white
  Embroidery
    silk, two-ply S-twist; white, dark brown, yellow, light green, light and medium red, light blue
    metallic
      core thread: cotton, two-ply S-twist; white
      strip: silver with copper, Z-twist; gold colored
  Lining
    warp: bast (linen), single-ply Z-twist; brown
    weft: bast (linen), single-ply Z-twist; brown
Techniques
  Balanced plain weave
  Embroidery
    flat stitches: invisible couching of braided elements; stem
    looped stitches: chain, chequered chain
  Pieced
  Interlining: warp-faced plain weave wool fabric
  Lining: balanced 2/2 diagonal twill weave
Thread count
  Basic fabric
    warp: 72   weft: 72
  Lining
    warp: 49   weft: 70

Catalogue Number 56

Catalogue Number 57
Iran
Furnishing Fabric, 19th century (?)
silk satin weave, pieced, embroidered with silk and metallic
  thread
42¼ x 41 (107.5 x 104) weft x warp
Eliza M. and Sarah L. Niblack Collection 33.821

The embroidered patterns on this square are reminiscent of
other Iranian designs, especially those on rugs. Here, lotuses
and carnations surround a central medallion worked on light
blue satin. These elements, executed in gold- and silver-
wrapped threads couched in twill and herringbone designs,
connect with a typical vining arabesque on a border of deep
red satin.

According to the literature, pieces such as this may have been
used for cushion covers.[19] Iranians usually furnished their
households with cushions and floor and wall coverings, which
the wealthy had executed in costly silks and metallic threads.
Occasionally the Iranians covered low dining tables or wrapped
bundles and gifts with fabrics: in such cases, the covers were
often as valuable as the contents.

Materials
  Basic fabric, center
    warp: silk, single-ply S-twist; light blue-green
    weft: silk, no twist; light blue-green
  Basic fabric, border
    warp: silk, single-ply S-twist; red
    weft: silk, no twist; light orange
  Embroidery
    silk, two-ply slight S-twist; dark blue-green, dark green,
      blue, white, light green, light yellow, two light oranges,
      black
    metallic #1
      core thread: silk, two-ply S-twist; yellow
      strip: gold and silver with copper, S-twist; gold colored
    metallic #2
      core thread: silk, two-ply S-twist; white
      strip: gold and silver with copper, S-twist; silver colored
  Backing, center
    warp: cotton, single-ply S-twist; white
    weft: cotton, single-ply S-twist; white
  Backing, border
    warp: silk, no twist; yellow
    weft: silk, no twist; yellow
Techniques
  Both center and border fabrics: warp-faced 6/1 satin weave
  Embroidery
    flat stitches: couching; satin, long and short satin
    combination flat stitches: couching over satin
  Pieced, then embroidered
  Backings: balanced plain weave; border fabric used on bias

Thread count
  Basic fabric, center
    warp: 383   weft: 77
  Basic fabric, border
    warp: 392   weft: 74
  Backing, center
    warp: 60   weft: 36
  Backing, border
    warp: 138   weft: 116

Catalogue Number 59
Town of Tabriz, Northwestern Iran
Rug, ca. 1860
silk and wool plain weave with silk supplementary
  weft knotted pile
69 x 51¾ (175 x 131.5) warp x weft
Gift of Gustave A. Efroymson 46.156

In the fourteenth century the Iranian court had its summer residence in Tabriz, a cultural center whose large library attracted many great painters, scholars, weavers, and other craftsmen.[23] Silk rugs made for the courts and for gifts to foreign rulers survive from the sixteenth century. The design of these rugs was often indebted to illuminated pages and highly decorated book covers, which frequently displayed compositions that, like this piece, had a centralized medallion.[24] Around 1860, Western demand stimulated a dramatic increase in the production of Iranian rugs, and these luxury items, once made solely for the court, became prized for their export value.

Materials
  Basic fabric
    warp: silk, three-ply tight S-twist; white
    weft: wool, four-ply S-twist; dark tan
    supplementary weft pile:
      silk, no twist; light red-orange, medium orange-red,
        light and dark blue, dark violet-red, blue-green,
        yellow, light orange, brown, white
Techniques
  Weft-faced plain weave with supplementary weft wrapping
    (knotted pile)
    symmetrical knots around two warps, alternate warps on
      different levels
    proportions: one row knots per two main wefts
  Selvedge: five single warps woven in plain weave with main
    weft
  No original finish at warp ends
Thread count
  Basic fabric
    warp: 36   weft: 44
    supplementary weft pile, warpwise: 18   weftwise: 22

Catalogue Number 60
Eastern Mediterranean
Man's or Woman's Coat, 19th century (?)
silk and cotton satin weave, quilted and stuffed (trapunto)
50½ (128) length, warp
Eliza M. and Sarah L. Niblack Collection 33.796

An important person must have owned this extraordinarily fine quilted coat. The labor expended on its execution underscores the status of textiles in this culture.

Materials
  Basic fabric
    warp: silk, no twist; light tan
    weft: cotton, single-ply Z-twist; light tan
  Lining
    warp: cotton, single-ply Z-twist; white
    weft: cotton, single-ply Z-twist; white
  Quilting thread
    cotton, two-ply S-twist; white, light tan

Cording
    cotton, four-ply S-twist; white
Techniques
  Warp-faced 4/1 satin weave
  Quilted and stuffed with cord
  Pieced garment
  Lining: balanced plain weave
Thread count
  Basic fabric
    warp: 172   weft: 88
  Lining
    warp: 78   weft: 86

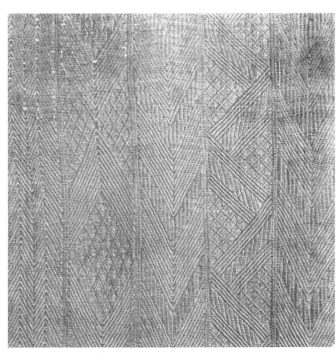

Catalogue Number 61
Turkey
Fragment of Garment Fabric, 16th century
silk velvet weave with silk supplementary warp and metallic
    supplementary weft (voided velvet with brocade)
48½ x 12¼ (123 x 31) warp x weft
John Herron Fund 18.142

This classic Turkish design, variously described as "clouds and
balls" or "tiger stripes and leopard spots," has its origins in the
uncertain past.[25] It has been proposed that the wavy lines originated in Buddhist China and that the combination of motifs
represents pearls borne on waves of the sea. This pattern may
have come to represent Rustam, one of the greatest Iranian
mythical heroes from the *Book of Kings*, or *Shāhnāme*, where the
pattern was associated with tiger and leopard pelts.[26]

Much of our knowledge about sixteenth-century Turkish
silks comes from a group of kaftans owned by various sultans
and later stored in the Topkapi Saray Palace in Istanbul. In that
collection there are two kaftans attributed to Mehmet the Conqueror (r. 1451-1481) that use the velvets of this pattern. In this
period, men and women wore long or short kaftans, with
sleeves of various lengths, over other garments.[27] The simplified cut of kaftans allowed for full appreciation of the dramatic
patterns typical in Turkish silks from the classical period. Yardage was used flat on back and front, with sleeves also cut flat
and set into straight shoulder seams: triangular gussets added
a bit of fullness to the sides. The triangular shape of this fragment implies that it was originally a side gusset for a kaftan.

Materials
  Basic fabric
    warp: silk, single-ply slight S-twist; yellow-tan
    weft: silk, no twist; yellow-tan
    supplementary warp:
      silk, single-ply slight S-twist; dark violet-red
    supplementary weft:
      metallic
        core thread: silk, single-ply S-twist; yellow-tan
        strip: gold and silver with copper and magnesium,
          S-twist; dark gray colored
Techniques
  Warp-faced woven pile, cut, (background) and warp-faced
    4/1 satin weave with small number of weft-faced floats
    remaining (figure); with supplementary warp pile and
    continuous supplementary weft, paired supplementary
    wefts
      proportions: one supplementary warp per two-three
        main warps, one supplementary weft and one velvet
        rod per two main wefts
  No selvedge
Thread count
  Basic fabric
    warp: 225   weft: 56
    supplementary warp: 90
    supplementary weft: 28 pairs (56 threads)
Pattern repeat
    warpwise: 4¼ in. (11.5 cm)   weftwise: 11¾ in. (30.0 cm)

Catalogue Number 62
Turkey
Fragment of Garment or Furnishing Fabric, ca. 1600
silk velvet weave with silk supplementary warp and metallic
  supplementary weft (voided velvet with brocade),
  embroidered with metallic thread
23½ x 15¾ (59.5 x 40) weft x warp
Eliza M. and Sarah L. Niblack Collection 33.1457

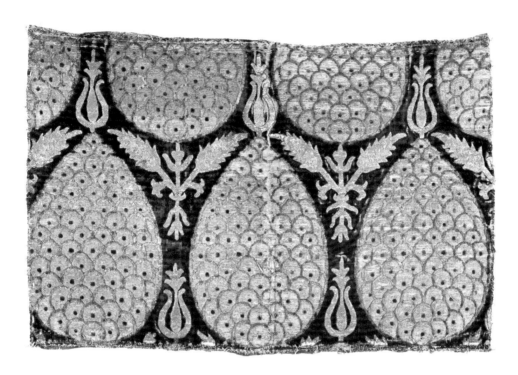

Ogive-patterned Chinese silk damask arrived in the Mediter-ranean, Mamluk Egypt, and Syria from 1250 to around 1350, then passed from Europe to Turkey, where it may have inspired fabric design from the sixteenth to the eighteenth centuries. Chinese models or Mamluk versions of them may be the specific source of this pattern.[28] In the sixteenth century both Turkish and Italian silk weavers employed this pattern of the pome-granate or pine cone (*pomme de pin*), often contained in an ogive (see cat. 94 and 95).

In this example the dark red velvet, patterned with pome-granates in gold-wrapped threads, is original to the seventeenth century, but the leaf patterns, embroidered with silver-wrapped thread, were added later. Like this example, silks of the period were commonly composed of three pattern units across the width, in staggered rows.

Materials
  Basic fabric
    warp: silk, single-ply Z-twist; light tan
    weft: silk, single-ply Z-twist; light tan, yellow
    supplementary warp:
      silk, single-ply slight S-twist; red, green
    supplementary weft:
      metallic #1
        core thread: silk, single-ply S-twist; light tan
        strip: gold and silver with copper, S-twist; gold
        colored
  Embroidery
    metallic #2
      core thread: silk, single-ply S-twist; light tan

strip: gold and silver with copper, S-twist; gold colored
    metallic #3
      core thread: silk, single-ply S-twist; tan
      strip: gold and silver with copper, S-twist; silver colored
  Backing
    warp: cotton, single-ply S-twist; light blue
    weft: cotton, single-ply S-twist; light blue

Techniques
  Warp-faced woven pile, cut, (background) and weft-faced
    floats bound in a diagonal twill alignment (figure); with
    supplementary warp pile and discontinuous
    supplementary weft
      proportions: two supplementary warps per seven main
        warps, one supplementary weft and one velvet rod per
        two main wefts
  Embroidery
    flat stitches: couching of doubled elements
  Backing: balanced plain weave

Thread count
  Basic fabric
    warp: 224   weft: 116
    supplementary warp: 64
    supplementary weft: 58
  Backing fabric
    warp: 52   weft: 48

Pattern repeat
  warpwise: 10 in. (25.5 cm) estimate
  weftwise: 8¼ in. (21.0 cm)

Catalogue Number 63
Turkey
Napkin (*peşkir*, *makrama*, *yāglik*), 19th century
cotton plain weave, embroidered with silk and metallic strips
52 x 21 (132 x 53) warp x weft
Gift of Mrs. M. B. Thomas 48.29

Turkish embroidered domestic linens such as these are known from the second half of the seventeenth century. In the eighteenth and nineteenth centuries, a great number were produced for trade.[29] Napkins were used not only for wiping the hands at mealtime, but also for covering food, wrapping small packages, and storing books and documents. They are usually patterned with flowers or, as here, with landscape scenes, in embroidery stitches that are reversible. Much of the metal thread in this embroidery was formed in long strips rather than wrapped around a fiber core. One end of the strip itself was sharpened so it could be worked in and out of the cloth like a needle. After the work was finished, the metal strips were gently hammered to flatten them.[30]

Embroidery enjoyed tremendous prestige in Turkey, where it symbolized the status of the wealthy. A professional guild of embroiderers, mostly men, worked for the court and wealthy individuals, and a group of city embroiderers made pieces to sell. In spite of this professional activity, embroidery in Turkey was largely a domestic occupation, done in the sultan's harem as well as the poorest laborer's hut. Every girl was expected to work embroidery for her dowry. Since textiles were so heavily used in the interior of Turkish dwellings, this task could take many years: in the common home, embroideries imitated the extremely costly woven silks of the wealthy and were used as cushion covers, wall hangings, bolsters, table covers, domestic linen, and decoration on clothing (see cat. 64).[31]

Materials

Basic fabric
warp: cotton, single-ply Z-twist; white
weft: cotton, single-ply Z-twist; white
Embroidery
silk, single-ply S-twist; tan, light, medium, and dark blue, three light greens, two light red-oranges, dark yellow, brown, gray, white
metallic #1
flat strip only: gold and silver with copper; gray-silver colored
metallic #2
flat strip only: gold and silver with copper, gold colored
Trim
metallic #3
core thread: silk, single-ply S-twist; light yellow
strip: gold and silver with copper, Z-twist; gold colored

Techniques

Balanced plain weave, loosely woven
Embroidery
flat counted stitches: double darning; satin; triangular two-sided Turkish
looped counted stitches: buttonhole
Selvedge: less than 1/8 in. wide (0.1 cm) warp-dominant plain weave, paired warps
Trim: needle lace edging of twisted buttonhole stitch with multiple elements

Thread count

Basic fabric
warp: 56   weft: 52

Catalogue Number 64
Turkey
Man's Belt (*uçkue, kuşak*), 19th century
linen plain weave, embroidered with silk and metallic thread
92¼ x 10 (234 x 25.5) warp x weft
Gift of Mrs. J. Ottis Adams Estate 55.57

Men wore decorated belts around their loose shirts and trousers year-round and around the layers of indoor coats during the winter. Belts may also have been worn as scarves.[32] Like napkins and towels, these are made of linen or cotton and decorated on each end with reversible gold designs. The delicacy of workmanship in this piece indicates it was probably professionally executed.

Materials
  Basic fabric
    warp: bast (linen), single-ply tight Z-twist; white
    weft: bast (linen), single-ply tight Z-twist; white
  Embroidery
    silk, two-ply S-twist; light and dark red, light and
      medium orange, light and medium yellow, light and
      medium green, light and dark blue, light blue-gray
    metallic
      core thread: silk, single-ply S-twist; yellow
      strip: gold and silver with copper, Z-twist; gold colored

Techniques
  Balanced plain weave, loosely woven with overspun warp
    and weft
  Embroidery
    flat stitches: satin
    flat counted stitches: double darning; handkerchief hem;
      pulled satin
    looped counted stitches: buttonhole
  Selvedge: ¼ in. (0.6 cm) wide, warp-dominant plain weave
    with single-ply slight Z-twist warps
  Pieced near center
  Finish: raw edges rolled under and stitched

Thread count
  Basic fabric
    warp: 68   weft: 63

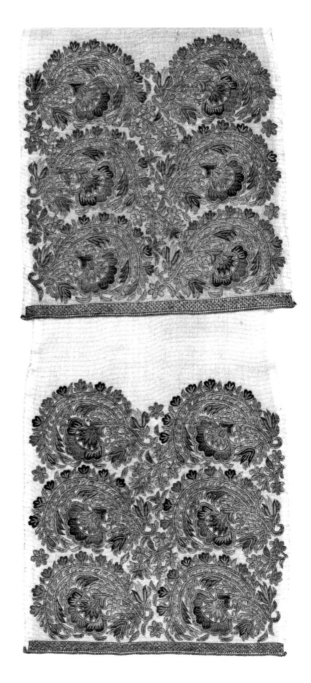

Catalogue Number 65
Town of Jannina, Epirus Region, Greece
Fragment of Border from Bed Cover, 1700-1850
linen plain weave, embroidered with silk
78½ x 15¼ (199 x 39) warp x weft
Eliza M. and Sarah L. Niblack Collection 33.1147

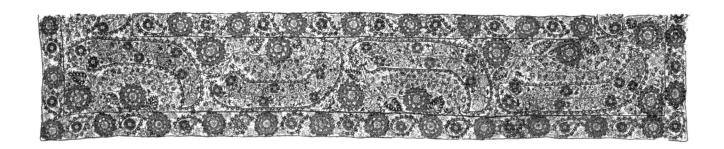

In the late twelfth century, Greece was part of the Byzantine Empire. When the European Crusaders' first sack of Constantinople in 1204 sapped the empire's strength, most of the Greek islands fell under Venetian control. During the fifteenth century the Ottoman Turks increasingly pressured Greece, and by the mid-sixteenth century they dominated the country. Thus, the Middle East has been a primary or secondary stimulus to Greek culture for almost 1,500 years.[33]

While most existing Greek embroideries date from the seventeenth to the mid-nineteenth centuries, the patterns they followed were used much earlier and later. Like most folk art, Greek embroidery favored traditional rather than innovative designs. Most of it was done in the home, most intensely when a girl was preparing her dowry. She was expected to make and decorate at least two dresses—one for the wedding and another for special occasions—a set of curtains and valances, a bed cover, and several covers for the household cushions used instead of formal furniture.[34]

Jannina, the capital of Epirus, probably borrowed from Turkish motifs more heavily than any other Greek tradition. At times in its history the town surpassed Athens in size and importance. Overrun by Turks in the late fourteenth and early fifteenth centuries, Jannina recovered to reach its pinnacle shortly before the turn of the nineteenth century, when the Turkish ruler Ali Pasha established a rich court there.[35] It created a huge market for brocaded textiles, embroidery, jewelry, and metalwork, and attracted hundreds of merchants and craftsmen.[36]

Most Jannina embroidery was done on cushion covers, bed covers, and hangings. The latter two were usually decorated around the edges and left plain in the center. This pattern, the most common, is a rose spray enclosed by an ogival compartment.[37] Turkish designs heavily influenced the smaller circular and teardrop flowers as well as the broader forms. These shapes are worked on linen with herringbone stitches in rich hues of blue, orange, green, and yellow.

In the mid-nineteenth century, lifestyle changed dramatically as mechanically manufactured goods flooded the region and replaced finely decorated embroideries. Very few full-size large pieces remain today: since traditional embroidery had ceased to be done, the owners cut up existing ones for their daughters' dowries.

Materials
Basic fabric
warp: bast (linen), single-ply Z-twist; white
weft: bast (linen), single-ply Z-twist, white
Embroidery
silk, two-ply Z-twist; white, red, blue, light orange, light
yellow-green, light and dark blue-green, yellow-orange
silk, two-ply tight Z-twist; black
Techniques
Balanced plain weave
Embroidery
flat stitches: closed herringbone; stem
looped stitches: chain
Selvedge: balanced plain weave with single warps
Thread count
Basic fabric
warp: 58   weft: 73

Catalogue Number 66
Island of Cos (?), Dodecanese Islands, Greece
Fragment of Bed Tent, 1700-1850
linen plain weave, embroidered with silk
34¾ x 15 (88.5 x 38) warp x weft
Eliza M. and Sarah L. Niblack Collection 33.1155

Compared with the free-flowing forms of Jannina embroidery (see cat. 65), those on Dodecanese pieces seem rigidly delicate. Most embroidery from this region is executed on linen in cross stitch in red, orange, yellow, and green silk. The patterns, like the stitches, are geometric. Triangular, leaflike shapes fill the borders, with stylized peacocks and double-headed eagles incorporated into the central band. The peacock is seen as a motif throughout the Middle East, particularly in Iran. From there it was probably transmitted to the Byzantine Empire, where it came to symbolize longevity. The Byzantine double eagle, another ancient Middle Eastern motif, has also been used throughout Greece, and after the fall of the Byzantine Empire, it became associated with Greek nationalism.[38] On the border is the leaf pattern called broad leaves (*platyphylla*) which has been widely used throughout the islands.[39]

In the Dodecanese, sparvers, or bed tents, have substituted for curtains since the Middle Ages. They are put on the bed for the wedding night, later used for festivals, and finally given to the daughter for her dowry.[40] The tents, made from decorated strips of linen that were fastened to the top of a circular wooden support, hung in a bell shape around the bed. The strips were heavily embroidered on the front, where the work showed, and left plain on the back. Characteristically, embroidered bands surround the central opening of the finest tents; these were usually worked in the leaf pattern seen here on the outside borders. Located above this main opening, the gable was frequently decorated with figures or birds. The central part of this piece probably came from such a gable.

Materials
Basic fabric
    warp: bast (linen), single-ply Z-twist; tan
    weft: bast (linen), single-ply Z-twist; tan
Embroidery
    silk, no twist; orange, light green, brown-yellow
Techniques
Balanced plain weave
Pieced, then embroidered
Embroidery
    flat counted stitches: pattern darning; double running; satin
Selvedge: balanced plain weave with single warps
Thread count
Basic fabric
    warp: 49   weft: 45

175

Catalogue Number 67 (see color plate, p. 42)
Uzbekistan, U.S.S.R.
Furnishing Fabric, ca. 1900
silk plain weave, resist-dyed warp (ikat), quilted
86 x 59¼ (218 x 150.5) warp x weft
Emma Harter Sweetser Fund 78.113

Detail

The technique of warp-ikat dyeing may have originated in central Asia and spread to other locales. Ikats made in Yemen during the tenth century have been found at Fustat, Egypt; and old written sources that allude to the technique's use in the south Arabian peninsula imply it was known as early as the seventh century.[41] The Turkmen region, however, may not have produced ikat-dyed cloth before the eighteenth century. Fabrics and coats made from it were traded with nomadic groups in surrounding areas.

In this region women traditionally provided much of the labor for wool textile production, but men dyed and wove silk ikat. Guilds of specialists made ikats such as this one in workshops located in the *tim*, or covered bazaar, of a town.[42] The plain woven silk taffeta (*adras*) illustrated here was used for robes, trousers, and wall hangings. Because they were luxury goods, ikats were given as presents for weddings and other important occasions.[43] This particular piece is lined and quilted, so it was probably made as a cover or a decorative hanging. The silk thread may have been produced in the area, long known for its sericulture.[44]

Here, the dramatic red designs were not matched from one panel to the next, undoubtedly for several reasons. Silk cloth was very costly, and aligning the patterns wasted it. More important, however, the aesthetic principle of bilateral symmetry was not a paramount concern in central Asia, as it was in Europe. Consequently, the alignment of these pieces is highly dynamic.

When Russia began to dominate this area at the end of the nineteenth century, traditions associated with such cloths, and finally the cloths themselves, disappeared.

Materials
Basic fabric
  warp: silk, no twist; white, light and medium red, yellow, dark blue, dark violet, dark green
  weft: silk, no twist; red
Quilting thread
  cotton, three-ply S-twist; light red, light blue, and light green all plied together
Backing
  warp: cotton, single-ply S-twist; tan
  weft: cotton, single-ply S-twist; tan
  dyes/pigments: green, red, dark brown
Techniques
Warp-faced plain weave
Resist-dyed warp
Four panels sewn together with seams at selvedges
Quilted
Backing: balanced plain weave, printed
Thread count
Basic fabric
  warp: 214   weft: 120
Backing
  warp: 50   weft: 51

176

Catalogue Number 68 (see color plate, p. 43)
Uzbekistan, U.S.S.R.
Garment Fabric, ca. 1900
silk velvet weave with silk supplementary warp (solid velvet),
   resist-dyed supplementary warp (ikat)
72 x 13¼ (182.5 x 33.5) warp x weft
Emma Harter Sweetser Fund 78.112

Ikat velvet (*baghmal*) such as this was used for men's coats
(*djoma*). In this region, the cut of such coats effectively conveyed
the drama of the fabric: the yardage was not shaped in the front
or back, and the sleeves were cut straight and attached at the
edges of the central panels. With this ease of fit, a man could
wear several garments at once, and thus fully display his rank.
Men's coats were traditionally custom-ordered from a tailor or
purchased ready-made.[45]

Velvet ikat was prestigious in itself because making its pile
required much more silk than was needed for plain taffeta ikat.
Only a long-standing regional tradition of ikat dyeing could
have fostered the development of such a process, for dyeing
the supplementary warp of velvet in ikat was enormously
complicated.

Materials
   Basic fabric
      warp: silk, single-ply Z-twist; red
      weft: silk, single-ply Z-twist; red
      supplementary warp: silk, no twist; dark blue, green,
        yellow, red, dark violet, white

Techniques
   Warp-faced woven pile, cut, with supplementary warp pile
   Resist-dyed supplementary warp
     proportions: two supplementary warps per three main
      warps, one velvet rod per four main wefts
   Selvedge: ⅜ in. (1.0 cm) warp-dominant 3/1 diagonal twill
     weave with green, yellow, and red stripes

Thread count
   Basic fabric
     warp: 123   weft: 288   supplementary warp: 82

Catalogue Number 69
Uzbekistan or Turkmenistan, U.S.S.R.
Woman's Coat, ca. 1900
silk plain weave, resist-dyed warp (ikat)
64½ (163.5) length, warp
Emma Harter Sweetser Fund 82.30

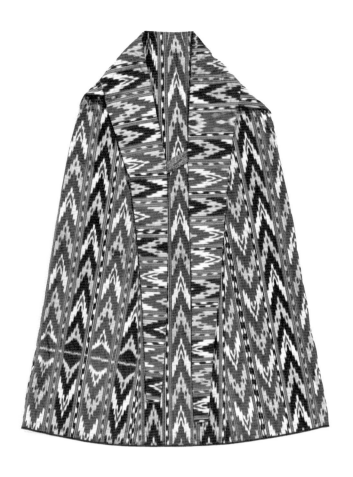

This coat was cut a bit narrower than a man's would have been, in a style adapted from earlier prototypes. The sleeves have become nonfunctional, flat bands. Women wore this type of coat draped over their heads or shoulders and used silk ikat for trousers, dresses, curtains, and wall hangings.[46]

Materials
  Basic fabric
    warp: silk, no twist; yellow, red, white, violet, light blue
    weft: silk, no twist; light red
  Lining 1
    warp: silk, no twist; red, green, yellow, white
    weft: cotton, two-ply Z-twist; white
  Lining 2
    warp: cotton, single-ply Z-twist; white
    weft: cotton, single-ply Z-twist; white
    dyes/pigments: red, green, yellow, blue, black
  Batting
    cotton
Techniques
  Warp-faced plain weave
  Resist-dyed warp
  Pieced garment, different patterns of basic fabric
  Quilted
  Trim: narrow band of vertical interlooping (plain knitting)
    in green silk
  Lining 1: warp-faced plain weave, resist-dyed warp
  Lining 2: balanced plain weave, printed
Thread count
  Basic fabric
    warp: 230   weft: 88
  Lining 1
    warp: 264   weft: 37
  Lining 2
    warp: 68   weft: 65

Catalogue Number 70
Tekke People, Turkmenistan, U.S.S.R.
Woman's Wedding Coat (*chyrpa*), ca. 1900
silk plain weave, embroidered with silk
47½ (120.5) length, warp
Gift of Mrs. Louis Wolf 62.206

Women wore coats like these over their headdresses. The sleeves have become mere strips of decorative fabric. The yellow silk ground, though associated with weddings, is comparatively rare in these coats, which are more commonly embroidered on dark blue silk. The geometric designs—in red, green, blue, black, and white—are reminiscent of leaves and flowers, particularly tulips.[47]

Materials
Basic fabric
  warp: silk, no twist; yellow
  weft: silk, single-ply slight Z-twist; yellow
Embroidery
  silk, two-ply Z-twist; light and medium red, dark green, blue, black, white
Facing 1
  warp: silk, single-ply Z-twist; red, yellow, black, green, white
  weft: silk, single-ply Z-twist; red, yellow, black, green, white
Facing 2
  warp: cotton, single-ply Z-twist; light brown, blue
  weft: cotton, single-ply Z-twist; light brown, blue
Lining
  warp: cotton, single-ply Z-twist; white
  weft: cotton, single-ply Z-twist; white
  dyes/pigments: yellow, green
Techniques
Warp-dominant plain weave
Embroidery
  flat stitches: back; Bokhara couching; stem
  looped stitches: buttonhole; chain, double chain, open chain; feather
Pieced garment
Quilted
Neck facings 1 and 2: balanced plain weave
Lining: balanced plain weave, printed
Thread count
Basic fabric
  warp: 178   weft: 104
Facing 1
  warp: 72   weft: 47
Facing 2
  warp: 39   weft: 40
Lining
  warp: 65   weft: 65

Catalogue Number 73
Yomut People, Turkmenistan, U.S.S.R.
Tent Band (*ǎk yüp*), ca. 1900
wool plain weave with wool supplementary weft (brocade),
  wool supplementary weft knotted pile, wool twining
619 x 11¼ (1,568 x 28.5) with fringe, warp x weft
Gift of Mrs. Anne Caroline Crane 54.9

Since at least the eighth century A.D., the felt-covered tent (*öy* or *yurt*) has served as the dwelling for vast numbers of nomadic herders in western Asia.[56] The supporting structure of this tent is made of lightweight, trellised cane, a material that is easily dismantled and transported. To preserve the shape of the tent, the cloth bands that envelop it are securely fastened to door struts, and the structure is subsequently covered with shaped felt. Since the tent is used only for welcoming guests or housing a newly wed couple, the interiors are decorated as sumptuously as possible: finely worked bands like this one are placed high on a wall with the pattern facing inward so it can be admired as luxurious decoration.[57]

These immensely long bands are woven on a horizontal loom, with the warp stretched out to its full length. A tripod structure above the warps supports the heddles. Straddling the warp, the weaver moves the tripod along as she works. The symmetrical red and blue knots are tied around three or four warp threads rather than two, as in most knotted rugs.

Materials
  Basic fabric
    warp: wool, two-ply S-twist; tan, red-brown
    weft: wool, two-ply S-twist; tan
    supplementary weft: wool, single-ply Z-twist; red-brown
    supplementary weft pile: wool, single-ply Z-twist; red-brown, dark blue, orange, dark green, yellow
    selvedge: wool, two-ply S-twist; dark blue
Techniques
  Warp-faced plain weave, weft-faced floats, countered compact twining, and supplementary weft wrapping (knotted pile); with tripled discontinuous supplementary weft, paired supplementary weft pile
    symmetrical knot around three or four warps
      proportions: three supplementary wefts or one group per one main weft
  Selvedge: single warps with a dark blue wool braid attached
  Finish: weft twining around grouped warps with grouped threads at both ends
  Fringe: warp ends and twining ends obliquely interlaced (braided); one end, flat braids, the other, round braids
Thread count
  Basic fabric
    warp: 61   weft: 14
    supplementary weft: 14 groups (42 threads)

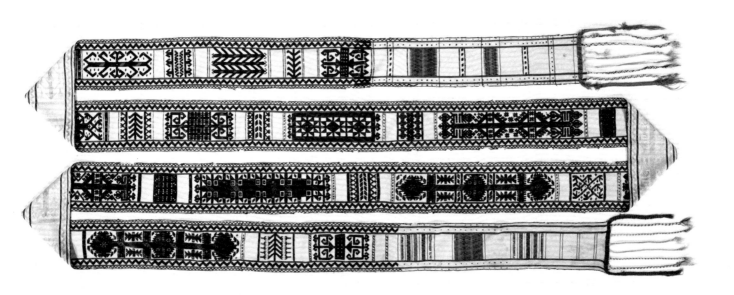

Catalogue Number 74
Shirvan Area, Caucasus, U.S.S.R.
Rug, ca. 1875
wool plain weave with wool twining (kilim)
130¼ x 64¾ (330 x 164) with fringe, warp x weft
Mrs. Lawrence Chambers Memorial Fund 70.55

The type of flat weave most often associated with the Caucasus is slit tapestry from the Shirvan region, just to the south of Kuba.[58] These rugs are usually made and used by nomads, most notably to cover their ox carts.[59] Slit tapestry weave is often called kilim, from the Arabic *gilim*, which appears in tenth- and eleventh-century sources.[60] Kilim creates a pliable cloth that is much less dense than soumak or pile weave. Since they were less durable than denser weave structures, slit tapestry woven rugs were the least expensive patterned wool weavings, and in fact were long excluded from the massive oriental rug export market. They were introduced to the West in the mid-twentieth century as wrappers for the more expensive knotted pile rugs.

To create such rugs, the colored patterning wefts were woven in weft-faced plain weave in the needed areas only. When the pattern changed color, a new thread was picked up and used as long as its color was called for. Worked back and forth within a particular area, the individual colored yarns created a finished edge on each pattern; these edges formed open slits between the design elements.

In the Shirvan region, men and women shared the preparation of weaving materials. While the men sheared sheep, the women prepared and wove the yarn. Older women taught these skills to very young girls, who learned to weave traditional patterns and techniques from memory. As part of their preparation for adulthood, girls strived for at least the level of excellence their peers had attained.

On these rugs the angular designs and reciprocal patterns, which interlace in both the foreground and background, belong to a design tradition that appears throughout the Islamic Middle East.[61]

Materials
  Basic fabric
    warp: wool, two-ply S-twist; brown and tan plied together
    weft: wool, two-ply S-twist; tan, red, brown, light, medium, and dark blue, yellow, light and medium green
    twining: wool, two-ply S-twist; tan, brown
Techniques
  Weft-faced plain weave, with continuous and discontinuous weft, slit tapestry joins, and countered compact weft twining
  Selvedge: two cords of paired warps woven in plain weave and wrapped with weft
  Fringe: looped warp ends at one end and individual warp ends at the other
Thread count
  Basic fabric
    warp: 16   weft: 58

Catalogue Number 75
Caucasus, U.S.S.R.
Rug, ca. 1900
wool plain weave with wool supplementary weft knotted pile
92 x 62¼ (233.5 x 157.5) with fringe, warp x weft
Director's Discretionary Fund 73.3

Throughout the Middle East rugs were, and still are, woven on a simple, two-beamed loom, which held the warp threads taut enough that knots could be easily inserted. Looms were usually placed vertically, so side poles had to be used to keep the structure rigid. Sitting on the ground in front of the loom, the weaver used balls of colored yarn to tie individual knots. She created the pile on this rug by tying symmetrical knots on two warp threads; the end of the threads came to the surface in the center of the knot. After completing one row of knots, she packed them down with a comb and passed one or more weft shots through the woven structure to hold the knots in place. Subsequently she beat the wefts in and continued with the next row of colored knots. After inserting several rows, she clipped the shaggy wool. Although vertical looms were the most common ones, certain nomadic groups laid the warp parallel to the ground and attached the two loom beams to pegs driven in the earth—a type of loom that was easily dismantled, rolled up, and carried to another site.

Kazak is a generic term for the rugs with bold patterns, vibrant colors, and long pile that are woven in the south central Caucasus. The small, highly abstracted animal forms, the bands of plain weave at the top, and the knotted fringe at the bottom are characteristic of rugs from this area. These medallion designs may be abstracted versions of a floral form from an earlier prototype,[62] or may have been inspired by Turks migrating west from central Asia.[63] *Kazak* rugs were very popular exports to the West during the late nineteenth century.

Materials
  Basic fabric
    warp: wool, three-ply tight S-twist; tan
    weft: wool, two-ply S-twist; tan
    supplementary weft pile: wool, single-ply slight Z-twist; tan, white, brown, yellow, light and medium red, light, medium, and dark blue, blue-green
    supplementary weft: wool, two-ply S-twist; red
Techniques
  Weft-faced plain weave with supplementary weft wrapping (knotted pile), paired supplementary weft
      symmetrical knot around two warps
      proportions: one row knots per four-five main wefts
  Selvedge: two cords of two warps each woven with a discontinuous supplementary weft in plain weave extending into knotted area in wedge shape every two or three rows of knots
  Headings: weft-faced plain weave
  Fringe: looped warp ends at one end and warps grouped by fours and interlaced, grouped by twelves and knotted at other end
Thread count
  Basic fabric
    warp: 14   weft: 12
    supplementary weft pile, warpwise: 7   weftwise: 6

187

Catalogue Number 76
Gendje Area, Azerbaijan Region, U.S.S.R.
Prayer Rug, 1312 Hejira, ca. 1900
wool and cotton plain weave with wool supplementary weft
    knotted pile
70½ x 51¼ (178.5 x 130) with fringe, warp x weft
Gift of George M. Chandler II 80.690

Niches on prayer rugs represent the *mihrab* (the prayer niche that faces Mecca in every mosque). That the Prophet Muhammed was buried in the *mihrab* of his mosque in Medina adds further importance to this shape. The origin of this form is unclear, but it may have been influenced by the apse of the classical basilica in early Christian architecture.[64]

Prayer rugs were, and continue to be, a luxury item. Wealthy men use them at home or during travel for devotional times each day, when the rug is placed so its niche points toward Mecca. The Islamic date 1312 woven above the niche assigns this rug to the turn of the twentieth century.

Materials
  Basic fabric
    warp: wool, three-ply S-twist; brown and tan plied
      together
    weft: cotton, two-ply S-twist; tan
    supplementary weft pile: wool, single-ply Z-twist; white,
      medium blue, dark blue-green, yellow-green, yellow,
      light green, red, red-violet
Techniques
  Weft-faced plain weave with supplementary weft wrapping
    (knotted pile), paired supplementary weft
      symmetrical knot around two warps
      proportions: one row knots per two-five main wefts
  Selvedge: two cords of doubled or tripled threads woven
    with main weft in plain weave with extra shots of weft in
    selvedge to compensate for knots
  Heading: weft-faced plain weave at one end
  Fringe: individual warp ends looped at one end, knotted at
    the other
Thread count
  Basic fabric
    warp: 16   weft: 22
    supplementary weft pile, warpwise: 8   weftwise: 11

Notes

[1] Cootner, 1981, p. 115.

[2] Gluck, 1977, p. 179.

[3] However, Louisa Bellinger concludes that the drawloom evolved independently in China and Syria (Wulff, 1966, p. 174).

[4] Dimand, 1973, pp. 6-7.

[5] Grube, 1966, p. 142.

[6] Pope, 1977, pp. 2069-70.

[7] Mackie, 1973, pp. 9-10.

[8] Petsopoulos, 1982, essay by Denny, p. 121.

[9] Mackie, 1973, p. 14.

[10] Mackie, 1980, p. 15.

[11] Reath, 1937, p. 14.

[12] Pope, 1977, p. 148.

[13] See the *Irene Emery Roundtable on Museum Textiles 1974 Proceedings: Archaeological Textiles* with articles by Dorothy Shepherd and by Nabuko Kajitani and the *Bulletin de Liaison du Centre International D'Etude des Textiles Anciens*, XXXVII, 1973.

[14] Mackie, personal communication.

[15] Mackie, personal communication.

[16] Gluck, 1977, p. 230.

[17] Dhamija, 1979, p. 43.

[18] Dhamija, 1979, p. 34.

[19] Pope, 1977, p. 2157.

[20] Petsopoulos, 1982, essay by Dragadze, p. 274.

[21] Landreau, 1978, essay by Housego, p. 12.

[22] Petsopoulos, 1982, p. 303.

[23] Dimand, 1973, p. 27.

[24] Mackie, 1980, p. 20.

[25] Mackie, 1973, p. 21.

[26] Petsopoulos, 1982, essay by Denny, pp. 126-28.

[27] Mackie, 1973, p. 12.

[28] Mackie, 1973, p. 13.

[29] Petsopoulos, 1982, p. 132.

[30] David Black Oriental Carpets, 1978.

[31] David Black Oriental Carpets, 1978.

[32] David Black Oriental Carpets, 1978.

[33] Johnstone, 1972, p. 7.

[34] MacMillan.

[35] Johnstone, 1961, pp. 31-32.

[36] MacMillan.

[37] MacMillan.

[38] Johnstone, 1961, pp. 24-25.

[39] Johnstone, 1972, p. 10.

[40] Johnstone, 1961, p. 43.

[41] Larsen, 1976, pp. 135-36.

[42] Larsen, 1976, p. 170.

[43] *Uzbek*, 1975, p. 50.

[44] Israel Museum, 1967.

[45] *Uzbek*, 1975, p. 50.

[46] *Uzbek*, 1975, p. 50.

[47] Gluck, 1977, p. 246.

[48] *Uzbek*, 1975, p. 50.

[49] Israel Museum, 1967.

[50] *Uzbek*, 1975, p. 61.

[51] Franses, 1978, p. 129.

[52] Landreau, 1978, essay by Tschebull, p. 46.

[53] Mackie, 1980, p. 20.

[54] Mackie, 1980, essay by Thompson, pp. 61-62.

[55] Landreau, 1978, essay by Tschebull, p. 57.

[56] Mackie, 1980, p. 45.

[57] Mackie, 1980, p. 53.

[58] Jenny Housego suggests that these rugs were woven farther south by the Shahsevan people in the Hastrud area, which is south of the Tabriz-Mianeh road in northwestern Iran (Landreau, 1978, essay by Housego, p. 43).

[59] Petsopoulos, 1982, p. 233.

[60] Petsopoulos, 1982, p. 11.

[61] Mackie, 1980, p. 21.

[62] Denny, 1979, p. 67.

[63] Tschebull, 1971, p. 15.

[64] Grube, 1966, p. 172.

Western Islam

The Phoenicians established their first North African outpost around 1100 B.C. in Tunisia and added a string of trading posts along the North African coast to the Atlantic, both north and south of Gibraltar. The great Tunisian city of Carthage, located on a peninsula jutting out into the Mediterranean Sea, was founded in the eighth century B.C. because of its strategically defendable position.[1] The city's location also made it particularly desirable for trade. In fact, great quantities of goods were exported, including precious metals from North and Subsaharan West Africa, grain, olive oil and, textiles, particularly cloth dyed with the famous Phoenician purple.[2] After the Punic Wars, Roman outposts replaced Phoenician ones; Rome was in turn supplanted by Byzantium in eastern coastal North Africa and by the Vandals in Spain and Morocco.

Early in the eighth century A.D., Arabs moved across North Africa to Spain and founded the first Muslim caliphate. Silk manufacture was introduced at this time, and Spain soon produced enough of this precious commodity for export to other European countries. Textile trade was further enhanced by the establishment of an important cultural center at Cordoba and of the great medieval fairs at Toledo, among other locations. In addition, annual pilgrimages brought large numbers of the faithful to Santiago de Compostela, an important religious sanctuary.[3]

Meanwhile native North African Berbers resisted the seventh-century Arab incursions that resulted in the formation of coastal trading towns. Nomadic and seminomadic Berbers, who were driven into the mountains and deserts, countered the Islamic caliphate during the eighth century A.D. and conquered Muslim Spain in 1090. The strength of the Berbers increased until they dominated an empire that stretched from Spain across North Africa to the frontiers of Egypt. Unification of Spain and North Africa under Berber Muslim rule led to an intense artistic and intellectual renaissance. Major universities and libraries were established both in Spain and North Africa, where art, literature, science, and philosophy flourished. European scholars flocked to these seats of learning to reestablish lost contacts with classical writers and to learn from Arabic scholarship.[4] When Berber dominance over Spain and North Africa ended in the thirteenth century, various Muslim rulers established control over smaller regions.

During the period that followed, Iranian artists came to the Spanish court, a number of them from the Mongol-devastated artistic center of Rayy. Foreign fabric designers borrowed Sasanian motifs as well as interlacing forms and arabesques. A consistent design vocabulary of these elements prevailed throughout North Africa and Spain, many traces of which are evident in North African design today. (see cat. 79 and 80). This brilliant era in Western Islam ended when Isabella and Ferdinand defeated the Muslims in Spain in 1492. Religious persecution engendered by these monarchs drove most Muslim and Jewish craftsmen from Spain into North Africa. Simultaneously the Ottoman Empire extended its sphere of influence from the East to Tunisia, Algeria, and Libya. In the late eighteenth century, European powers finally defeated Ottoman rulers in North Africa, and in the nineteenth century, France colonized the area.

During Muslim rule of North Africa, cultural styles were established that were like those in the rest of the Islamic world. As with other regions of the Middle East, the fundamental difference between herder-nomadic and city-court textiles is marked. A constant dichotomy existed between the people who settled in coastal metropolitan centers and the Berbers who lived in the interior. Urban dwellers used silk, wore more elaborate, highly decorated costume, and used embroidery to embellish their houses. The design vocabulary consisted of typical Islamic arabesques and abstracted floral forms. These more delicate, convoluted forms contrast strongly with the strident angularity of the woven woolen garments and carpets the seminomadic Berbers produced. Like other nomadic Muslims, they preferred bold, geometric patterns and vibrant color combinations, the prototypes for which may have developed in the centuries before Islamic rule.

Catalogue Number 77 (see color plate, p. 46)
Spain
Furnishing or Garment Fabric, ca. 1500
silk satin and plain weaves with silk complementary weft
20¼ x 16 (51.5 x 41) weft x warp
Eliza M. and Sarah L. Niblack Collection
    33.1507 and 33.1719

By the ninth century Moorish artists in Spain had developed a unique style that borrowed from eastern Islamic arabesques, interlacings, and Kufic writing. Silks patterned on Eastern models—particularly silks produced in Baghdad—must have been among the ninth-century Hispano-Mooresque textiles listed in papal inventories. The Hispano-Mooresque vocabulary included Sasanian rondels that enclosed animal and human forms, and a parallel tradition based on banded geometric interlace had developed by the thirteenth century. Fourteenth- and fifteenth-century artists in Granada used this type of design, which has been dubbed the "Alhambra Style" after wall decoration in that famous Islamic building.

In the fifteenth century a strong influence from European Gothic design introduced motifs such as the pomegranate and leaf patterns seen here.[5] Confronted animals belonged to the textile decorative imagery inherited from Sasanian design. Moorish Mudejar craftsmen favored the combination of animal motifs, pomegranates—which here look more like pine cones—palmettes, and lotuses,[6] which may have been based on Egyptian prototypes.[7] Similarly, many of these forms, including the arabesques, are related to designs in media such as architectural stucco and metalwork.

Pieces like this one are thought to have been woven in Toledo,[8] one of the sites of the great medieval fairs.

Materials
    Basic fabric
        warp: silk, single-ply Z-twist; dark green
        complementary weft: silk, no twist; white, yellow, red, green
        supplementary warp: silk, single-ply Z-twist; white
Techniques
    Warp-faced 4/1 satin weave (background) and weft-faced floats in plain weave alignment (figure), with supplementary binding warp and continuous complementary weft, grouped weft
        proportions: one supplementary warp per five main warps
    No selvedges
Thread count
    Basic fabric
        warp: 170   complementary weft: 76 groups
        supplementary warp: 34
Pattern repeat
    warpwise: 11 in. (28.0 cm)   weftwise: 6 in. (15.0 cm)

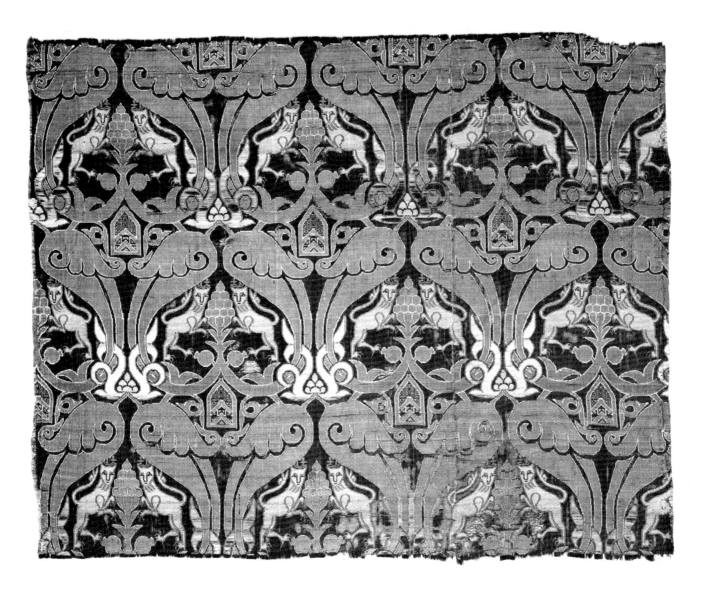

Catalogue Number 78
Town of Hammamet, Tunisia
Woman's Wedding Shirt (*qmajja*), 19th century
silk and cotton satin weaves (damask), cotton twill and satin
    weaves (damask), silk plain weave, silk and cotton plain
    weave with silk supplementary warp; embroidered with
    silk, metallic thread, and sequins
49 (124.5) length, warp
Eliza M. and Sarah L. Niblack Collection 33.313

Historically, Tunisia was sharply divided between the thriving coastal cities and the interior, peopled mostly by Berbers. Certain art forms produced in the seaside towns reflected their relaxed atmosphere but also showed urban influence: the capital of Tunis, for example, affected the fine embroidery made in the many coastal villages to its south. As in other areas of North Africa, Tunisian embroidery was made in the home and the professional workshop with both silk and metal threads. The Tunisians embellished clothing more often than they did domestic linens, a preference directly opposite the Moroccans'.

Among the most important embroidered items were bridal garments. On her wedding day a girl donned a pointed headdress, pants, a bodice, finely decorated slippers, and an elaborately decorated shirt[9] like the one illustrated here.[10] The flat central panel is covered with couched silver- and gold-wrapped threads (*tenbit*) embellished with metallic sequins. To the side of the central panel, embroidered purple silk damask panels alternate with bands of red and yellow braid. The prophylactic patterns seen here, based on the hand of Fatima and the tree of life, protected the wearer from the "evil eye" (see cat. 79 and 89). In a culture which was not wealthy, such a costly garment was considered security for the future. In fact, money was earned from renting out *qmajja* to brides who could not afford their own.[11]

Materials
  Fabric 1
      warp: silk, single-ply slight S-twist; violet
      weft: cotton, two-ply Z-twist; light violet
  Fabric 2
      warp: cotton, single-ply Z-twist; yellow
      weft: cotton, single-ply Z-twist; yellow
  Fabric 3
      warp: silk, single-ply slight S-twist; red
      weft: silk, single-ply slight S-twist; red
  Fabric 4
      warp: silk, no twist; red, white, black
      weft: cotton, two-ply S-twist; black
      supplementary warp: silk, no twist; yellow
  Embroidery
      silk, two-ply S-twist; white, yellow
      metallic #1
          core thread: silk, single-ply Z-twist; yellow
          strip: silver with gold and copper, S-twist; gold colored
      metallic #2
          core thread: silk, single-ply Z-twist; white
          strip: silver with copper, S-twist; silver colored

Techniques
  Fabric 1: warp-faced 4/1 satin weave (figure) and weft-faced 4/1 satin weave (background)
  Fabric 2: warp-faced 7/1 twill weave (figure) and weft-faced 4/1 satin weave (background)
  Fabric 3: weft-dominant plain weave, loosely woven, weft heavier than warp
  Fabric 4: warp-dominant plain weave and warp-faced floats, with supplementary warp
      proportions: one supplementary warp per one main warp
  Embroidery
      flat stitches: couching of single and doubled elements
      sequins attached by two straight stitches
  Pieced garment
  Selvedge of fabric 1: ⅜ in. (0.8 cm) wide, warp-faced 4/1 satin weave of green and white stripes

Thread count
  Fabric 1
      warp: 240   weft: 100
  Fabric 2
      warp: 69   weft: 62
  Fabric 3
      warp: 50   weft: 36
  Fabric 4
      warp: 124   weft: 74   supplementary warp: 124

Catalogue Number 79
Town of Fez, Morocco
Woman's Belt (*hzūm, hzām*), 18th century
silk twill weave with silk supplementary weft (brocade)
130½ x 12 (331 x 30.5) with fringe, warp x weft
Eliza M. and Sarah L. Niblack Collection 33.239

Moulay Idriss I founded Fez in A.D. 789, and his son named it the capital in A.D. 807. Throughout its history the city's importance rose and fell, but it remained a leading cultural center for craftsmen and scholars because of its university. Fez was judiciously located at the crossing of two ancient trade routes, one from Algeria to the Moroccan cities on the Atlantic and the other from the Mediterranean, south across the Sahara, to the ancient kingdoms of West Africa.

The *Prolegomenes*, by the fourteenth-century historian Ibn Khaldoun, contains the first known reference to the fancy belts Moroccan women wore. Women of royalty or the wealthy merchant class donned these intricately woven belts for their weddings, and afterwards for special occasions.[12] The belt was folded in half lengthwise, wrapped around the waist, and tied with the upper portions of the fringes from each end, while the remaining fringes hung down to each side. The changes in pattern characteristic of these belts allowed the wearer to show different sides of it; one belt could thus appear to be several different ones, according to which pattern was exposed.

Designs for these belts owe a great deal to Hispano-Mooresque fourteenth- and fifteenth-century textile patterns in the so-called Alhambra style. This example's bright colors and red ground are typical of these belts, as are the arabesques and bands of interlacings.[13] The geometric interlace, very carefully rendered here, is an important feature of this type of Islamic design and was used on tiles, ceramics, and architectural decoration as well as fabric. At the bottom edges of this piece are two designs whose placement is also common on the belts. The first is an eight-point star derisively called the "Seal of Solomon," and the other an abstracted hand that represents the hand (*khama*) of Fatima, Muhammed's daughter. These symbols were thought to dispel the dangerous effects of the evil eye, a belief widely held in North Africa (see p. 210).[14]

The complicated structure evident here was executed on a drawloom, a kind of patterning loom used early in China and the Middle East. It employed a system of pulleys to lift the warp threads required by the pattern. At the top of the loom, threads tied to patterning warps were strung over pulleys with weighted ends. The weaver's assistant, located on a platform at the top of the loom or on the floor to one side of it, pulled the desired cord when the weaver called for it. The pattern shed opened, and the weaver inserted the design weft. Preparing the loom for weaving with such a device was time-consuming and tedious, and the fabrics made on it were consequently quite expensive.

The numerous colored patterns on this piece were produced with supplementary wefts; all of them were carried in the cloth simultaneously and passed from selvedge to selvedge across the width of the fabric. When a particular color was needed, it came to the surface, and when completed, fell back into the weave structure. Another color then replaced it. Each of these colored wefts was secured to the surface with an additional red warp. Furthermore, a red structural weft was introduced between each pattern row. The presence of these extra threads in the structure created a dense, solid weave that was durable enough for a belt.

Materials
  Basic fabric
    warp: silk, single-ply Z-twist; red
    weft: silk, no twist; red
    supplementary warp: silk, single-ply Z-twist; red
    supplementary weft: silk, no twist; white, light and
      medium yellow, red, light and medium blue, light
      green, black
    selvedge cord: silk, single-ply tight Z-twist; tan
Techniques
  Warp-faced 2/1 diagonal twill weave (background) and
    weft-faced floats bound in a diagonal twill alignment
    (figure), with supplementary binding warp and
    continuous supplementary weft, grouped supplementary
    wefts
    proportions: one supplementary warp per three main
      warps, one group of supplementary wefts per one
      main weft
  Selvedge: outer warp end of three cords
  Fringe: warp ends grouped and obliquely interlaced
    (braided) forming round braid with wrapped ends
  Starch on back side
Thread count
  warp: 147   weft: 45
  supplementary warp: 49
  supplementary weft: 45 groups
Pattern repeat (top to bottom)
  warpwise: 3½ in. (6.4 cm) to 4¼ in. (10.5 cm)
    weftwise: 2⅞ in. (7.3 cm)
  warpwise: 3⅛ in. (8.0 cm)
    weftwise: 2⅞ in. (7.3 cm)
  warpwise: mirror image   weftwise: 2⅞ in. (7.3 cm)
  warpwise: none   weftwise: 2⅞ in. (7.3 cm)

Catalogue Number 80 (see color plate, p. 47)
Town of Fez, Morocco
Woman's Belt, 19th century
silk twill weave with silk and metallic supplementary weft
   (brocade), resist-dyed warp (ikat)
119 x 13¼ (302 x 33.5) with fringe, warp x weft
Eliza M. and Sarah L. Niblack Collection 33.243

During the nineteenth century the inspiration for embellishment on women's belts changed from Hispano-Mooresque to European and, to a lesser extent, oriental patterns. Characteristically, these belts employ floral forms, often interwoven with geometric interlace. Such floral decoration was probably derived from the curving bands popular on European silks in the third quarter of the eighteenth century (see cat. 124).[15] Changes in the background color—from both side to side and end to end—further differentiate the various zones. The latter change is accomplished by ikat dyeing the two differently colored warps so there are four background zones of color. Added to the marked change in design character from one end to the other, this color shift created four different faces on the belt when it was worn. Furthermore, evidence indicates that one quarter of the piece was also folded in on each side, so that a two-toned background could be seen. This folding gave the wearer the appearance of having six different belts, a variety certainly desirable for such an expensive garment. Another noteworthy feature of this design is the change in pattern on the bottom zones at each end, where the hand of Fatima and the eight-point star appear. At one end, the star and hand motif alternate, and on the other, there is only a smaller hand motif.

In the nineteenth century belts became longer and wider. To make them look even more impressive, they were stiffened with a starch backing; the density of this piece was further increased by the use of paired warps, which packed twice the number of threads into the structure. No longer produced, these magnificent costume accessories fell out of use in the late nineteenth century.

Materials
   Basic fabric
      warp: silk, single-ply Z-twist; red, yellow, light
         green, blue
      weft: silk, single-ply Z-twist; red
      supplementary warp: silk, single-ply Z-twist; red
      supplementary weft (weave structure 1):
         silk, no twist; orange, yellow, white, light red, black,
            light green
      supplementary weft (weave structure 2):
         silk, single-ply Z-twist; tan
         metallic
            core thread: silk, single-ply S-twist; yellow
            strip: gold and silver with copper, S-twist; gold colored
      supplementary weft (weave structure 3):
         silk, single-ply Z-twist; tan
         metallic
            core thread: silk, single-ply S-twist; yellow
            strip: gold and silver with copper, S-twist; gold colored
         silk, no twist; dark green, yellow
      selvedge cord: silk, single-ply tight Z-twist; yellow

Techniques
   Three areas with different weave structures
      Weave structure 1: warp-faced 2/1 diagonal twill weave
         (background) and weft-faced floats bound in a diagonal
         twill alignment (figure), with supplementary binding
         warp and continuous supplementary weft; paired main
         warps and grouped supplementary wefts
            proportions: one supplementary warp per six main
               warps, one group supplementary wefts per one
               main weft
      Weave structure 2: warp-faced 2/1 diagonal twill weave
         (background) and weft-faced floats bound in a diagonal
         twill alignment (figure), with supplementary binding
         warp and continuous supplementary weft, paired main
         warps and paired supplementary wefts
            proportions: one supplementary warp per six main
               warps, one pair supplementary weft per two main
               wefts
      Weave structure 3: warp-faced 2/1 diagonal twill weave
         (background) and weft-faced floats bound in a diagonal
         twill alignment (figure), with supplementary binding
         warp and two sets of continuous supplementary wefts;
         paired main warps, one set of paired supplementary
         wefts and one set of single wefts
            proportions: one supplementary warp per six main
               warps, three supplementary wefts per two main
               wefts
   Selvedge: outer warp end of three cords
   Fringe: warp ends grouped and obliquely interlaced
      (braided) forming round braids with wrapped ends
   Starch on back side
Thread count
   Basic fabric
      warp: 135 pairs (270 threads)   weft: 48
      supplementary warp: 45
      (1) supplementary weft: 48 groups
      (2) supplementary weft: 24 pairs (48 threads)
      (3) supplementary weft: 144 threads
Pattern repeat (top to bottom)
   (1) warpwise: 3⅞ in. (9.8 cm)   weftwise: 2¼ in. (5.7 cm)
   (2) warpwise: 9¾ in. (24.7 cm)   weftwise: 3⅛ in. (8.0 cm)
   (3) warpwise: 4¾ in. (12.0 cm)   weftwise: 3⅛ in. (8.0 cm)

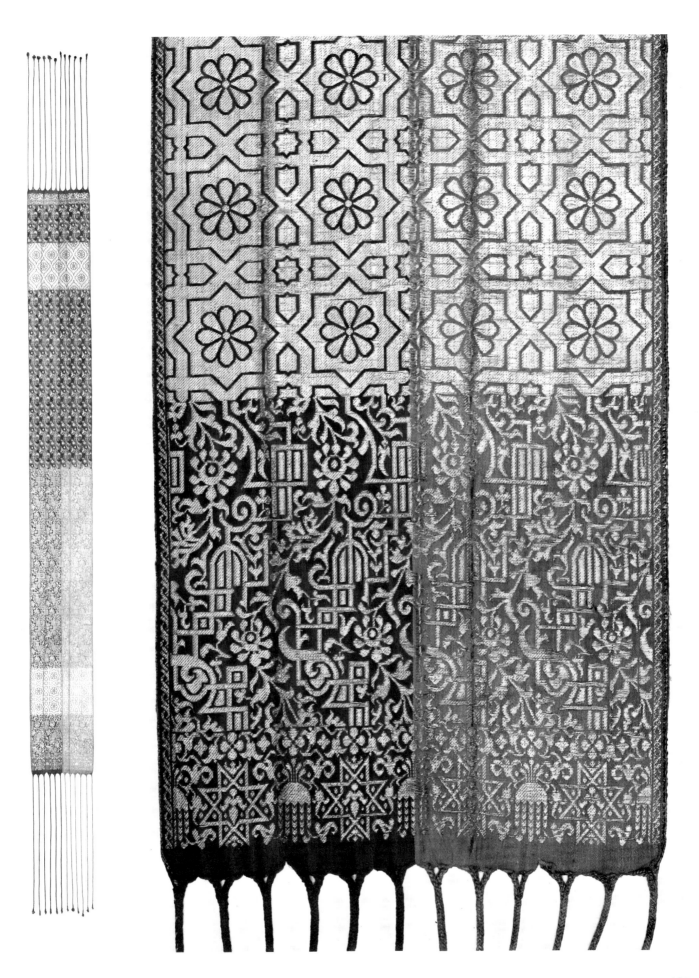

Catalogue Number 81 (see color plate, p. 48)
Town of Fez, Morocco
Wall Hanging (*häiti*), 19th century
silk velvet weave with silk supplementary warp (solid velvet),
   embroidered with metallic thread, pieced
167½ x 66 (424.5 x 167) weft x warp
Eliza M. and Sarah L. Niblack Collection 1983.66

The writer Muhammed al-Saghīr makes the first historical reference to *häiti* in his *Nuzhat al-Hādī*, a history of the Sa'adian Dynasty (A.D. 1511–1690): ". . . Curtains embroidered with gold, of perfect workmanship were embroidered in it, so that the four sides of the Kubba al-Khamsiniya might be covered with them. These were called by the Arabs 'Hā'iti.' "[16] According to the literature, pieces like this were owned by only the wealthiest families, who used them for special occasions—especially the seven-day celebration following a marriage ceremony. If a family could not afford such a piece, they could rent one from a *neggāfa* (the mistress of ceremonies) or from a wealthy family, who would entrust the *neggāfa* with responsibility for its care.[17] During nuptials the *häiti* was placed on the wall facing the room's entrance.[18] It hung behind the bride (or, if used for other occasions, behind the honored guest). The bride, dressed in rich clothes and a highly decorated belt (see cat. 79 and 80), was seated on a fancy chair, which was often surrounded by rich fabrics. The total effect of the gold embroidered hanging and sumptuous silks must have been magnificent indeed.

The most prestigious of these cloths was made of velvet worked in gold embroidery and consisted of five, seven, or nine panels, alternately in red and green, with arched patterns. The cloths were reportedly made under the supervision of the leatherworkers' guild, which also oversaw their embroidering.[19] This piece is constructed of seven panels that were individually executed and then sewn together. The template for the gold embroidery was cut from leather and then completely covered with gold-wrapped thread, in underside couching. This stitch allowed the costly metal thread to lie on the surface, so that the valuable commodity would be entirely visible. To stiffen the background further and help support the enormous weight of the piece, parts of it were glued or stitched to cardboard. The bottom band of damask was concealed by cushions on the divans or benches that stood in front of it, in the interior of the dwelling.

The design consists of typical interlaced patterns arranged in an arch, probably a reference to the *mihrab*. This kind of decoration was widely used in architectural design. It was appropriate to translate architectural designs into textiles that, when placed on a wall, created a special setting for an important ceremony.

Materials
   Fabric 1
      warp: silk, no twist; tan
      weft: silk, no twist; tan
      supplementary warp: silk, no twist; red
   Fabric 2
      warp: silk, no twist; dark green
      weft: silk, no twist; dark green
      supplementary warp: silk, no twist; dark green
   Embroidery
      metallic from panel 1 and 2
         core thread: silk, single-ply S-twist; yellow
         strip: gold, silver, and copper, S-twist; gold colored
      metallic from panel 3 and 4
         core thread: silk, single-ply S-twist; yellow
         strip: gold, silver, and copper, S-twist; gold colored
   Trim
      warp: silk, single-ply slight S-twist; red or yellow
      weft: silk, no twist; red or yellow
   Cording
      silk, two-ply S-twist; white and green plied together
   Lining of panels
      warp: bast (linen), single-ply Z-twist; tan
      weft: bast (linen), single-ply Z-twist; tan
   Lining of trim fabric
      warp: cotton, single-ply Z-twist; tan
      weft: cotton, single-ply Z-twist; tan
   Backing
      warp: cotton, single-ply Z-twist; brown
      weft: cotton, single-ply Z-twist; brown
Techniques
   Fabric 1: warp-faced woven pile, cut, with supplementary
   warp pile
      proportions: one velvet rod per three main wefts, one
         supplementary warp per two main warps
      selvedge: ¼ in. (0.5 cm) wide, white, brown, and dark
         green strips of warp-faced 3/1 diagonal twill weave
   Fabric 2: warp-faced woven pile, cut, with supplementary
   warp pile
      proportions: one velvet rod per three main wefts, one
         supplementary warp per two main warps
      selvedge: ⅜ in. (0.9 cm) wide, brown and yellow stripes
         of warp-faced 3/1 diagonal twill weave
   Embroidery
      flat stitches: invisible couching worked over
         leather form
   Pieced
   Trim: cording and fabric of warp-faced 2/1 diagonal twill
      weave and weft-faced 2/1 diagonal twill weave
   Lining of panels: balanced plain weave, loosely woven
   Lining of trim fabric: balanced plain weave
   Backing: balanced plain weave, glazed

Thread count
Fabric 1
    warp: 92   weft: 141   supplementary warp: 46
Fabric 2
    warp: 90   weft: 138   supplementary warp: 45
Trim fabric
    warp: 147   weft: 146
Lining of panels
    warp: 22   weft: 12
Lining of trim fabric
    warp: 64   weft: 60
Backing
    warp: 72   weft: 67

Catalogue Number 82
Town of Fez, Morocco
Furnishing Fabric (*gelsa*), ca. 1900
cotton plain weave, embroidered with silk
35 x 34 (89 x 86.5) warp x weft
Eliza M. and Sarah L. Niblack Collection 33.254

Domestic embroidery was widely practiced in the urban cultures of Morocco. The *ma'allema,* or professional embroiderer, not only instructed young girls but also worked pieces ordered by her patrons.[20] Girls were expected to decorate clothing for their wedding chests as well as cushion and divan covers, wall hangings, and bed covers for their future homes. A *gelsa,* shown here, marked the seating place reserved for an honored guest.[21] This particular type of domestic piece is known to have been made only in Fez.

Unlike most domestic items embroidered in Fez, this square's motifs radiate from the dark blue pattern concentrated in the center; usually, the border is decorated and the corner designs point inward. More characteristic of Fez designs are the carefully executed triangles, diamonds, crosses, and eight-petalled flowers that compose these tightly controlled patterns. The ground fabric is used as a structural grid, an embroidery technique termed counted stitch. In it, each warp and weft thread is counted to determine the spaces between entry of the needle into the cloth and its return to the surface. This method produces a meticulously controlled, geometric pattern. By working back over the reverse side of a previously completed area, the embroiderer easily made the piece reversible, a technique that was widely used in Morocco. In Fez the cloth to be embroidered was stretched on a frame before it was worked, a practice that held the ground fabric taut so the threads were more easily counted.

Most Fez embroideries were monochromatic, and dark blue was one of the most common colors. By the twelfth century southern Morocco was a major producer of indigo and Fez an important dyeing center.[22] Cotton was also cultivated in sufficient quantities for export in southwest Morocco and immediately around Fez,[23] so silk embroideries were most often worked on a cotton ground or, in older examples, on linen.

The pattern elements are strongly reminiscent of Greek island embroideries. In fact, there are many other parallels between Greek and North African embroidery. Islamic influence was pervasive in both areas, but active trade also persisted throughout the Mediterranean from early times. Certainly textiles, because of their high prestige value and easy portability, were part of that trade. Another factor important in the dissemination of style was the mobility of craftsmen, impelled by the rise and fall of various regimes.

Materials
Basic fabric
warp: cotton, single-ply Z-twist; tan
weft: cotton, single-ply Z-twist; tan
Embroidery
silk, no twist; dark blue
Techniques
Balanced plain weave
Embroidery
flat counted stitches: Algerian eye; Bosnian, reinforced Bosnian worked diagonally; double running; variation of long-armed cross
looped counted stitches: buttonhole
Finish: rolled hem
Thread count
Basic fabric
warp: 41   weft: 45

Catalogue Number 83
Town of Fez, Morocco
Handkerchief (*mherma*), ca. 1900
cotton plain weave, embroidered with silk
9½ x 8¾ (24 x 22) with tassels, warp x weft (?)
Eliza M. and Sarah L. Niblack Collection 33.360

Moroccan women carried small, elaborately embroidered squares such as this green and white one, much as Western women carried fancy handkerchiefs (see cat. 139 and 140): they were less a practical item than a sign of prestige and wealth. For walking in the street, a well-dressed, urban Moroccan woman might wear wide pants, a shirt, one or more caftans over the shirt, a belt (see cat. 79 and 80), an elaborately tied headkerchief, a veil over her nose and mouth, a large shawl (*haik*), and embroidered slippers. Completely dressed, she resembled a moving mountain of cloth.

Materials
Basic fabric
  warp: cotton, single-ply Z-twist; white
  weft: cotton, single-ply Z-twist; white
Embroidery
  silk, no twist; light green
Techniques
Balanced plain weave, loosely woven
Embroidery
  flat counted stitches: Bosnian, reinforced Bosnian
    worked diagonally
  looped counted stitches: buttonhole
Finish: rolled hem and attached tassels
Thread count
Basic fabric
  warp: 90   weft: 98

Catalogue Number 84
Town of Meknès, Morocco
Table or Cushion Cover, ca. 1900
cotton plain weave, pieced, embroidered with silk
50 x 40 (127 x 101) warp x weft
Eliza M. and Sarah L. Niblack Collection 33.246

Located to the southwest of Fez, Meknès served as Morocco's capital for a short time but never enjoyed the sustained importance of its northern neighbor. Meknès embroideries resemble those made in Fez in design and technique, but not in character: the arbitrary placement of abundant, strong color gives the Meknès examples a dramatic and spontaneous quality, compared with the meticulous, monochromatic embroideries of Fez. In this silk embroidery the asymmetrical placement of bright color accents enlivens the geometric character of the counted stitch technique, for the glowing purples and pinks punctuate the reds, yellows, and greens of the composition. The artful balance of these seemingly incompatible elements accounts for the charm of this piece.

Materials
Basic fabric
warp: cotton, single-ply Z-twist; tan
weft: cotton, single-ply Z-twist; tan
Embroidery
silk, no twist; black, light and medium red, light orange-red, yellow, yellow-brown, yellow-green, light and dark green, green-blue, blue-violet, light and medium violet, violet-red

Techniques
Balanced plain weave
Embroidery
flat counted stitches: Algerian eye; back; Bosnian, reinforced Bosnian, double reinforced Bosnian; overcast edge; double running, double running in two colors
Pieced, then embroidered
Finished with rolled hem

Thread count
Basic fabric
warp: 58   weft: 62

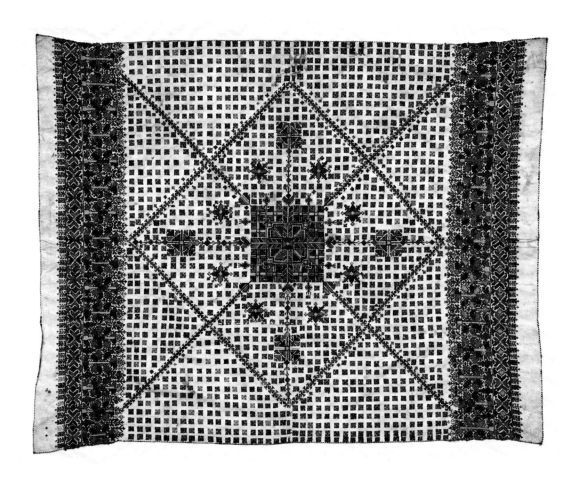

Catalogue Number 85
Town of Chechoman, Morocco
Furnishing Fabric (*arid*), 19th century
silk plain weave, pieced, appliquéd, embroidered with silk
    and metallic thread
83 x 14½ (210.5 x 37) weft x warp
Eliza M. and Sarah L. Niblack Collection 33.281

In many parts of the Muslim world, including Morocco, fine embroideries were brought out to decorate homes for festivals and rituals. On these occasions an *arid* was hung from wall shelves across an alcove, so it faced the bedroom.[24] Central to this composition are three eight-point stars, prophylactic devices believed to protect the owner from the evil eye (see p. 210). Executed in gold-couched embroidery on a cardboard base, the star motifs were sewn to the central area of the strip. In the square areas at both ends of the fabric strip are motifs that imitate the central stars. The geometric character of the pattern is related to the Fez and Meknès examples in this exhibition, but its overall effect differs markedly. While Fez embroideries display delicate, netlike designs on an open background, this Chechoman piece exhibits multicolored patterns that appear to have been influenced by woven designs, although, as in the Meknès example, the color placement is somewhat arbitrary. Interestingly, the design in the squares at each end recalls embroideries made in the region of Russia to the west of the Caspian Sea, where the Caucasus, northwest Iran, and eastern Turkey are adjacent.

Materials
  Basic fabric
    warp: silk, single-ply Z-twist; white
    weft: silk, single-ply Z-twist; white
  Embroidery
    silk, no twist; white, yellow, light and medium red, light
      blue, two medium blues, light green, violet, black
    metallic
      core thread: silk, single-ply S-twist; yellow
      strip: copper with gold and silver, Z-twist; gold colored
Techniques
  Balanced plain weave
  Pieced, appliquéd with red-violet cotton plain weave fabric
  Embroidery
    flat counted stitches: invisible couching worked over
      paper form; cross, long armed cross; variation of
      double running
  Finish: raw edges folded under
Thread count
  Basic fabric
    warp: 23   weft: 31

206

Catalogue Number 86
Town of Azemmour, Morocco
Furnishing Fabric, ca. 1900
linen plain weave, embroidered with silk
92¼ x 14¼ (234 x 36) with fringe, warp x weft
Eliza M. and Sarah L. Niblack Collection 33.1127

The practice of embroidering the background of a design while leaving the pattern unworked originated in Renaissance Europe. In many narrow bands that still exist from that period, the backgrounds are worked in tightly pulled threads that are often dyed red. A number of Renaissance Italian pattern books illustrate these designs, which were preserved for centuries in Mediterranean folk embroidery. The one location in North Africa that seems to have been most thoroughly influenced by this tradition is Azemmour. The geometric peacock and the vase with three extensions also closely tie these patterns to the embroidery of the Greek islands, where both motifs were widely used. The red, long-armed cross stitch in the background of this piece was also common in the Greek islands. In Azemmour long bands like this one were used to cover the sides of mattresses.

Materials
  Basic fabric
    warp: bast (linen), single-ply Z-twist; tan
    weft: bast (linen), single-ply Z-twist; tan
  Embroidery
    silk, no twist; red, dark blue
Techniques
  Balanced plain weave
  Embroidery
    flat counted stitches: back; long-armed cross, cross-
      marking; straight
Thread count
  Basic fabric
    warp: 42   weft: 44

Catalogue Number 87
Town of Tétouan, Morocco
Furnishing Fabric (*tensifa*), ca. 1800
linen plain weave, embroidered with silk
73 x 19¾ (185 x 50) warp x weft
Eliza M. and Sarah L. Niblack Collection 33.227

Located on the Mediterranean coast north of Fez and Meknès, Tétouan was founded early in the fourteenth century, only to be razed in A.D. 1400 as punishment for its inhabitants' acts of piracy. The town was resettled at the beginning of the sixteenth century by Andalusians whom Ferdinand and Isabella had expelled from Granada.[25]

A professional needleworker (*ma'allema*) drew this design directly on the linen. The patterns used on this piece are highly reminiscent of eighteenth-century Ottoman embroideries. What appear to be tulips and artichokes surrounded by curving forms may come from Ottoman ogival design, but here the design elements are crowded together and broken down because the original model was reinterpreted to suit another taste.

These long scarves, worked on the ends and left plain in the middle, were used ceremonially to adorn the windows and doorways of the bed chamber for forty days after the wedding. Like this one, older examples were executed with multicolored silk threads on linen, while later pieces used silk on silk.

Materials
Basic fabric
warp: bast (linen), single-ply Z-twist; white
weft: bast (linen), single-ply Z-twist; white
Embroidery
silk, no twist; violet, light and medium yellow, red, light
blue, two light greens, black, white
Techniques
Balanced plain weave
Embroidery
flat stitches: double darning; double running; satin;
slanting Slav; stem; woven hem
Finish: rolled hem on one side and selvedge on the other
Fringe: individual warp ends
Thread count
Basic fabric
warp: 58   weft: 44

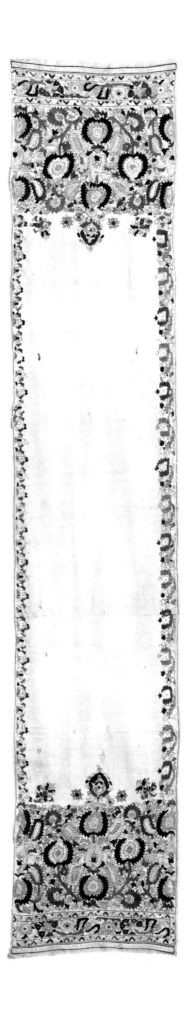

Catalogue Number 88
Jbala People (el-Jaia?), Western Rif Region, Morocco
Woman's Belt (*kerziya*), ca. 1900
wool twill weave (herringbone) and cotton and wool plain
    weave, resist dyed
161½ x 14¾ (409.5 x 37.5) with fringe, warp x weft
Eliza M. and Sarah L. Niblack Collection 33.1988

The el-Jaia are a subgroup of Jbala living in the Rif, a north-western section of Morocco. Jbala belt weavers used a horizontal treadle loom. This loom activated the heddles with foot pedals that alternately raised each set of warps while the weft was shot from side to side in a shuttle. Much faster than the vertical fixed heddle loom used by Berbers farther to the south, the horizontal loom easily created the herringbone twill structure of this piece by using extra heddles, or pattern sticks, to raise the appropriate sheds. Decorative white and blue cotton wefts were inserted at one end of the belt.

After it was woven, the belt was dyed yellow. Portions of it were then wrapped and tied with twine, a procedure that created a resisted pattern during the second dipping, in dark red. When the desired value was reached, the belt was removed, the tying strings cut, and the whole piece washed. Dye and mordant solutions were prepared in such a way that they colored the wool and not the cotton, thus preserving the natural white and blue of the end border.[26]

A woman wore the finished belt to fasten her outer wrapper, or *haik*, at the waist. Compared with Fez belts (see cat. 79 and 80), the patterning on this piece appears haphazard. The feathery dyed patterns' random placement on the rigid, geometric ground of the twill weave creates a dynamic interplay not evident in the more structured Fez pieces.

Materials
  Basic fabric
    warp: wool, single-ply Z-twist; yellow
    weft (weave structure 1);
      wool, single-ply Z-twist; yellow
    weft (weave structure 2):
      cotton, single-ply Z-twist; white, light blue
    dye: brown
Techniques
  Two areas with different weave structures
    (1) Balanced 2/2 herringbone twill weave
    (2) Weft-faced plain weave, paired warps and wefts
  Resist dyed with tied resists
  Fringe: obliquely interlaced warp ends (braided), silk fabric
    added to braid at ends
Thread count
  Basic fabric
    warp: 30   (1) weft: 26   (2) weft: 140

Catalogue Number 89 (see color plate, p. 49)
Shluh (Chleuh) Subgroup, Berber People, High Atlas Region,
    Morocco
Man's Cape (*akhnif*), 19th century
wool plain weave with wool and cotton supplementary weft
    wrapping, wool and silk supplementary weft knotted pile,
    wool and cotton twining; embroidered with wool
66 (167) length, warp
Eliza M. and Sarah L. Niblack Collection 33.1984

The Berbers of the High Atlas are remnants of Morocco's original inhabitants, who may have migrated from the East in the
third or second millenium B.C. to mix with the indigenous pop-
ulations. The Greeks called them the *libou* (Libyans) and the
Romans, *barbarus*, from which the designation "Berber" came.[27]
The large numbers of Arabs who invaded Morocco, first in the
seventh and eighth centuries and again in the eleventh century,
forced the Berbers either to convert to Islam or flee to less
hospitable regions. Most adopted Islam as a belief but refused
to acknowledge Arab political dominance. Even today, some
descendants of these independent peoples live a seminomadic
existence as they follow the seasonal needs of their herds. As
was typical of the Muslim world, marked differences between
fiercely independent, largely self-sufficient groups such as the
Berbers and settled, more specialized urbanites were reflected
in textiles.

Like nomadic weavers in other Muslim areas, Berber women
did—and some still do—most of the preparation of wool, as
well as the weaving itself. Wool was shorn by men and then
washed, combed, and spun by women, who also prepared the
warp and set up the loom. When it had been tightly spun and
firmly beaten, a mixture of goat hair and sheep's wool created
a virtually waterproof material well suited to a cape. Goat hair
fiber shrinks when it is dry, allowing air to circulate, and ex-
pands when wet, keeping dampness out.[28] An extremely wide
loom was needed to make this garment, since it was woven in
one piece from the top of the hood to the curved bottom. The
actual weaving of these capes is not described in the literature,
but the method used can be seen in the garment's structure;
subtle curves at the shoulder and across the back were formed
by additional wefts inserted in wedge-shaped configurations.
In fact, the entire red oculus on the back was added in this
manner, and these insertions created most of the curvature of
the hem as well. Further details were patterned with twining,
wrapping, and knots. After the piece was woven, a tailor sewed
it together and possibly also executed the embroidery at the
chest.[29]

A robe such as this was mentioned by Olfert Dapper in 1659,
when he described the costume of ambassadors who came to
Amsterdam from the court of the Sultan of Fez. Over his
wrapped garment (*haik*) one of them wore

> une robe fort large, qui lui couvroit là moitié du corps,
> faite de poil de chèvre, ou de laine noire, avec un ca-
> puchon par derrière, & boutonné par devant. On ap-
> pelle cette robbe *Chanyf*.[30]

More specific nineteenth-century descriptions referred to High
Atlas Berbers' wearing cloaks of black wool and goat hair that
displayed lozenge-shaped patterns on the back. Today, the
Shluh and Ouaouzguite of the High Atlas Mountains, as well
as Jews of the same region, frequently wear such cloaks.[31] A
rather romanticized image of the Berber man is given by
Budget Meakin:

Yonder stalwart form, contrasting strangely with the
lighter hues around him, in a thick, stiff robe of goat-
hair, fringed, shaped like to an extinguisher, with tas-
seled hood to match; jet black except an assagai-
shaped patch across the back about the level of the
knees—the patch bright-yellow with designs in red or
black—that form is an Atlas Berber, a Shluh. He represents the original Moor: no mixed blood in him, but
a pride of independence dearly bought, and still to
some degree maintained. He might be Mephistophe-
les, to see him stalking there, his bare and bony shanks
beneath that curious robe, thrust into leather bags now
brown, that once were heel-less yellow slippers.[32]

The dominant design on this piece is the magnificent red oculus
in the center back, which probably represents the evil eye:

> Belief in the evil eye is both ancient and widespread—
> throughout North Africa, the Middle East and south-
> ern Europe—by Jews and Muslims alike. The eye is
> believed to mirror man's soul; therefore it is said to be
> the seat of special powers which can have an evil effect.
> The evil eye may be an intentionally vicious glance or
> transmitted involuntarily through a look of fascination
> or curiosity. Certainly, the best advice is to avoid the
> evil eye altogether, by shunning those suspected of
> having it. However, although one cannot count on
> being able to escape it, there are a multitude of means
> to make it innocuous. The representation of an eye or
> pair of eyes is said to throw back the energy of the
> baneful eye . . . thus the design itself may have been
> created in response to the belief in the evil eye.[33]

Materials
  Basic fabric
    warp: wool (goat), two-ply S-twist; black
    weft: wool (goat), single-ply Z-twist; black
            wool, single-ply Z-twist; orange-red, red, green
    supplementary weft wrapping:
      wool, single-ply Z-twist; orange-red, red, violet-red,
        blue, light green
      wool, two-ply S-twist; orange-red, red, violet-red, blue,
        light green
      cotton, three-ply S-twist; white
    supplementary weft pile:
      silk, single-ply S-twist; orange, dark red-violet, light
        green
      wool, single-ply S-twist; orange, light green, dark
        violet-red
      cotton, three-ply S-twist; white, yellow
    twining: wool, two-ply S-twist; red, white
      cotton, three-ply S-twist; white
  Embroidery
    wool (goat), two-ply S-twist; black

Techniques

  Weft-faced plain weave with continuous and discontinuous
    eccentric weft (loom-shaped weaving), and discontinuous
    supplementary weft wrapping, discontinuous
    supplementry weft (knotted pile) countered compact weft
    twining
      symmetrical knots placed in pairs with each knot around
       two warps and both knots sharing one warp
      proportions: one supplementary weft wrapping per one
       main weft
  Embroidery at chest:
    flat stitches: trellis couching; closed herringbone;
      overcast bars
    looped stitches: variation of chain
  Trim: leather binding at front opening
  Fringe: added wrapped tassels of black goat hair
  Hood tassel: oblique interlacing (braiding) of black
    goat hair

Thread count

  Basic fabric
    warp: 16   weft: 38
    supplementary weft wrapping: 38

Catalogue Number 90
Berber People, High Atlas Region, Morocco
Man's Wrapper or Rug (*hanbel*), ca. 1900
wool plain weave with wool twining, wool and cotton
    supplementary weft knotted pile
159 x 59½ (403 x 151) warp x weft
Eliza M. and Sarah L. Niblack Collection 33.1993

The nomadic peoples of the Middle East greatly prized sheep, and fittingly so, since the animals afforded their owners food and wool for physical comfort. In his preface to *Moroccan Carpets*, Prosper Ricard wrote:

> North Africa has been ever a country of shepherds and of sheep—of sheep which provide man with flesh and wool, that is to say with the staple of his food, clothing and furniture.
>
> What a noble and beneficent textile wool is, too! Listen to the tale of the virtues attributed to it by the transhumant or migratory tribes of the Central Atlas, whose mode of life remains what it was in Biblical times, and which were once believed in throughout the whole of Barbary.
>
> Wool is white, a colour of good omen.
>
> Its charms are powerful, since a flock tucked into her headdress suffices to ensure the protection of the spinster; since a bit of yarn tied round a mule's or mare's foot, or to the tail of the cow just bought, brings down blessings upon them; since on her wedding morn a thread is twined round the bride's fingers, to be untwined in the evening by her bridegroom.[34]

According to the literature, rugs (*hanbels*) were used in Andalusia and Egypt in the twelfth century, and in northern Tunisia in the fifteenth century.[35] Important to Portuguese trade with Subsaharan West Africa in the fifteenth and sixteenth centuries, they were exchanged for gold and slaves. Their status in this trade is illustrated by a 1480 law giving Prince John exclusive rights to export *hanbels* to the Gold Coast factory of El Mina. In Safi, a town near the mouth of the Tennsift River on Morocco's west coast, weaving workshops established to meet the demand wove *hanbels* to Portuguese specifications. With the decline of Portuguese trade at the end of the sixteenth century, however, *hanbel* production returned to the domestic sphere.[36]

Hanbels served as sleeping covers, ground cloths, and domestic decoration. They were usually executed in flat weave, which produced a supple fabric easily adapted to a number of uses. Four different techniques mark this piece: slit tapestry weave, twining, knots, and simple weft striping. Typical of High Atlas pieces are the patterns arranged in bands from edge to edge. Here they are worked in brown, with red and white contrasts.

Materials
  Basic fabric
      warp: wool (goat), two-ply S-twist; dark brown
      weft: wool (goat), single-ply Z-twist; dark brown
          wool, single-ply Z-twist; tan, light red, blue, blue-green, light red-violet
      twining: wool (goat), three-ply S-twist; tan, dark brown
      supplementary weft pile:
          wool, single-ply S-twist; light red, blue, blue-green, light red-violet
          cotton, three-ply S-twist; white
Techniques
  Weft-faced plain weave with continuous and discontinuous weft, slit tapestry joins, countered compact weft twining, and discontinuous supplementary weft wrapping (knotted pile)
      symmetrical knots around two warps in short, single rows twining is over one, two, and three warps with ends left as fringe at selvedges
  Selvedge: three outer warps doubled, woven with extra weft
  No original finish at warp ends
Thread count
  Basic fabric
      warp: 10   weft: 40

Catalogue Number 91
Berber People, Middle Atlas Region, Morocco
Man's Wrapper or Rug (*hanbel*), ca. 1900
wool plain weave with wool complementary wefts (weft
    substitution), wool supplementary weft knotted pile
168½ x 64¼ (427 x 163) warp x weft
Eliza M. and Sarah L. Niblack Collection 33.1997

Most Berber textiles were, and continue to be, woven on a vertical loom, which traditionally was fixed to the central tent pole of a family's portable dwelling. The simple loom used a string heddle that was fastened to a pole or wall behind the weaver to create one shed, and a shed stick to create the alternate opening. The weaver, seated on the ground before the loom, raised and lowered the shed stick with one hand and introduced the weft with the other. Weft threads were worked with fingers only; no shuttle was used. This method suited the equipment since weft substitution, a technique frequently used in these regions, was easily executed with the fingers. Whether the technique developed because of the equipment or vice versa is probably impossible to determine. Since the fixed heddle mechanism put little stress on the frame of the loom, the poles did not need to be heavy, a feature well adapted to a transient lifestyle.

In Salé, flat-woven rugs were commercially manufactured on a large scale. At the end of the nineteenth century, when this piece was probably made, Salé *hanbels* were traded throughout Morocco, and even as far as Oran, Algeria.[37] These pieces use one or more bands of knotted patterns, a distinguishing feature that was influenced by the "oriental" rug designs popular in Rabat (see cat. 92). Because of the Salé rug's popularity, such patterns were widely adapted to *hanbels* made throughout the region.[38] These knotted bands—here in multicolored yarns alternating with yellow, tan, and red bands of weft striping—were frequently placed on the side of the rug next to the floor, where they provided extra padding, while the back of the knots were on the face of the rug.

Materials
  Basic fabric
    warp: wool, single-ply Z-twist; tan
    weft: wool, single-ply slight Z-twist; tan, light orange,
      red, black, yellow, blue, green, brown
    complementary weft:
      wool, single-ply slight Z-twist; tan, light orange, red,
        black, yellow, blue, green, brown
    supplementary weft pile:
      wool, no twist; tan, light orange, red, black, yellow, blue,
        green
Techniques
  Weft-faced plain weave with continuous weft and
    discontinuous complementary weft, (weft substitution or
    skip plain weave), and discontinuous supplementary weft
    wrapping (knotted pile), paired complementary wefts
      symmetrical knot around two warps
      proportions: one supplementary weft wrapping per one
        main weft, one row knots per two ground wefts
  No original finish at warp ends
Thread count
  Basic fabric
    warp: 12   weft: 31
    complementary weft: 31 pairs (62 threads)
    supplementary pile, warpwise: 4   weftwise: 6

Catalogue Number 92
Berber People, Middle Atlas Region, Morocco
Man's Wrapper or Rug (*hanbel*), ca. 1900
wool plain weave with wool complementary wefts (weft
    substitution), wool supplementary weft knotted pile
140½ x 68¾ (356 x 174.5) with fringe, warp x weft
Eliza M. and Sarah L. Niblack Collection 33.1994

Patterning on this *hanbel* seems to have come from two different sources. Geometric designs in alternating weft substitution bands are typical of Berber flat-weave patterns; the designs in the knotted zones, however, are more directly related to Turkish rugs. Medallions with latch-hook extensions were used from Turkmenistan in southern Russia and through Turkey to Spain. It is difficult to determine whether the inspiration for these patterns belonged to the original design vocabulary that various Muslim invasions transmitted or came from a popular pattern that had been consciously appropriated to make the pieces marketable. Regardless of the origin, the combination is richly effective.[39]

Materials
  Basic fabric
      warp: wool, single-ply Z-twist; tan
      weft: wool, single-ply Z-twist; light and medium blue,
        orange, yellow, green, black, white
      complementary weft:
        wool, single-ply Z-twist; light and medium blue, orange,
          yellow, green, black, white
      supplementary weft pile:
        wool, single-ply Z-twist; light and medium blue, orange,
          yellow, green, black, white
Techniques
  Weft-faced plain weave with continuous weft,
    discontinuous complementary weft, (weft substitution or
    skip plain weave) and discontinuous supplementary weft
    wrapping (knotted pile), paired complementary weft
      symmetrical knot around two warps
      proportions: one supplementary weft per one main
        weft, one row knots per three or four wefts
  Selvedge: wrapped with extra weft
  Fringe: eight to sixteen warp ends obliquely interlaced
    (braided)
Thread count
  Basic fabric
    warp: 11   weft: 25
    complementary weft: 25 pairs (50 threads)
    supplementary weft pile, warpwise: 5   weftwise: 4

217

Catalogue Number 93
Beni Ouarain Subgroup, Berber People,
    Middle Atlas Region, Morocco
Woman's Wrapper (*handira*), 19th century
wool and cotton plain weave with wool and cotton
    complementary wefts (weft substitution), wool and linen
    supplementary weft wrapping, wool and cotton twining
79 x 33¼ (200 x 84.5) with fringe, warp x weft
Eliza M. and Sarah L. Niblack Collection 33.1986

Berber women wore a large wrapped shawl (*izar*) fastened with clips and a wrapped belt (see cat. 88) as an outer garment.[40] For added warmth they draped a shaggy shawl (*handira*) over the shoulders and secured it with braided ties. Some of the most intricate of all Berber weavings are the *handiras* made by Beni Ouarain women in the eastern portion of the Middle Atlas. These pieces are patterned through meticulously worked weft substitution, or complementary weft, weft wrapping, and twining; long, loose ends are left on the garment's reverse side to create shaggy insulation. The weaver of this magnificent piece saved it for special occasions, when she could display her weaving skills.

Black, white, and a rich, dark red dominate the color scheme of this piece, which is punctuated by small areas of yellow. The names of geometric patterns such as these have been documented: some are descriptive—a jagged line, for example, may represent a saw—while others have prophylactic meaning, such as "tongue of a serpent." The significance of many of the patterns, however, has been lost.[41]

Materials
Basic fabric
    warp: wool, single-ply Z-twist; tan
    weft: wool, two-ply S-twist; red, dark violet-red, dark
      yellow, white, black
            cotton, three-ply S-twist; white
    complementary weft:
      wool, two-ply S-twist; red, dark violet-red, dark yellow,
        white, black
      cotton, single-ply Z-twist; white
    supplementary weft wrapping:
      wool, two-ply S-twist; red, dark violet-red, dark yellow,
        white, black
      linen, two-ply S-twist; white
    twining: wool, two-ply S-twist; black
      cotton, three-ply S-twist; white
Techniques
Weft-faced plain weave with continuous weft,
    discontinuous complementary weft (weft substitution or
    skip plain weave), discontinuous supplementary weft
    wrapping and countered compact twining
        proportions: one supplementary weft per one
          main weft
Selvedge: two doubled warps wrapped with weft
Trim: ties of oblique interlacing (braiding), four-part round
    braids grouped and braided into a four-part flat braid for
    each tie
Fringe: three-ply S-twist of six warp ends, knotted; weft
    ends left as fringe on one side
Thread count
Basic fabric
    warp: 19   weft: 72
    complementary weft: 72 pairs

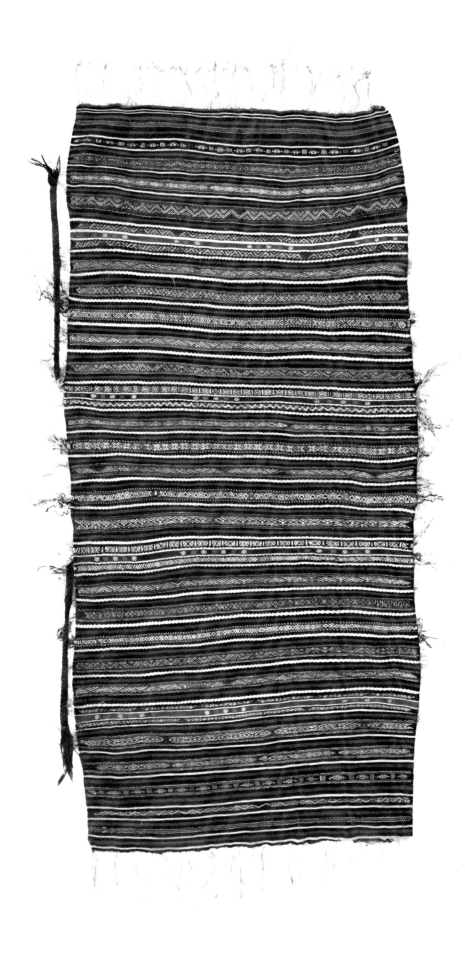

patterned" silks came to the fore. Naturalism did not influence these patterns until about 1730. As the century progressed, so did the influence of Rococo playfulness over fabric—and later, lace—design, which became increasingly delicate. The larger, dense needle laces that had laid nearly flat on seventeenth-century costume gave way to softer laces, which fell gracefully when gathered at a woman's sleeve and hem or a man's collar and cuff.

While eighteenth-century fabric patterns changed annually in both women's and men's clothing, the cut of women's clothes evolved more slowly. The basic open robe with stomacher and petticoat remained a fashion staple throughout the century. The few alterations of this garment focused on the treatment of the back and the drape of the skirt. Since a dress went out of style because of its fabric rather than its cut, wealthy women could not alter last year's dress to make it fashionable. If one considers that at the time, a prosperous merchant's house cost £500 and a lady's dress from £10 to £60, of which the mantua maker[6] charged only about £2, one can appreciate the economics of keeping in style.[7]

The eighteenth century was a time of exotic influences in Europe. Things "oriental" were considered prestigious, and people clamored over porcelains and silks from China and dyed cottons from India. Patterns for these materials were often sent from Europe so they would be made especially to suit taste at home. Soon European textile manufacturers began to produce their own fabrics to compete with the lush imported goods.

Although the manufactory of Christophe-Philippe Oberkampf (1738-1815) at Jouy was most famous for large-scale, copper-printed furnishing fabrics, they composed only about ten percent of total production. The rest of it consisted of *indiennes*, or copies of the famous Indian cottons that were flooding the European market in the late eighteenth century (see cat. 27 and 29). The manufactory's main innovation was the introduction of *bon teint*, a new technique that guaranteed colorfastness in *indiennes*. Originally the Oberkampf firm had printed with blocks, in imitation of Indian dyeing techniques—though this process was more akin to European models than it was to India's Asian ones. Block printing on fabric was known in Europe during the Middle Ages; Cennino Cennini described in his 1437 *The Art of the Old Masters* the method for applying patterns to cloth with an engraved woodblock.[8] Nonetheless, European printed fabrics had never been colorfast. That the brightly colored Indian goods were washable greatly contributed to their popularity, and later to that of the *indiennes*.

Political turmoil in Europe in the late eighteenth and early nineteenth centuries wholly disrupted the production of traditional goods. Furthermore, the mounting Industrial Revolution had already displaced thousands of traditional European craftsmen. English textile manufacturing spurred the Industrial Revolution in the mid-eighteenth century with the development of the flying shuttle, a device that allowed wider fabrics to be woven in less time. Automated spinning devices and net and lace making machines followed. These British inventions, along with the semiautomated loom Joseph Marie Jacquard (1752-1834) patented in France in 1805, ultimately forced many craftsmen to abandon a trade their families may have practiced for generations: those who could not adapt to mechanized production lost their means of employment. The shrinking market for handmade material caused other craftsmen to leave Europe for the United States, where they established weaving traditions that would create necessary goods for homesteaders. Reflecting this transition, nineteenth-century novels are full of concern for the turmoil and social displacement caused by the evolution from the handcraft to the machine age.

The democratization of fashion was one of the most significant developments during the nineteenth century. While industrial jobs were increasing the affluence of the middle classes, automation was decreasing prices of fashionable items previously affordable only by the wealthy. Shopkeepers and even domestics mimicked their masters, but the uppermost strata still preferred handmade luxury goods.

To twentieth-century eyes, nineteenth-century Europe appears to be an artistic mélange. Early in the century, Indian muslins and Neoclassic taste held sway. Designs were simple: ladies dressed in clinging, thin cotton gowns that were decorated with small, delicate patterns. In the 1830s, with the beginning of Victoria's reign, tastes changed. Past designs imbued these years of rapid industrialization with a feeling of stability. Victorian designers combined Gothic tracery and other architectural elements with Renaissance and eighteenth-century floral and decorative motifs, and infused them with an overriding, romantic naturalism.

The shape as well as the embellishment of fashion changed rapidly as the tempo of life increased. Although the voices of serious reformers were often heard, women still preferred corsets, hoops, and bustles, which completely altered the shape of their bodies, to comfortable styles. At the same time, the tendency toward overelaboration affected style from clothing to interiors. The visually chaotic ambience mirrored contemporary social upheaval.

Toward the end of the century, several decades of philosophical and practical concern over the mechanization of society and life in an industrialized age culminated in the Arts and Crafts Movement in England. It began as an attempt to simplify design, which its practitioners perceived as a reaction to the engulfing style and the ubiquity of high Victorian taste. To a greater or lesser degree, participating artists were concerned with the effect of a tasteless social and physical environment on the common man's ability to appreciate beauty. Some practitioners aligned themselves with the socialist cause and proselytized about the rights of the common man in an industrialized age. Ironically, it was primarily the wealthy elite that appreciated these artists, who nonetheless precipitated the two great design movements of the future, Art Nouveau and the Modern movements.[9]

The aesthetic principles of the Arts and Crafts Movement were most strongly stated in architectural decoration and the decorative arts. That a major artistic movement should devote itself to the so-called "minor arts" was fitting, for in a number of places, schools of design had been founded as a foil for royal academies, which concerned themselves mainly with painting and sculpture.[10] Impelled by this interest, a small group of Arts and Crafts adherents gave design an unprecedented status in late nineteenth-century England and laid the foundation for twentieth-century tastes.[11]

The early decades of the twentieth century were rather like an extension of the Victorian period. Though huge extensions of the body in bustles and leg-o'-mutton sleeves were no longer stylish, elaborate decoration was still preferred by Edwardian taste. Beginning about 1909, forward-looking Parisian designers like Vionnet and Poiret fell under the influence of the colorful Ballet Russe and began to strip female bodies of their corsets to create soft, draped fashion. Dresses made in bright, clear colors were cut on the bias to reveal the wearer's body, a style that differed radically from the pastel, heavily corseted "pouter pigeon" fashions of the Belle Epoque. These innovative designs had some effect on taste in the second decade of the century, but it was ultimately the First World War that caused a major shift in life style and consequently, in the clothes women chose to wear.

The war prompted many of the developments that democratized fashion. When the men went off to fight, the women took over their jobs at home and worked for the war effort as well. Because upper- and middle-class women labored side-by-side, sometimes in the same uniforms, the importance of clothing as an indicator of status was mitigated. Furthermore, the much better wages lower-class women now received enabled them to spend more on their wardrobes.

During the war years the practical garb whose straight, simple lines and shorter hems allowed for ease of movement led to a major change in women's fashion after the war. Marked by the geometric, decorative mode of Art Deco, the early twenties witnessed a straighter silhouette in dresses that hung from shoulder to hem. Hemlines rose and waistlines dropped; by 1925, skirts rested just below the knee. While the full, mature figure was favored in the first decades of the century, the minimally endowed adolescent body was now the height of fashion. Those unlucky enough to be graced with rounded curves suppressed them with tight undergarments.

At the close of the flamboyant twenties, America experienced its great stock market crash. Artists and designers were instantly put out of work since those who had previously bought their creations were now financially ruined. Franklin Roosevelt's New Deal, which attempted to bring the country some measure of economic relief, extended employment to the artists' community through the Works Project Administration/Federal Arts Project (WPA/FAP). By the time a degree of financial stability was achieved, the Second World War was imminent. As the country mobilized, wartime strictures were placed on the fashion industry.

The war effectively severed American fashion from Parisian influence, and after the war had ended, Norman Norell led the American ready-to-wear industry to international prominence. His designs bridged the gap between Parisian made-to-order couture and American mass-garment manufacture. Norell and fashion luminaries Bill Blass and Halston, all born in Indiana, characterize the various directions American fashion has followed. While Norell excelled at meticulous detailing and classic design of clothing, Blass injected fashion into virtually every level of society through his franchising efforts. Halston made his mark by simplifying American women's dress. Typically American, all three tendencies were also symptomatic of their times.

Catalogue Number 94 (see color plate, p. 50)
Italy
Garment or Furnishing Fabric, ca. 1475
silk velvet weave with silk supplementary warp and metallic
    supplementary weft (pile-on-pile and voided velvet with
    brocade)
80¼ x 23¾ (203.5 x 60.5) warp x weft
Roger G. Wolcott Fund 82.7

One of the most popular designs of the late Gothic period was the so-called pomegranate pattern executed here in silk velvet. The name, which became associated with the design in the nineteenth century, probably evolved from the term *pomme de pin*, or pine cone, which appeared in old inventories. Antecedents for the design were probably Middle Eastern and Chinese patterns (see cat. 62) and late Gothic naturalism. The palmette and twisting floral tendrils of earlier designs came to be immensely enlarged[12] and took on a monumental grandeur that was reminiscent of the spirit of the Italian Renaissance.

Silk velvet weaving in Europe may have originated in Venice. The city had traded with the Near East, where velvets were also produced in great abundance. By 1425, Venetian velvet weavers were organized into two groups of specialists: one wove plain velvet and the other patterned velvet.[13] But it was in fifteenth-century Florence that velvet was first combined with the technique of brocade with precious metal-wrapped threads[14] to produce grand-scale fabrics such as the one illustrated here. Not until the Industrial Revolution was Italy's leadership in manufacturing large-scale furnishing fabric actually eclipsed.

Producing velvet is complicated, particularly when it is patterned. During the course of weaving, the supplementary warps used to make the pile are first secured to the ground structure and then brought up and over metal rods that lie parallel to the wefts. Loops formed by this method are then cut by running sharp knives along a ridge on the top of the rods. This basic construction is considerably more difficult if, as in cut and uncut velvet, some of the pile is cut and some left looped or, as in voided velvet, the pattern is worked and the ground structure left uncovered. Finally, including a metallic wrapped supplementary weft—whether flat, looped, or both—challenges the craftsmen even further. Numerous paintings of the period show fabrics like this one being used for religious hangings and vestments, but despite their large scale, they were apparently also employed in clothing, as can be seen in a painting from the Museum's collection (see illustration, p. 225).[15] Rarely seen in velvets of this design, the blue was not in fact an ecclesiastical color dictated for use during the liturgical year but was probably intended for secular purposes.

Materials
Basic fabric
    warp: silk, single-ply S-twist; yellow
    weft: silk, no twist; yellow, brown-yellow
    supplementary warp:
        silk, single-ply slight S-twist; dark blue
    supplementary weft:
        metallic
            core thread: silk, single-ply S-twist; yellow
            strip: silver with gold and copper, S-twist; gold colored,
                core exposed
        silk, no twist; yellow

Techniques
Warp-faced woven pile, cut long; warp-faced woven pile,
    cut short; warp-faced woven pile, cut short with weft
    loops; weft-faced floats bound in plain weave alignment;
    and weft-faced loops; with supplementary warp pile and
    continuous supplementary weft
        proportions: one supplementary warp per three main
            warps, two supplementary wefts and one velvet rod
            per three main wefts
Selvedge: ⅝ in. (1.6 cm) wide, warp-faced plain weave of
    light green and light red stripes

Thread count
Basic fabric
    warp: 228   weft: 78   supplementary warp: 76
    supplementary weft: 26 pairs

Pattern repeat
    warpwise: 41¾ in. (106.0 cm)   weftwise: full width

The Ciervales Master, Aragon
Legends of St. James, 1500-1510
oil on panel (26¾ x 12½)
James E. Roberts Fund 24.3

Catalogue Number 95
Italy or Turkey
Chasuble Back, ca. 1470
silk velvet weave with silk supplementary warp (voided velvet)
30¼ x 26 (77 x 66) warp x weft
Orville A. and Elma D. Wilkinson Fund 76.163

This delicate velvet with ogival patterning is difficult to attribute. It could have been made either in Italy or Turkey, so similar were the designs and techniques of the two countries during this period. The most unusual feature of this piece is its use of green and yellow in combination with the more common red and blue.

Materials
Basic fabric
  warp: silk, single-ply Z-twist; yellow-tan
  weft: silk, no twist; white
  supplementary warp: silk, no twist; red, yellow, blue, green
Lining
  warp: bast (linen), single-ply Z-twist; light blue
  weft: bast (linen), single-ply Z-twist; light blue

Techniques
Warp-faced woven pile, cut, and warp-faced 4/1 satin weave, with supplementary warp pile, striped areas have paired supplementary warps
  proportions: one or one pair supplementary warp per six main warps; one velvet rod per three main wefts
Lining: balanced plain weave

Thread count
Basic fabric
  warp: 216   weft: 108
  supplementary warp: 36 threads or 36 pairs (72 threads)
Lining
  warp: 40   weft: 36

Pattern repeat
  warpwise: 14 in. (35.5 cm)   weftwise: 6¼ in. (16.0 cm)

Catalogue Number 97
Spain
Garment or Furnishing Fabric, ca. 1500
silk velvet weave with silk supplementary warp and metallic
    supplementary weft (voided, cut and uncut velvet with
    brocade), trimmed with silk and metallic band
52¼ x 22¾ (133 x 58) warp x weft
Orville A. and Elma D. Wilkinson Fund 76.165

The ubiquitous "pomegranate" pattern is reinterpreted here to suit the Spanish taste for grandeur. The sixteenth century was a glorious time for Spain: reaping vast amounts of gold from the New World, the country displayed its wealth magnificently. The Muslims who invaded in the eighth century established a vigorous silk industry and, with it, the dominant Islamic decorative motif of interlaced arabesques (see cat. 77). Charles V's (1506-1558) banishment of Moorish weavers left a vacuum that Spain filled by importing Italian fabrics. The few local craftsmen that remained combined the best of Italian and Mudejar design in the Baroque style[20] to create complicated velvets such as this one. The design has lost the basic clarity of the original Italian model (see cat. 95 and 98) in a curvilinear tangle of vines and flowers that interweave with the ogival structure. This intricate design, along with the lavish flat and looped brocading in gold- and silver-wrapped thread and the voided velvet pattern, epitomizes Spanish design in the sixteenth century.

Materials
Basic fabric
    warp: silk, single-ply S-twist; yellow
    weft: silk, no twist; yellow-tan
    supplementary warp: silk, single-ply S-twist; red
    continuous supplementary weft:
        metallic #1
            round wire only: silver with gold and copper;
                gray-gold colored
    discontinuous supplementary weft:
        metallic #2
            core thread: silk, single-ply S-twist; yellow
            strip: silver with gold and copper, S-twist; gold colored
        metallic #3
            core thread: silk, single-ply S-twist; yellow
            strip: silver with gold and copper, S-twist; gold colored
        metallic #4
            core thread: silk, single-ply S-twist; yellow
            strip: silver with gold and copper, S-twist; gold colored
        metallic #5
            core thread: silk, single-ply S-twist; white
            strip: silver with gold and copper, S-twist; silver
                colored
        metallic #6
            core thread: silk, single-ply S-twist; white
            strip: silver with copper, S-twist; silver colored

Trim
    warp: silk, single-ply slight S-twist; yellow
    weft:
        metallic #3
            core thread: silk, single-ply S-twist; yellow
            strip: silver with gold and copper, S-twist; gold colored
    supplementary warp:
        metallic #3
            core thread: silk, single-ply S-twist; yellow
            strip: silver with gold and copper, S-twist; gold colored
        metallic #6
            core thread: silk, single-ply S-twist; white
            strip: silver with copper, S-twist; silver colored

Techniques
Warp-faced woven pile, cut; warp-faced woven pile, looped; weft-dominant twill weave; and weft-dominant weave with looped weft; with supplementary warp pile and continuous and discontinuous supplementary weft, paired continuous supplementary weft
    proportions: one supplementary warp per three main warps; one pair continuous supplementary weft, one discontinuous supplementary weft and one velvet rod per three main wefts
Trim: warp-faced plain weave and warp-faced loops, with supplementary warp
    proportions: three supplementary warps per one main warp

Thread count
Basic fabric
    warp: 117   weft: 72
    supplementary warp: 39
    continuous supplementary weft: 48 pairs (96 threads)
    discontinuous supplementary weft: 24
Trim
    warp: 16   weft: 42   supplementary warp: 48

Literature
Weibel, *2000 Years of Silk Weaving*, plate 55.

Exhibition
2000 Years of Silk Weaving, Los Angeles County Museum of Art, 1944

231

Catalogue Number 98
Italy
Garment or Furnishing Fabric, ca. 1550
silk plain and twill weaves (damask) with metallic
    supplementary weft (brocade)
65½ x 33 (166 x 84) warp x weft
Emma Harter Sweetser Fund 78.160

A typical smaller-scale pattern from the fifteenth and sixteenth
centuries features a palmette surrounded by an ogive. The rigid
character of this design stresses both the vertical and horizontal
axes through the placement of the palmettes, and the diagonal
through that of the shafts of wheat. In the piece shown here,
this rather formal device is softened by background images
woven in damask.[21] This technique has produced a shiny
ground of red twill with background pattern of plain weave,
on top of which lie supplementary gold-wrapped threads. The
resulting very subtle interplay between shiny and dull surfaces
heightens this silk's exciting effect.

Materials
  Basic fabric
      warp: silk, single-ply S-twist; red
      weft: silk, no twist; red
      supplementary weft:
        metallic
          core thread: silk, two-ply S-twist; yellow
          strip: silver with gold and copper, S-twist; gold colored
Techniques
  Warp-faced 4/1 diagonal twill weave (background),
      weft-dominant plain weave (figure), and weft-faced floats
      bound in a diagonal twill alignment (figure), with
      discontinuous supplementary weft
        proportions: one supplementary weft per two main
          wefts
  Selvedge: ⅜ in. (0.8 cm) wide, warp-faced plain weave of
    green, yellow, and white stripes
Thread count
  Basic fabric
    warp: 290   weft: 82   supplementary weft: 41
Pattern repeat
  warpwise: 7¼ in. (18.5 cm)   weftwise: 5½ in. (14.0 cm)

Catalogue Number 99 (see color plate, p. 52)
Andalusia Region of Spain, Portugal or Italy
Panel, ca. 1600
silk satin and twill weaves (damask)
29¼ x 21¼ (74.5 x 54) warp x weft
Stanley Zweibel Fund and Eliza M. Niblack Textile Fund
  50.60

The image of opposing animals with a central tree is an old one that has been employed in silks at least since the Sasanian dynasty in Iran. Also used in the Byzantine world, the motif was diffused to a number of other locations, including Moorish Spain (see cat. 77), through Muslim influence. What infuses a different, more animated spirit into this heraldic design, in red and yellow damask, is the activity of the other animals leaping into the spatial voids. Little tufts of grass hint at a landscape, but no real attempt is made to put the animals in a relative scale or a determinable space. The strictly bilateral composition is on a central axis against which the curving, active forms play. The design is much influenced by earlier hunting scenes from Near Eastern and European fabrics as well as by the new interest in the natural world typical of the sixteenth century.

Materials
  Basic fabric
    warp: silk, single-ply slight S-twist; red
    weft: silk, single-ply slight S-twist; yellow
Techniques
  Warp-faced 4/1 satin weave (background) and weft-faced
    4/1 diagonal twill weave (figure)
  Selvedge: ³⁄₁₆ in. (0.4 cm) wide, warp-faced 4/1 satin weave
Thread count
  Basic fabric
    warp: 265   weft: 68
Pattern repeat
  warpwise: 15 in. (38.0 cm)   weftwise: point repeat
Literature
  Lubell, *Textile Collections of the World*, p. 318.

Catalogue Number 100 (see color plate, p. 53)
Switzerland
Furnishing Fabric, ca. 1520
linen and cotton plain weave; embroidered with silk, linen
    and metallic thread; trimmed with silk interknotted fringe
    (macramé)
42¼ x 22¾ (107 x 58.5) warp x weft
Emma Harter Sweetser Fund 81.210

During the Middle Ages in Northern Europe, much embroidery used ecclesiastical themes. While there was an active tradition of professional needleworking, perhaps the majority of
work was produced in the home or convent. It is difficult to
determine which Swiss embroideries were executed in the
home, for domestic use, and which were made in the convent,
for the church. Because of its small size and side fringe, this
panel was probably used domestically as a furniture cover on a
table, chest, or sideboard. In a church such panels were used
as antependia and altar cloths.[22] These embroideries are rarely
signed and seem to be modeled after woodblock prints, especially those in illustrated Bibles, the most widely circulated
books of the time. In fact the design on this piece, its rather flat
and crisp forms often outlined in a contrasting shade, is reminiscent of a woodblock print.[23] Of the few pieces that have been
found, only two[24] are known to be from the same design.[25]

The depiction of the four Evangelists is drawn from the
Apocalypse. Each of them is placed in a corner, surrounding a
medallion that contains a version of the sacrificial offering of
Isaac. Of the few hundred known examples of this type of
textile—only a few of which are in American museum collections—most depict scenes from the New Testament; thus this
example is rather rare. A characteristic feature of these embroideries is floral rondels that set off various elements of the
design. This popular Gothic design was used from the thirteenth century (when the development of Swiss linen embroidery began) until the seventeenth. The decorative device may
have been indebted to Early Christian mosaic design and illuminated books.[26] Patterning began to change at the end of the
fifteenth century, when figural scenes were introduced, and
continued to evolve during the sixteenth and early seventeenth
centuries, when the relation of figures to ground became more
elaborate and the embroidery stitches more various. Because
this piece still retains the flat treatment and rather limited vocabulary of stitches common to Gothic works, it has been dated
to the early sixteenth century.

These pieces have been described as being embroidered with
linen thread on a linen ground. Our technical analysis revealed
that the ground cloth is woven of a linen warp and cotton weft.
According to the literature, the brown tone of the background
cloth in this and other pieces may have resulted from the use
of a rusty cotton weft, dyed with iron salts.[27] The coloring,
though stained, does seem to be integral to the piece. Linen
threads, it was thought, were dyed in only blue, yellow, and rust
brown; other colors were worked in silk or wool. Technical
analysis of all the colored threads in this piece reveals, however,
that only the white threads are linen, and the rest are silk. The
amount of dark brown remaining in St. John and in the names
of the Apostles is unusual since the iron oxide dyes used at the
time caused original fibers to become brittle and drop off. In
fact, the brown yarns are missing in areas of the altar and
Jacob's boots.

Materials
  Basic fabric
    warp: bast (linen), single-ply Z-twist; tan
    weft: cotton, single-ply Z-twist; tan
  Embroidery
    silk, two-ply S-twist; yellow, brown, tan, violet-red, light
      blue, light green
    bast (linen), two-ply S-twist; white
    metallic #1
      round wire only: copper with iron and zinc;
        gray-copper colored
    metallic #2
      core thread: silk, two-ply S-twist; tan
      strip: copper, S-twist; gold colored
  Trim
    silk, two-ply S-twist; tan
Techniques
  Balanced plain weave
  Embroidery
    flat stitches: Bokhara couching; couching; satin, padded
      satin, surface satin
    looped stitches: bullion knot
  Trim: attached interknotted fringe
Thread count
  Basic fabric
    warp: 58   weft: 53

Catalogue Number 101
England
Bed Valance, ca. 1550
linen plain weave, embroidered with wool and silk
72½ x 13½ (184 x 34) warp x weft
Martha Delzell Memorial Fund 75.737

The history of English embroidery in the Middle Ages is lustrous indeed. One of the earliest known, and perhaps the most notable, of all these embroideries is the Bayeux Tapestry, produced to commemorate the victory of William the Conqueror in 1066. In the thirteenth and fourteenth centuries "Opus Anglicanum" became the most highly prized embroidery in all of Europe.

In 1561, during England's Elizabethan period (1558-1603), the Broderers Company received official recognition—although the guild had undoubtedly been operating in some form for hundreds of years.[28] Like other guilds, this one controlled the quality of its members' designs, work, and materials as well as the scale of their prices. By 1580, eighty-nine master craftsmen were listed in the guild. Embroiderers labored in workshops or in the great households typical of the period. Some craftsmen stayed in one household or workshop for long periods while others moved from one place to another according to local demand and their patrons' wealth.

Certainly not all Elizabethan embroidery was executed by professionals; in fact, this was one of the great ages of domestic embroidery, when any woman in a household of means was expected to be accomplished with the needle—as were women of the lower classes, who executed domestic embroidery for hire as well as for their own families. Unfortunately, little of the domestic embroidery used by the poor remains because, unlike that used by wealthy families, it was worn out.

Regardless of the embroiderer's economic status, she needed patterns. The wealthy hired artists to draw them, but the vast majority of women followed the patterns frequently printed in books. The earliest known book of popular ornament was printed in Augsburg, Germany, about 1523; and by 1590, a number were available in Italy, France, and England. The designs were based on classical forms, Mediterranean and Islamic motifs, and Gothic ornament.[29] Other important sources were illuminated Bibles, herbal and flower illustrations, books—such as those devoted to natural history—and lining papers from boxes and coffers.[30]

Valances commonly display figural scenes taken from fables, myths, and Biblical narratives.[31] The images on this embroidery come from a variety of sources. The seven panels depict significant events in the Virgin's life, arranged in chronological order from right to left. The first scene depicts the angel's announcement to Joachim; the second, the meeting between Joachim and Ann at the Golden Gate; the third, the birth of the Virgin; and the fourth, her education. The fifth panel shows the marriage of Mary and Joseph; the sixth, the Annunciation; and the last, the Visitation of Mary and Elizabeth. Surrounding these vignettes is a border replete with animals and flowers that fully expresses the Elizabethan love of flowers and gardens. Popular contemporary publications demonstrated the great interest in botany, which was expressed through the cultivation of new species of flowers from the Middle East and the Americas. The enjoyment of flowers, reflected in their appearance in paintings of the late fifteenth and early sixteenth centuries, is further evidence of this developing obsession.

> Cut flowers were to be seen in Elizabethan houses as well as potted plants and strewn herbs, for Livimus Lemnus, a Dutchman who visited England in 1560 wrote: "their chambers and parlours strewed over with fresh herbes refreshed mee; their nosegays finely intermingled with sundry of fragraunt flowers, in their bed-chambers and privy rooms, with comfortable smell cheered me up, and entirely delighted all my senses."[32]

Tulips and irises, seen here, were exotic imports. Particular qualities were attached to many flowers: the iris was the "flower-de-luce"; the rose comforted the heart; the pansy was Cupid's flower;[33] and carnations represented pure love.[34] In this particular embroidery daffodils, carnations, tulips, irises, hyacinths, lilies, morning glories, and roses can be seen.

In addition to plants, animals reflect the natural world in this embroidery: the flowers and tendrils, rendered in the flat Gothic style, are interspersed among deer, hounds, peacocks, pelicans, and a squirrel. The pelican is a Christian symbol of the sacrifice of Christ and the peacock represents immortality. According to legend, only a virgin could tame the unicorn, so it is associated with Mary. The crane eating a snake, found in the border, represents the victory of good over evil. Although these animals are symbolic, others are purely decorative and spring from the same interest in documenting natural life evident in millefleur tapestries.

It was not thought unusual at the time to combine such secular observations with religious iconography in a domestic embroidery and to place it on top of a bed. The bed was a very important piece of furniture in Elizabethan England and was decorated as lavishly as possible. To allow for some modicum of privacy and comfort, these imposing structures were surrounded by hangings and covered at the top. To mask the curtain rail, two valances were placed on the sides and one on the end. The valance illustrated here must have been for the left side because of its length and its arrangement of the vignettes. Stretched and secured to the top of the bed, these items—unlike curtains and coverlets—have survived because they were rarely handled.

Materials
  Basic fabric
    warp: bast (linen), single-ply Z-twist; tan
    weft: bast (linen), single-ply Z-twist; tan
  Embroidery
    wool, single-ply Z-twist; dark blue, green, brown,
      yellow-green, light blue, light orange, light red
    silk, single-ply slight Z-twist; white, tan, two yellows, gray,
      black, light, medium and dark blue, three browns,
      light red
Techniques
  Balanced plain weave, woven with space between every two
    warps and every two wefts
  Embroidery
    flat stitches: long and short satin; split; straight
    flat counted stitches: cross; tent
    combination flat stitches: Roumanian and split over long
      and short satin; stem over long and short satin
Thread count
  Basic fabric
    warp: 22   weft: 22

Catalogue Number 102
Germany
Ecclesiastical Furnishing Fabric, ca. 1675
linen twill weaves (damask)
33 x 22½ (84 x 57) warp x weft
Stanley Zweibel Fund and Eliza M. Niblack Textile Fund
  50.61

European linen damask weaving with geometric patterns probably evolved in the Netherlands and began to use pictorial design in the fifteenth century. Further developments took place
in the flax-producing areas of Saxony, Flanders, and northern
France, where such fabrics were most commonly employed as
bed and table cloths. Apparently they were acquired as much
by the growing merchant class as by wealthy landowners. Many
napkins and large table cloths showed secular themes, including
heraldic devices and plant forms,[35] as well as biblical motifs.

A particular type of design developed which may have had
its origin in the early woodcuts of the Flemish and German
schools.[36] In the late sixteenth century, Schleswig, Saxony, and
Friesland were the first areas of Germany to execute picture
weaving. Although the majority of white linen damasks were
woven as bed and table covers, blue and white, and red and
white pieces with Old and New Testament themes were made
as altar cloths for country churches. The region of Ober Lausitz
produced fabrics similar to this piece. In them, professional
weavers executed the patterns with both horizontal and vertical
repeats. In this particular region the weavers seemed not to
care if, as in this example, woven script was reversed on one
side of the vertical axis[37] and thus created a mirror image of
the other side. Certainly this is not sophisticated draftsmanship
or execution but it does nonetheless have a certain charm and
directness.

Materials
  Basic fabric
    warp: bast (linen), single-ply Z-twist; white
    weft: bast (linen), single-ply Z-twist; dark blue
Techniques
  Warp-dominant 7/1 diagonal twill weave (figure) and
    weft-faced 7/1 diagonal twill weave (background)
  No selvedge
Thread count
  Basic fabric
    warp: 65   weft: 88
Pattern repeat
  warpwise: not discernible   weftwise: point repeat

Catalogue Number 103
Workshop of Karel van Mander (1579-1623), Belgium
Set of Six Wall Hangings (tapestries), ca. 1640
wool and silk plain weave with wool warp
Anthony Conquers Pelusium
105½ x 143 (267.5 x 362.5) warp x weft
Cleopatra Entertains Anthony
159 x 145½ (403 x 368.5) warp x weft
Anthony Catches a Salted Fish
152.5 x 144 (286.5 x 365) warp x weft
Anthony Aids Ventidius to Achieve Victory Over the
Parthians
133 x 144¼ (337 x 366) warp x weft
Octavia Effects the Concord of Tarentum
159½ x 143½ (404 x 363.5) warp x weft
Cleopatra Dies at the Tomb of Anthony
132½ x 144 (335.5 x 365) warp x weft
Gift of Mr. and Mrs. Herman C. Krannert 66.1-6

These tapestries portray six exploits from the life of Marc Anthony, as related by Plutarch.[38] In chronological order they are:

1) *Anthony Conquers Pelusium* (55 B.C.)
Anthony restores Ptolemy XI to the throne as Pharaoh of Egypt and receives a reward of ten thousand talents. Ptolemy XII, then six years old, stands in the background.

2) *Cleopatra Entertains Anthony* (41 B.C.)
Cleopatra sails up the River Cydnus on her golden barge. Anthony invites her to dine, but she thinks it more proper for him to join her. He complies and is dazzled by the magnificent preparations.

3) *Anthony Catches a Salted Fish* (41 B.C.)
Anthony catches nothing when he sets out to fish with Cleopatra, so he orders his fishermen to dive underwater and put fishes on his hook. The next day Cleopatra invites Anthony to her barge again; when he lets down his line, one of her servants hooks a salted fish to it. Great merriment follows, and Cleopatra exhorts him to abandon fishing and go forth to conquer kingdoms.

4) *Anthony Aids Venditius to Achieve Victory Over the Parthians* (38 B.C.)
After struggling with the Parthians, Anthony's lieutenant Venditius learns of Anthony's acceptance of three hundred talents to end the struggle. Anthony publicly recognizes Venditius's role in the battle.

5) *Octavia Effects the Concord of Tarentum* (37 B.C.)
Anthony's wife Octavia entreats her brother Octavius (later the Emperor Augustus) to make a peaceful settlement with her husband. Though massive troops have already gathered, various legions are exchanged, and each leader sets off on a different campaign.

6) *Cleopatra Dies at the Tomb of Anthony* (30 B.C.)
After her husband has summoned her to leave Egypt, Cleopatra arranges one final visit to Anthony's tomb. After bathing and dining, she receives a basket of figs containing a deadly asp and succumbs to its bite in the presence of her ladies, Iras and Charmoin, who die with her.

Noble subjects from classical literature were favored in tapestry design from the fourteenth century on, and the story of Anthony and Cleopatra was particularly popular in the seventeenth and eighteenth centuries. Though Renaissance artists such as Raphael—perhaps the best known among them—executed cartoons or sketches, it was Peter Paul Rubens who revitalized tapestry weaving, in Brussels, when he drew his first cartoons in 1618.

Karel van Mander II probably drew the central panels of this set. The son of an artist-scholar who maintained an art academy in Haarlem, he became a painter and then official designer of cartoons for the Spierincx tapestry works at Delft. Though he probably sketched them in 1620, the panels were executed after his death in 1623. The elaborate borders were not designed until perhaps a decade later. Raphael was among the first artists to emphasize the border, and by the late sixteenth century, this framing device had taken on a life of its own. Rubens reintegrated the tapestry and its frame by creating a kind of proscenium arch for his Achilles tapestry cartoons, under way from 1630 to 1635. In the set shown here, a richly architectural, three-sided arch springs from a simple molding at the bottom of the work. Because of the combination of the frame, after Rubens, and the design by van Mander, the set must have been executed between 1635 and 1650.

European tapestries were woven on a vertical loom without heddles or a shed stick. On the warp threads, here of wool, stretched between the top and bottom of a rigid frame, the weaver inserted the threads manually while working in the colored areas one at a time. He often placed a large drawing, or cartoon, of the finished piece behind the warps so he could refer to it while working. If the tapestries were very large, they were sometimes worked sideways, with the warps running across the width of the tapestry, as they are here.

It appears that these tapestries were originally designed in 1623 for the third Duke of Richmond, who planned to put them in a banquet room he was adding to Cobham Hall, which is located near the Thames, between Gravesend and Rochester. The estate passed through that family and later into the family of the Earl of Darnley whence it became a part of the National Trust in 1959.

Catalogue Number 103 *Anthony Captures Pelusium*

Materials
  Basic fabric
    warp: wool, three-ply S-twist; light gray-tan
    weft: wool, two-ply S-twist; gray, blue-gray, blue, green-
      blue, green, yellow, brown-yellow, brown, red-brown,
      tan, white
        silk, single-ply Z-twist; white, light and medium
          yellow, light blue, light brown, light red

Techniques
  Weft-faced plain weave, with discontinuous wefts; slit and
    double interlocking tapestry joins, some eccentric wefts
  Silk wefts in groups, wool weft sometimes of two plies of
    different colors

Thread count
  Basic fabric
    warp: 14   weft: wool, 48   silk, 55

Literature
  Pantzer and Weinhardt, *Art Association of Indianapolis
    Bulletin*, March 1966, pp. 4-30.

Catalogue Number 103 *Cleopatra Entertains Anthony*

Catalogue Number 103 *Anthony Catches a Salted Fish*

Catalogue Number 103 *Anthony Aids Ventidius to Achieve Victory*
Over the Parthians

Catalogue Number 103 *Octavia Effects the Concord of Tarentum*

Catalogue Number 103 *Cleopatra Dies at the Tomb of Anthony*

Catalogue Number 104
France
Pair of Screens, ca. 1725
linen plain weave, embroidered with wool and silk
each screen: 104¾ x 97¼ (265.5 x 246.5) warp x weft
each textile panel: 101¾ x 23¾ (258 x 60.5) warp x weft
Gift of the family of J. K. Lilly, Jr.
    67.10.125.1 and 67.10.125.2

Until the second quarter of the seventeenth century, most of the furnishings of wealthy Europeans' homes were temporary and portable. Screens, cushions, and wall hangings could be moved from residence to residence, brought out for special celebrations, and stored when not in use. By the mid-seventeenth century interior decoration became more important; as their wealth increased, people could afford to dress their houses as lavishly as they dressed themselves. Woven silks, wool tapestries, and embroideries were nailed to a framework and inserted in panelling or fastened directly to walls.[39] These embroidered panels originally may have been attached to walls since they are cut at the top to fit onto the screens seen here.

The drawing in these panels reflects textile design in the 1720s and 1730s, which attempted to create naturalism in flowers through a three-quarter view, interlaced stems, curling leaves, and color shading. Moralizing Latin inscriptions ornament the decorative cartouches.[40]

Materials
  Basic fabric
      warp: bast (linen), single-ply Z-twist; light brown
      weft: bast (linen), single-ply Z-twist; light brown
  Embroidery
      wool, two-ply S-twist; light, medium, and dark blue, medium and dark blue-green, red, dark brown-orange, five shades of brown, yellow-brown, orange-brown
      silk, no twist; light and medium yellow, light, medium, and dark blue, light green, light orange
Techniques
  Balanced plain weave, woven or pulled so that there is a space between every two warps and every two wefts
  Embroidery
      flat counted stitches: cross; tent
  Finish: mounted in wood frames
Thread count
  Basic fabric
      warp: 22   weft: 22

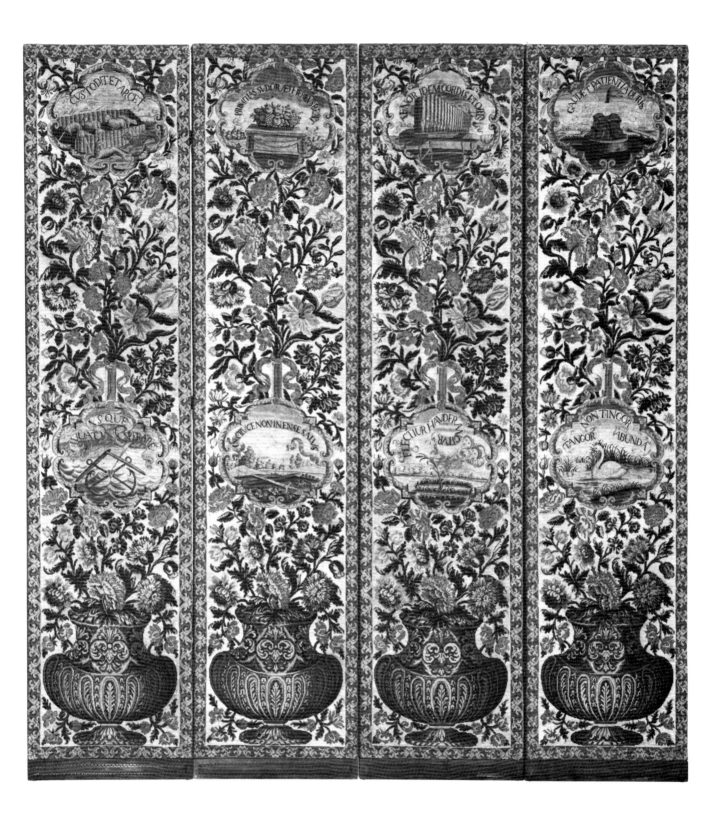

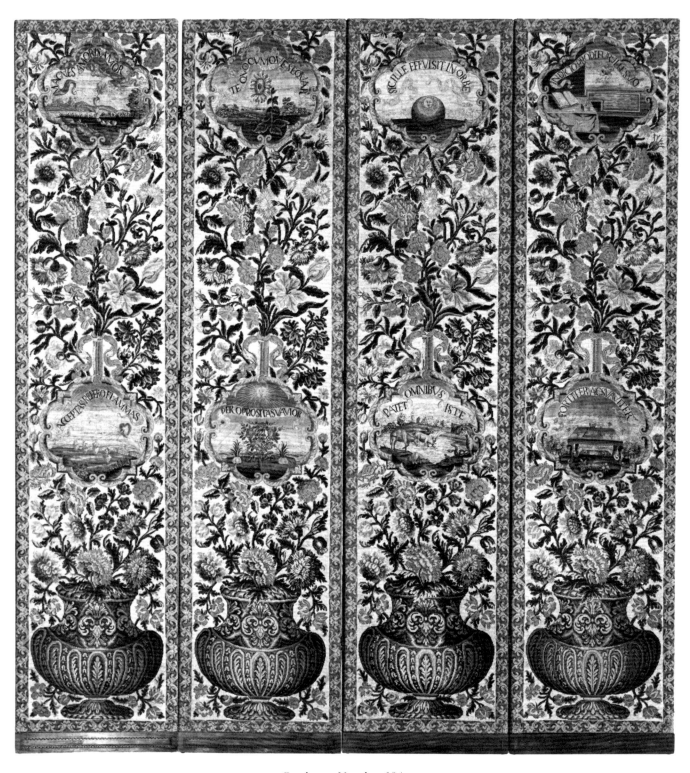

Catalogue Number 104

Catalogue Number 105
Italy or France
Valance, ca. 1705
silk satin weave, embroidered with silk and metallic thread,
   trimmed with silk and metallic fringe
100½ x 28½ (255 x 72.5) with fringe, warp x weft
Gift of Mrs. Albert J. Beveridge 37.131

The function of this magnificent embroidery remains an enigma since it is too large to serve as a shawl and shows no signs of wear.[41] It was probably executed as a furnishing fabric for a bed. By the mid-seventeenth century bed hangings became more complex; fabrics were fastened to walls and even hung over windows. As the century passed, architects were employed to design whole interiors.[42] The decorations at Versailles for Louis XIV are the most opulent expression of this trend.

The design and execution of this embroidery reflect the prevailing Baroque taste. In Europe, the style was most pervasive in Italy, where the greatest amount of furnishing silk with large-scale patterns was produced. This piece demonstrates late seventeenth-century naturalistic design elements such as the use of perspective to give depth—here created by leaves that turn under and over each other—and the juxtaposition of silk threads of differing hues to make shading.[43] Since large-scale flowers reentered textile's design vocabulary from about 1712 to 1720, this piece could have been made then, but the rather abstracted and almost imaginary shapes of the flowers are reminiscent of "bizarre" silks and thus suggest an earlier date. The glory of this piece lies in the movement of the design, the overblown quality of the flowers, and their dramatic relation to each other.

Materials
Basic fabric
   warp: silk, single-ply slight S-twist; light yellow-white
   weft: silk, no twist; light yellow-white
Embroidery
   silk, no twist; light and dark yellow, light, medium, and
      dark orange, light and medium violet-red, light and
      medium yellow-green, light, medium, and dark blue-
      green, tan, light and medium brown
   metallic #1
      core thread: silk, single-ply Z-twist; white
      strip: silver with gold and copper, S-twist; gold colored
   metallic #2
      core thread: silk, single-ply Z-twist; white
      strip: silver with gold and copper, S-twist; silver
         colored
   metallic #3
      core thread: silk, two-ply overspun Z-twist; white
      strip: silver with gold and copper, S-twist; silver
         colored, core exposed
   metallic #4
      core thread: silk, two-ply S-twist; white
      strip: gold and silver with copper, Z-twist; silver
         colored, wrapped with light yellow silk thread

Trim
   warp: silk, two-ply S-twist; light orange
   weft: silk, two-ply S-twist; light orange
   metallic #5 (visual identification)
      core thread: silk, two-ply overspun Z-twist; white
      strip: silver colored; S-twist; core exposed
   supplementary warp:
      metallic #6 (visual identification)
         core thread: silk, single-ply Z-twist; white
         strip: gold colored; S-twist
   tassels: silk, no twist; white, light yellow
      metallic #7 (visual identification)
         core thread: silk, two-ply S-twist; white
         strip: silver colored; Z-twist
Backing
   warp: silk, single-ply slight S-twist; light orange
   weft: silk, no twist; light orange
Techniques
Warp-faced 7/1 satin weave
Embroidery
   flat stitches: couching of single and doubled elements,
      pattern couching; satin, encroaching satin, surface satin,
      long and short satin; split; stem
Trim: band of warp-faced plain weave and warp-faced
   floats, with supplementary warp; fringe and added tassels;
   tassels of wrapped, twisted, and looped threads at ends
Backing: warp-faced 4/1 diagonal twill weave
Thread count
Basic fabric
   warp: 384   weft: 128
Backing
   warp: 125   weft: 148

Catalogue Number 105

Catalogue Number 105, Detail

Catalogue Number 106 (see color plate, p. 251)
Master of the Pagan Paradise, Andalusia Region of Spain or
    Portugal
Fragment of Furnishing Fabric, ca. 1675-1725
silk satin weave with silk supplementary weft (brocade)
34 x 22½ (86.5 x 57) warp x weft
Gift of Miss Lucy M. Taggart 29.73

This panel was probably woven by a particular craftsman who
has been identified as Master of the Pagan Paradise. He makes
no attempt to put flowers, trees, animals, and figures in relative
scale.[44] There are cypress trees, turkeys, peacocks, and fabulous
fountains, here woven in multicolored silk and chenille threads
on a grey-green silk satin ground. In addition, there are finishing upper and lower borders that may indicate the panel was
intended for use above decorative wall paneling or moldings.
The effective use of chenille fibers, which are tied to the ground
weave in a diagonal twill, gives variation to the surface. A won-
derful world of imaginary gardens with bird-filled trees and
fanciful animals is depicted here, in a style that is an exception
to the usual massive Baroque or delicate Rococo style of the
period.

Materials
  Basic fabric
    warp: silk, single-ply slight S-twist; white
    weft: silk, single-ply slight S-twist; white
    continuous supplementary weft:
      silk, no twist; dark green, white
    discontinuous supplementary weft:
      silk, no twist; four shades of brown, yellow, light blue,
        light orange
      silk, chenille Z-twist; yellow, blue, orange, light and
        medium brown, green
      silk, two-ply S-twist with one ply overspun; each ply a
        different color, yellow and light green, tan and light
        green, and solid white

Techniques
  Warp-faced 7/1 satin weave (background) and weft-faced
    floats bound in a diagonal twill alignment (figure), with
    continuous and discontinuous supplementary weft, some
    grouped supplementary weft
      proportions: two continuous and one or two
        discontinuous supplementary wefts per two main wefts
  Selvedge: ⅜ in. (1.0 cm) wide, warp-faced 7/1 satin weave

Thread count
  Basic fabric
    warp: 292   weft: 88
    continuous supplementary weft: 44 pairs (88 threads)
    discontinuous supplementary weft: chenille, 22   silk, 44

Catalogue Number 107
Town of Venice (?), Italy
Garment or Furnishing Fabric, ca. 1670
linen needle lace
110 x 9 (279 x 23)
Martha Delzell Memorial Fund 82.151

Italian needle lace dominated the lace market until the eighteenth century. To make needle lace, a backing paper with the pattern drawn on it was prepared, and linen threads were laid along the design contours and attached to the backing. The lace maker worked the first row of buttonhole stitches on those threads, the next row on those stitches and then returned back and forth between the two until a solid patterned area (*toilé*) was formed. The solid areas were joined together by bars of thread (*brides*) that were worked over with buttonhole stitches and embellished with loops (*picots*). The name *point plat* describes the surface quality of this lace, which is worked flat (*plat*) with a needle (*point*) and has no raised edges.

Characteristic of late seventeenth-century style are large, flat flowers and the curved stems, which often terminate in C scrolls. The abstract openwork patterns of this piece further accentuate the flat quality of the design, though an organic richness and feeling of growth pervade the whole. A piece like this was probably made to serve as a decorative flounce on the edge of a cuff, skirt, apron, collar, or even on household linen. It also might have been used on a clerical garment or an altar linen.

Materials
  Basic fabric
    outline: bast (linen), two-ply S-twist (thick); white
    figure and ground: bast (linen), two-ply S-twist; white
Techniques
  Needle lace; buttonhole stitches
    flat figures (*toilé*), no visible outline (*cordonnet*), figures
    connected with bars (*brides*) with loops (*picots*)
Thread count
  Basic fabric
    stitches: 76

252

Catalogue Number 108
France
Garment Fabric, ca. 1700
linen needle lace
201 x 16½ (510 x 42)
Martha Delzell Memorial Fund 82.150

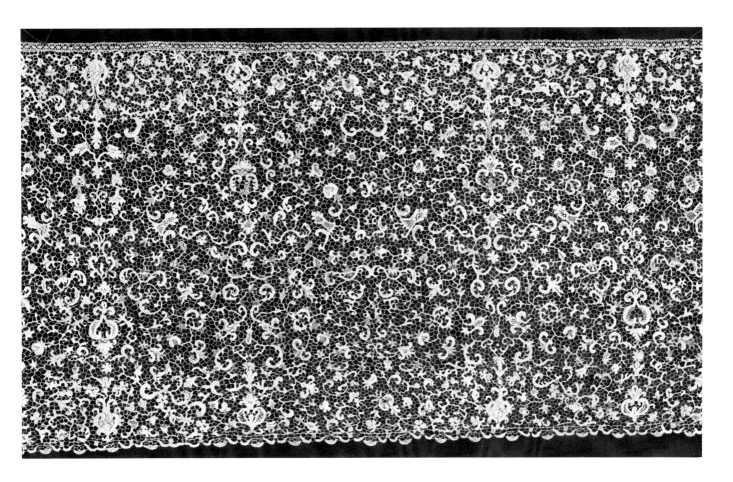

In the third quarter of the seventeenth century, Colbert established the lace making industry in France by importing Flemish and Italian workers. Compared with earlier lace (see cat. 107), the design of this piece is much lighter and more diffuse; scroll shapes and individual flowers float in the field. Though these elements appeared earlier, in Italian lace, they are recombined here in a way that is typically French. Another French device in this piece is the stacking of forms in long vertical axes, reminiscent of ironwork candelabra.[45]

This new design vocabulary prompted a change in technique. As motifs became smaller, the ground, or *réseau*, assumed more importance and the joining bars, or *brides*, eventually became more regular: in this piece they are arranged in a hexagonal configuration. These changes all reflect a different taste that eventually led into the Rococo style. In fact, laces made in late seventeenth-century France and Flanders were lighter than Italian laces, and the innovation of a mesh ground to replace the old *brides* and *picots* came about as pattern elements were spaced more widely apart, leaving larger negative spaces (see cat. 122).

A panel of this width might have been used to trim the bottom of a clerical vestment, the alb. Albs are known to have been worn as liturgical vestments in the thirteenth century, although they were probably used much earlier. They were usually made of linen because it was associated with Christ's burial wrappings and was a material that grew directly from the earth.[46] The alb was worn next to the body, underneath the chasuble or dalmatic, so decoration at the bottom was visible below the hem of the outer garment.

Materials
    Basic fabric
        outline: bast (linen), two-ply S-twist; white
        figure and ground: bast (linen), two-ply S-twist; white
Techniques
    Needle lace; buttonhole stitches
        flat figures (*toilé*), raised outline (*cordonnet*), figures
            connected with bars (*brides*) with loops (*picots*) arranged
            in irregular hexagons
Thread count
    Basic fabric
        stitches: 66

Catalogue Number 109
Europe
Fragment of Garment Fabric, ca. 1670
linen plain weave, embroidered with linen
46 x 22 (117 x 22) warp runs diagonally
Gift of Eliza M. Niblack 16.1047

The intricate patterning and curvilinear character of this design with large-scale floral patterns may place it in the late seventeenth century. As in cat. 107, the elaborate decorative designs negate the volumetric quality of the natural forms. Patterns in these areas are produced by withdrawing and deflecting threads of the woven linen ground and working them with a variety of embroidery stitches. At the time, such work was considered "poor man's lace" since it duplicated lace forms, though in a much simpler and thus far less costly manner. The extreme delicacy, finely drawn pattern, and variety of fill stitches make this piece remarkable.

Materials
Basic fabric
warp: bast (linen), single-ply Z-twist; white
weft: bast (linen), single-ply Z-twist; white
Embroidery
bast (linen), two-ply S-twist; white
Techniques
Balanced plain weave, loosely woven
Embroidery
flat stitches: couching; overcast edging; satin
looped stitches: buttonhole; French knot
deflected and withdrawn element stitches: back, variation
of double back; upright cross; cushion filling; detached
eyelet; diagonal drawn filling; diagonal raised band;
faggot, variation of faggot; Greek cross, variation of
Greek cross filling; oblique filling; pulled satin; step
Thread count
Basic fabric
warp: 133   weft: 126

Catalogue Number 110
Western Czechoslovakia
Baby's Cap, ca. 1800
cotton plain weave, quilted and stuffed (trapunto),
    embroidered with linen, trimmed with cotton bobbin lace
6¼ (16) length
Gift of Mrs. May Wright Sewall 46.88

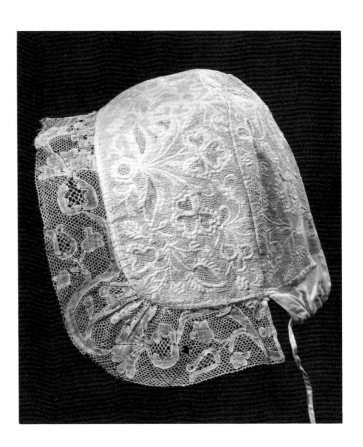

Czech embroidery, first documented in the twelfth century, had
long been a very important art by the eighteenth.[47] As in many
traditional cultures, the women learned embroidery skills and
patterns in childhood and spent many years preparing linens
and clothing for their dowries. The patterns came from other
forms of folk art as well as from textiles, which traders carried
through the country. Once adopted, such patterns were used
for long periods of time. Thus, although this example may have
been worked at the turn of the nineteenth century, the designs
probably originated at least a century earlier. This traditional
vocabulary remained intact in Czechoslovakia until the mid-
nineteenth century, when an educational reform movement
that introduced embroidery patterns and devalued folk designs
eventually caused a decline in creative embroidery.[48]

Materials

Basic fabric
    warp: cotton, single-ply slight Z-twist; white
    weft: cotton, single-ply slight Z-twist; white
Embroidery
    bast (linen), two-ply S-twist; white
Lace trim
    figure and ground: cotton, two-ply S-twist (thin); white
    outline: cotton, two-ply S-twist (thick); white
Lining
    warp: bast (linen), single-ply Z-twist; white
    weft: bast (linen), single-ply Z-twist; white

Techniques

Balanced plain weave
Quilted and stuffed with cord
Embroidery
    flat stitches: back, double back
    looped stitches: French knot
    flat counted stitches: deflected element faggot
Pieced garment
Trim: bobbin lace
    flat figures (*toilé*), outlined with thick thread (*cordonnet*),
        with a hexagonal-shaped mesh (*réseau*) consisting of six
        triangles around a hexagon with twisted threads (*Point
        de Paris*)
Lining: balanced plain weave

Thread count

Basic fabric
    warp: 92   weft: 112
Lace trim
    figure, horizontal: 60   vertical: 72
    mesh, horizontal: 14   vertical: 18
Lining
    warp: 82   weft: 66

Catalogue Number 111
Town of Binche, Belgium
Baby's Cap, ca. 1710
linen bobbin lace
7 (18) length
Emma Harter Sweetser Fund 82.75

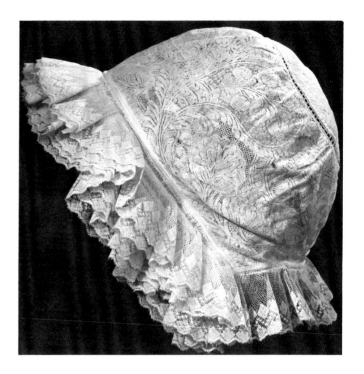

By the beginning of the eighteenth century, various cities in France and Belgium had developed differing traditions of lace making that distinctly characterized their products. The towns of Valenciennes and Binche were related to the lace making center of Anvers, Belgium, where lace had been made since the sixteenth century. Laces made during the seventeenth century in Binche and Valenciennes, both then in Flanders, are easily confused with those made at Anvers; and in fact the five-holed *cinq trous* ground, characteristic of Binche lace and seen here, was first used at Anvers.[49]

One feature that typifies all laces from this region is the use of a continuous thread to form both the *toilé* and the ground. Bobbin lace is made of a number of threads that are wound on bobbins; the lace maker works these around pins that are stuck through a parchment pattern and into the pillow it lies upon. The threads are twisted around each other and/or plaited to create the openwork of the ground (*réseau*) and "woven" to form the solid areas of the *toilé*. The design can be worked in one of two ways: either the solid elements are executed first and the ground is added later, or the *toilé* and ground are worked at the same time. The second method was used at Anvers, Valenciennes, and Binche and characterizes lace from that region. Another trait of Binche lace is its use of two types of ground patterning: five corners (*cinq trous*) and snowflake (*fond de neige*). The latter may have evolved from the rather spotty appearance of early eighteenth-century *point de Paris* lace (see cat. 108),[50] but regardless of its origins, Binche lace is extremely delicate. It is often difficult to see the forms of the design, especially in pieces from the early eighteenth century, when, as in this example, solid patterns were large and the grounds rather dense. Since the design has been cut to accommodate the cap, the pattern is hard to see, but it seems to share some qualities with "bizarre" silk designs (see cat. 112 and 116).

Materials
  Basic fabric
    bast (linen), two-ply S-twist; white
Techniques
  Bobbin lace
    flat figures (*toilé*), no outline (*cordonnet*), no mesh (*rèseau*)
  Pieced garment
Thread count
  Basic fabric
    figure, horizontal: 152   vertical: 148

Catalogue Number 112
Town of Lyon (?), France
Garment Fabric, ca. 1710
silk plain, satin and twill weaves with silk and metallic
    supplementary weft (brocade)
90 x 84 (228 x 213) warp x weft
Emma Harter Sweetser Fund 82.29

Its location between two major rivers made Lyon the focal point for trade to Paris, Italy, Switzerland, and Germany.[51] The important position held by its pattern designers contributed to the city's dominance over the silk industry. Well paid and highly regarded, they consequently produced the best work in Europe at the time. Their active relationship with merchants who distributed the fabrics set the standard for the annual change of silk patterns, which were imitated all over Europe.

This particular silk was designed in what is known as the "bizarre" style. There has been much speculation about the origins of and influences on silk design during this period, which lasted from about 1705 to 1720,[52] but it appears to be a perfectly logical combination of several previous developments and new elements. The illogic of these pieces resides in their designs, where large sweeping volutes end in delicate flowers, and writhing columns have draped baldachinos tied at the bottom with tiny ribbons. Tables that turn into balustrades support delicate oriental vessels, which hold bouquets of flowers executed in a completely different scale. In fact, the fashion for archways, diagonal screens, and balustrades was a new idiom in textile design introduced in 1707.[53]

This entire design is underlaid with a delicate trellis shadow pattern of other floral forms that are apparently unrelated to what lies on top of them. The shadow effect of the background weave was rooted in seventeenth-century subpatterns, which were introduced in an attempt to imbue design with depth.[54] Twisted columns and large-scale flowers with turning leaves also expressed Baroque taste in the late seventeenth-century manner. All the elements that compose this design are easily traced, but the way in which they are rearranged is clearly unique. This particular phenomenon must have arisen from the general desire for the exotic that marks the early eighteenth century. Many foreign influences were flowing into Europe during the period, and this eclectic fashion merely reflects the resulting diversity of taste.

Materials
  Basic fabric
    warp: silk, single-ply slight Z-twist; white
    weft: silk, no twist; white
    continuous supplementary weft:
      silk, no twist; dark green
    discontinuous supplementary weft:
      silk, no twist; light green, light blue, light red, light
        violet, two light oranges
    metallic #1
      core thread: silk, no twist; white
      strip: silver with gold and copper, S-twist; gold colored
    metallic #2
      core thread: silk, two-ply overspun Z-twist; white
      strip: silver with gold and copper, S-twist; gold colored,
        core exposed
Techniques
  Warp-faced 3/1 diagonal twill weave (background), warp-
    faced 4/1 satin weave (background), warp-faced plain
    weave (background), weft-dominant 3/1 diagonal twill
    weave (figure), and weft-faced floats bound in a diagonal
    twill alignment (figure); with continuous and
    discontinuous supplementary weft
      proportions: one continuous and one discontinuous
        supplementary weft per one main weft
  Selvedge: ½ in. (1.1 cm) wide, warp-faced satin weave in
    light red-orange and white stripes and with outer three
    warps of thick white silk cord
  Four panels sewn together at selvedges with seams
Thread count
  Basic fabric
    warp: 153   weft: 47
    continuous supplementary weft: 47
    discontinuous supplementary weft: 47
Pattern repeat
  warpwise: 16–18 in. (41.0–46.0 cm)
  weftwise: 17 in. (43.0 cm)

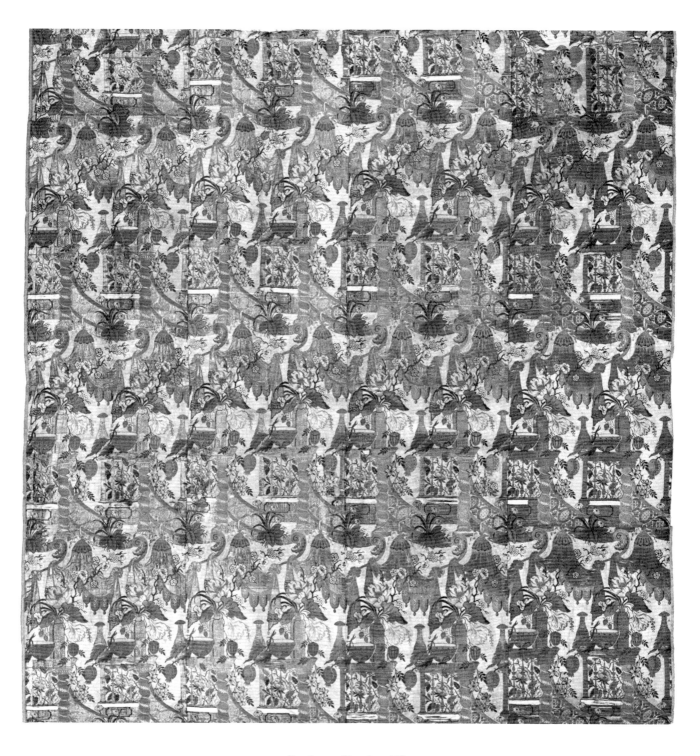

Catalogue Number 112

Catalogue Number 112, Detail

Catalogue Number 113
Town of Lyon, France
Garment or Furnishing Fabric, ca. 1735
silk plain and twill weaves with silk supplementary warp and
    silk and metallic supplementary weft (brocade)
90½ x 61½ (229.5 x 156) warp x weft
Gift of Mr. and Mrs. R. Kirby Whyte 70.114.2

In this piece the grace of the flowers' drooping petals indicates it belongs to the period of silk design that followed the one in which "bizarre" and "lace" patterning were popular. Another favorite device during this time was introducing landscape and architectural elements seen through a grotto.[55] Here, the little buildings contain chinoiserie elements, which were also popular at the time. The ribbed brown background is figured with colored flowers and the architectural vista, in black and white.

Materials
  Basic fabric
    warp: silk, single-ply slight S-twist; brown
    weft: silk, no twist; brown
    supplementary warp: silk, single-ply slight S-twist; brown
    supplementary weft:
      silk, no twist; white, light and medium blue, light and
        medium red, light and medium orange, light and
        medium green, brown
      metallic #1
        core thread: silk, single-ply S-twist; white
        strip: silver with gold and copper, S-twist; silver
          colored
      metallic #2
        core thread: silk, two-ply S-twist with one ply
          overspun; white
        strip: silver with gold and copper, S-twist; silver
          colored, core exposed
Techniques
  Warp-faced plain weave (background) and weft-faced floats
    bound in a diagonal twill alignment (figure), with
    supplementary warp and discontinuous
    supplementary weft
      proportions: two supplementary warps per one main
        warp, one or one pair supplementary weft per one
        main weft
  Selvedge: ¼ in. (0.6 cm) wide, weft-dominant plain weave
    with six thick white silk cords as warp
  Three panels sewn together with seams at selvedges
Thread count
  Basic fabric
    warp: 118   weft: 62   supplementary warp: 23
    supplementary weft: 62 threads or 62 pairs (124 threads)
Pattern repeat
  warpwise: 17¼–17¾ in. (44–45 cm) weftwise: point repeat

Catalogue Number 114 (see color plate, p. 55)
Town of Lyon, France
Garment or Furnishing Fabric, ca. 1735
silk plain and twill weaves with silk supplementary warp and
    silk and metallic supplementary weft (brocade)
95 x 84½ (240.5 x 214) warp x weft
Emma Harter Sweetser Fund 81.5

In the 1730s large-scale, naturalistic, heavy fruits and flowers dominated French fabric design. Jean Revel, probably the most famous Lyon designer, was credited with developing the particular aspects of drawing and shading associated with these patterns. Born in 1684, Revel was designing silks by 1730. He invented "points rentrés," a technique that used interlocking joins of two differently colored supplementary wefts to heighten the subtle effects of shading and give a fuzzy quality to outlines.[56]

Here, the realism achieved with silk threads is astounding. Unlike the vessel in cat. 104, this shell-shaped container is volumetric and shoots out into space with a prowlike form, an effect created by the dramatic use of light and shade. Surrounding the fruit filled container are swirls of silver threads reminiscent of the ogival borders of earlier centuries, but here they are softened into Rococo clouds. Underlying all of this is a lovely pattern of small flowers that covers the entire background—a magnificent design conception worthy of Revel himself.

Materials
Basic fabric
    warp: silk, single-ply S-twist; green
    weft: silk, no twist; dark green
    supplementary warp: silk, single-ply S-twist; light green
        or green
    continuous supplementary weft:
        silk, no twist; brown
    discontinuous supplementary weft:
        silk, no twist; two yellows, two light greens, two light
        reds, red, light and medium brown, light and medium
        blue, two light oranges, white
    metallic #1
        core thread: silk, no twist; white
        strip: silver with gold and copper, S-twist; silver
            colored
    metallic #2
        core thread: silk, two ply overspun Z-twist; white
        strip: silver with gold and copper, S-twist; silver
            colored, core exposed
Trim
    warp: silk, single-ply Z-twist; white
    weft:
        metallic #3
        core thread: silk, single-ply Z-twist; white
        strip: silver with gold and copper, S-twist; silver
            colored
    supplementary weft:
        metallic #4
        flat strip only: silver with gold and copper; silver
            colored

Techniques
Weft-dominant plain weave (background), warp-faced
    floats in plain weave alignment (background), and weft-
    faced floats bound in a diagonal twill alignment (figure);
    with supplementary warp and continuous and
    discontinuous supplementary weft
    proportions: two supplementary warps per one main
        warp, one continuous and one discontinuous
        supplementary weft per two main wefts
Selvedge: ¼ in. (0.7 cm) wide, warp-faced diagonal twill
    weave of yellow, light red, green, and white stripes
Four panels sewn together at selvedges with seams
Trim: woven band of weft-faced plain weave and
    weft-faced floats, with discontinuous supplementary weft

Thread count
Basic fabric
    warp: 112   weft: 50   supplementary warp: 224
    continuous supplementary weft: 50
    discontinuous supplementary weft: 50

Pattern repeat
    warpwise: 17 in. (43.0 cm)   weftwise: full width

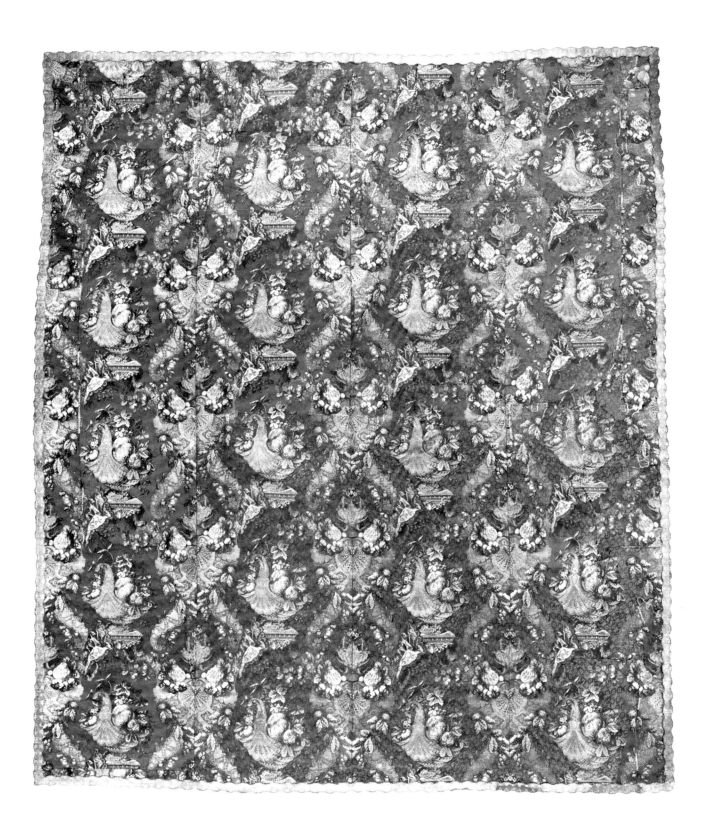

263

Catalogue Number 115
Spain
Fragment from Ecclesiastical Vestment, ca. 1700
silk plain weave with silk supplementary warp and metallic
    supplementary weft (brocade)
45 x 35 (114 x 89) warp x weft
Gift of Eliza M. Niblack 30.916

This extraordinary black silk patterned with gold probably belonged to a vestment. Black vestments were worn during times of mourning, either for a funeral or Good Friday. The symbols woven into this cloth are emblematic of the famous pilgrimage shrine of Santiago de Compostela. In the center of the panel is a cartouche containing a sword with decorative pommel that is flanked by shells. This emblem is reported to represent the Order of St. James of the Sword, which protected pilgrims from Moorish attack.[57] Beneath and above it is the papal emblem of the three-tiered hat and the staffs with three graduated bars, an allusion to Pope Urban II's placement of Santiago de Compostela under control of the Holy See in the eleventh century.[58] The pilgrim's wide-brimmed hat and staff, which appear beneath the papal crown, are symbolic of St. James,[59] as well as of the archbishop of the See of Santiago (who was also a cardinal). On either side of these devices are stools or thrones topped with crowns. These symbols allude to the diocese's fealty to its patron, the King of Spain. Above and beneath the thrones are urns with two stars, symbolizing the Sepulchre of St. James. According to Spanish tradition, *Campus Stellae* is his burial place. The name later degenerated to Compostela, and these devices are also found on the coat of arms of that city.[60] The scroll-shaped floral vines and cartouche belong to the late Baroque decorative vocabulary, combined with a hint of Chinese design influence. In sum, this glorious fabric must have been a dramatic vestment.

Materials
  Basic fabric
    warp: silk, single-ply slight S-twist; brown
    weft: silk, no twist; brown
    supplementary warp:
      silk, single-ply slight S-twist; yellow
    supplementary weft:
      metallic #1
        core thread: silk, single-ply Z-twist; light yellow
        strip: gold and silver with copper, S-twist; gold colored
      metallic #2
        core thread: silk, two-ply Z-twist with one ply
          overspun; white
        strip: gold and silver with copper, S-twist; gold colored,
          core exposed
Techniques
  Warp-faced plain weave (background) and weft-faced floats
    bound in a diagonal twill alignment (figure), with
    supplementary binding warp and discontinuous
    supplementary weft, some paired supplementary weft
      proportions: one supplementary warp per four main
        warps, one or one pair supplementary weft per one
        main weft
  Selvedge: ¼ in. (0.5 cm) wide, balanced plain weave of
    white and dark green stripes
Thread count
  Basic fabric
    warp: 84   weft: 42   supplementary warp: 21
      supplementary weft: 42 threads or 42 pairs (84 threads)
Pattern repeat
  warpwise: 22 in. (56.0 cm)   weftwise: point repeat

Catalogue Number 123 (see color plate, p. 57)
Germany (?)
Woman's Apron, ca. 1760
silk plain weave, embroidered with silk and metallic thread
39 x 26 (99 x 66) weft x warp
Gift of Mr. and Mrs. W. J. Holliday, Sr. 70.46

The complexity of iconography and method of its combination into a decorative whole make this apron an interesting study.[71] In the eighteenth century an apron was worn over a skirt or open robe, under the stomacher. This particular piece still retains pleat marks and creases as well as stitch marks on the top, where it was probably folded over and sewn to a waist band. The pattern and creases dip in the center of the garment to accommodate the stomacher. When the apron was pleated, the five embroidered columns remained rigid and thus protruded, while the intervening blank silk fell to the back. Since the bottom panel was less disrupted by pleating, it was fully decorated.

On the top tier of the five decorative columns are various plants and flowers. The palm and tulip, both native to distant lands, suit the eighteenth-century taste for the exotic. Interspersed between each of the vignettes are arrangements of flora and fauna reminiscent of "bizarre" patterning (see cat. 112 and 116). The next row of the design is a series of "oriental" figures related more to the European vision of Cathay than to accurate ethnic costume types. Seated under parasols, the three central figures hold attributes, so they are probably rulers; the standing figures on the two outer bands may be servants. Below this group is another set of decorative elements, among them a shell, swags, and exotic birds and fruits.

The set of medallions in the next row, the largest group on the apron, represents mythological scenes. The first, on the far left, depicts a duel on a bridge in front of a castle. In the background, as on the rest of the apron, are buildings with steep roofs and towers. The next scene, showing the same architecture in the background, probably represents the Judgment of Paris. The dominant medallion in the center of the apron depicts the Colossus of Rhodes, the sixth of the Seven Wonders of the World. Though the other mythological scenes are taken from Ovid's *Metamorphosis*, this image is not: it may have been derived from a dictionary or compendium that illustrated the Seven Wonders. The next medallion, showing two groups of warriors battling on a bridge, may depict the siege of Troy. The final panel on the far right clearly illustrates the myth of Athena and Arachne. Since Arachne challenged Athena to a weaving contest in this tale, the scene certainly befits a textile of such magnificence.

Beneath the upper medallions is a variety of images, including symbols of war, more "bizarre" elements, and several kinds of birds and flowers. Near the bottom of the apron is another rank of medallions. On each end are blue and white cameos: the left one holds a woman with Roman hairdo in between the initials "F," on the left, and "I A," on the right; the companion cameo on the far right holds a man crowned with a laurel wreath and the initials "Q E." The two smaller medallions on either side of the central figure depict, on the left, Apollo and Daphne, who is changing into a laurel tree, and on the right, possibly Cepheus and Procris; the figure on the ground is run through with a spear, and the one standing is distraught. The central medallion may contain a portrait of the garment's owner. Seated in a typically Rococo, twisted pose, she wears a

flower-trimmed bergère hat and a necklace. Her laced bodice is decorated with a bosom flower, and she holds a feather muff and green fan. The artistic quality of this picture is far lower than that of the other scenes and figures: the pose is stiff and the face less expressive. Furthermore, the right arm is much too fat and the left one hard to place; the hat floats on the head; and the shading at the neck is very poorly handled. The background is done in cream and gold—two colors that are not juxtaposed elsewhere—and unlike the rest of the apron, has no shading. This portrait may have been drawn by an artist of less skill than the one who drew the rest of the apron or possibly even by an amateur. Along the bottom edge are various devices that could have come from printed pattern books: cornucopia, "oriental" figures (one of whom may be smoking an opium pipe), swans in a fountain, and other decorations.

After comparing this piece with other embroideries of the period, it was decided that, because of its eclectic combination and stiff organization of decorative elements, the apron probably was not executed in France or England. The two other possible places of origin are Germany or Holland.

Materials
   Basic fabric
      warp: silk, single-ply slight S-twist; white
      weft: silk, no twist; white
   Embroidery
      silk, no twist; white, tan, light and medium yellow, yellow-green, light and medium blue, light and medium blue-gray, light and medium brown-orange, light, medium and dark brown, light, medium and dark green, light and medium green-blue
   metallic #1
      core thread: silk, single-ply Z-twist; white
      strip: gold and silver with copper, S-twist; gold colored
   metallic #2
      core thread: silk, single-ply Z-twist; white
      strip: silver with gold and copper, S-twist; silver colored
   metallic #3
      core thread: silk, two-ply Z-twist; yellow
      strip: silver with copper, S-twist; silver colored
   metallic #4
      core thread: silk, two-ply Z-twist with one ply overspun; white
      strip: silver with copper, S-twist; silver colored, core exposed

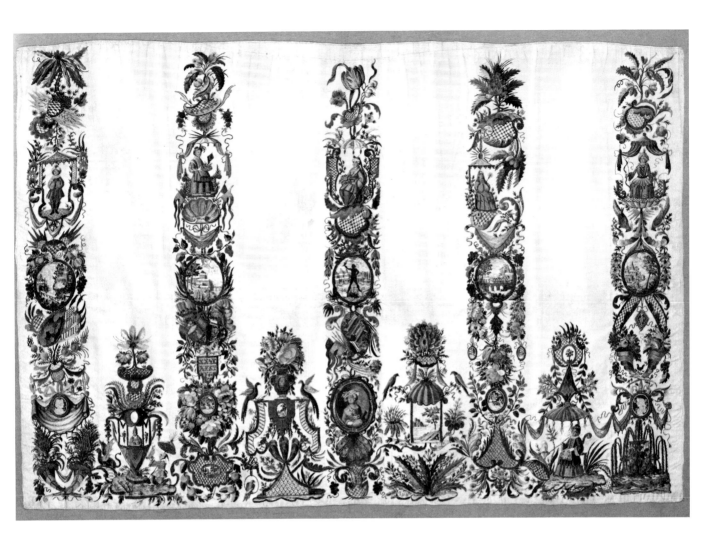

Techniques

Warp-dominant plain weave

Embroidery

flat stitches: pattern couching, couched braid; cross; fishbone; satin, long and short satin; back stitched seeding; stem; split; straight

looped stitches: Chinese knot; French knot

combination flat stitches: back over long and short satin; satin over long and short satin; stem over long and short satin; split over long and short satin; straight over long and short satin; couching held down with arrowhead; couching held down with cross

combination flat and looped stitches: trellis couching held down with back-stitched seedling or cross, interspersed with stitch or French knot

Thread count

Basic fabric

warp: 170   weft: 108

Literature

Lubell, *Textile Collections of the World*, p. 221.

Catalogue Number 124 (see color plate, p. 58)
France
Woman's Dress with Sleeve Ruffles, ca. 1760
dress: silk plain weave with silk supplementary warp and silk
   supplementary weft (brocade), trimmed with silk and
   chenille threads
sleeve ruffles: cotton plain weave, embroidered with linen
53½ (136) length, warp
Emma Harter Sweetser Fund 81.290, 82.10, and 82.11

The fabric in this gown is certainly in the delicate High Rococo mode, which from 1740 to 1770 was characterized by a retreat from naturalism. In the 1760s imitations of lace, ribbons, and even fur were added in interlaced meandering patterns.[72] Here the meanders consist of flowering vines and patterned areas reminiscent of lace or white work.

The cut of fashionable dress in the eighteenth century did not show dramatic changes from 1730 to 1770. The open robe seen here consists of a floor-length dress that opens in the front to reveal a stomacher at the top and a petticoat below. In the eighteenth century, dress backs were treated in three different ways: with yardage falling straight from the shoulders to the floor, called the sack; fitted at the back with the skirt to the floor, called the English gown (see cat. 125); and later, with the skirt drawn up by swags to expose the petticoat, called the *polonaise*.

This dress belongs to the type of open robe known as the sack. It has changed little since its creation. The form of the sack that had evolved by 1730 featured a long, flowing back. These dresses were made of costly silks with lavish trim for formal wear, and with sleeve ruffles of cheaper muslin drawnwork and a kerchief instead of expensive lace for daily wear.[73] This particular dress design probably originated in France. French styles were disseminated to England and elsewhere through fashion dolls which, until the end of the century, substituted for women's fashion periodicals.[74] A woman's stays, which were made to measure, shaped the small waist and rigid torso. The gown, then, was designed to conform to the shape of the stays rather than to that of the body.

Materials
   Basic fabric
      warp: silk, single-ply slight S-twist; light blue
      weft: silk, single-ply slight S-twist; light blue
      supplementary warp: silk, single-ply slight S-twist;
         light blue
      supplementary weft: silk, single-ply S-twist; white
   Sleeve ruffles
      warp: cotton, single-ply Z-twist; white
      weft: cotton, single-ply Z-twist; white
      embroidery: bast (linen), two-ply S-twist; white
Techniques
   Balanced plain weave (background), warp-faced floats and
      weft-faced floats in patterned alignment (figure), with
         supplementary warp and continuous supplementary weft
            proportions: one supplementary warp per one main
               warp, one group of three wefts per two main wefts
   Trim: pleated basic fabric, silk chenille yarn and silk floss
   Pieced garment with two-pieces: fitted bodice with attached
      skirt and underskirt
   Sleeve ruffles: balanced plain weave
   Embroidery
      flat stitches: back; eyelet; closed herringbone; satin
      looped stitches: buttonhole
      deflected element: back; variation of cushion filling;
         chessboard filling; detached eyelet; variation of
         diagonal chained border; variation of diagonal cross
         filling; diagonal drawn filling; double back filling;
         faggot; various Greek cross fillings; various pulled satin
         fillings; reversed faggot; reversed four sided; ridge;
         satin; variation of wave filling
Thread count
   Basic fabric
      warp: 176   weft: 98   supplementary warp: 176
      supplementary weft: 49 groups (147 threads)
   Sleeve ruffles
      warp: 60   weft: 76

Catalogue Number 125
Spitalfields Area, London, England
Woman's Dress, ca. 1760
silk plain and twill weaves with silk supplementary warp and
 weft (brocade), trimmed with silk and chenille thread
53 (134.5) length, warp
Orville A. and Elma D. Wilkinson Fund 76.255

The Worshipful Company of Weavers was founded in London in 1155. During the reign of James I in the seventeenth century, the English planted mulberry trees to develop sericulture and encouraged French silk weavers to immigrate to England and thus further strengthen its already important wool industry. Around 1675 Protestant Huguenot refugees settled just outside London, in a quarter near the Spitalfields market.[75]

A number of events aided the British silk weaving industry in the eighteenth century. The economic depression in France during the first two decades of the century and British dominance of sea trade allowed England a commanding position economically. Yet unlike France, England lacked a group of designers that worked within the weaving industry, and its internal regulation of quality control was far less strict. England finally was unable to compete profitably with France, though its silk weaving retained a character all its own.[76]

Through the Spitalfields sample books at the Victoria and Albert Museum, it has been determined that the silk in this garment was made between 1755 and 1760.[77] Its adaptation of full Rococo patterning is unusual in its use of pink, grey, and black to create flowers and zigzag striping. The dress underwent a number of alterations during its lifetime, and is pictured here in its second phase, as an open robe.

While the sack was worn for more formal occasions, the English gown, or night gown, as it was called in the eighteenth century, was informal wear developed from an earlier loose gown. The English gown was frequently worn with a quilted petticoat for warmth, and the usual hoops were then put aside.[78]

This garment was altered into all three of the fashionable forms of the eighteenth century.[79] First, the fullness was removed from the original sack, and the fabric combined with the extra sleeve ruffles to make a full petticoat. This petticoat replaced the old one, which probably had silk in the front alone. When the *polonaise* style became popular later in the eighteenth century, skirts were raised in a swag fashion through cords that were attached to buttons at the back waistline. This style had to be worn with a petticoat made of a fine fabric all the way around. The dress shown here, which retains its buttons, came to us with a considerably pieced petticoat. Both the dress and the petticoat were reconstructed in the English gown style.

Materials
 Basic fabric
  warp: silk, single-ply slight S-twist; light gray
  complementary weft: silk, single-ply slight S-twist; light red, black
  supplementary warp: silk, single-ply slight S-twist; light gray
  supplementary weft: silk, single-ply slight S-twist; light gray
Techniques
 Warp-faced plain weave, weft-faced floats in a diagonal twill alignment, weft-faced floats, and warp-faced floats forming weftwise ribbing; with paired complementary wefts, supplementary pattern warp and continuous supplementary binding weft
  proportions: one supplementary warp per two main warps, one supplementary weft per eight complementary wefts
 Trim: pleated basic fabric, chenille yarn and wrapped yarns
 Pieced garment with two pieces: bodice with attached skirt and underskirt
Thread count
 Basic fabric
  warp: 220   complementary weft: 84 pairs
  supplementary warp: 110   supplementary weft: 21
Pattern repeat
 warpwise: 10 in. (25.5 cm)   weftwise: 5 in. (13 cm)

Catalogue Number 126
France (?)
Man's Suit, ca. 1775
silk plain weave, embroidered with silk
36 (91.5) length of coat
21½ (54.5) length of waistcoat
23½ (60) length of breeches
Martha Delzell Memorial Fund 76.475

In the first half of the eighteenth century, the same fabrics were used in men's and women's clothing. When garment fabrics became lighter and less decorated around 1750, embroidery was increasingly used, especially in men's attire. Embroidery had for quite some time been popular, however, and during certain periods a heavily worked garment was often more costly than one of patterned silk. Earlier in the eighteenth century, heavy brocades and embroideries with lace collars and cuffs were *de rigueur* but taste in decoration later changed radically, especially toward the end of the century. The lighter, playful mode of the late Rococo often used single flowers or small clusters in delicate arrangements.

An eighteenth-century suit of clothes included a coat, a waistcoat, and breeches. Often, the waistcoat was of a different color than the other two garments, and was the most highly decorated of the three.[80] By the third quarter of the eighteenth century, the long jacket skirts of earlier periods had become abbreviated: the front was cut back and pleats fell to the rear. With the bulk of the coat and waistcoat in the back, breeches were altered so they covered the front opening with a flap. White stockings and closely fitted breeches were characteristic of the 1700s.[81] A gentleman probably wore a cravat, delicately patterned with end panels of lace, with this embroidered brown silk suit.

Materials
  Basic fabric
    warp: silk, no twist; dark brown
    weft: silk, no twist; yellow-brown
  Embroidery
    silk, no twist; light and medium blue, light and dark orange, light and medium green, light and medium blue-green, yellow-green, white, light brown
    silk, two-ply Z-twist; white
  Lining
    warp: bast (linen), single-ply Z-twist; light tan
    weft: bast (linen), single-ply Z-twist; light tan
Techniques
  Warp dominant plain weave
  Embroidery
    flat stitches: satin, padded satin; split; stem; straight
    looped stitches: French knot
    combination flat stitches: satin over satin
  Selvedge: ½ in. (1.3 cm) wide of warp-faced plain weave in orange and white stripes
  Pieced garment with three pieces: coat, waistcoat, and breeches
  Trim: embroidered cloth covered buttons
  Lining: balanced plain weave
Thread count
  Basic fabric
    warp: 192   weft: 66
  Lining
    warp: 46   weft: 60

Catalogue Number 127
France (?)
Yardage for a Man's Vest, ca. 1780
silk satin weave, embroidered with silk, metallic thread, and
    sequins
36 x 22 (91.5 x 56) warp x weft
Eliza M. and Sarah L. Niblack Collection 33.1096

At the end of the eighteenth century, embroidery became increasingly delicate and discreet; tiny isolated flower buds and
sprigs decorated the edges of garments. This particular piece
is noteworthy because it is uncut white satin yardage for a man's
waistcoat. Such pieces were executed in shops, where professional male and female embroiderers worked on lengths of silk
stretched on a frame. The finished yardage was purchased and
taken to a tailor, who cut the forms and assembled them; he
used the extra flowers that had been worked at the bottom of
the fabric to cover the buttons. The back of the garment was
made of cotton. The embroidery is so ingeniously placed that
barely a scrap of fabric was wasted. In the 1780s there was a
mania for men's embroidered waistcoats, and a wealthy man of
fashion might have owned several hundred of them.[82]

Materials
    Basic fabric
        warp: silk, single-ply S-twist; white
        weft: silk, single-ply slight S-twist; white
    Embroidery
        silk, no twist; light green, light red, light blue, yellow
        silk, two-ply S-twist; light red, brown-yellow
        metallic
            core thread: silk, no twist; white
            strip: silver, S-twist; gray-silver colored
        metallic sequins: flat and convex round discs; silver
            colored
Techniques
    Warp-faced 4/1 satin weave
    Embroidery
        flat stitches: Roumanian; satin; straight
        looped stitches: chain
        sequins attached with back stitch
Thread count
    Basic fabric
        warp: 245   weft: 131

Catalogue Number 128
France (?)
Garment or Furnishing Fabric, 1775
silk plain weave with metallic supplementary weft,
    embroidered with silk, metallic thread, sequins, and gems
24½ x 18½ (47 x 62) warp x weft
James V. Sweetser Fund 80.378

This elegant embroidered silk epitomizes Louis XVI style.
Small motifs are arranged in alternating rows that are rather
widely spaced to create an open, airy effect. The yellow silk
background is shot with gold supplementary wefts and embroidered with rose and white, with additional bands of sequins
applied to the surface.

Materials
Basic fabric
    warp: silk, no twist; yellow
    weft: silk, no twist; yellow
    supplementary weft:
        metallic #1
            core thread: silk, single-ply S-twist; white
            strip: silver with gold and copper, S-twist; gold
                colored
Embroidery
    silk, no twist; violet-red, white
    silk, two-ply S-twist; white
    metallic #2
        round wire and flat strips only: silver with gold and
            copper; silver colored
    sequins: flat discs, convex discs, violet glass gems, and
        violet-red metallic discs

Techniques
Warp-dominant plain weave and weft-faced floats bound
    in a plain weave alignment, with continuous
    supplementary weft
        proportions: one supplementary weft per two main
            wefts
Selvedge: ¼ in. (0.4 cm) wide of seven cords of two-ply
    S-twist white silk in plain weave
Embroidery
    flat stitches: satin
    looped stitches: French knot

Thread count
Basic fabric
    warp: 152   weft: 40   supplementary weft: 20

Catalogue Number 129
United States or England
Furnishing Fabric, ca. 1775
cotton plain weave, resist dyed
78 x 70 (198 x 177.5) weft x warp
Emma Harter Sweetser Fund 81.289

These indigo blue dyed textiles have caused much controversy because of their rarity and technique as well as the lack of documentation of their manufacturer's location. One theory proposes that they were made in England and exported to America,[83] while another states it is more likely they were actually made in America.[84] One piece[85] carries an English excise stamp dated 1766 (similar to the one found on cat. 133), and several of the finished bed coverings have edgings known to have been imported from England to America. No pieces of this type have ever been found in Europe, however; all those of known origin have come from New England, in the area surrounding the Hudson River. Their origin is thus frequently designated "Hudson River Valley."

There is also disagreement on the method of the patterns' production. One scholar believes they were made with the "china blue" technique,[86] another, with pattern-resisted indigo dye.[87] Indigo blue dye has an ancient history: the first records date from the first century A.D., and both Vitruvius and Dioscorides refer to the dye plant. The *Periplus of the Erythrian Sea*, a navigational guide for the Indian Ocean from around A.D. 60, mentions the export of Indian indigo to Egypt. *Indigofera tinctoria*, the plant that produced the most potent color, was—and still is—grown in parts of Africa, Asia, the Americas, and Australia.[88]

Unlike other dye materials, indigo is insoluble in water. It requires an alkaline solution to suspend it in the dyebath and oxidation to develop its lustrous, permanent blue color. Because controlling the oxidation proved to be quite a difficult feat, dyeing with resists, which required dipping the whole cloth into a dye vat, was the accepted way to use this dye before the nineteenth century in Europe. In 1730 a method was invented to slow the oxidation process by adding the thickening agent orpiment. By 1846 the indigo mixture had been improved enough that it could be printed directly with woodblocks. "China blue," another advance in the application of indigo, was developed early in the nineteenth century. In this method the viscous medium holds the indigo in suspension; the dye oxidizes and bonds with the cloth after it has been dipped in vats of ferrous sulphate and lime.[89] This technique was also used in printing with copper plates and rollers.

This piece appears to have been colored through resist application to the surface and vat dyeing. The first step was to apply resist paste with blocks, and probably also by hand, to all of the areas to remain white. After the resist dried, the cloth was dipped into the indigo vat and exposed to the air to achieve the light blue color. When the indigo had dried, the dyer again placed the cloth on the table and used blocks to apply more resist to the areas that would remain light blue. Finally, the cloth was redipped several times into the indigo vat; when sufficiently dark, the cloth was removed and the resist paste washed out to reveal the white and the light and dark blue patterns.[90] The general appearance of the cloths, which show drips of resist material and irregular design outlines, indicate they were patterned with a resist technique. Because it directly printed a

viscous material, "china blue" should have been a more precise method, but evidence indicates that this technique was not perfected until late in the eighteenth century, and printing a lighter color over a darker one was particularly difficult.[91] The problems of the textiles' origin and method thus remain unresolved.

Materials
   Basic fabric
      warp: cotton, single-ply Z-twist; white
      weft: cotton, single-ply Z-twist; white
      dye: medium and dark blue
Techniques
   Balanced plain weave
   Resist dyed with printed or painted wax resist
   Two panels sewn together at selvedges after dyeing
Thread count
   Basic fabric
      warp: 56   weft: 46
Pattern repeat
   warpwise: 27½ in. (70.0 cm)   weftwise: 20 in. (51.0 cm)

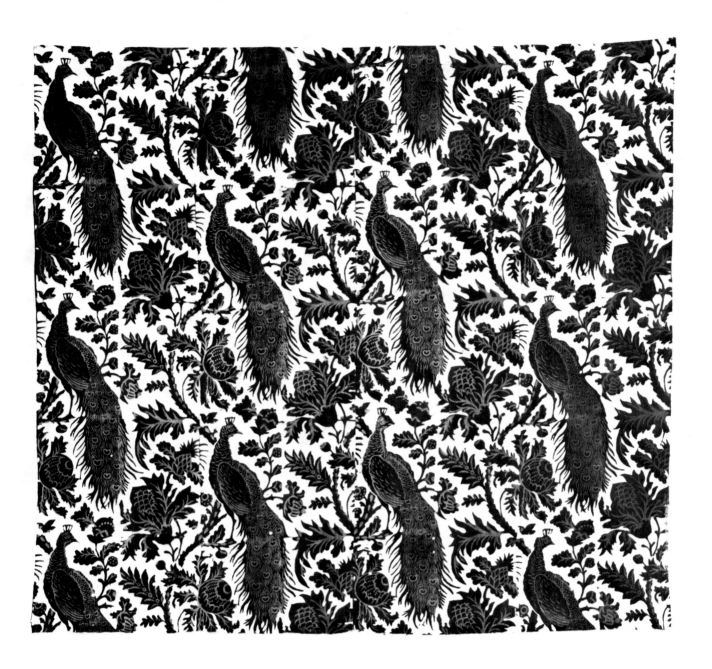

Catalogue Number 130
Jean-Baptiste Huet (1783-1811), Town of Jouy, France
Furnishing Fabric, *Le Sacrifice à l'Amour*, 1804
cotton plain weave, copper plate printed
50½ x 38¾ (128 x 98.5) warp x weft
Eliza M. and Sarah L. Niblack Collection 33.1257

The Oberkampf manufacturing plant established at Jouy, on the Bievre River, produced its first printed goods in 1760—just after government edicts that prohibited cotton printing had been revoked. A major innovation in this technology occurred in 1770, when the first press for copper plate printing was installed. It involved placing the plate in a carriage that slid back and forth under a pressure roller. Engraving the plate, which originally measured 3 ft. 9 in. x 2 ft. 3½ in., was a lengthy process that often took as long as six months. Although only a small percentage of the total volume of the Jouy manufactory was involved with making these fabrics, the prestige of the company rested so completely on their excellence that any large-scale monochromatic furnishing fabric made on this model continues to be known as *toile de Jouy*.

Perhaps the height of Christophe Oberkampf's career came on June 20, 1806, when the Emperor Napoleon and the Empress Josephine paid a surprise visit to the plant. Napoleon was so impressed with what he saw that he bestowed his own Cross of the Legion of Honor on Oberkampf.[92]

Chief designer Jean-Baptiste Huet, who executed his first Jouy pattern in 1783, greatly contributed to the prestige of this fabric. Huet's figural compositions have been described as "translating the entire universe in terms of Dresden figures."[93] The figures may be markedly idealized, but the liveliness of the animals is the true hallmark of his style. He imparts a kind of Neoclassic romanticism to the scene: a women in Neoclassic dress offers a sacrificial lamb to the god of love, who is installed on a pedestal like a classical statue. Below him is a knife and a basin for the sacrificial blood. Furthermore, cavorting children and a mother in contemporary dress are combined with other classical elements, such as a stone relief, in the idealized landscape. All of these allusions are rooted in the seventeenth- and eighteenth-century fascination with *fête champêtre*, or idealized people cavorting in an imaginary landscape. This taste was to change when the full effects of the revolution and the ensuing financial depression were realized.

Materials
  Basic fabric
    warp: cotton, single-ply Z-twist; tan
    weft: cotton, single-ply Z-twist; tan
    dye/pigment: brown
Techniques
  Balanced plain weave
  Copper plate printed, one color, printed to within ⅝ in. (1.7 cm) of selvedge on one side, 1⅝ in. (4.0 cm) on the other side
  Selvedge: ¼ in. (0.6 cm) wide, warp-dominant plain weave with doubled warps
Thread count
  Basic fabric
    warp: 45   weft: 51
Pattern repeat
  warpwise: 39 in. (99.0 cm)   weftwise: full width

Catalogue Number 131
Louis-Hippolyte Lebas (1782-1867), Town of Jouy, France
Furnishing Fabric, *Là Marchande d'Amour*, ca. 1817
cotton plain weave, copper roller printed
52½ x 38¼ (133 x 97) warp x weft
Eliza M. and Sarah L. Niblack Collection 33.1256

At the turn of the nineteenth century, style in design was changing from free-flowing, elaborate scenes to a new architectural composition that was framed by a figured ground.[94] A technical innovation, the copper roller eased the stylistic change, and the Oberkampf plant, the first to employ the copper plate in mass production, led the industry. The image was engraved on a cylinder rather than printed from a flat plate. The continuous printing saved enormous amounts of time: one machine could produce 5,400 yards of printed goods a day, an amount that previously would have taken the time of forty-two block printers. Coupled with an invention that mechanized engraving, this innovation reduced a process that had lasted six months to five or six days. The Oberkampf company was consequently able to supply even its competitors with superior goods.[95]

The company's peak, during the Napoleonic years, was soon curtailed by war and depression. In 1813 the Oberkampf establishment showed its first deficit and laid off workers. The strain probably contributed to Christophe Oberkampf's death in 1815, after which the family reorganized control of the operation. Their master designer Huet had also died, and they now hired eminent artists of the day to execute their designs. Among these artists was architect Hippolyte Lebas, who produced four designs for the firm from 1815 to 1818.[96] The classicism then in vogue is fully displayed here through cameo medallions and putti. *The Merchant of Love*, the title design shown in the main medallion, comes from a Roman painting discovered in 1759 at Gragnano, a suburb of Naples. During a 1776 trip to Rome, Jacques-Louis David made a copy of the engraving Vien did after the Gragnano painting. Entitled *Marchand à la Toilette*, the engraving was originally published in *Le Antichità de Ercolano* in 1762. Lebas's version is very close to the David drawing.[97] Underneath this medallion is one that may represent Hercules, who is shown riding a lion. His attributes—a bow, a club, and a distaff—are displayed above the medallion.

The other large medallion is more enigmatic. The winged figure who breaks a bow as he stands on a wing may represent Time. If so, the image could allude to Time overcoming Love, for Venus consoles a wingless Cupid while Time breaks his bow. Above this medallion are Time's attributes, a winged hourglass surrounded by a snake biting its tail. In the shell-shaped medallion, Cupid sails on his quiver and bow, using arrows as oars and his torch as a mast. None of these scenes is known from Greek mythology, although they may be after Roman paintings. The small, round medallions contain vignettes of Cupid sharpening his arrows and of Cupid and Psyche, who is shown winged like a butterfly, her symbol. Below Cupid's torch is a medallion holding a butterfly, and below the pair of doves representing Venus are two loving cherubs.

Materials
 Basic fabric
  warp: cotton, single-ply Z-twist; light tan
  weft: cotton, single-ply Z-twist; light tan
  dye/pigment: violet-red
Techniques
 Balanced plain weave
 Copper roller printed, one color, printed to selvedges
 Selvedge: ³⁄₁₆ in. (0.5 cm) wide, balanced plain weave with
  slightly denser warp
Thread count
 Basic fabric
  warp: 86   weft: 92
Pattern repeat
 warpwise: 20 in. (51.0 cm)   weftwise: full width

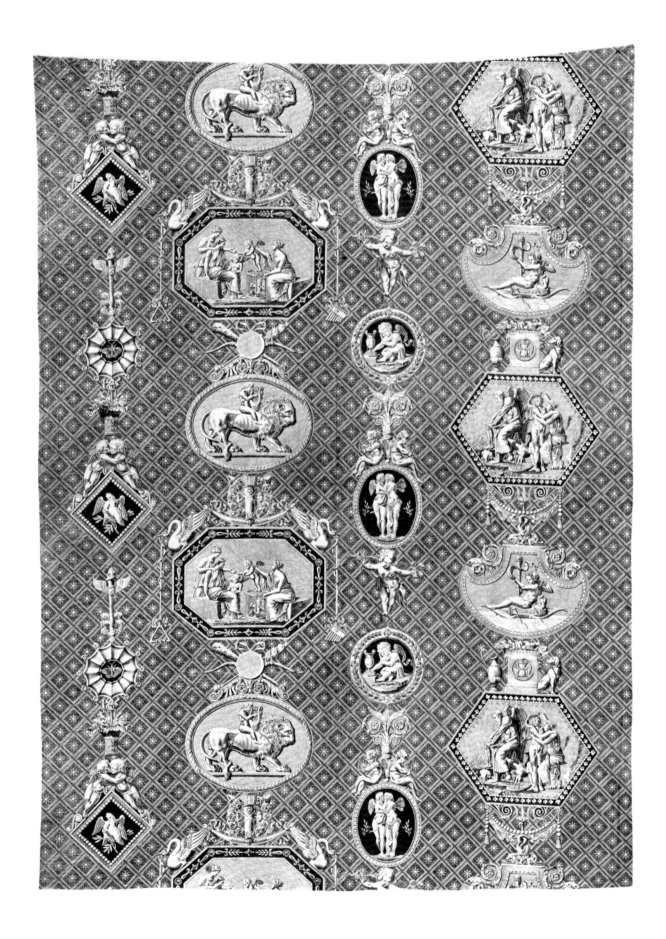

Catalogue Number 132
Town of Nantes or Rouen, France
Furnishing Fabric, ca. 1820
cotton plain weave, copper roller printed
92¾ x 28½ (235.5 x 72.5) warp x weft
Gift of Mrs. Louis H. Levey 51.61

Though none of them held the status that Jouy did (see cat. 130 and 131), a number of other towns in France were known for printed cotton goods and supplied them in great quantities to all levels of society. This particular roller print of romantic scenes in the countryside is typical of its genre. Each of the scenes carries a subtitle: *Le Délassement* (Diversion), *L'Agneu* [sic] *Chéri* (The Beloved Lamb), *Le Berger Constant* (The Loyal Swain), and *La Déclaration* (The Announcement).

The large scale and complicated compositional arrangement apparent in the Huet Jouy piece (see cat. 130) are here smaller and rather more blocky. The shorter pattern repeat is characteristic of roller prints because they could be made only so large; copper plate sizes were less restricted. Certainly no designer working at the time could equal the inspiration of Huet: this piece obviously has charm, but lacks the monumental scope that typifies work from the Jouy manufactory. The piece is signed "Duquet D S" in the plate *La Déclaration*.[98]

Materials
    Basic fabric
        warp: cotton, single-ply Z-twist; white
        weft: cotton, single-ply Z-twist; white
        dye/pigment: red
Techniques
    Balanced plain weave
    Copper roller printed, one color, printed to selvedges
    Selvedge: 1/16 in. (0.3 cm) wide, balanced plain weave with
      outer two warp ends tripled
Thread count
    Basic fabric
      warp: 59   weft: 66
Pattern repeat
    warpwise: 22 in. (56.0 cm)   weftwise: full width

Catalogue Number 133
John Lowe & Co., Shepley Hall, Town of Lancashire,
    England
Furnishing Fabric, ca. 1830
cotton plain weave, roller and block printed
38¾ x 26 (98.5 x 66) warp x weft
Eliza M. and Sarah L. Niblack Collection 33.1271

By the turn of the eighteenth century English printers had mastered colorfast block printing in a limited range of colors, and edicts banning the import, use, and wear of Indian cottons had stimulated local industry. By 1752 Francis Nixon had set up the Drumcondra Printworks in Dublin. In 1761 he moved his company to Lancashire,[99] which was to become the major center in Britain for cotton printing. Designs for cottons were largely controlled by London drapers such as Richard Ovey of Covent Garden, who commissioned patterns from artists and sent them to printing establishments to be executed.

Around the turn of the nineteenth century, madder, indigo, and quercitron were being used to color cottons in red, blue, and yellow.[100] This particular piece was printed in red with an engraved roller and overprinted in blue and yellow with woodblocks or a wooden surface roller. It has been suggested that misregistered colors, as are apparent here, were printed with the "Union Printing Machine" patented by Adam Parkinson in 1810. This device combined engraved and surface printing into one operation.[101] The graceful intertwining vines and delicate flowers are reminiscent of the Rococo, mixed here with a healthy dose of Indian cotton design. The mark of the manufactory and the excise stamp are printed on the bottom of the reverse side of this piece (see detail below).

Materials
  Basic fabric
    warp: cotton, single-ply Z-twist; tan
    weft: cotton, single-ply Z-twist; tan
    dyes/pigments: red, yellow, blue, green
Techniques
  Balanced plain weave
  Copper roller and woodblock (or roller) printed in three
    colors, producing four colors, printed to selvedge, glazed
  Marker printed on back side "JOHN LOWE and COMPY,
    Shepley Hall, Furniture Printers"
Thread count
  Basic fabric
    warp: 83   weft: 86
Pattern repeat
  warpwise: 14½ in. (37.0 cm)   weftwise: full width

297

Catalogue Number 134 (see color plate, p. 59)
William Morris (1834-96), England
Furnishing Fabric, *Honeysuckle*, 1876
cotton plain weave, block printed
70 x 40 (177.5 x 101.5) warp x weft
Gift of Miss Charity Dye 20.112

The firm of Morris, Marshall, Faulkner and Company was founded on April 11, 1861, to execute mural designs, architectural sculpture, metalwork, furniture, and furnishing fabrics. At the International Exhibition in South Kensington in 1862, the firm was awarded two gold medals and, consequently, achieved its first commercial success that year.[102] Nonetheless the company did not begin to manufacture textiles until 1873, after establishing its reputation in wallpaper design.

William Morris's production methods were particularly difficult because he wanted to print fabrics with woodblocks and use natural dyes. Because late nineteenth-century textile manufacture was highly industrialized and accustomed to chemical dyes, Morris had great difficulty finding a firm that would meet his standards in printing with such materials. *Honeysuckle*, one of his first printed cottons, was done at Thomas Wardle's Dyeworks in Leek, Staffordshire. Morris wrote Wardle in 1876 that "Honeysuckle has cost me a lot of blocks, and is one of the most important we have or are likely to have."[103] All the dyes on this piece were applied with blocks, except for the resist-dyed indigo. Morris believed that natural dyes should be used because, unlike the chemical dyes of the period, they were intrinsically beautiful and permanent; furthermore, he thought the rules imposed by their use would discipline patterning.[104]

At this time Morris was working at the South Kensington Museum (later to become the Victoria and Albert Museum) as an examiner of student work. His earlier experience designing woven textiles had aroused his interest in the medieval textiles in the museum's collection, which he had studied in some depth. The mirror image or "turn over" evident in this piece is more characteristic of a woven pattern than it is of one drawn for woodblock printing,[105] and Morris's use of it probably stemmed from his interest in historical weaving.

Morris's influence on future design was as significant to the twentieth century as Oberkampf's had been to the nineteenth. A hallmark of the Industrial Revolution, Jouy's efficiency made Europe dominant in printed fabrics and set the stage for the reaction of the late nineteenth century. In stimulating this response, Morris helped to launch a new fashion.

Materials
Basic fabric
warp: cotton, single-ply Z-twist; tan
weft: cotton, single-ply Z-twist; tan
dyes/pigments: two light reds, medium red, light blue, medium blue, light brown, medium green, black

Techniques
Balanced plain weave, weft thicker than warp
Block printed, six colors, printed to within 1¾ in. (4.5 cm) of selvedge on one side, 2½ in. (6.5 cm) on the other
Marker printed in selvedge "MORRIS & COMPANY, 449 OXFORD STREET"

Thread count
Basic fabric
warp: 55   weft: 35

Pattern repeat
warpwise: 29¾ in. (75.5 cm)   weftwise: point repeat

Catalogue Number 135
Town of Paisley, Scotland or France
Woman's Wrapper (plaid), ca. 1855
wool and silk twill weave with wool supplementary weft
145½ x 62½ (369 x 158.5) with fringe, warp x weft
Gift of Mary Alice Sloan 30.133

The history of the "Paisley" shawl is bound up in the annals of the Indo-European trade. Just as dyed cottons (see cat. 27 and 29) from India were the fashion rage of the eighteenth century, woven wool shawls from the northern Indian region of Kashmir became a craze in the nineteenth. By 1777 the Indian shawls had become popular in England as a costume accessory and were especially valued for their warmth and softness.[106] Around the turn of the nineteenth century, European fashion made a major shift from stiff, corseted costume to soft, form-revealing dress, so the simultaneous introduction of this luxury item of trade was propitious. Women abandoned their heavy, enveloping cloaks for softly draping Kashmiri shawls that enhanced the clinging character of Empire dress. The most popular shawl shape was the plaid, a long rectangle, measuring twelve by five feet, which was worn folded in the middle and draped over the shoulders. Square shawls (see cat. 31) and smaller scarves were next in popularity.

In Europe, both Norwich and Edinburgh were pioneers in early shawl weaving. The first shawls these centers produced were woven on harness patterning looms, which were popular at the time. The weavers soon discovered that the fine wool yarn, used in India to pattern shawls on a tapestry loom, broke on a harness loom. Because silk fibers were stronger and more elastic than wool, as well as more familiar to the weavers, the warps of European shawls came to be made completely of silk or of a combination of silk and wool. Once these technical problems were resolved, European shawls were able to compete with their imported Indian prototypes.

Paisley, Scotland, eventually became the center of European shawl weaving. During the eighteenth century emigrating Spitalfields weavers had helped to develop a Scottish silk industry.[107] Around 1800 a decline in the popularity of silk in favor of cotton muslin forced Paisley weavers to adapt to the vagaries of fashion. Initially, they copied successful Norwich and Edinburgh shawls, but developed a more efficient system of production and took the lead in about 1820. Until its shawls fell out of use about 1870, the city dominated the field so completely that all shawls of this type, whether European or Indian, were called "Paisleys," and even the basic teardrop motif used today is referred to as a paisley.

Until about 1840 shawl weaving in Paisley was a cottage industry. Weavers worked alone, or in groups of four to six in the cottage of the master weaver.[108] In the early days of the industry when the drawloom was still used, the master weaver frequently executed his own designs. Between 1825 and 1840, however, a number of specialists became involved in the process, among them a pattern drafter; tiers of the warp thread and the pattern strings; the warp stainer, who colored the warps; the beamer, who fixed the warp on the loom; the weaver; the clipper, who trimmed the excess from the floating threads on the back of the shawl and prepared its fringe; and others, who were involved with finishing and pressing.[109] It was this system of specialists that enabled Paisley to dominate shawl production, for

the city consistently produced fine products at relatively low prices.

Widely used after 1845, the Jacquard attachment (see cat. 142) could produce the extremely complicated patterns Europe demanded. The cost and unwieldiness of this new, semiautomated attachment caused a shift from small production units in homes to large ones in factories, and thus a once highly personalized production moved closer to industrialization.

The changes in technology prompted an evolution in design. The first shawl to become popular in Europe was the Indian wrap. At the bottom edges of its plain central field were single bands of flowered forms whose outline was related to the teardrop paisley; a rather abstracted floral border often ran along the outside edge. These delicately patterned, softly draping shawls closely resembled their Iranian and Indian models and reflected the simple taste of the time, but the rather understated designs fell out of favor as the Victorian spirit evolved in the 1830s.

For almost 150 years France had been the leader in silk textile design. French shawl patterns, sent to India to be copied, were in turn reinterpreted in Scotland. Hence, Europe drew from a well-established artistic and technological base to inspire the final evolution of the Paisley design, just as it had Indian dyed cottons. It is difficult to imagine anything further removed from an Indian prototype than the shawl illustrated here. What was originally a narrow decorative band marking the ends now consumes the central field, except for a small hint of black. Extremely attenuated here, the original teardrop shape stretches from the center of the bottom into the first third of the field, where it becomes interlaced with vegetal forms. The shape of the small palmettes in the field are reminiscent of Renaissance design (see cat. 98), and their arrangement on the broad side borders is similar to French silks of about 1730 (see cat. 118); the mixture of elements from various textile traditions is typically Victorian.

Technically, this piece is a marvel. Along the bottom edge are multicolored tabs whose weave imitates the pieced and embroidered edges of Indian shawls. To create these tabs, certain areas of the warp are dyed various colors and the supplementary wefts are used on the surface to make a solid field. In fact, the warp is dyed red up to the central medallion in the field, where it turns black. Unusual structural devices were employed to imitate effectively the irregular qualities of the Indian twill tapestry shawls. Only one structural warp was dyed to correspond with desired colors in particular areas, but there are nine different colored supplementary wefts and one structural weft. The structural weft never appears on the surface. All surface patterning is done with supplementary wefts, which are anchored to the warp in a 2/1 twill; interestingly, the structural weft is used in a 5/1 twill that can be seen only on the back. One line across the fabric could be composed of up to nine colors, each requiring a different shed. Once this line was completed, the supplementary wefts were beaten down to cover the struc-

300

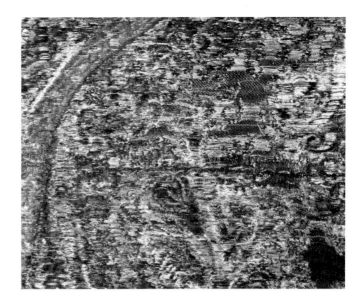

tural weft so that the only wefts seen on the surface were supplementary.

Another interesting feature of this piece is the documentation that accompanied it when the Museum acquired it:

This remarkable Kashmir doshal is the property of Miss Mary Alice Sloan, and has an unusual history. It was woven for the first Paris International Exposition in 1855, and was made of the fleece of the unborn kid of the Kashmir goat, sacrificing [sic] the lives of both goat and kid for each tiny fleece. The material could not be obtained fast enough to complete the shawl (four yards long and two yards wide) in time for the Exposition, so when it was a little more than half finished the shawl had to be cut from the loom and sent to Paris, where it was exhibited and attracted the attention of many visitors. Among those most interested was the beautiful Empress Eugénie, wife of Napoleon

Catalogue Number 135, Detail

III, and as she was making a collection of fine shawls, she ordered it returned to the loom and completed for her.

After the close of the Exposition it was sent back to the Vale of Kashmir, returned to the loom, and after a long period it was finally completed and started on its way to become the property of the Empress. But the Fates decreed otherwise. Before it had reached its destination the son of the Empress had been killed in the Zulu War and she went into mourning. Then she no longer wished [sic] the shawl and it was offered for sale in Paris, . . . Attached to this shawl is a satin print of the gold medals awarded for workmanship and design when it was on exhibition at the Paris Exposition, also [sic] the tape bearing the number identifying it at that exhibition.

One would normally attribute such a tale to the romantic imagination of a loving relative, but the many curiosities displayed on this piece are not so easily dismissed. First of all, there is a break in the warp just above the black central field (see detail p. 301). Secondly, one set of warps were cut and another set substituted. Finally, stitch marks remain on the back side of the long portion where the woven medallion (see detail left) was placed. This piece was not made in India, of course, but the physical evidence nonetheless lends itself to speculation.

Materials
Basic fabric
  warp: wool and silk, two-ply S-twist; white, blue, red, red-violet, black
  weft: wool, single-ply Z-twist; white, red, black
  supplementary weft:
    wool, single-ply Z-twist; white, two yellows, green, light blue, red, black, very light red, very light yellow, very light green

Techniques
Weft-dominant 5/1 diagonal twill weave (main weft) and weft-dominant 2/1 diagonal twill weave (supplementary weft), with continuous supplementary weft, weft floats on back side trimmed after weaving
  proportions: one supplementary weft per one main weft
Space dyed warp and individual warp replacements for color changes
Complete warp replacement dividing weaving into approximately one-third and two-third sections
Selvedge: ½ in. (1.3 cm) wide of weft dominant 2/1 diagonal twill weave in green silk
Fringe: individual warp ends, knotted area of fringe from selvedge in about 2 in. (5.0 cm)

Thread count
Basic fabric
  warp: 198   weft: 218   supplementary weft: 218

Catalogue Number 136
Chantilly Area, France
Woman's Wrapper, ca. 1860
silk bobbin lace
96 x 53 (243.5 x 134.5)
Gift of Mrs. Fisk Landers 74.133

Many black lace shawls like this one were made in the nine-teenth century. At Chantilly they were bobbin-made, and after 1840 the Pusher machine produced excellent imitations. A dull black silk thread stiffened with gum arabic was employed to create the typical mid-Victorian patterns of realistic flowers, swags, and ribbons. Here the pattern is nicely composed with a teardrop-shaped border.

Materials
Basic fabric
outline, figure and ground: silk, two-ply S-twist; black
Techniques
Bobbin lace
flat figures (*toilé*), thick outline (*cordonnet*) of grouped threads and a hexagon-shaped mesh (*réseau*) with four sides twisted and two sides crossed (*Fond Simple*); figure and ground worked together
Thread count
Basic fabric
mesh, horizontal: 16   vertical: 15

Catalogue Number 137
Belgium
Wedding Veil, ca. 1860
cotton needle lace
114 x 57 (289 x 145)
Gift of Mrs. Charles S. Crosley 36.71

In 1851 *point de gaze* was shown at the Crystal Palace Exposition.[110] Although the exhibition catalogue contains the first published account of this type of lace, it was probably made before that year. Since the ground is worked with one row of a single twist of the thread alternating with another of double twist, it is one of the finest and most delicate in needle lace. Designs in this lace exhibit virtuosic technique in the flowers, whose appliquéd petals give a particularly naturalistic dimension to the surface. The primacy of the rose in these designs led to its second name, *point de rose*.[111]

Lace wedding veils became popular in the mid-nineteenth century, when a "set" of lace for the wedding might include a veil, a flounce ten to twelve inches deep and six yards wide, a garniture four inches wide and eight yards long, a handkerchief, a fan, and, if the wedding was at night, lappets.[112] Only the very rich could afford to have this type of lace in their wedding attire. This veil is made of fine cotton thread, a material often used in the nineteenth century, and typifies Victorian laces at the height of their popularity. Curving scrollwork surrounds bouquets of naturalistically rendered flowers. The many kinds of eighteenth-century design elements—such as rococo scrolls, trailing flowers with turning stems, and elaborate fill patterns—are combined in a rather confused and overly elaborate form in this mid-nineteenth-century piece.

Materials
Basic fabric
outline: cotton, single-ply S-twist; white
ground: cotton, single-ply S-twist; white
Techniques
Needle lace; buttonhole stitches
layered figures (*toilé*), padded outline (*cordonnet*) and mesh (*réseau*) of simple looping with alternating number of twists; figure and ground worked separately
Thread count
Basic fabric
mesh, horizontal: 30   vertical: 16

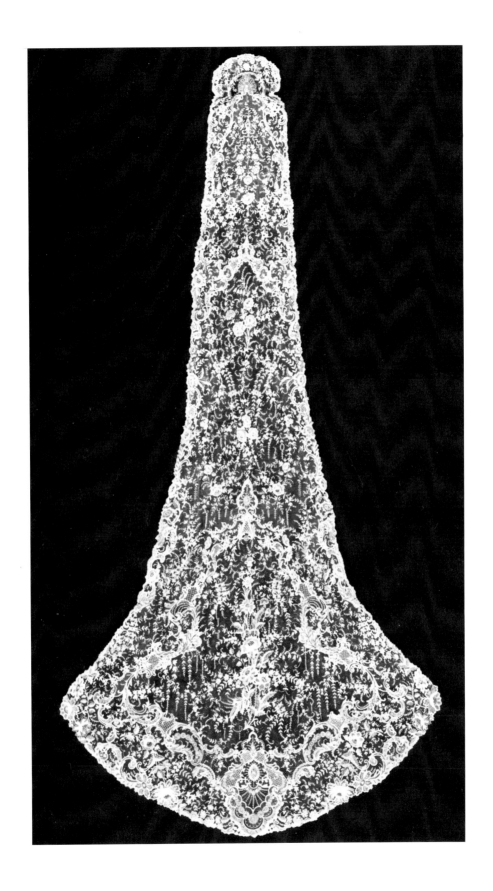

Catalogue Number 138
Belgium (?)
Bed Cover, *The Romance of Real Lace*, ca. 1900
cotton bobbin lace
99 x 93 (251 x 236)
Gift of Mrs. Charles S. Crosley 36.66

This delightful tour-de-force of bobbin lace making is a glossary of lace ground patterns as well as an illustration of a wide variety of flowers. Putti cavort in a garden as they make bobbin lace. In the central area, two putti manipulate bobbins to make a large sunflower; another putto holds a pin, and at the bottom a fourth enters, carrying scissors. In the lower right corner is another, gathering flax and another holding a distaff. Flax springs from the vase, amid other naturalistically rendered flowers and plant forms. At the time this piece was made, machinery had eclipsed handmade lace, and it was appropriate to commemorate "real" lace in such a magnificent form.

Materials
 Basic fabric
  figure: cotton, single-ply Z-twist; white
  ground: cotton, single-ply Z-twist; white
Techniques
 Bobbin lace
  flat figures (*toilé*) connected with bars (*brides*) with loops (*picots*) and a hexagon-shaped mesh (*réseau*) plaited on all sides with small holes at each angle (*Round Valenciennes*); figure and ground worked separately
Thread count
 Basic fabric
  figure, horizontal: 74 vertical: 68
  mesh, horizontal: 6 vertical: 6

Catalogue Number 139
Europe
Handkerchief, ca. 1890
linen plain weave, embroidered with cotton, trimmed with
    cotton bobbin lace
22 x 22 (56 x 56) warp x weft
Gift of Mrs. William James Reid 43.50

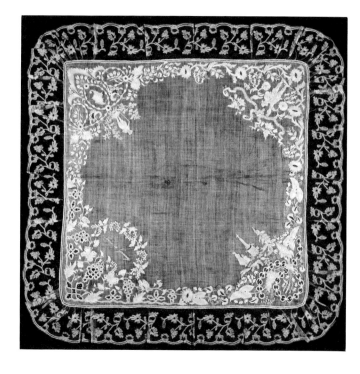

Since the eighteenth century the handkerchief had belonged
to fashionable attire as a decorative rather than functional accessory. Consequently, many handkerchiefs were highly decorated with lace and openwork. The imagery on this piece
suggests it was made for mourning. In one corner, what appear
to be a mother and daughter reverently visit a grave. In another
corner is a man wearing what appears to be an interpretation of eighteenth-century costume. In the ribbon bands above
his head is the inscription *plutôt mourir que me tacher; je ne
change que n'mourant.* Another corner bears a name, Louise de
Gournay.

Materials
    Basic fabric
        warp: bast (linen), single-ply slight Z-twist; white
        weft: bast (linen), single-ply slight Z-twist; white
    Embroidery
        cotton, single-ply Z-twist; white
        cotton, two-ply S-twist; white
    Lace trim
        cotton, two-ply S-twist; white
Techniques
    Balanced plain weave, loosely woven
    Appliquéd with white linen plain weave that is ground of
      embroidery
    Embroidery
        flat stitches: eyelet hole; padded satin
        looped stitches: buttonhole; chain; French knot
        needle lace insertions of buttonhole stitches
    Trim: bobbin lace
        flat figures (*toilé*), no outline (*cordonnet*), and a diamond-
          shaped mesh (*réseau*) plaited on all four sides
          (*Valenciennes*); figure and ground worked together
Thread count
    Basic fabric
        warp: 139   weft: 135
    Lace trim
        figure, horizontal: 80   vertical: 76
        mesh, horizontal: 16   vertical: 16

Catalogue Number 140
Europe
Handkerchief, ca. 1890
linen plain weave, embroidered with cotton
16 x 16 (40.5 x 40.5) warp x weft
Gift of Mrs. Charles S. Crosley 36.83

This exquisitely executed handkerchief, worked with densely spaced embroidery stitches, has openwork panels and a border ornament of needle lace fills. The flowers and leaves that lie over the trellis background create a marvelous interplay of patterns.

Materials
    Basic fabric
        warp: bast (linen), single-ply slight Z-twist; white
        weft: bast (linen), single-ply slight Z-twist; white
    Embroidery
        cotton, two-ply S-twist; white
        cotton, three-ply S-twist; white

Techniques
    Balanced plain weave, loosely woven
    Embroidery
        flat stitches: eyelet; padded satin; seeding
        looped stitches: buttonhole
        needle lace insertions of buttonhole stitches

Thread count
    Basic fabric
        warp: 161   weft: 179

Catalogue Number 141
William Craig, Sr. (1800-1880), James Craig (1823-89),
    William Craig, Jr. (1824-90s), Decatur County, Indiana,
    United States
Bed Cover (coverlet), *Liberty,* 1846
cotton and wool double weave with complementary warp
    and weft
94¼ x 77 (239 x 197) with fringe, warp x weft
Gift of Mrs. Ferdinand L. Mayer 21.127

Coverlet weaving was an important pastime in nineteenth-century Indiana. At least forty professional weavers worked in the state, and there may have been more.[113] Most of the weavers who settled in Indiana had emigrated from Scotland, England, and Germany. In the first decades of the nineteenth century, steam-powered mills were common enough in Europe to cause many weavers who had been apprenticed at the turn of the century on the newly patented Jacquard loom to be put out of work. Finding few opportunities in Europe, many left to seek employment in America.

Transportation to Indiana was readily available from the East Coast. In fact, the greatest number of weavers settled in communities surrounding the National Road (U.S. Route 40), which bisects the state from east to west. The influx of weavers coincided with the growing prosperity in farming communities, and farmers were all too willing to show their affluence in brightly colored, professionally woven coverlets for their homes. Most coverlet weavers in Indiana were also farmers and listed themselves as such in the census. Many of them became wealthy landowners on the profits of their weaving, for coverlets were highly esteemed, and the best weavers were eagerly sought out.

Perhaps the best known Indiana coverlet weavers were the Craigs: William, Sr., and his two sons, James and William, Jr. William, Sr., was born in 1800 in Kilmarnock, Ayrshire, a Scottish city that was famous for its ingrain carpet weaving. He came to the United States in 1820, around the time a number of other Indiana coverlet weavers who had apprenticed in Kilmarnock did. His sons were born in South Carolina, and after a brief stay in Rhode Island, the family settled in the 1830s in Mount Carmel in Franklin County, Indiana, where William's brother was a Presbyterian minister. Although William was weaving during this period, and his sons probably assisted him, no coverlets remain from the time prior to his move to Decatur County in 1840.

During the time this coverlet was produced, the father and two sons were all weaving and all using the same signature block. The building on the signature blocks on all four corners of the coverlet may represent the Decatur County Courthouse. Built in 1827, it was a source of community pride. By the late 1840s the three weavers had established their own weaving shops and started to use different signature blocks.

All four corners of Craig coverlets commonly hold a signature square; most coverlet weavers use only two, on the bottom edge. The lily end borders and mosque and bird side borders are fairly common on Craig coverlets from this period. This coverlet's complicated pattern, further varied by the bands of red, white, and blue, superbly expresses the weaver's art and underscores the family's reputation for some of the finest coverlets in Indiana.

Materials
Basic fabric
    complementary warp:
        cotton, three-ply S-twist; white
        wool, two-ply S-twist; red, dark blue
    complementary weft:
        cotton, three-ply S-twist; white
        wool, two-ply S-twist; red, dark blue
Techniques
Double-cloth weave; two layers of balanced plain weave,
    with warps and wefts interchanging singularly; with
    continuous complementary warp and continuous
    complementary weft
Two panels sewn together at selvedges
Fringe: individual warp ends at bottom edge
Finish: rolled hem at top edge
Thread count
Basic fabric
    warp 1: 17   warp 2: 17   weft 1: 15   weft 2: 15
Pattern repeat
Center
    warpwise: 22¾ in. (58.0 cm)
    weftwise: 20¾ in. (53.0 cm)
Border
    warpwise: 23¼ in. (59.0 cm)
    weftwise: 21 in. (53.5 cm)

311

Catalogue Number 142
Charles Adoph (1815-70s), Wayne County, Indiana,
    United States
Bed Cover (coverlet), 1847
cotton and wool double weave with complementary warp
    and weft
87 x 76 (220.5 x 193) with fringe, warp x weft
Gift of Miss Anne Locke 41.1

Both this coverlet and the preceding one (see cat. 141) were woven on the semiautomated Jacquard loom. Even though Joseph Marie Jacquard held an 1805 patent for this loom, it was the culmination of several centuries of devices. All of them attempted to streamline the weaving of fancy patterns on the drawloom. To execute these patterns, holes were punched in large, rectangular cards placed in the Jacquard loom frame. The cards were drawn over a cylinder with holes that allowed certain pegs to pass. These pegs then activated strings that lifted pattern threads on the loom. Different weavers did use the same patterns, so pattern books and prepunched cards must have been available, though none have surfaced. The composition of this particular coverlet is masterly; its side and end borders gracefully relate to the central field. Some patterns are inexplicably cropped and others assembled so arbitrarily that it seems the weaver must have been blindfolded when he picked them from a bin. This feature may, however, reflect the customer's lack of taste rather than that of the weaver's.

Though Charles Adolph was known as one of the best dyers among Indiana coverlet weavers, this piece is woven of blue-black indigo dyed wool yarn and white cotton. Sometimes, the customer produced the raw materials for coverlets by preparing the yarn, dyeing it, and taking it and an indication of the desired pattern to the weaver. As customers became wealthier, they removed the malodorous indigo dye pot from the hearth and left preparation of the yarn to the weaver's assistants. Indigo was by far the most common dye in Indiana coverlets, and madder for red the next. Falling far behind these two were colors obtained from natural substances found in the Indiana countryside. Madder and indigo dyes, as well as manufactured cotton, could be purchased in most shops in Indiana that served weavers. Indiana coverlet weavers seldom used the chemical dyes developed in Europe in the 1850s, perhaps in part because by the time they were widely distributed in the state, handwoven coverlets were rarely made.

An emigrée from Alsace, Charles Adolph travelled directly to Cambridge City, in Wayne County, where he joined Henry Adolph, who may have been an Alsatian kinsman. This coverlet was woven at that time, before he moved away to Henry County. He stayed there—except for an interval back in Cambridge City—until 1870, when he sold his Indiana property and moved to Kansas. Very few coverlets were woven after 1870, perhaps because of the Civil War, which may have placed a strain on supplies. Two other developments may have been more influential, however: the change in fashion to the late Victorian Mauve Decade and the ever-encroaching age of industrialization. The very mechanized systems that the weavers had escaped when they left Europe now stymied them in this country, though not before they had left an indelible and beautiful legacy in thousands of colorful coverlets.

Materials
Basic fabric
    complementary warp:
        cotton, two-ply S-twist; white
        wool, two-ply S-twist; dark blue
    complementary weft:
        cotton, two-ply S-twist; white
        wool, two-ply S-twist; dark blue
Techniques
    Double-cloth weave; two layers of balanced plain weave
        with warps and wefts interchanging singularly; with
        complementary warp and continuous complementary weft
    Two panels sewn together at selvedges with zigzag running
        stitch
    Fringe: individual warp ends at bottom edge
    Finish: rolled hem at top edge
Thread count
    Basic fabric
        warp 1: 17   warp 2: 17   weft 1: 19   weft 2: 19
Pattern repeat
    Center
        warpwise: 13½ in. (34.0 cm)
        weftwise: 15 in. (38.0 cm)
    Border
        warpwise: 13¼ in. (33.5 cm)
        weftwise: 15¼ in. (39.0 cm)

313

Catalogue Number 143 (see color plate, p. 60)
Northeastern United States
Bed Cover (quilt), 1853
cotton plain weave, pieced, appliquéd, embroidered with
    cotton and silk, quilted
88¼ x 87 (224 x 220.5) warp x weft
Orville A. and Elma D. Wilkinson Fund 75.107

American appliquéd quilts reached their pinnacle in the mid-nineteenth century, perhaps as a development from *broderie perse*, the late eighteenth- and early nineteenth-century practice of appliquéing small motifs from Indian printed cotton on fabric, in imitation of more costly and time-consuming embroidery.[114] Whatever the origin, quilt making became a truly American art form.

American quilt designs are patterned and arranged in several different ways. Eighteenth-century quilt patterns are usually larger and frequently are composed with a central focus and surrounding decorative elements, as this one is. This particular composition is more common on quilts of appliquéd fabric and on those that are plain; the latter have no piecing or appliqué, so the design is rendered in needlework only. Throughout their history quilts made of small pieces of fabric have usually been designed with a geometric grid, and therefore display an overall pattern rather than one central focus. Like other art forms of the nineteenth century, quilts reflect the taste of the times but, in addition, mirror the presence of past folk art, whose conventions allowed traditional patterns to continue in popularity. This quilt, a good example of that continuity, combines the basic eighteenth-century compositional device of central forms with the star, a primary motif from geometric, pieced quilts.

Quilt making was an important part of an American woman's life. The early settlers made quilts from used scraps. As homesteaders grew more affluent, quilts also began to reflect social status. Almost as soon as she could walk, a girl was expected to learn needlework and to execute small piecework projects. Girls from well-to-do families attended needleworking classes where they learned quilt piecing as well as painting and decorative paper cutting.[115] Needleworking remained in public and private school curricula until the mid-nineteenth century. Before becoming engaged, a girl was supposed to execute a number of quilt tops for her dowry, or trousseau. The worked tops were stitched to padded backings at a quilting bee. An important social event, it was usually arranged as an all-day affair with quantities of good food and gossip. One participant wrote:

> Aunt Sally had her quilt up in her landlord's east room, for her own house was too small. However, at about eleven she called us over to dinner; for people who have breakfasted at five or six have an appetite at eleven.
>
> We found on the table beefsteaks, boiled pork, sweet potatoes, kohl-slaw, pickled tomatoes, cucumbers, and *red* beets (thus the "Dutch" accent lies), apple-butter and preserved peaches, pumpkin- and apple-pie, with sponge-cake and coffee. . . .
>
> The first subject of conversation was the fall housecleaning; and I heard mention of "die carpet hinaus an der fence," and "die fenshter und die porch;" and the exclamation, "My goodness, es war schlimm." I quilted faster than Katy Groff, who showed me her hands, and said, "You have not been corn-husking, as I have."

> So we quilted and rolled, talked and laughed, got one quilt done, and put in another. The work was not fine; we laid it out by chalking around a small plate. Aunt Sally's desire was rather to get her quilting finished upon this great occasion, than for us to put in a quantity of needlework.
>
> About five o'clock we were called to supper. I need not tell you all the particulars of this plentiful meal. But the stewed chicken was tender, and we had coffee again. . . .[116]

Women usually worked in a group to make a quilt. In larger cities a professional might prepare the pattern to be executed in needlework and spend from two to five days drawing it on the quilt top.[117] In rural areas a woman known for her creative abilities could be called upon to draw the pattern. Lacking such assistance, the quilt maker could trace a design from any number of sources to make a template.

Materials for padding the bottom layer of the quilt have varied according to the maker's time and resources. Because it was cheaper and more easily obtained, wool was much more common in padding of the eighteenth century than cotton was. Cotton cultivated on the large English plantations of America during the seventeenth and eighteenth centuries was very costly because of the lengthy process of removing the seeds. The invention of the cotton gin in 1793 prompted both the growth of the cotton weaving industry and production of cotton batting in the late eighteenth to early nineteenth centuries.[118] All of these developments precipitated the explosion of creative quilt making that occurred from 1825 to 1875.

County fairs, first held in the nineteenth century, offered prizes for the best quilts,[119] and the quilt display in the Women's Building of the Indiana State Fair still occupies a large area. Quilt making has in fact been revived periodically in the twentieth century, perhaps because of social conditions, or the timeless need to create an object of beauty.

Materials
Basic fabric
    warp: cotton, single-ply Z-twist; white
    weft: cotton, single-ply Z-twist; white
Appliquéd fabric 1
    warp: cotton, single-ply Z-twist; red, blue, green, yellow-orange, or white
    weft: cotton, single-ply Z-twist; red, blue, green, yellow-orange, or white
    dyes/pigments: yellow, red, green (on white only)
Appliquéd fabric 2
    warp: silk, single-ply Z-twist; white
    weft: silk, single-ply Z-twist; dark brown
Embroidery
    cotton, two-ply S-twist; blue-green, green, brown, yellow, black
    silk, two-ply S-twist; white

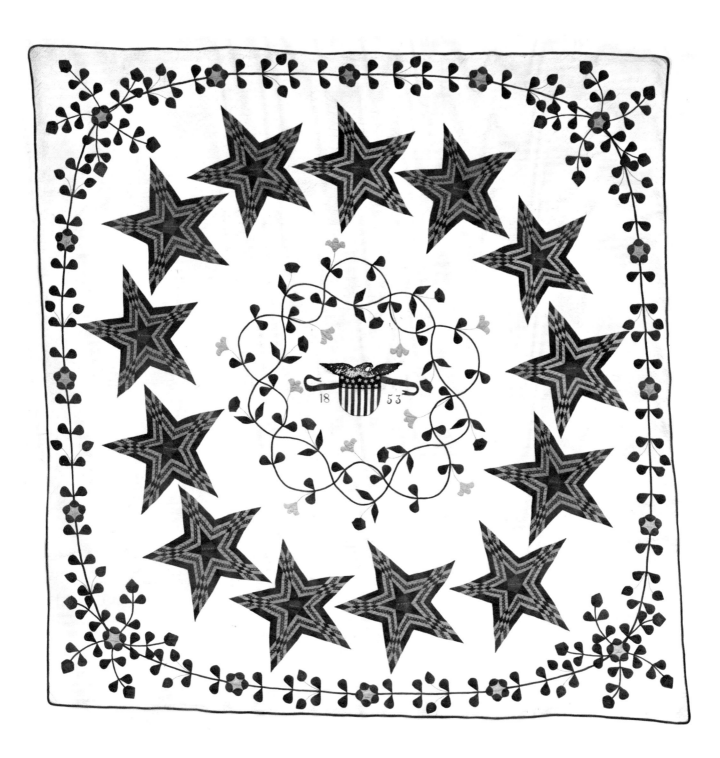

Batting
  cotton
Backing
  warp: cotton, single-ply Z-twist; white
  weft: cotton, single-ply Z-twist; white
Techniques
  Balanced plain weave
  Appliquéd with fabric of balanced plain weave and pieced
    balanced plain weave
  Embroidery
    flat stitches: cross
    looped stitches: buttonhole; chain

Quilted
Finish: edges bound with fabric of balanced plain weave cut
  on bias
Backing: balanced plain weave
Thread count
  Basic fabric
    warp: 86   weft: 76
  Backing
    warp: 55   weft: 55

Catalogue Number 144
Hawaii, United States
Bed Cover (quilt), ca. 1900
cotton plain weave, appliquéd, quilted
77 x 71¼ (195 x 180.5) warp x weft
Gift of Mrs. Albert P. Niblack 48.56

On the morning of April 3, 1820, the American Board of Missions held the Sandwich Islands' first sewing circle, aboard the Brigand Thaddeus, which was 162 days out of Boston. Kalakua, the dowager queen, and four of her friends and relatives started to work on the geometric pieced patterns so familiar to New England missionary wives.[120] An art form inspired by the native islanders arose from this auspicious beginning.

Before the arrival of Europeans and Americans, the islanders had used *tapa* (see cat. 21) as the basic material for their clothing and furnishing fabric. Since they had no scraps from sewing or old garments with which to fabricate quilts, Hawaiians had to purchase cotton goods for quilt making and logically decided that a method closer to their traditional way of designing *tapa* patterns would be a more efficient use of cloth. This method involved folding the fabric into eighths and cutting out the pattern—much as we make paper snowflakes—to create a single unit of design. A unique vocabulary of patterns consequently arose. The inventor, who named her own design, may have been inspired by fruit, flowers, sea life, a beautiful spot in nature, biblical themes, public events, or other seemingly disparate elements.[121] In fact, patterns were sometimes "stolen" from their originators and reinterpreted.

Hawaiians learned to sew with a needle and thread, a technique foreign to them, from especially imported American teachers. Domestic arts such as sewing and wool weaving, which were not originally part of the missionary school curriculum, were offered beginning in the 1830s.[122] Quilts had been made with wool padding, as was common in New England in the early nineteenth century. Used in the piece illustrated here, wool stuffing produced deeper crevices between the quilted rows, a form Hawaiians called *kulipu'u*, or lump hill.[123] The design of the stitched quilting followed the appliquéd patterns in traditional Hawaiian quilts; independent or geometric patterns were not used.[124]

Materials
  Basic fabric
    warp: cotton, single-ply Z-twist; white
    weft: cotton, single-ply Z-twist; white
  Appliquéd fabric
    warp: cotton, single-ply Z-twist; white
    weft: cotton, single-ply Z-twist; white
    dye/pigment: dark violet-brown
  Batting
    wool
  Backing fabric
    warp: cotton, single-ply Z-twist; white
    weft: cotton, single-ply Z-twist; white
Techniques
  Balanced plain weave
  Appliquéd with printed fabric of balanced plain weave
  Quilted
  Finish: edges bound with fabric of balanced plain weave
  Backing: balanced plain weave
Thread count
  Basic fabric
    warp: 68   weft: 78
  Appliquéd fabric
    warp: 86   weft: 76
  Backing
    warp: 51   weft: 51

Catalogue Number 145
Victoriene Parsons Mitchell (1829-1916)
Bed Cover (quilt), 1883-93
silk, cotton, wool and linen; various weaves; appliquéd;
 embroidered with silk and cotton; pieced
74½ x 64½ (188 x 162.5)
Gift of Mrs. Jaema C. Ryan 77.363

Victorian crazy quilts emerged after 1850. If quilting is characterized by needlework through all three layers, then crazy
quilts are wrongly named, for at most their top layer is fastened
to the bottom one by widely spaced thread tacks. In this piece,
manufactured quilted backing was attached around the edges
only. The enormous variety of embroidery stitches in this piece,
however, certainly compensates for any lack of creative quilting
stitches. Crazy quilts are usually composed of small pieces of
silk that are sometimes eccentrically joined and other times assembled into regular squares whose seams are then embroidered, as they are here. *Godey's Lady's Book* recommended:

> The greater the diversity in stitches the better . . . It
> saves time if a few of the smaller pieces are joined by
> a sewing machine, but we would suggest only a little
> of this being done, as it gives straight lines. If, on com-
> pletion, there are any angularities offending the eye,
> they can be hidden by the application of ovals or other
> curved forms of silk being put on the top and worked
> around.[125]

There is certainly a variety of stitches here, as well as many
motifs. Several different people may have executed these
squares, and similarities that emerge in the drawing, subject
matter, and stitches indicate that one individual made four or
five of them. Though some of the images must have been original, others may have come from a commercial source such as
Godey's, where the following advertisement appeared in Janu-
ary, 1885:

> Crazy Patchwork. We send ten sample pieces of ele-
> gant silk, all different and cut so as to make one 12
> inch block of crazy patchwork with a diagram showing
> how to put them together, and a variety of new stitches,
> for 35¢. We send a set of thirty-five perforated pat-
> terns, working size, of birds, butterflies, bugs, beetles,
> spiders and web, reptiles, Kate Greenaway figures,
> flowers, etc., with materials for transferring to the silk
> for 60¢.[126]

This piece might be a "friendship quilt," in which case friends
of Mrs. Mitchell would have executed the squares, that she then
assembled. It also might be a family piece, since five squares
are embroidered with the final initial "G" and one square with
the names Mama, Papa, Clarence, Leslie and Robbi.

 Crazy quilts were used not just in bedrooms but also in parlors
as lap throws or as covers for daytime naps. The quilts' effusive
color and varied, even confusing, mixture of design elements
typify the high Victorian taste also displayed in lace, fabric,
costume, architecture, and interiors.

Materials
 Fabric at borders
  warp: silk, single-ply slight S-twist; red, yellow or blue
  weft: silk, no twist; red, yellow or blue
 Embroidery
  silk, two-ply S-twist; yellows, oranges, reds, violets, blues,
   greens, white, black
  cotton, two-ply S-twist; yellows, oranges, reds, violets,
   blues, greens, white, black
Techniques
 Fabrics of cotton, wool, silk, and linen in various weave
  structures including plain, twill, satin, and pile weaves
 Fabric at borders: warp-faced 7/1 satin weave
 Pieced and appliquéd
 Embroidery
  flat stitches: Algerian eye; arrowhead; back; couching;
   Croatian; cross, tied cross, double cross, tied double
   cross, long-armed cross, upright cross; dot; fishbone;
   herringbone, double herringbone, tied herringbone,
   variations of herringbone; ray, tied ray; Roumanian;
   running, double running; satin, encroaching satin,
   padded satin; seeding; variation of spider web;
   stem; straight
  looped stitches: bullion knot; buttonhole; chain,
   detached chain, open chain, Russian chain, twisted
   chain, variations of chain; feather, double feather,
   closed feather, long-armed feather, variation of feather;
   fly, variations of fly; French knot; petal; sheaf;
   turkey knot
 Trim: silk cord
 Backing: machine quilted fabric
Thread count
 Fabric at borders
  warp: 200   weft: 88
Pattern repeat
 size of blocks, 4 in. x 4 in. (10.0 cm x 10.0 cm)
Literature
 McMorris, *Crazy Quilts.*

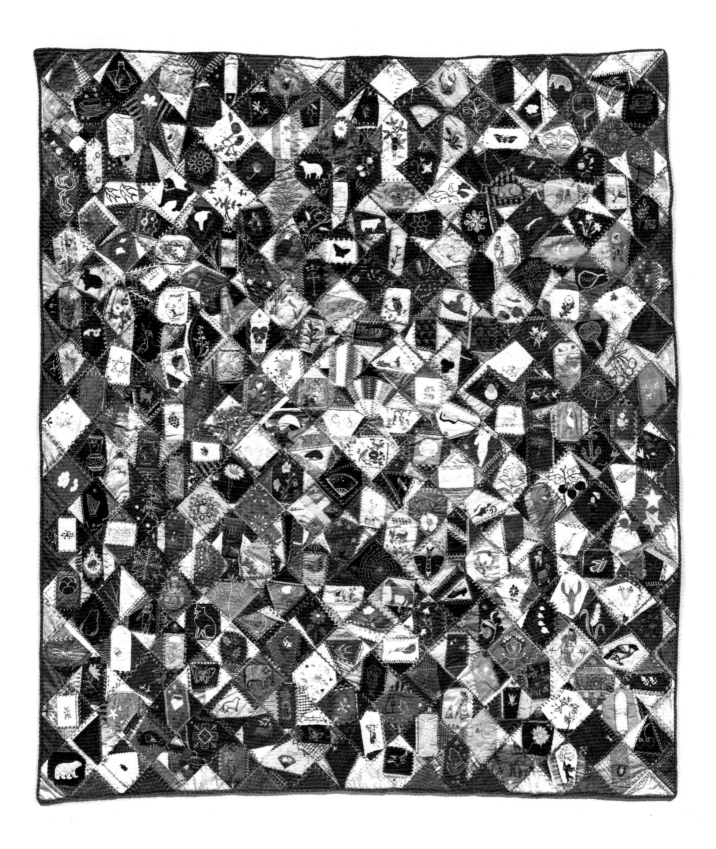

Catalogue Number 146
United States
Wedding Dress, 1871
silk plain weave (taffeta), trimmed with cotton bobbin lace
64 (162) length
Gift of Mr. Robert C. Martindale 74.372

On May 11, 1871, at 8:30 p.m., Alice Morrison married Robert Weir Cathcart. The wedding took place at the residence of her parents, Mr. and Mrs. John J. Morrison, on the southwest corner of Tennessee and Vermont streets in Indianapolis. The bride wore this rich brown dress. By the mid-nineteenth century white was the usual color for wedding dresses, although there were a few individualistic young women who preferred to be married in colored gowns.

Although rather sedate and conservative, this dress is characteristic of early 1870 design, most visibly in the asymmetrical overskirt trimmed with ruffles and ruching. Many elements in this dress are related to designs of the previous century. The overskirt imitates the eighteenth-century *polonaise* draped skirt; the flat panel in front mimics an eighteenth-century apron; and the deep V of the bodice front and the decorative bands from waist to shoulder are reminiscent of bodice treatment in the eighteenth century (see cat. 124). Nonetheless, no one would mistake this dress for one made in the eighteenth century. In particular, the shape of the garment differs significantly from those seen in the 1700s: here, the corset, crinolette, and hoop create a decidedly nineteenth-century silhouette.

Materials
Basic fabric
    warp: silk, no twist; orange-brown
    weft: silk, no twist; orange-brown
Lining 1
    warp: cotton, single-ply tight Z-twist; orange-brown
    weft: cotton, single-ply tight Z-twist; orange-brown
Lining 2
    warp: cotton, single-ply Z-twist; light tan or light
        orange-brown
    weft: cotton, single-ply Z-twist; light tan or light
        orange-brown

Techniques
Warp-dominant plain weave, weft thicker than warp
Pieced garment with three pieces: bodice, skirt, and
    overskirt
Trim: cotton bobbin lace collar, pleated basic fabric with
    frayed raw edges, pleated flaps and cloth-covered buttons
    on front of skirt; white silk satin and pleated white ribbon
    on inside of sleeves; cloth- and cord-covered buttons
Lining 1: warp-faced 4/1 satin weave in bodice
Lining 2: glazed balanced plain weave

Thread count
Basic fabric
    warp: 226   weft: 88
Lining 1
    warp: 127   weft: 75
Lining 2
    warp: 61   weft: 52

Catalogue Number 147
United States
Day Dress, 1871
silk plain weave (taffeta), trimmed with silk satin and cotton
   tape lace
55 (140) length
Gift of Mr. Robert C. Martindale 74.379

Mrs. Cathcart wore this delicate pink silk dress as part of her
trousseau (see cat. 146). The very simple day dress still displayed the fashion of the 1870s in the detachable skirt panel,
which imitates draped swags.

Materials
   Basic fabric
      warp: silk, no twist; light red
      weft: silk, no twist; light red
   Lining 1
      warp: silk, single-ply Z-twist; white
      weft: silk, single-ply Z-twist; white
   Lining 2
      warp: cotton, single-ply tight Z-twist; light tan
      weft: cotton, single-ply tight Z-twist; light tan
Techniques
   Warp-dominant plain weave, weft thicker than warp
   Pieced garment with two pieces and belt: bodice and skirt
   Trim: cotton tape lace collar, tape appliquéd to machine-
      made cotton square net, white silk satin, and cord-covered
      buttons
   Lining 1: warp-faced 5/1 satin weave in bodice
   Lining 2: balanced plain weave, loosely woven and glazed,
      in skirt
Thread count
   Basic fabric
      warp: 214   weft: 100
   Lining 1
      warp: 116   weft: 78
   Lining 2
      warp: 50   weft: 62

Catalogue Number 148
G & E Spitzer, Vienna, Austria
Evening Dress, ca. 1891
silk plain and satin weaves, printed warp (chiné), trimmed
    with silk satin and cotton tape lace
77 (195) length
Gift of Mrs. Addison C. Harris 32.189

During the final decade of the nineteenth century, the desire
for freedom and the tendency to retain familiar modes of fem-
ininity clashed in dress design.[127] Bustles and elaborate skirts
were replaced by the slim hourglass, a silhouette that followed
the shape of the hips and then flared at the bottom hem. A long
corset and gored skirt, of eight panels in this example, accomplished this shape. The elaborate surface decoration typical of
the 1880s is subtly present here in the woven patterning of the
silk chiné fabric. Bows and ruffled swags sweep from the center
to the back of the skirt, over delicate background flowers. Near
the bottom of the skirt, these swags are embellished with narrow
bands of ruching.

This gown was worn by Mrs. Addison Harris, the Indian-
apolis-born wife of the Ambassador to Austria.

Materials
Basic fabric
    warp: silk, no twist; white, light red, light yellow, light
        blue, light green
    weft: silk, no twist; white
Lining 1
    warp: silk, no twist; white
    weft: silk, single-ply S-twist; white
Lining 2
    warp: silk, no twist; white
    weft: silk, no twist; white

Techniques
Warp-dominant plain weave (background), warp-faced
    satin weave (figure) and weft-faced floats (figure)
Warps printed before weaving
Trim of basic fabric: narrow, gathered satin ribbons
    appliquéd to skirt; machine-made net with appliquéd tape
    lace and layered machine-made lace at neck and sleeves
Trim of lining 2: two machine-made lace ruffles at inside
    hem, pleated tulle flounce with three rows of gathered
    ribbon on outside hem, and one wide ruffle of machine-
    made net with appliquéd tape lace on outside hem
Pieced garment with two pieces: bodice and skirt
Waist tape labelled "G & E Spitzer"
Lining 1: warp dominant plain weave in bodice
Lining 2: warp dominant plain weave in skirt

Thread count
Basic fabric
    warp: 360   weft: 57
Lining 1
    warp: 224   weft: 104
Lining 2
    warp: 224   weft: 88

Pattern repeat
warpwise: 9½ in. (24.0 cm)   weftwise: 9½ in. (24.0 cm)

Catalogue Number 149
G. Giuseffi Ladies' Tailoring Co. (active ca. 1890-1934),
    St. Louis, Missouri, United States
Day Dress with Jacket, ca. 1903
silk velvet weave with silk supplementary warp (solid velvet);
    trimmed with cotton tape lace, silk satin, piping;
    embroidered with silk
dress, 69½ (183) length
jacket, 25 (63.5) length
Estate of Caroline Ella Burford Danner 76.298

The small-waisted, smoothly fitted skirt is one of the many features of late nineteenth-century design that continued into the
early twentieth century. This silhouette was significantly altered, however, by a new type of corset that flattened the front
of the abdomen, and consequently pushed the bust forward
and the hips back. Called the "health corset," it was then
thought to improve the disposition of a woman's internal or-
gans by liberating them from the constriction of older corsets.
The ample, rounded bosom of the new "pouter pigeon" style
was further enhanced by dangling ornaments and layers of
ruffling and overdraping.

This outfit belongs to a collection of forty-two ensembles
given to the Museum in 1976 by Mrs. Danner's daughter. They
provide a unique glimpse of a wealthy Indianapolis woman's
taste and appearance, from around 1900 to the late 1920s. Mrs.
Danner purchased most of her garments from a dressmaking
family headed by Girolamo Giuseffi (d. 1934).[128] Giuseffi maintained a custom dressmaking firm in St. Louis, where the
clothing industry was then very strong and active. As exhibited
in her garments and her home, Mrs. Danner's taste leaned
toward the effusive decorative styles of the high Edwardian
period. Typical of Giuseffi's garments is the elaborate embellishment, composed of piping, beadwork, lace, ruffles, and silk
flowers.

Materials
  Basic fabric
      warp: silk, single-ply slight S-twist; black
      weft: silk, no twist; dark blue
      supplementary warp: silk, no twist; dark blue
  Lining 1
      warp: silk, no twist; white
      weft: silk, no twist; white
  Lining 2
      warp: silk, no twist; dark blue
      weft: silk, no twist; dark blue
  Lining 3
      warp: silk, single-ply slight S-twist; white
      weft: silk, no twist; white
Techniques
  Warp-faced woven pile, cut; with supplementary warp pile
      proportions: one supplementary warp per one main
      warp, one velvet rod per three main wefts
  Pieced garment with three pieces: bodice, skirt, and jacket
  Trim: cotton tape lace, machine made hexagonal net,
      gathered satin spheres, appliquéd with satin fabric strips,
      velvet-covered cording, satin covered cording
  Embroidery
      flat stitches: couched
      looped stitches: chain
  Lining 1: balanced plain weave in bodice
  Lining 2: balanced plain weave in skirt
  Lining 3: balanced plain weave and warp-faced 4/1 satin
      weave in jacket
  Waist tape labelled "G. Giuseffi L T Co Saint Louis"
Thread count
  Basic fabric
      warp: 112   weft: 112   supplementary warp: 88
  Lining 1
      warp: 198   weft: 124
  Lining 2
      warp: 200   weft: 124
  Lining 3
      warp: 280   weft: 120

Catalogue Number 150
Europe (?)
Evening Dress, ca. 1910
silk satin weave, embroidered with silk, metallic thread, and
  beads
86 (218) length
Gift of Mr. Henry Lane Wilson 28.299

Heavily influenced by European designers, the shape of the
body had shifted to an even straighter silhouette by 1910.
Achieving this straight, "natural" style often required corsets,
though the Europeans had intended to free the body from such
constraints. The Edwardian emphasis on the bosom was abandoned in around 1910, when the whole torso was compressed
to create a straight, smooth appearance. This dress seems to
combine several earlier periods in its form and decoration,
much as Victorian dress melded various influences. The high
waist and straight lines may be derived from early nineteenth-
century garments, and the rich, beaded embroidery from a
Neoclassical interpretation of seventeenth-century fashions.

Materials
  Basic fabric
    warp: silk, single-ply slight Z-twist; white
    weft: silk, single-ply slight Z-twist; white
  Embroidery
    silk, no twist; white
    silk, two-ply Z-twist; yellow
    metallic #1
      flat strip only: copper; gold colored
    metallic #2
      core thread: silk, two-ply S-twist; tan
      strip: copper with silver, S-twist; gray-gold colored
    metallic #3
      core thread: silk, two-ply S-twist; yellow
      strip: copper with iron, S-twist; gold colored
    beads
      imitation pearls, round; white
      round; white, clear
      cylindrical; gold-colored
  Lining 1
    warp: silk, no twist; white
    weft: silk, no twist; white
  Lining 2
    warp: cotton, single-ply Z-twist; white
    weft: cotton, single-ply Z-twist; white
Techniques
  Warp-faced 7/1 satin weave
  Embroidery
    flat stitches: couching; satin, padded satin; straight
    looped stitches: chain, French knot
    combination flat stitches: stem over satin; straight over
      satin
    combination flat and looped stitches: chain over satin
  Pieced garment with one piece
  Trim: machine-made hexagonal net, fringe of beads
  Bodice linings (1 and 2): balanced plain weave, loosely
    woven

Thread count
  Basic fabric
    warp: 312   weft: 66
  Lining 1
    warp: 216   weft: 132
  Lining 2
    warp: 88   weft: 88

Catalogue Number 151 (see color plate, p. 61)
Callot Soeurs (active 1895-1937), France
Evening Dress, ca. 1925
silk plain weave, embroidered with silk, trimmed with silk and
    metallic net and imitation pearls and opals
41 (104) length
Gift of Mrs. Anton Hulman, Jr. 77.360

Callot Soeurs was a design firm of three sisters who were born
in France of Russian heritage. Their father was an antiques
dealer, and their first shop, which carried lace, lingerie, and
ribbons, opened in Paris in 1895.[129] Perhaps true to their childhood upbringing, the sisters exhibited a love for the exotic,
whether Rococo or oriental. Their earliest dresses were made
of lace, but around 1915 they adopted the straight line typical
of the advanced Paris fashion of that day. Their garments were
known for very fine, detailed workmanship and deluxe fabrics.
The sisters' designs reached the height of their popularity from
1916 to 1926, when sheath dresses were characterized by scal-
loped and panelled hemlines decorated with beading, tassels,
and embroidery,[130] as in the piece shown here.

   This epitome of the "flapper" dress is made in layers of soft,
exotic materials—chiffon, metallic lace, and embroidered chiffon—and topped with a huge hanging "jewel," a confection
guaranteed to shimmer to the beat of the latest dance craze.
This garment typifies the 1920s dress: it hangs nearly to the
knee, barely indicates the waist, and has a deep, if modified,
décolletage in the design. Actually, the garment is no more than
an embellished slip hanging from thin, chiffon shoulder straps.
To this simple, basic cylinder have been added layers of sheer
decoration intended to give an aura of elegance to the body
as it moves. Dresses of this period are completely unrealized
unless they are worn, for they are shaped by the wearer's
movements.

Materials
   Basic fabrics
      warp: silk, single-ply Z-twist; light red or light blue
      weft: silk, single-ply Z-twist; light red or light blue
   Net fabric
      silk, two-ply S-twist; white
      metallic #1
         core thread: cotton, single-ply slight Z-twist; white
         strip: copper, Z-twist; gray-copper colored
   Embroidery
      silk, no twist; two light reds, two oranges, three light
         greens, two light yellow-greens, light and medium blue,
         brown
      metallic #2
         core thread: cotton, single-ply S-twist; yellow
         strip: copper with silver, Z-twist; gold colored
      metallic #3
         core thread: cotton, four-ply S-twist; yellow
         strip: copper and gold with silver, Z-twist; gold colored
   Lining
      warp: silk, single-ply slight S-twist; light red
      weft: silk, single-ply overspun S-twist; light red
Techniques
   Balanced plain weave, loosely woven
   Embroidery
      flat stitches: running; spaced satin, spaced surface satin

Pieced garment with two pieces
Trim: machine-made hexagonal netting, silk and metallic
    thread lace, imitation pearls and opals
Lining: warp-faced 5/1 satin weave
Thread count
   Basic fabric
      warp: 122   weft: 104
   Lining
      warp: 340   weft: 113

Catalogue Number 152
George Philip Meier (d. 1932), L. S. Ayres & Co.,
    Indianapolis, Indiana, United States
Evening Cape, ca. 1925
silk velvet weave with silk supplementary warp (solid velvet),
    trimmed with metallic thread embroidery and silk satin
45 (114.5) length
Gift of Mrs. Otto N. Frenzel 81.338

This elegantly finished, velvet evening cape is characteristic of
George Philip Meier designs. Meier operated a large workshop
at L. S. Ayres & Co., the leading Indianapolis department store
of his day. He and his wife Nellie, a palmist, entertained both
their local friends and visiting notables at weekly salons. The
Meiers travelled to Europe twice a year to obtain designer orig-
inals for the Parisian fashion shows Meier staged at Ayres. Undoubtedly, many of these acquisitions were used as models for
clothing that would be sold at the store.

Over a lissome body, unconstructed garments of the 1920s
fall from shoulder to hem. The ideal evening cape for a col-
umnar dress would be soft enough to wrap around the body,
as this one does. It is interesting that Meier placed his beautifully worked decorative details on the inside rather than the
outside of the garment.

Materials
    Basic fabric
        warp: silk, two-ply S-twist; black
        weft: silk, two-ply S-twist; black
        supplementary warp: silk, three-ply Z-twist; black
    Lining
        warp: silk, single-ply S-twist; black
        weft: silk, single-ply S-twist; black
        embroidery:
            metallic
                core thread: cotton, four-ply S-twist; yellow
                strip: copper, Z-twist; gold colored
Techniques
    Warp-faced woven pile, cut; with supplementary warp pile
        proportions: one supplementary warp per two main
            warps, one velvet rod per three main wefts
    Pieced garment with one piece
    Lining: warp-faced 7/1 satin weave; tucks in lining, front
        facings shaped
        embroidery: couched stitches
    Labelled with embroidered ribbon, "Meier"
Thread count
    Basic fabric
        warp: 98   weft: 148   supplementary warp: 49
    Lining
        warp: 376   weft: 111

Catalogue Number 153
Raoul Dufy (1877-1953), manufactured by Bianchini-Ferrier,
    France
Furnishing Fabric, *La Moisson*, ca. 1920
cotton and linen plain weave, block printed
55½ x 47 (141 x 119.5) warp x weft
Gift of Mrs. Mary Quinn Sullivan 27.126

When Raoul Dufy became a painter, the art world was exploring the nature of color and form. These influences were not lost on him. Around 1910 he began to design furnishing fabric for the firm of Bianchini-Ferrier. Dufy was stimulated by the precise requirements of color chemistry for cloth and the mechanics of the printed image.[131] Around 1908 he had begun to engrave woodblocks[132] and as a result the forms in this piece seem more geometrically disposed, a quality that relates them to woodblock prints. Richness of pattern is created here through the opposition of the parallel, straight lines and the curved forms of the wheat, much as it does in his 1928 drawing of the same subject.[133] In addition to his cotton furnishing prints, Dufy designed printed shawls, handkerchiefs, and wall hangings, as well as brocades for furnishings and garments. His subject matter and presentation are not typical of flowery fabric patterns of the time, for he sought inspiration in decorative arrangement, wherever it could be found.[134]

Materials
  Basic fabric
      warp: cotton, single-ply Z-twist; tan
      weft: bast (linen), single-ply Z-twist; tan
      dye/pigment: medium brown
Techniques
  Balanced plain weave
  Block printed in one color, printed to selvedges
  Selvedge: ⅛ in. (0.3 cm) wide of warp-dominant plain
    weave with paired warps
  Metal stud in selvedge at top, "BF"
Thread count
  Basic fabric
      warp: 51   weft: 38
Pattern repeat
  warpwise: 29 in. (73.5 cm)   weftwise: 15¼ in. (39.0 cm)

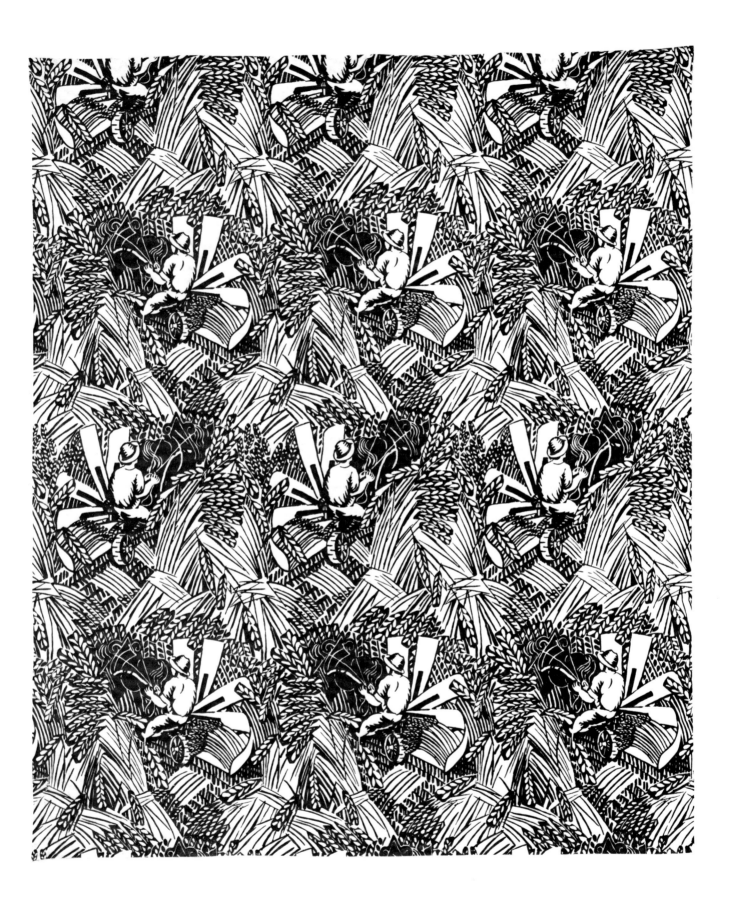

Catalogue Number 154
Mariano Fortuny (1871-1949), Venice, Italy
Furnishing or Garment Fabric, 20th century
silk velvet weave with silk supplementary warp (solid velvet),
    discharge dyed, printed
80½ x 51¼ (204 x 130) warp x weft
Emma Harter Sweetser Fund 77.308

Fortuny, a painter, turned to fabric and costume design to express his belief that painting, etching, photography, textiles, and clothing were all works of art. He worked equally well in each medium and was an innovator in stage design, lighting techniques, and many other creative ventures. Though born in Granada, Fortuny spent much time in Italy, and his family finally moved to Venice. His style was evolving just as the Arts and Crafts, the Aesthetic, and the Modern movements were grappling with what they perceived as the artificiality of art. All three sought to find simpler, more direct methods of creating furnishings, architecture, and clothing, and advocated the use of manual techniques and natural materials. Fortuny realized such goals by experimenting with natural dyes and applying patterns by hand.

His most famous applications of these principles are the form-revealing, pleated silk gowns he dyed in rich colors and the printed velvets he used for furnishing or wall covers and for soft-draped jackets and capes. His patterns on velvet—often based on Renaissance and seventeenth-century European, as well as Turkish and Iranian models—prompted innovations in production methods. The crinkled, flaky surface of this velvet was achieved by applying pigment over a natural paste and pressing the color into the cloth with a roller or other mechanical device.[135] Frequently his patterns were so thoroughly worked with hand-applied pigment and metallic powders that no two areas looked the same, as in this piece.

Fortuny closely supervised the workshops that produced innovative dresses and patterned velvets in his thirteenth-century Venetian palazzo. His first costumes, the Knossos scarf and the Delphos dress, were designed in 1906 through 1907, and his velvet printing soon followed. He varied the basic styles of his first pieces only marginally throughout his career, so his pieces are not datable stylistically.[136] Because of his family's wealth, Fortuny worked as he wished—outside the couture system—and never abandoned his high standards or personal supervision of production.

Materials
  Basic fabric
    warp: silk, single-ply S-twist; light violet
    weft: silk, no twist; light violet
    supplementary warp: silk, no twist; light violet, gray
    pigments:
      blue colored; major metallic element copper, minor
        magnesium
      gray colored; major metallic element copper, minor
        magnesium
      white colored; major metallic element copper, minor
        aluminum
      yellow colored; major metallic element copper, minor
        magnesium
  Backing
    warp: silk, no twist; light green
    weft: silk, no twist; light green

Techniques
  Warp-faced woven pile, cut; with supplementary warp pile
      proportions: one supplementary warp per two main
        warps, one velvet rod per three main wefts
  Discharge-dyed and stencil-printed in three colors
  Backing: balanced plain weave
  Labelled with "Mariano Fortuny Venice"
Thread count
  Basic fabric
    warp: 90   weft: 130   supplementary warp: 45
  Backing
    warp: 128   weft: 119
  Pattern repeat
    warpwise: 15¼ in. (39.0 cm)   weftwise: 24 in. (61.0 cm)

Catalogue Number 155
Florence Kawa, Milwaukee WPA Handicraft Project,
    Wisconsin, United States
Wall Hanging, *The Workers*, ca. 1936
cotton plain weave, block printed
63¾ x 41¾ weft x warp
Museum purchase supplementing the
    Eliza M. and Sarah L. Niblack Collection 39.41

A federally funded artists' relief program, the Works Project Administration's Federal Arts Project (WPA/FAP) followed several less effective efforts to help artists impoverished by the collapse of the art market in the Great Depression. Funded from the fall of 1935 until 1943, it was part of President Franklin Roosevelt's New Deal, which created work relief projects throughout the country.[137]

The WPA/FAP funded many kinds of artistic media, including murals, sculpture, easel paintings, prints, and decorative arts. Frame and diorama makers also benefited from the Project. A number of artists were employed to instruct the public in the art centers that were established and in the schools. Because artists were funded regardless of the type or quality of their work, the effort was truly democratic. Interpretations of the American scene, particularly the worker, were popular in these artists' pieces. Portrayals of these laborers did not embody an ideology, but expressed the simple dignity of their contribution toward building a community.[138]

In this block-printed panel, which was probably made as a decorative wall hanging, working men and women are shown as abstracted forms, removed from the normal noise, dirt, and sweat of a factory. No social commentary is delivered through the worker, however; his relation to the gears and cogs of the machines is aesthetic rather than political.

Materials
Basic fabric
    warp: cotton, single-ply Z-twist; light brown-yellow
    weft: cotton, single-ply Z-twist; light brown-yellow
    pigments: yellow-green, blue-green, blue, brown-red,
    black
Techniques
Balanced plain weave
Block printed in five colors
Selvedge: ¼ in. (0.8 cm) wide, warp-dominant plain weave
Finish: edges turned under and whip stitched
Thread count
Basic fabric
    warp: 68   weft: 66
Pattern repeat
Center
    warpwise: 6 in. (15.0 cm)   weftwise 11½ in. (29.0 cm)
Borders
    warpwise: 13¼ in. (33.5 cm)   weftwise: 8 in. (20.5 cm)

335

Catalogue Number 156
Richard Lindner (1901-1978), United States
Wall Hanging, *Untitled #1*, 10/20, 1964
wool felt, synthetic satin, and vinyl; pieced, appliquéd
83 x 47 (210.5 x 118)
Gift of the Contemporary Art Society 69.35.2

In cultures that consider painting an important art form, artists have used designs derived from painting in their textiles (see cat. 40 and 103). The contemporary artist does not always execute the piece s/he has designed, particularly if the medium allows for duplication, as appliqué does. The appliqué illustrated here was issued in an edition of twenty. The flat planes of color intrinsic to this technique effectively mirror Lindner's own painting style. The motif of an aggressive, robust woman is one of the principal images in his work. Sexual overtones and almost violent imagery are expressed through flat planes of differently textured fabric in strident colors.

Materials
   Basic fabrics
      wool felt; blue, black, yellow, orange, violet, red, gray, green-blue
      synthetic satin; white, pink, light red-orange
      synthetic vinyl; brown, black
   Backing
      warp: synthetic, two-ply S-twist; blue
      weft: synthetic, two-ply S-twist; blue
Techniques
   Fabrics of natural and synthetic fibers; felt, satin weave, and nontextile structures
   Pieced and appliquéd with straight and zigzag machine stitches
   Backing: balanced plain weave
   Labelled "Made by Betsy Ross Flag & Banner Co., Inc." and signed "10/20 Richard Lindner N.Y. 1964"
Thread count
   Backing
      warp: 32   weft: 32
Exhibition
   Painting and Sculpture Today, 1969, Indianapolis Museum of Art, 1969
   New Accessions USA, Colorado Springs Fine Arts Center, 1970

Catalogue Number 157
Norman Norell (1900-1972), United States
Evening Dress, 1966
silk plain weave (crepe) and nylon net, embroidered with
    beads
38 (96.5) length
Gift of Mrs. Lyn Revson 80.266

"Arty talk about *haute couture* gives me a swift pain."[139] This down-to-earth statement articulates Norman Norell's fundamental attitude toward fashion. This designer was born Norman David Levinson on April 20, 1900, just north of Indianapolis. At the age of 19, he left Indiana to study at Parsons School of Design in New York. After an additional stint at the Pratt Institute, he designed theatrical costumes until he became Hattie Carnegie's designer in 1928.

At that time Paris couture was the symbol of social status: Carnegie purchased fashions in Paris twice a year and her designer reinterpreted them to suit American taste. During his years with Carnegie, Norell learned to perfect detail, a skill that became his trademark. After a disagreement with her in 1940, he left her employ and joined Anthony Traina, a producer of moderately expensive dresses for the mature, larger woman. With a combination of expertise in American ready-to-wear and creative craftsmanship, Norell launched one of the most successful fashion careers ever known in the United States.

Norell's timing couldn't have been better, for when he created his first collection with Traina in 1941, France was in the midst of World War II. Separated from the Parisian influence that had marked the fashions of Hattie Carnegie and her contemporaries, newer American designers were eager to fill the void. Norell's most important contribution to fashion design was his ability to combine elegance and ease with meticulous craftsmanship, in garments that became classic style statements. He said:

> Fashion's function is to enhance the beauty of a woman. It must also serve her needs in a constantly changing world. Fashion follows very quickly on the heels of a new way of life. It changes constantly because women want it to.[140]

One of his enduring classics was the chemise. A straight chemise was shown in his first collection, and he retained the shape throughout his career. It was made in jersey for daytime wear under superbly constructed coats (see cat. 158) or made of silk and covered with beads for evening wear, as here. While simplicity was his hallmark, superb fabrics and meticulous workmanship enhanced his classic design. Other designers were content to subcontract the production of each line of garments, but Norell personally supervised every aspect of his collections and always demanded perfection.

His garments are classics in the best sense of the word. They integrate aspects of the changing times, yet also remain timeless. Although well-constructed classics such as suits, coats, and dresses for day were an important part of Norell's lines, he also relished glamour at night. He has said of his fashions, "They can never be too simple during the day or too elaborate at night, as far as I'm concerned."[141]

This evening dress in peach silk crepe de chine combines two of Norell's most important elements, the straight chemise and the surface of glittering rhinestone beads. The mermaid or siren dress encrusted with beads or sequins was one of Norell's perennial favorites and was designed in both short and long lengths. This short version was made during the late sixties, when miniskirts were the rage.

Materials
    Basic fabric
        warp: silk, no twist; light orange
        weft: silk, single-ply overspun S-twist; light orange
    Outer fabric
        vertical element: synthetic (nylon), single-ply S-twist;
            light orange
        horizontal element: synthetic (nylon), single-ply S-twist;
            light orange
    Embroidery
        beads, round and cylindrical; clear
Techniques
    Basic fabric: warp-dominant plain weave, overspun wefts
    Outer fabric: machine-made hexagonal net
    Embroidered with round faceted beads
    Pieced garment with one piece
    Trim: fringe of faceted cylindrical beads
Thread count
    Basic fabric
        warp: 120   weft: 66
    Outer fabric
        mesh, vertical: 23   horizontal: 24

Catalogue Number 158
Norman Norell (1900-1972), United States
Coat, 1962
wool twill weave
36½ (93) length
Gift of Mrs. John E. Miklozek 80.278

Beautifully conceived and constructed coats were important in Norell's work. This classic coat made in gray wool combines a silhouette that follows the figure and a dramatic cape collar. Here, Norell not only calls attention to the upper part of the torso but also to the neckline, which on this coat is gracefully rounded to stand away from the neck of the wearer—a feature that is a hallmark of his design. This kind of elegant simplicity is the basis of Norell's fashion philosophy:

> My approach to design consists of a great deal of thinking and not much designing. I believe in thinking out what the next logical and natural trend in fashion will be. Once I have decided, the rest is easy. I simply take the most straightforward approach to it, without any extra, fancy trimmings. I don't like over-designed anything.[142]

Norell set the standard for a whole generation of designers. In 1943 he won the first Coty Award and after receiving two more, was inducted into the Coty Hall of Fame in 1956. He received a number of other awards and accolades both here and abroad.

His biannual showings were held at nine at night, a time no other designer dared to try. Clients attended these formal affairs because they adored Norell and wanted to experience the excitement of the presentation of his new line. In fact, his generous, self-effacing, and good-humored manner endeared him to his co-workers as well as his clientele.

Materials
Basic fabric
  warp: wool, single-ply S-twist; gray-tan
  weft: wool, single-ply S-twist; gray-tan
Lining
  warp: silk, no twist; gray
  weft: silk, no twist; gray
Techniques
Balanced 2/2 diagonal twill weave
Pieced garment with one piece
Trim: plastic buttons
Lining: warp dominant plain weave
Thread count
Basic fabric
  warp: 64   weft: 59
Lining
  warp: 188   weft: 110

341

Catalogue Number 159
Bill Blass (b. 1922), United States
Evening Dress, 1981
silk plain weave (crepe) and silk plain weave (taffeta)
55 (140) length
Gift of Mrs. Ronald Reagan and Bill Blass 82.50

On May 7, 1981, Nancy Reagan wore this strikingly simple red silk taffeta and chiffon evening dress to a state dinner for Japan's Prime Minister Zenko Suzuki and his wife, Sachi Suzuki. The First Lady also donned the dress on February 3, 1982, for a state dinner for the new President of the Arab Republic of Egypt, Hosni Mubarak, and his wife, Suzan Mubarak.

Another fashion luminary from Indiana, Bill Blass was born in Fort Wayne. He started in the business as a sketcher during the late forties and early fifties. Like Norell, he joined an established manufacturer, Maurice Rentner, and eventually purchased the firm outright. Since then, Blass has changed the American perception of the designer as a recluse. His wit and charm are in demand for numerous social events, and Blass believes that social mingling with the potential customer is necessary. He said:

> Anyone who thinks a designer works in an ivory tower is mad. It's a people-oriented profession. I've always enjoyed being with people. I've never had trouble meeting them or getting along with them. It was a necessity to me as a designer. You have to understand people to make clothes for them because the clothes don't exist in the abstract.[143]

Blass was among the first clothing designers to exert artistic influence over areas such as linens, car interiors, and even chocolates, which bear his name. He said:

> In the 1970s the designer became a brand name. His name on the product gave it validity. This helps establish design standards and, on the whole, is a good thing, providing it is not abused.[144]

Blass designs are basic and mirror the easy practicality that Americans expect from domestic designers. His flair for pleasing the public emerges when he shows a new line. His assistant, Tom Falen, carefully choreographs the show's staging, presentation, and music as the models appear in pairs or groups.

Materials
  Basic fabric
    warp: silk, single-ply tight S-twist; red
    weft: silk, single-ply tight S-twist; red
  Trim fabric
    warp: silk, no twist; red
    weft: silk, no twist; red
Techniques
  Balanced plain weave, loosely woven
  Pieced garment with one piece
  Trim: warp-dominant plain weave, weft thicker than warp;
    at sleeves and belt
Thread count
  Basic fabric
    warp: 116   weft: 120
  Trim fabric
    warp: 176   weft: 110

Catalogue Number 160
Halston (b. 1932), United States
Evening Dress, 1980
silk twill weave (organza) and silk velvet weave with silk
   supplementary warp (solid velvet)
63 (160) length
Gift of Halston, Limited 80.262

Roy Halston Frowick grew up in Evansville, Indiana, and later attended the Art Institute of Chicago. Subsequently, he opened a successful millinery shop in Chicago and left there in 1952 to work for Lily Daché in New York. Halston later joined the custom millinery department at Bergdorf Goodman in New York, and in 1966 his clothing designs were first featured in the Halston Boutique at the store. In 1968 he established his own firm, Halston Limited, where his former Bergdorf Goodman customers followed him. He was on his way to success.

Halston's major contribution was to create an easy, elegant, and comfortable line a great many people could wear. He said:

> I think, probably, it's that I cleaned up Amercian fashion at a particular point in time—I was actually called Mr. Clean. It was just getting rid of all the extra details that didn't work—bows that didn't tie, buttons that didn't button, zippers that didn't zip, wrap dresses that didn't wrap. I've always hated things that don't work. And it had to do with all different kinds of dressing, not just sweater-dressing. It was also daytime dressing for women in business, things to make them look neat and feminine, not too dressed up and not too dressed down. And for evening, it was saying: okay, take off your underpinnings. You've got a damn good figure; you can show it off in an attractive way. The Greeks did it, and the Romans, and everybody else—there's really nothing prettier than the female figure.[145]

Halston's attitude toward design is visible in this garment. The black silk velvet skirt wraps around the waist and creates a slit in front that opens as the wearer walks. The softly draped, white silk l'organza top is articulated with ruffles in the front. The lines are easy and the dress comfortable, yet it displays enough elegance to make the wearer feel she is well dressed.

Halston, like Blass, has given his name to a host of products. He is involved in every aspect of his franchising:

> I have to be involved in every aspect, because it's interesting and it's fun. And I want the success, not just for my own ego. It's a big business, you know, and the livelihoods of thousands and thousands of people depend on your productivity. You have to be serious about it.[146]

Halston has joined Norton Simon Enterprises in order to divest himself of bookkeeping and some managerial responsibilities and devote more time to creativity. He claims the creative process is not easy for him:

> Any new design I do myself. I drape it on a mannequin or on my model. I cut it on the floor, really— and it can be at two in the morning—and I extend it on paper to all its different possibilities. That is, if it is a new idea for a collar, you extend it on paper so that you can see every possibility for a coat, blouse, dress, suit, or whatever. To me, this is the most interesting part—to invent new cuts and new points of view in fashion. And how that happens isn't that a light bulb goes on and click! you have it. You have to pull it out of yourself—and pull and pull and pull until it comes.[147]

From Halston's workrooms come a range of styles designed for both the made-to-order and ready-to-wear markets. Models move gracefully to the beat of contemporary music in his jazzy showings. There are no theatrics and no announcements of the numbers of the designs.

Halston has received public acclaim as a symbol of American ease. Not only the customer, but also the design industry appreciates his comfortable styles: his colleagues have given him four Coty Awards and in 1974 placed him in the Hall of Fame.

Materials
   Basic fabric 1
      warp: silk, no twist; white
      weft: silk, no twist; white
   Basic fabric 2
      warp: silk, two-ply S-twist; black
      weft: silk, two-ply Z-twist; black
      supplementary warp: silk, no twist; black
   Lining
      warp: silk, no twist; black
      weft: silk, no twist; black
Techniques
   Basic fabric 1: warp dominant diagonal twill weave
   Basic fabric 2: warp-faced woven pile, cut; with
      supplementary warp pile
         proportions: one supplementary warp per two main
            warps, one velvet rod per three main wefts
   Pieced garment with two pieces and belt: blouse and skirt
   Skirt lining: balanced plain weave
Thread count
   Basic fabric 1
      warp: 220   weft: 92
   Basic fabric 2
      warp: 88   weft: 136   supplementary warp: 44
   Lining
      warp: 146   weft: 136

Notes

[1] Wilson, 1979, p. 151.

[2] Wilson, 1979, pp. 153-54.

[3] Rissenlin-Steenebrugen, 1980, p. 183-185.

[4] Thornton, 1965, p. 21.

[5] Rissenlin-Steenebrugen, 1980, pp. 245-46.

[6] The term "mantua maker" originated in the seventeenth century, when seamstresses made women's undergarments and accessories (mantuas were a type of jacket) and male tailors made women's gowns. By the mid-eighteenth century seamstresses provided most parts of a woman's apparel. (Buck, 1979, p. 160).

[7] Thornton, 1965, pp. 80-81.

[8] Clouzot, 1927, p. 76.

[9] Naylor, 1980, p. 8.

[10] Naylor, 1980, p. 98.

[11] Naylor, 1980, p. 7.

[12] Weibel, 1944, viii-ix.

[13] Weibel, 1972, p. 66.

[14] Weibel, 1944, ix.

[15] The Ciervales Master, Aragon, *Legends of St. James* (1500-1510) oil on panel (26¾ in. x 12½ in.), James E. Roberts Fund, 24.3.

[16] Mayer-Thurman, 1975, p. 48.

[17] Mayer-Thurman, 1975, p. 44

[18] Mayer-Thurman, 1975, p. 40.

[19] Anthony Janson, personal communication.

[20] Weibel, 1972, p. 67.

[21] This damask is a patterned weave that alternates plain and satin weaves which reverse on the back side of the cloth.

[22] Trudel, 1950, pp. 2879-90.

[23] Wardwell, 1980, p. 285.

[24] Our piece is virtually identical to one published in *Sammlung Leopold Ikle, St. Gallen Textilian*; the few variations are most noticeable in the drawing of Jacob and in the flowers (1923, vol. II, pl. 67).

[25] Trudel, 1950, p. 2888.

[26] Janson, personal communication.

[27] Trudel, 1950, p. 2874.

[28] Digby, 1963, p. 28.

[29] Sonday, 1978.

[30] Digby, 1963, p. 52.

[31] Digby, 1963, p. 27.

[32] Digby, 1963, p. 43.

[33] Digby, 1963, p. 42.

[34] Mayer-Thurman, 1975, p. 49.

[35] Meyer-Heisig, p. 27.

[36] Weibel, 1972, p. 68.

[37] Meyer-Heisig, pp. 27-28.

[38] The Museum published this set of six tapestries when it acquired them in 1966. The research was prepared by Carl Weinhardt, Jr., then Director of the Museum and Kurt Pantzer, trustee and noted Turner scholar and collector. It is from that publication that the following information is drawn (*IMA Bulletin*, Weinhardt, 1966, pp. 5-10, Pantzer, 1966, pp. 11-24).

[39] Thornton, 1965, p. 82.

[40] They are translated as follows: (screen from left to right)

Panel 1. *Magnes Amoris Amor* (Great love of love); *Acceptas Refero Flammas* (I shall give back the flames received)

Panel 2. *Te Quo Cum Que Sequar* (I shall follow you anywhere); *Per Oprositas Vavior* (?)

Panel 3. *Sic Ille Effulsit In Orbe* (Thus that one shone in the world [orb]); *Fortiter Ac Svaviter* (Bravely and agreeably)

(screen from left to right)

Panel 1. *Custoditet Arcet* (He guards and wards off evil); *Ivuat Isque Sperare* (It helps to hope)

Panel 2. *Primitias Sudor Aethereus Beat* (For the first time heavenly sweat [moisture] blesses [?]); *In Cruce non In Ense Salus* (Salvation lies in the cross, not in the sword)

Panel 3. *Tenor Idem Cordis Et Oris* (I am considered to be the same of heart and of face); *Flectiur Haud Frangitur* (It is bent but by no means broken)

Panel 4. *Gaudet Patientia Duris* (Patience rejoices in difficult things); *Tangor Non Tingor Abunda* (I am touched but not imbued excessively)

[41] It appears that the lining and fringe are original to the piece.

[42] Thornton, 1965, p. 82

[43] Thornton, 1965, p. 92.

[44] Weibel, 1972, p. 151.

[45] Risselin-Steenebrugen, 1980, p. 250.

[46] Mayer-Thurman, 1975, p. 25.

[47] Vaclavir, p. 48.

[48] Vaclavir, p. 53.

[49] Risselin-Steenebrugen, 1980, pp. 433-35.

[50] Risselin-Steenebrugen, 1980, pp. 341-42.

[51] Thornton, 1965, p. 37.

[52] Irwin, 1955, pp. 153-54.

[53] Thornton, 1965, pp. 95-98.

[54] Thornton, 1965, p. 90.

[55] Maeder, 1983, essay by Rothstein, p. 83.

[56] Thornton, 1965, pp. 116-17.

[57] Cox, 1957, p. 102.

[58] Herrera, personal communication.

[59] Sill, 1975, p. 10.

[60] Herrera, personal communication.

[61] Gervers, 1977, essay by Levey, p. 185.

[62] Mayer-Thurman, 1975, pp. 34-35.

[63] Rothstein, 1983, p. 85.

[64] Gervers, 1977, essay by Levey, p. 185.

[65] Thornton, 1965, p. 109.

[66] Gervers, 1977, essay by Levey, p. 186.

[67] Mayer-Thurman, 1975, p. 31.

[68] Mayer-Thurman, 1975, p. 49.

[69] Herrera, personal communication.

[70] Maeder, 1983, essay by Ratzi-Kraatz, p. 117.

[71] The following description and conclusions were provided by Dorit Paul, a longtime Museum docent and ardent researcher.

[72] Thornton, 1965, pp. 128-29.

[73] Buck, 1979, p. 26.

[74] Buck, 1979, p. 33.

[75] Thornton, 1965, pp. 53-54.

[76] Thornton, 1965, pp. 57-58.

[77] Rothstein, personal communication.

[78] Buck, 1979, pp. 41-43.

[79] Information concerning its various stages and present restoration can be found in a paper given by conservator Harold Mailand and published in the proceedings of the International Textile Conference at Como, Italy, in 1980 (Pertegato, 1982, essay by Mailand, pp. 229-38).

[80] Buck, 1979, p. 28.

[81] Buck, 1979, p. 31.

[82] Maeder, 1983, essay by Scheur, p. 103.

[83] F. Montgomery, 1970, pp. 194-211.

[84] Pettit, 1975, pp. 33-57.

[85] F. Montgomery, 1970, fig. 187.

[86] F. Montgomery, 1970, pp. 198-99.

[87] Pettit, 1975, pp. 45-46.

[88] Katzenberg, 1973, pp. 4-5.

[89] Katzenberg, 1973, pp. 29-31.

[90] Pettit, 1974, pp. 45-46.

[91] F. Montgomery, 1970, pp. 199-200.

[92] Clouzot, 1927, pp. 23-24.

[93] Clouzot, 1927, p. 33.

[94] Clouzot, 1927, p. 34.

[95] Clouzot, 1927, pp. 21-22.

[96] Clouzot, 1927, pp. 37-39.

[97] Rosenblum, 1967, plates 2 and 5.

[98] Metropolitan Museum of Art, 1927, cat. no. 144, p. 44.

[99] Floud, 1955, p. 6.

[100] Victoria and Albert Museum, 1960, p. 37.

[101] Floud, 1955, p. 32.

[102] The Arts Council, p. 5.

[103] Clark, 1973, p. 56.

[104] Clark, 1973, p. 55.

[105] Clark, 1973, p. 57.

[106] Irwin, 1955, p. 19.

[107] Rossbach, 1980, p. 37.

[108] Rossbach, 1980, p. 55.

[109] Irwin, 1955, p. 30.

[110] Simeon, 1979, p. 101.

[111] Risselin-Steenebrugen, 1980, p. 471.

[112] Wardle, 1968, p. 38.

[113] This information on Indiana coverlet weavers comes from Pauline Montgomery's thorough study, *Indiana Coverlets & Their Weavers*, (P. Montgomery, 1974).

[114] Holstein, 1973, p. 4.

[115] Orlofsky, 1974, p. 26-27.

[116] Orlofsky, 1974, pp. 51-52.

[117] Orlofsky, 1974, p. 136.

[118] Orlofsky, 1974, p. 97.

[119] Orlofsky, 1974, p. 57.

[120] Jones, 1973, p. 7.

[121] Jones, 1973, pp. 13-15.

[122] Jones, 1973, p. 10.

[123] Jones, 1973, p. 12.

[124] The quilt shown here is virtually identical to one illustrated in Jones (Jones, 1973, p. 34).

[125] Orlofsky, 1974, p. 61.

[126] Orlofsky, 1974, pp. 61-62.

[127] Cunningham, 1970, p. 538.

[128] Schoelwer, 1979.

[129] International Cultural Corporation of Australia, p. 20.

[130] The Viking Press, 1977, p. 60.

[131] Berr de Turique, 1930, p. 94.

[132] Berr de Turique, 1930, p. 260.

[133] Berr de Turique, 1930, p. 62.

[134] Berr de Turique, 1930, pp. 262-64.

[135] de Osma, 1980, p. 119.

[136] de Osma, 1980, p. 28.

[137] O'Conner, 1973, pp. 27-28.

[138] O'Conner, 1973, p. 22.

[139] Lee, 1975, p. 349.

[140] Lee, 1975, p. 353.

[141] Lee, 1975, p. 353.

[142] Lee, 1975, p. 377.

[143] Walz, 1978, pp. 46-47.

[144] Walz, 1978, p. 47.

[145] Gross, 1980, p. 238.

[146] Gross, 1980, p. 163.

[147] Gross, 1980, p. 238.

Africa and the Americas

Catalogue Number 161 (see color plate, p. 62)
Paracas Style; probably from the Paracas Necropolis,
    South Coast, Peru
Burial Wrapper, Early Intermediate Period, Epoch 1 or 2,
    400–200 B.C.
wool plain weave, embroidered with wool
42½ x 15¾ (108 x 40) warp x weft
Mrs. A. W. S. Herrington and
    the Eliza M. Niblack Textile Fund 47.88

The Paracas Peninsula is located on the south coast of Peru between the Pisco and Ica river valleys. The first scientific excavations of the region took place in 1925, when Julio Tello, a Peruvian archaeologist, discovered two major burial sites. Having been systematically examined, the 429 burial bundles retrieved from these sites yielded numerous spectacular textiles.[1]

Making fabrics is an ancient art in Peru, where cotton was cultivated by 3000 B.C. Cotton fragments not constructed on a loom have been excavated from the preceramic period. The first loom with heddles that has been found dates to the time of the introduction of pottery (2000–1400 B.C.).[2] Textile patterning in the Early Horizon (1400–400 B.C.) was limited primarily to tapestry weave, but embroidery and working with camelid fibers had quickly become dominant[3] by the beginning of the next period, the Early Intermediate.

Part of burial wrappings that formed a bundle, the piece illustrated here was probably executed during the first two centuries of the Early Intermediate. When a wealthy individual died, his body was dried in the fetal position and then wrapped in his own precious garments and other, gift textiles; ritual objects were tucked into the folds.[4] The wrapped body was placed in a basket, which was then enveloped with other textiles. The finished bundle was formed like a mound, which may have inspired later Andean mound shrines.[5] Certainly this elaborate treatment of the corpse demonstrates the importance placed upon the afterlife as well as the elevation of the dead to the status of ancestor, the intermediary between the living and the world beyond.

In southern Peru, the innovative and turbulent period in which these textiles were produced created a new set of mythical images. What precipitated this new development is unclear, but the images on Paracas textiles obviously reflect new religious precepts. One of the most interesting and prevalent motifs, the Oculate Being, represents a mythical personage, or a human impersonating such a creature.[6] Many of these images translate observation of the real world into needle and thread, a process that fits their function as ideographs of the cult of nature as well as the culture's belief in life after death.[7]

Agricultural fertility was a primary concern to the early Peruvian peoples, and fittingly so, since the success or failure of crops could cause the increase or disappearance of the society. The Nasca People attempted to control this aspect of nature through the gods they created. The figure shown here is a Nasca supernatural being who has gold forehead and whisker ornaments, which are partially obliterated by the fan he holds. The stooped position of the figure is somewhat unusual; gods are usually depicted as falling or flying. Alan Sawyer tentatively interprets the iconography as follows:

> The figure holds a trophy head in its upraised hand while the other holds a fan and a tassled cord commonly associated with trophy head cult warriors. Serpent-like streamers are attached to both wrists; the

upper one terminating in a stylized otter head with tongue protruding (symbolic of water), the lower one ends in an animal figure (probably a fox in view of its pointed ears and bicolour pelt). A monkey figure may be seen on the end of a short band emerging from the figure's head. It is an important symbol of the trophy head cult and it may be significant that it takes the place of the triangular obsidian beheading knife usually found in this position. The long tresses of the figure lie across its back. The torso is bare showing chevron-like ribs and large navel—shamanistic symbols of death and rebirth. The skirt of the figure is composed of serpent-like trophy head elements.[8]

This fragment represents one quarter of a large mantle's central field. In the Early Intermediate, such wrappers customarily displayed a central field with squares, alternately decorated and undecorated, and a wide, embellished border. Embroidery was the most common decorative technique during this period: the stem, satin, and running stitches, as well as edgings of cross-knit looping, were among the few stitches used. This piece almost exclusively uses stem stitch, in an over-four-under-two execution—that is, the yarn passes over four threads of the ground fabric and then back under two. Specialists in spinning, dyeing, weaving, and embroidering may have made cloths like this one. Although women wove the ground fabric, as they did in virtually all pre-Columbian Peruvian weaving, men who were particularly well versed in, and thus sensitive to, the rapidly changing ritual iconography probably executed the embroidery.[9] These pieces commemorate an extraordinary people who initiated the fantastic variety of decorative techniques and dramatic imagery typical of pre-Columbian Peruvian textiles.

Materials
    Basic fabric
        warp: wool, two-ply tight S-twist; dark violet
        weft: wool, two-ply tight S-twist; dark violet
    Embroidery
        wool, two-ply S-twist; light and medium yellow, green,
            violet, light and dark blue, light orange, red-violet,
            yellow-brown
Techniques
    Balanced plain weave
    Embroidery
        flat counted stitches: padded satin; stem
Thread count
    Basic fabric
        warp: 21   weft: 22

Catalogue Number 162 (see color plate, p. 63)
Kingdom of Chimor, North Coast, Peru
Fragment of Shirt, Late Intermediate Period 6-8
   (ca. A.D. 1350-1476)
cotton plain weave, embroidered with feathers
28¾ x 13½ (73 x 34) warp x weft (?)
Emma Harter Sweetser Fund 82.58

The Kingdom of Chimor, which lasted from about A.D. 1300 until the sixteenth-century European conquest, encompassed an area of northern Peru that stretched south from the present border with Ecuador for 650 miles. The kingdom's capital, now known as Chanchan, was a great city esteemed for its pomp and extraordinary wealth. Now in ruins near the mouth of the Moche River overlooking the ocean, it may have been the largest city in ancient Peru. It consisted of modest structures that surrounded more elaborate compounds, some of which contained burial platforms for the distinguished dead.[10] Glorious objects such as elaborate textiles, featherwork, magnificent gold ornaments, and dinnerware have been taken from these burial sites, largely by looters. The animals on this piece may be foxes, which are uncommon on textiles.[11]

   This piece is made of three panels of woven cotton, and each of its feathers is individually knotted to the structure. The two left-hand panels retain three selvedges and two of the images cross slightly over the joining seam, an indication that these two pieces were sewn together before the featherwork was added. The right panel is cut on the far right edge, and the stitching joining it to the two left panels differs from the stitching that joins those two. These features imply that the piece originally composed the bottom of a tunic with a slit in the center. The two left panels were probably on one side of the garment and the right panel on the other.

Materials
   Basic fabric
      warp: cotton, single-ply tight S-twist; brown
      weft: cotton, single-ply tight S-twist; brown
   Embroidery
      feathers; green, yellow, orange, blue
      cotton, two-ply S-twist; light brown
Techniques
   Balanced plain weave
   Continuous warp with four selvedges
   Embroidered with feathers attached to ground in knotted
      running stitches
   Three panels sewn together at selvedges
Thread count
   Basic fabric
      warp: 49   weft: 30

Catalogue Number 163
Charasani Region, Department of La Paz, Bolivia
Bag (*chuspa*), ca. 1900
wool plain weave with wool complementary warp,
 embroidered with beads, trimmed with wool tassels
11½ x 15½ (29 x 40) without strap, weft x warp
Eliza M. and Sarah L. Niblack Collection 33.718

The La Paz region of Bolivia borders on the Peruvian highlands. When the Inca captured the territory south of Lake Titicaca, on the border between Peru and Bolivia, they discovered the ancestors of the Indians who live in that region today. Bags like this one were used in male attire during the time of Inca civilization.[12] In particular, the *callawaya*, or diviners and healers (*q'olla*, medicine; *wayu*, bag), used them to hold their ritual paraphernalia. In ancient times *callawaya* purportedly performed brain surgery and employed compounds such as penicillin long before its development in Europe. The woven pattern on this bag is known as *wayrapallay*, a pattern associated with the *callawaya* that may represent a snail or cornucopia. *Wayra* means to encourage prosperity, joy, and supernatural powers[13]—attributes certainly suited to a healer and diviner.

Materials
 Basic fabric
 warp: wool, two-ply S-twist; black, orange-red, orange,
 light green, light violet
 wool, two-ply Z-twist; red-violet
 complementary warp: wool, two-ply S-twist; white, black,
 orange-red, light green
 weft: wool, two-ply S-twist; black
 Strap
 warp: wool, two-ply S-twist; orange, black, light green,
 light violet
 weft: wool, two-ply S-twist; light green, light violet
 Embellishments
 beads: round; clear, light and dark blue, red, green,
 yellow, orange-yellow, light red
 cylindrical; clear, white, dark green, dark blue
 tassels: wool, no twist; orange, light and dark green, dark
 blue, yellow, red, white, light red, light blue-green, dark
 brown, gray
Techniques
 Warp-faced plain weave and warp-faced floats with
 complementary warp, loom shaped flaps
 Embroidered with beads
 Trim: wrapped tassels and woven binding
 Strap: warp-faced plain weave, paired wefts
Thread count
 Basic fabric
 warp: 77   weft: 16
 complementary warp: 77 pair
Pattern repeat
 warpwise 1¾ in. (4.5 cm)

Catalogue Number 164
Achiri Area, Altiplano Region, Department of La Paz, Bolivia
Ceremonial Cloth (*awayo*), ca. 1900
wool plain weave with wool complementary warp
37½ x 29¼ (95 x 74) warp x weft
J. E. Koffenberger Fund 80.214

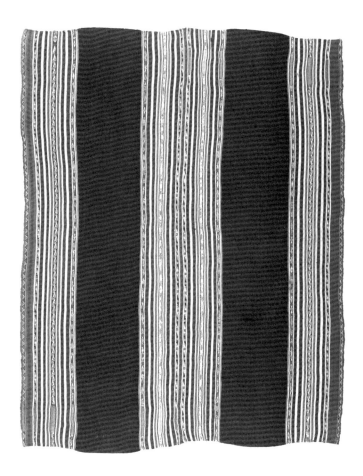

The people living near Lake Titicaca are the descendants of the largest community of Indians in ancient Bolivia. Considered sacred, the lake attracted many to its environs even though the climate was forbidding. Textiles such as these were used to wrap ceremonial gifts and offerings. Woven on simple body-tensioned looms, they were unusually constructed, with two panels of cloth that were edged by four selvedges. In order to make this cloth, the weaver wove from top to bottom and then from bottom to top to meet the previously finished cloth near the bottom edge. Finally, the string heddle was removed and the last few rows were woven by hand with a needle. This section is easily detected since the customary pattern is interrupted and the fabric more loosely woven. Typical textile patterns from this region feature a large plain central field and subtly colored edge stripes, which contain small, geometric designs.[14]

Materials
Basic fabric
  warp: wool, two-ply S-twist; dark blue, light and medium
    red, light blue, yellow-green, yellow
  complementary warp: wool, two-ply S-twist; white, dark
    red, dark blue
  weft: wool, two-ply S-twist; dark blue

Techniques
  Warp-faced plain weave and warp-faced floats, with
    complementary warp
  Continuous warp with four selvedges
  Two panels sewn together at vertical selvedges with zigzag
    running stitch

Thread count
  Basic fabric
    warp: 90   weft: 21
      complementary warp: 90 pairs (180 threads)

Catalogue Number 165
Town of Santo Tomas Chichicastenango, Guatemala
Ceremonial Cloth, ca. 1930
cotton plain weave with silk and cotton supplementary weft
 (brocade)
34½ x 27¾ (87.5 x 70.5) warp x weft
Gift of Mrs. C. E. Smith from the Carolyn Bradley Collection
 62.96

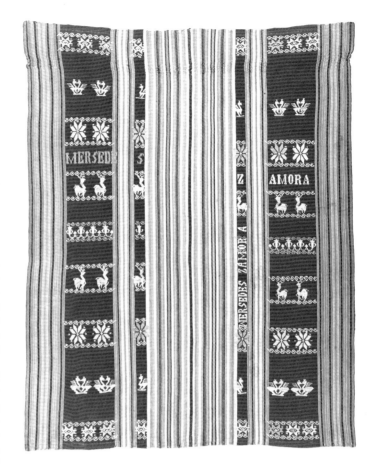

Since their languages are related, the Indians in Guatemala today were probably influenced by the ancient Maya, as well as by the other classical cultures of Mexico. The only artifacts of early textile traditions in the highlands are clay spindle whorls (600–300 B.C.) and figurines dressed in skirts and loincloths (ca. 300 B.C.–A.D. 1000). Spain conquered the area in 1720 and it became independent in 1821.[15]

The town of Santo Tomas Chichicastenango is best known in the highlands for its biweekly market. In fact, most people in the region live outside the town and visit it only on market and festival days. Fabrics from this region are characterized by thin stripes with decorative bands that are worked in as the cloth is woven. The needleworker joined these two, four selvedged panels with brightly colored embroidery stitches on a dark blue ground.

A member of the Cofradiá probably used a finely decorated piece like this while caring for statues dedicated to particular saints. The Spanish established these brother- and sisterhoods to take care of churches and religious paraphernalia in the absence of permanent priests. These caretakers covered their hands with cloths when they handled materials related to various celebrations, such as firecrackers, flowers, candles, and food. Mercedes Zamora, the name embroidered on this piece, was probably the owner of the cloth.

Materials
Basic fabric
　warp: cotton, two-ply Z-twist; dark blue, yellow, light
　　blue-green, light green, light blue, red, white
　　　cotton, two-ply S-twist; light violet, light red-violet
　weft: cotton, two-ply S-twist; dark blue, red, white
　supplementary weft:
　　silk, no twist; light violet, light red, light green, yellow
　　　white
　　cotton, single-ply S-twist; white
　　cotton, two-ply S-twist; light red-violet

Techniques
Warp-faced plain weave (background) and weft-faced floats
　in plain weave alignment (figure), with discontinuous
　supplementary weft, supplementary wefts paired or in
　groups of four
　　proportions: one group supplementary weft per one
　　　main weft
Continuous warp with four selvedges
Two panels sewn together at vertical selvedges with zigzag
　running stitch

Thread count
Basic fabric
　warp: 92　weft: 25
　　supplementary weft: 25 groups (50 threads)

Catalogue Number 166
Town of Saltillo, Mexico
Man's Wrapper (*sarape*), 19th century (?)
cotton and wool plain weave (tapestry)
98 x 51¼ (248.5 x 130) with fringe, warp x weft
Eliza M. and Sarah L. Niblack Collection 33.1229

The Saltillo *sarape* appears to be a happy marriage of Mexican Indian and Spanish traditions.[16] The source of the classical design is probably Indian: it has a diamond-shaped central medallion with a serrated edge and a minutely patterned background and border. The fine wool and treadle loom used to execute the pattern, and the prestige it attained, however, are Spanish.

Blankets with or without neck openings were worn throughout Mexico for centuries before the European incursion. When the Spanish overtook central Mexico, the Tlaxcalan Indians who lived near Puebla were one of their important allies. The Spanish introduced horses, cattle, and wool-bearing sheep as well as the treadle loom to the area, and the Indian weavers there adopted the latter two. As the Spanish expanded their empire northward, they sent the Tlaxcalan to "civilize" the obstreperous Chichimec Indians. It was one of these moderating expeditions that took a group of Tlaxcalan Indians to Saltillo. Eventually, more of them settled in San Esteban, where they wove the now famous Saltillo *sarapes*.[17]

When Mexico gained independence in 1821, the Saltillo *sarape* became an expression of national pride. It had formerly been worn by the wealthy Spanish *charros* who had developed horse culture to a high art. One can imagine the superb image of a Spanish gentleman—dressed in highly embroidered garments, a sombrero, and a Saltillo *sarape*—astride a steed elaborately adorned with silver ornaments.[18] The highly prestigious garment, once worn by the conquerers, was adapted by local wealthy citizens as an expression of their own importance.

This finely woven blanket is a masterly composition that balances the rather nervous serrated and dotted patterns in the central medallion with the regular geometric, zigzag grid of the central field. Filled with smaller dots, triangular motifs border all these elements and contain the flamboyant character of the design.

Saltillo *sarapes* were traded throughout Mexico and the southwestern United States through the great Mexican fairs, which distributed other local materials as well as fancy goods from Europe and the Orient. Because of its status, this *sarape* later strongly influenced Rio Grande and Navajo weavers.

Materials
  Basic fabric
    warp: cotton, two-ply S-twist; white
    weft: wool, single-ply Z-twist; white, black, blue
      cotton, two-ply S-twist; white
Techniques
  Weft-faced plain weave with discontinuous wefts, slit tapestry joins
  Two panels sewn together at selvedges
  Headings: cotton weft-dominant plain weave
  Fringe: four warp ends, knotted
Thread count
  Basic fabric
    warp: 18   weft: 71

Catalogue Number 167
Nupe Subgroup, Yoruba People, Nigeria
Woman's Wrapper, 20th century
cotton plain weave with rayon supplementary weft (brocade)
74 x 58 (187.5 x 147.5) warp x weft
Emma Harter Sweetser Fund 81.394

West African women weave cotton on a vertical loom. Though this loom probably has an ancient history in Subsaharan Africa, its existence prior to European contact is difficult to substantiate; the humid, warm climate quickly destroys wooden looms and the textiles woven on them. By the eleventh century A.D., production of cotton was widespread in Africa, and a contemporary site in Mali has yielded scraps of cotton and wool woven textiles.[19] Vertical looms may have been used through much of Africa long before the Muslim incursion probably introduced the treadled horizontal loom. This evidence implies that men used the vertical loom until the more efficient horizontal loom was known. After that time, women wove domestic articles in the home on the vertical loom.

While most male weavers now produce cloths for the market, women weave mainly for themselves and their families and sell only the surplus. With the vertical loom, usually set up in the home, the weaver wraps the warp continuously around top and bottom beams. To raise alternate sheds, she inserts a shed stick for one and string heddles for the other. The woven portion is slipped to the back as a section of cloth is completed. The woman works the piece until just a small section of warp is left unwoven, and then removes it from the loom either by cutting through the middle of the remaining warps or by loosening the end beams and slipping the cloth off uncut. The fabric illustrated here is formed of two strips that were woven as one panel before they were cut and sewn together. She introduced patterns by manually inserting small bobbins of colored threads onto the surface of the cloth. Some of the motifs probably represent combs, stools, bracelets, an hourglass drum, and an umbrella.

West African costume has been documented since the fifteenth century, when various types of draped and wrapped dress were described. Some women still wear cloths such as this one, wrapped around their bodies and tucked in at the top. In many areas women abandoned weaving when cheap, printed European cloth became available. However, Nupe weavers still produce many textiles because of the prestige now attached to them, and numerous traditional cloths continue to be used today—although Western influence has altered their importance.

Materials
Basic fabric
 warp: cotton, single-ply Z-twist; red, black, light and medium blue
 weft: cotton, single-ply Z-twist; black
 supplementary weft: synthetic (viscose rayon), no twist; yellow, orange, white, red, light brown, light and medium green, light and medium blue, black
Embroidery
 synthetic (viscose rayon), two-ply S-twist; two yellows, white
Techniques
Warp-dominant plain weave (background) and weft-faced floats in plain weave alignment (figure), with discontinuous supplementary weft, paired warps and tripled wefts
 proportions: one supplementary weft per four group main weft
Two panels sewn toegther at selvedges with machine stitching
Finish: raw edges turned under and embroidered with machine stitches
Thread count
Basic fabric
 warp: 58 pairs (116 threads)
 weft: 26 groups (78 threads)
 supplementary weft: 13

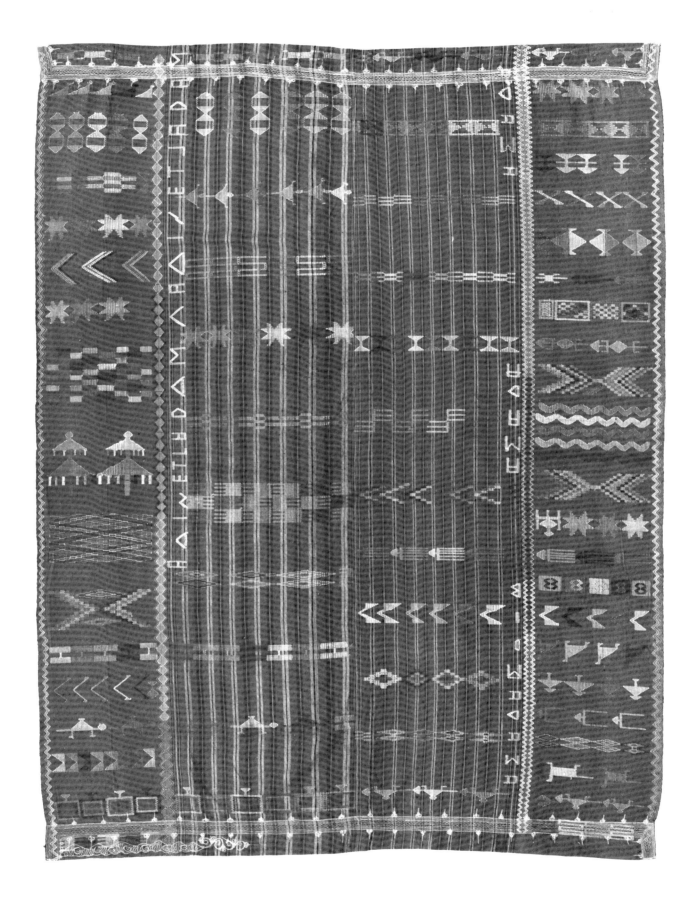

Catalogue Number 168
Kuba People, Zaire
Garment or Furnishing Fabric, 20th century
raffia plain weave, embroidered with raffia
82.61: 26½ x 24½ (76.5 x 62) warp x weft (?)
82.62: 27 x 26 (68.5 x 66) warp x weft (?)
Helen Adams Bobbs Fund 82.61 and 82.62

Before cotton was introduced, bast and raffia fibers were probaby widely used in Subsaharan Africa. The earliest example of bast fiber textiles was excavated from the ninth-century site of Igbo-Ukwu in southeastern Nigeria. While bast comes from the inner bark of a tree, the raffia used in these examples comes from the leaf of a raffia palm. The fibers are peeled from a leaf and used in the lengths in which they come. Rather than spun, these fibers are put on the loom straight, so textiles woven from them usually range from 16 to 24 inches. The wefts are pulled through the shed with a hook, and the loose ends left at each side are cut and hemmed to keep the cloth from unravelling.

Today looms using straight lengths of raffia are found in Zaire, Angola, Gabon, and parts of Ghana. In 1917, H. Ling Roth reported seeing them in Sierra Leone, southeastern Nigeria, and Cameroon as well. This rather random sampling hints at an earlier and wider distribution of this loom, which easier technologies later displaced.[20] That men weave on these looms today implies that tradition predating the horizontal treadle loom has been retained. Where these looms are used, the horizontal loom is not, and women do not weave to any great extent.

Among the Kuba, women decorate woven squares with embroidery. As can be seen here, both flat stitches and cut pile are worked on the surface with a needle. Since the embellishing thread passes under the top crossing of the weave structure alone, the embroidery stitches do not show on the reverse of the cloth. The geometric patterns used for fabric decoration are the same ones used in woodcarvings and on the body for scarification. Many patterns have names, some of which are purportedly related to particular Kuba kings. For the last century the pile cloths have been executed mainly by the Kuba and their neighbors along the Kasai River. Examples brought to England in the mid-eighteenth century from the Kongo people living at the mouth of the Congo River indicate, however, that the practice was more widespread at that time.[21]

In the eighteenth century embroidered raffia cloths were used as clothing and blankets and on stools and chairs for people of rank, functions some of these items still perform today. The edges of the squares are sewn together to make larger cloths or smaller garments. Olfert Dapper documented the joining of small raffia fiber squares for an overskirt in 1686,[22] and Lopez's sixteenth-century report describes "a surprising Art in making various Sorts of Cloths, as Velvet, cut and uncut, Cloth of Tissue, Sattins, Taffeta, Damasks, Sercenets, and such like" from palm-tree fibers.[23]

82.61

Materials
Basic fabric
  warp: leaf fiber (raffia), no twist; light yellow-brown
  weft: leaf fiber (raffia), no twist; light yellow-brown
Embroidery
  leaf fiber (raffia), no twist; light brown
Techniques
Balanced plain weave
Embroidery
  flat counted stitches: loose running stitch cut to form pile
Finish: edges folded to front and stitched
Thread count
Basic fabric
  warp: 20   weft: 23

82.62

Materials
Basic fabric
  warp: leaf fiber (raffia), no twist; light red-orange
  weft: leaf fiber (raffia), no twist; light red-orange
Embroidery
  leaf fiber (raffia), no twist; light yellow-brown, black
Techniques
Balanced plain weave
Embroidery
  flat counted stitches: stem; loose running stitch cut to
  form pile
Finish: edges folded to front and stitched
Thread count
Basic fabric
  warp: 17   weft: 19

Notes

[1] Paul, 1979, p. 11.

[2] Rowe, 1977, p. 11.

[3] Dwyer, 1971.

[4] In fact, the artifacts found in these bundles have provided much of the information now available on Paracas culture (Paul, 1979, p. 293).

[5] Paul, 1980, p. 298.

[6] Dwyer, 1971.

[7] Paul, 1980, pp. 294-95.

[8] Sawyer, personal communication.

[9] Dwyer, 1971.

[10] Menzel, 1977, pp. 21-22.

[11] Rowe, personal communication.

[12] Wasserman, 1981, pp. 1-2.

[13] Wasserman, 1981, p. 10.

[14] Wasserman, 1981, p. 11.

[15] Rowe, 1981, pp. 12-14.

[16] Information for the following comments was derived from Joe Ben Wheat's excellently concise chapter on the Saltillo *sarape* in the exhibition catalogue *Spanish Textile Traditions of New Mexico and Colorado* (Museum of International Folk Art, 1979).

[17] Museum of International Folk Art, 1979, essay by Wheat, p. 75.

[18] Museum of International Folk Art, 1979, essay by Wheat, p. 74.

[19] Picton, 1979, p. 28.

[20] Picton, 1979, p. 86.

[21] Picton, 1979, p. 198.

[22] Sieber, 1972, p. 25.

[23] Sieber, 1972, p. 28.

L. P. Stodulski, D. Nauman, and M. Kennedy

Technical Appendix
Analysis of Precious Metal Threads

Introductory Comments

The identification and study of precious metal threads has, in the past, been the province of the textile curator and conservator. These scholars attempt to accomplish their task through *in situ* visual observation of thread color in order to distinguish between threads of different metallic composition, and by microscopic observation of individual sampled specimens to determine thread construction. Using these techniques, four different types of metallic threads have been identified and reported:

1. Small diameter solid metal wires.
2. Thin sheets of precious metal which have been cut into narrow strips, called *lamellae*, and spun around a fine linen or silk thread, called the core. These narrow strips can be of gilded silver.
3. Thin sheets of metal applied onto animal membrane—such as leather—or paper, cut into strips, and then wound onto a core thread.
4. Gilt leather or paper strips, not wound on a core but attached to the fabric as flat strips.

Visual and microscopic determinations of thread and strip construction by *in situ* examination of textiles are difficult at best. The microscopic examination of sampled threads provides more information about thread type and strip construction, but neither of these methods provide a positive identification of the metallic composition of the thread (if it is a wire) or the strip. The best the curator can do is to speculate that two wires or strips are composed of different metals, or mixtures of metals, based on the respective colors of their surfaces. The situation is further complicated by the frequently subtle color differences. Thus, in order to be certain of metallic composition, small specimens must be subjected to material analyses.

Very few analytical studies of precious metal threads have been conducted. To the best of our knowledge, only one such study, involving the scanning electron microscopic analyses of medieval gilt silver threads (ca. 1250-1350) taken from eight similar, excavated textiles has been reported.[1] It was therefore our purpose to investigate the construction and metallic composition of golden- and silver-colored threads from the Museum's exhibition pieces with a combination of optical microscopic, atomic emission spectrographic and scanning electron microscopic/x-ray analytical methods. The types of information generated by these analyses, and the significance of the data in providing a much more detailed picture of thread and strip composition and construction, will be discussed here. Fifty-four individual objects were sampled by the Museum's textile curatorial and conservation staff, and as many different thread types as could be visually recognized were taken from each piece. Thus, specimens were chosen for study based on surface color differences (golden- or silver-colored), obvious differences in construction (wires, narrow strips wound on cores, and narrow strips without cores), and differences in use within the piece (woven into fabric, used in embroidery, or in the trim). In all, 124 specimens were submitted for analysis.

Analytical Studies:
Microscopic observation of samples

Prior to the spectrographic analyses, an approximately 3 mm length of each specimen was carefully observed under reflected tungsten light, at magnifications of either 40X or 100X, using a Nikon optical microscope. Certain specimen characteristics were used as initial clues to thread and strip construction: top surface color and condition—cracks in or losses of surface layer, for example; presence of corrosion products of different color from unreacted metal, either on the surface or lying under the thin metal layer; and the presence of other materials under surface metal layers. The back surfaces of many strips were observed as well. The specimens observed fell into one of these general categories:

a. strips clearly exhibiting a thin golden-colored surface layer on top of a silver or black (corroded silver) substrate—indicative of a gilded silver strip

b. golden-colored strips with surfaces so intact that no different metal underlayers were observed—suggesting either a very well preserved gilded silver strip, or a gold metal strip

c. silver- or black-colored (corroded silver) strips with no definite golden surface layer detected

d. small diameter solid metal wires, either golden- or silver-colored

e. strips with thin, golden- or silver-colored layers over much thicker fibrous backings, presumably of paper, and

f. strips consisting of thin golden- or silver-colored surface layers on top of a colored claylike material, which was itself on top of a fibrous (paper?) backing.

Even though the identities of the metals contained in these samples could not be determined by this method, the above data were not only very helpful, but indeed often critical, to classifying these threads in a later part of this study.

Atomic Emission Spectrographic Analyses

Immediately after microscopic analysis, each specimen was transferred to a pure graphite sample electrode, packed with graphite powder, carefully positioned in an Applied Research Laboratories Spectrographic Analyzer, and heated to about 4000°F by means of the instrument's powerful DC electric arc. This instrument allows the analyst to determine the elemental composition of an unknown sample in the following way: when subjected to intense heat, the atoms of each of the different chemical elements within the sample emit a series of wavelengths of ultraviolet and visible light. It is well known that this series of wavelengths emitted by atoms of a particular element, called the emission spectrum of that element, is characteristic of that element alone. Thus, if a sample containing gold, silver, copper, and other metallic and certain nonmetallic elements were strongly heated, the sample would simultaneously emit the characteristic wavelengths, that is, the emission spectra of each of the different elements present. A portion of the light emitted from the vaporized sample would pass through the spectrograph, be separated into its component wavelengths by a diffraction grating, and finally expose a strip of special photographic film. Upon development, the film would reveal the record of the spectrum of the sample as a series of closely spaced lines of varying intensities. Since the exact wavelengths of the emission lines of all the elements are accurately known, the analyst can determine which elements were present in the unknown sample by identifying their emission lines on the film. Conversely, the absence of elemental emission lines would prove that either that element was absent, or if present, was there in very low concentration.

Quantitative analyses are also possible. It has been shown that the intensity of an emission line is roughly proportional to the amount of the element giving rise to it, that is, the amount of that element originally in the unknown sample. Thus, elements present in large or major concentrations give rise to intense lines while those present in minor or trace amounts exhibit proportionately less intense lines. The relationship between the amount of a given element in a sample and the intensity of its emission line must be experimentally established with standard materials that contain accurately known amounts of the elements being determined.

Further discussion of the principles of qualitative and quantitative atomic emission spectrographic analyses is beyond the scope of this appendix. This study determined the presence or absence of about fifty metallic and nonmetallic elements for each specimen analyzed. Also, the presence of silver, gold, and copper as either major, minor, or trace constituents was determined through comparison of the appropriate emission lines of these metals with those measured from vaporization of a standard containing a known amount of each of them. The concentrations of the other elements reported below, usually present in trace quantities, were determined through the relative line intensity values of these elements as given in the literature.

Classification of Metallic Threads

The visual, microscopic, and compositional data generated by the methods described above were combined (see Table) and analyzed in order to classify the strips more precisely. The first column of the table gives the catalogue number of the textile sampled and the number and use description of the individual threads. The second column gives the provenance of each piece. The third column gives the color of each thread or strip as visually determined during sample selection and removal. The microscopic description of each laboratory specimen submitted for analysis is given in the fourth column, followed by the major, minor, and trace elemental composition of the specimen as determined by spectrographic analysis. The final column lists the class to which each thread was assigned, based on the foregoing data.

The various classes established were:
  I. Gold metal layer on silver strip
 II. Silver metal strip, containing impurity metals
III. Wire threads—solid gold, silver or copper metal, with other metals present
 IV. Strip made of other kinds of metals, or of metal alloys
  V. a. Gold or gold alloy layer on fibrous backing strip
     b. Silver or silver alloy layer on fibrous backing
 VI. a. Gold or gold alloy on claylike layer over fibrous backing strip
     b. Silver or silver alloy on claylike layer over fibrous backing
     c. Other type of metal alloy over claylike layer and fibrous backing
VII. Miscellaneous strips or threads

The specimens listed in the table were judged to be in the type I category based on clear observation of a thin golden-colored layer over a silver, or a black corroded silver, strip. In some cases, observation of the back of these types of strip revealed a silver-colored surface that greatly helped to confirm the assignment. For the majority of cases, however, the back surface color of the strip was rendered very doubtful by the presence of a thin layer of corrosion product that imparted a golden color to the surface under the lighting conditions employed. All type I strips were spectrographically determined to contain a major amount of silver (Ag), a major or minor amount of gold (Au), and a minor or trace amount of copper (Cu). This data allowed us to decide that the surface metal layer was indeed gold, and that the substrate was silver metal containing some copper as an impurity. The elements silicon (Si), calcium (Ca), magnesium (Mg) and lead (Pb) were also commonly found as impurities in these types of strips. There were twenty-one definite type I strips identified. In many cases, the strip surface was intact, and it could not be definitely determined that it was really a gold layer over a silver substrate. These kinds of specimens (twenty-five of them) were given the designation I or IV, since, even though the elemental profile closely resembled definite type I gilded silver strips, this elemental composition could also indicate a gold-colored strip made of an alloy of silver containing enough gold and copper to give the material a golden color.

The twenty-eight specimens in the type II category had either silver-colored or blackened surfaces, and were shown to contain major amounts of silver, together with minor to trace amounts of gold and copper. With the exception of three Indian (cat. 22, cat. 23-#2 and cat. 28-#4) and one Chinese (cat. 36-#3) specimen, all silver strips contained appreciable amounts of one or both of these other metals. Their presence in these materials was attributed to accidental inclusion and lack of removal during refining of the silver rather than purposeful addition. Traces of lead were also detected in several specimens.

Six examples of wire threads were found—two definitely gold-colored (cat. 97-#3 and 117-#1), one possibly golden-colored (cat. 119-#3), one a coppery-gold (cat. 100-#1), and two definitely silver-colored (cat. 117-#8 and cat. 128-#2). All of the golden-colored specimens contained major amounts of silver and minor amounts of copper. Only one specimen (cat. 117-#3) contained a major amount of gold, strongly indicating that these three specimens were silver alloys with enough gold, and perhaps also copper, added to give them the desired color. The two silver-colored wires contained major silver and minor amounts of gold and copper. The reason for the presence of gold in these wires is not certain. They could represent impurities in the silver. It is also possible that the original manufacturers required an alloy with a more golden and less bright silvery color, and therefore added some gold and copper to the silver. The coppery-gold colored wire is basically copper metal with minor amounts of iron (Fe) and zinc (Zn), and only a trace of silver. Though presently corroded, the original color of this wire would probably have been a golden-yellow; alloys containing copper and smaller amounts of zinc are classified as brass. The diameters of these wires were measured during microscopic observation. The gold and silver specimens were approximately 0.06 mm in diameter and the coppery/brass (?) wire was 0.33 mm in diameter.

Thirteen golden to coppery-golden colored specimens are listed as belonging to the type IV category of strips, based mostly on their respective elemental compositions. All but one of these strips (cat. 23-#3) contained copper as the major element. In this one case, silver was the major and copper the minor element; gold was not detected. Five of these specimens (cat. 150-#1, 151-#1, 100-#2, 152 and 7-#3) were almost pure copper, with only trace amounts of other metals detected. The objects from which these samples came were, in all but one case, nineteenth- or twentieth-century textiles. The remaining specimen (cat. 100-#2) was taken from a Swiss piece

dated to 1520. Two silver-colored strips (cat. 23-#5 and #6) may also belong in this category. Both may very well be silver, copper, and lead alloys, rather than silver strips with copper and lead impurities. Unfortunately, the data available does not allow us to distinguish between these two possibilities.

Type V strips were all clearly identified by microscopic observation. The thin layer on the strip surfaces was sometimes partially missing, and usually extensively cracked where intact. The metallic layer appeared to have been applied directly on the backing, without the aid of an adhesive. In all, six such samples were encountered—all golden-colored and all from Japanese textiles. Gold was the major element in all but one specimen (cat. 45), and that one had a major silver concentration and a minor amount of gold and copper.

Type VI strips were also easily identifiable microscopically. In all but three specimens, a layer of what appeared to be a particulate, red-colored, claylike material was observed between the thin metallic surface layer and the fibrous backing. The other three specimens exhibited a yellow-colored, claylike material underneath the surface of the strips. The red under layer was reminiscent of red bole, a fine-ground clay containing small amounts of red Fe_2O_3 (hematite) and often used in the gilding of paintings, and of stone and wooden objects, to provide a smooth surface layer upon which the gold leaf is applied. The detection of minor amounts of silicon in several of the larger specimens analyzed would tend to support this speculation. The absence of iron is explained by the fact that most of the Chinese specimens submitted for analysis were extremely small—and therefore the iron, which was present in rather small amounts, escaped detection. Twelve of these strips were golden-colored: the compositions of their metallic layers ranged from almost pure gold (cat. 34 and 35) and pure copper (cat. 38-#1) to various mixtures of gold, silver, and copper. Only one silver-colored strip was provided for analysis (cat. 36-#4), and its metallic layer contained a major amount of silver, a minor amount of copper, and only a trace of gold.

Scanning Electron Microscopic/X-Ray Analysis Studies

It has already been pointed out that, in several cases, the assignment of a particular strip to a given class on the basis of optical microscopic and spectrographic compositional data was not always definite. Most notably, some gold-colored strips could not be unequivocally determined to have gold metal layers on silver substrates and had to be identified as being either type I or IV. Also, laboratory specimens of several strips that were silver-colored in the textile exhibited quite corroded surfaces, and were found to contain minor amounts of gold—making it difficult to decide whether these specimens were type II strips containing some gold, or type I strips with the underlying silver corrosion products covering the gold metal surface layer.

An attempt to resolve these problems, and to further our knowledge of the details of metal strip construction, was made by submitting several representative specimens for Scanning Electron Microscopic (SEM) examination.

The instrument used in these studies was an Etek Autoscan Scanning Electron Microscope fitted with an energy-dispersive x-ray Analyzer. The specimens to be examined were mounted in epoxy resin and sectioned perpendicular to the length of the thread with an Ultramicrotome employing a diamond knife. Successive four ten-thousandths of an inch slices were removed from the mounted specimen surface until a representative—that is, an uncorroded—section was obtained. The sectioned specimen was then coated with a very thin layer of material, capable of conducting electricity, placed in the instrument's vacuum chamber, and scanned with a high energy beam of electrons.

Several processes occur when the surface of a sample is scanned by an electron beam.

1. Electrons (called secondary electrons) are emitted by the atoms of the sample itself;

2. The atoms in the sample reflect some of the electrons from the beam (called back scattered electrons), and

3. The energy inherent in the beam disrupts the electronic structure of the sample atoms, causing them to emit x-radiation of characteristic energies.

Each of these different processes provides information about either the surface structure or composition of the sample scanned. The instrument provides information about the surface of the sample by translating the secondary electrons emitted into electrical signals of varying intensities, to produce an image of the surface scanned on an oscilloscope screen. This image, called a secondary electron (SE) image, can be photographed with Polaroid film to produce a permanent record of the sample's surface. The electron beam can be focused down to a very small diameter and be used to scan very small areas. The secondary image is then magnified on the oscilloscope screen to produce SE images of any desired magnifications, up to about 1,000,000X.

The second process described previously allows an analyst to obtain information about the elemental composition of a sample's surface. The back scattered electrons can also be translated into an image (called a back scattered electron, or BSE, image) on the oscilloscope screen. In this case, however, the atoms of those elements having the highest atomic number (that is, the heaviest atoms) reflect more electrons than the lighter element atoms. As a result, the BSE image shows those areas of the surface containing the higher atomic number species as brighter than those containing the lower atomic number species. For example, if the sectioned surface of a strip having a thin layer of gold on a silver substrate were scanned by the SEM operating in the "back scatter" mode, the resultant image would show the gold layer as a bright line next to a grey-colored layer, since gold atoms have a much higher atomic number than silver atoms. BSE images of strip cross-sections showing exactly this effect are

presented below. Furthermore, since the magnification of any SE or BSE image is accurately known, the dimensions of features shown in the photograph of the image can be determined by simple measurement.

The third process, emission of x-rays from the sample surface, is used to identify the elements within the sample area scanned. Atoms of the different elements emit x-rays of different, but characteristic, energies. Thus, an SEM fitted with an x-ray analyzer detects and separates emitted x-rays on the basis of their various energies, and thereby identifies the elements present. Also, the intensities of the x-rays of different energies are used to determine the relative amount of each element present in the sample scanned.

In summary, SEM analyses provide information about sample topography, qualitative and quantitative elemental composition, and the distribution of the various elements throughout the sample surface. All this information can be obtained about a large or very small area of the sample, depending upon the magnification chosen. Also, measurements of the size of various sample features can be made from photographs of SE and BSE images.

The SE image (300X magnification) of a mounted and sectioned specimen of thread (cat. 96-#1) is shown in fig. I. The individual fibers of the core thread are clearly seen in this photograph, as well as the cross-section of the strip. Measurements made from this photograph revealed that the diameter of the thread is of the order of 0.30 mm. Fig. IIa is a higher magnification (5000X) BSE image of the strip cross-section. The bright line on the left is the surface gold layer, as proved by x-ray analysis of the spots indicated on the photo. Fig. IIb shows the results of x-ray analyses of areas 1 and 7. Analysis of area 1, the outermost part of the surface layer, shows the presence of a large amount of gold, and only traces of silver and copper. Analysis of area 7 (just beyond the gold layer) shows that only silver and a small amount of copper are present. Analysis of area 5 (back surface of strip) and area 6 (another part of gold layer) gave the same results.

The thickness of the gold layer was measured from the BSE image and found to be 0.7 micrometer (μm) at the thickest point and 0.2 μm at the thinnest point.[2] The thickness of the entire strip is approximately 8.4 μm. These results show that without a doubt, thread sample cat. 96-#1 is a core thread wrapped by a strip having a very thin layer of gold on a much thicker silver substrate.

Several other threads were analyzed by SEM techniques. Figs. IIIa and IIIb show the SE and BSE images (2000 and 5000X magnification, respectively) of sample cat. 118-#3. The section of the strip scanned is highly corroded but the gold layer (bright line, right surface underneath corrosion layer in fig. IIIb) is intact. The identification of this material as gold was again done by x-ray analysis. The corrosion layer above the gold, and the interior of the strip contained silver. Copper was not detected by this technique, which cannot detect elements in concentrations of less than 1 percent. A trace of copper

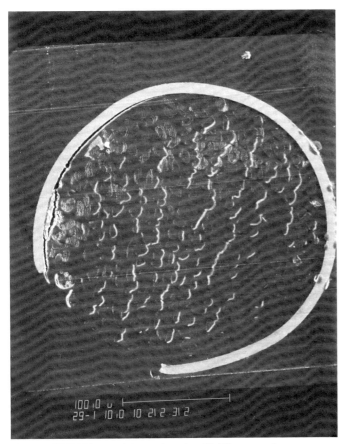

Figure I: 300X SE image of the specimen (cat. 96-#1) cross-section.

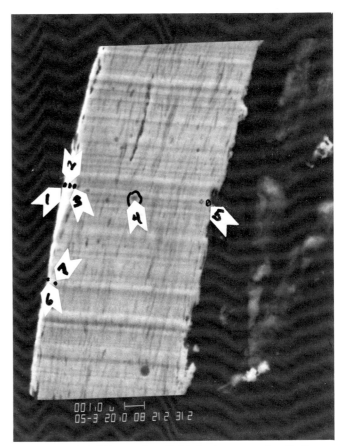

Figure IIa: 5000X BSE image of cat. 96-#1, showing areas analyzed by X-ray Analyzer.

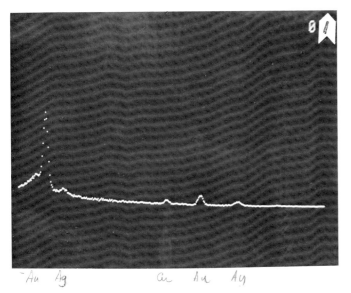

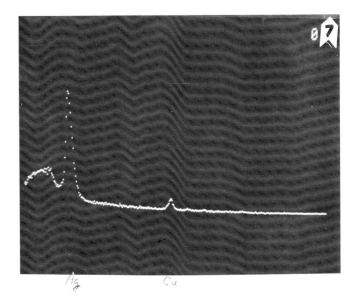

Figure IIb: Results of x-ray analyses of areas 1 and 7, indicated in fig. IIa.

was, however, detected spectrographically. A very surprising result of this analysis was the detection of another gold layer on the *inside* of the strip (see bright line, bottom left of fig. IIIb). The identity of this second surface layer was proven to be gold by x-ray analysis. The thread was 0.22 mm in diameter; the strip (measured in an uncorroded area) was about 10 μm thick and 0.20 mm wide.

The front and back gold layers, as measured from fig. IIIb, were about equally thick—0.22 μm.

Fig. IVa shows the SE image of the Japanese strip (cat. 44). Unfortunately, the fibrous backing strip split into two pieces during mounting in the epoxy resin. The metallic layer is seen on the top surface of the upper fragment. A 10,000X blow-up of this top surface is shown in

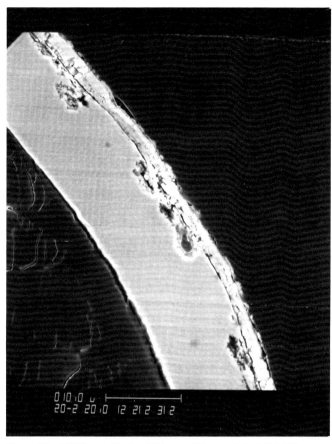

Figure IIIa: 2000X magnification SE image of the sample (cat. 118-#3).

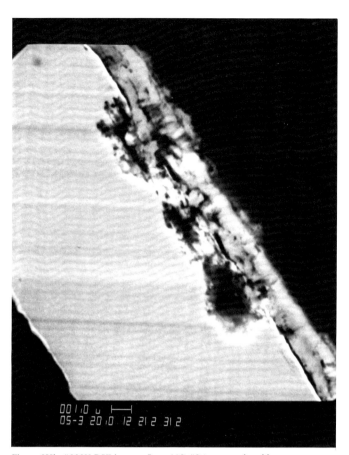

Figure IIIb: 5000X BSE image of cat. 118-#3 (areas analyzed by x-ray indicated).

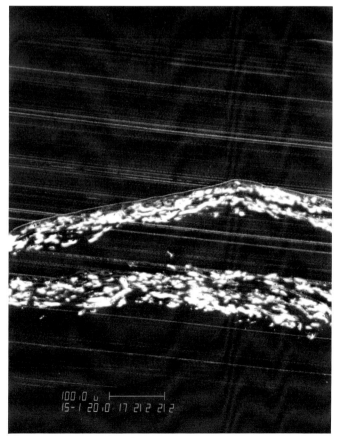

Figure IVa: 150X SE image of the Japanese strip (cat. 44) with gold-silver alloy layer on top.

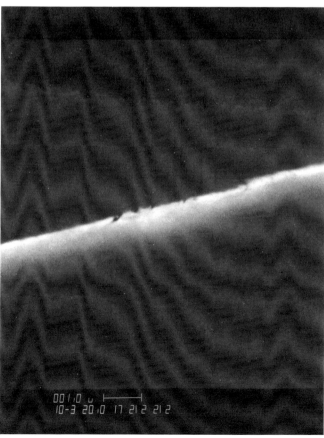

Figure IVb: 10,000X BSE image of gold-silver layer (top bright line—fibrous backing below) cat. 44.

366

Figure Va: 300X SE image of the thread (cat. 34).

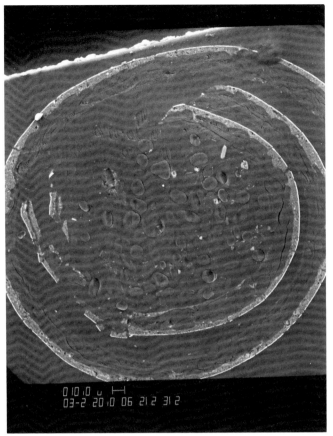

Figure Vb: 300X BSE image of cat. 34.

Figure Vc: 3000X BSE image of cat. 34, showing areas analyzed by x-ray.

fig. IVb. X-ray analysis of this surface layer revealed the presence of major gold and a minor amount of silver, indicating that this material is a gold/silver alloy. The thickness of the layer is 0.1 to 0.2 μm. The entire strip is about 0.62 mm wide and approximately 0.11 mm (110 μm) thick.

Figs. Va and Vb show the 300X magnification SE and BSE images, respectively, of the mounted and sectioned Chinese thread (cat. 34). It appears that the strip was under tension before mounting since, like a stretched-out watch spring, it relaxed and coiled up when placed in the epoxy resin. The surface metal layer is clearly seen (bright line) in the BSE image. The less bright layer underneath the top layer is the material previously suspected of being a red claylike layer. The darkest bottom layer is the fibrous backing. Fig. Vc shows a 3000X magnification blow-up of these layers. The areas indicated were analyzed by x-ray and found to contain gold (only) in the surface layer (area 1), a large amount of silicon, and smaller amounts of aluminum (Al) and iron (Fe) in areas 2 and 4, and very small amounts of silicon, aluminum and iron in area 5. One of the higher average atomic number particles (bright spot—area 3) was shown by x-ray to contain a large concentration of iron. These results are consistent with the previously postulated construction of Chinese strips. Silicon, and to a lesser extent, aluminum are always present in clays. Red bole is colored red by the presence of iron oxide compounds—especially red-colored hematite—Fe_2O_3. It can also be seen in these images that the gold layer lies quite evenly on the smooth surface of the claylike layer underneath, which fills in irregularities in the underlying fibrous backing. The gold layer is about 0.3 μm average thickness; the claylike layer varies from about 3 to 10 μm at its thinnest and thickest points. The thread diameter is 0.22 mm and the strip 0.40 mm (400 μm) wide and 23 μm thick.

Concluding Remarks

This discussion has amply demonstrated the value of material analysis techniques in furthering our knowledge of precious metal threads. Much more remains to be learned, however, about the interesting examples of the weaver's and the metallurgists's arts. The results presented here represent only the first phase of the cooperative art historical and scientific study of the Museum's extensive textile collection.

Notes

[1] Hoke and Petrascheck-Heim, 1977, pp. 49-62.

[2] For comparison—one mm is about four one-hundredths of an inch (0.04 in.) and one μm is about four one-hundred-thousandths of an inch (0.00004 in.).

Sample Number	Curatorial Description	Strip Color (Visual)	Microscopic Description	Elemental Composition of Strip			Strip/Thread Type
				Major	Minor	Trace	
cat. 117	European, ca. 1730-40						
#1 (embroidery)		gold	gold-colored strip	Au, Ag	Cu	Si, Al, Pb, Ca, Mg	I or IV
#2 (embroidery)		gold	gold-colored strip—black corrosion underneath	Au, Ag	Cu	Si, Pb, Mg	I
#3 (embroidery)		gold	0.06 mm diameter golden-colored wire	Au, Ag	Cu	Si	III
#4 (embroidery)		gold	golden-colored strip—black corrosion underneath	Au, Ag	Cu	Si, Pb, Mg	I
#5 (embroidery)		gold	golden-colored strip—corrosion underneath	Au, Ag	Cu	Si, Pb, Ca, Mg	I
#6 (embroidery)		gold	golden-colored strip—black corrosion	Au, Ag	Cu	Si, Pb, Ca, Mg	I
#7 (embroidery)		silver	silver-colored strip—black corrosion in some areas	Ag	Cu	Au, Si, Pb, Mg	II
#8 (embroidery)		silver	0.06 mm diameter silver-colored wire	Ag	Au, Cu	Si	III
#9 (embroidery)		silver	narrow golden-colored strip	Au, Ag	Cu	Si, Pb	I or IV
#10 (embroidery)		silver	very corroded (black) strip	Ag	Au, Cu	Ca, Mg	II or IV
cat. 128	European, 1775						
#1 (weft)		gold	few golden patches on black strip	Ag	Au, Cu	Mg, Ca, Si	I
#2 (embroidery)		silver	0.06 mm diameter silver-colored wire	Ag	Au, Cu	Mg	III
cat. 150	European, ca. 1910						
#1 (embroidery)		gold	dark golden surface w/black corrosion	Cu	—	Ag, Zn	IV
#2 (embroidery)		gray-gold	strip, golden-colored top surface, silver-colored on reverse	Cu	Ag	Au, Si, Ca	IV
#3 (embroidery)		gold	bright golden-colored strip	Cu	Fe	Au, Ag, Ni, Cr, Si	IV
cat. 116	French, ca. 1707						
#1 (weft)		gold	golden-colored strip—black corrosion underneath	Ag	Au	Cu, Si, Ca, Mg	I
#2 (weft)		gold	extensively corroded strip; possible golden surface	Ag	Au	Cu, Si, Ca, Mg	I
#3 (weft)		silver	bright silver-colored strip w/some yellowish highlights	Ag	Au, Cu	Si, Ca, Mg	II
#4 (weft)		silver	black (corroded) surface—only one possible golden patch	Ag	Au, Cu	Si, Fe, Ca, Mg	II

*Assignment also based on SEM analysis for these samples.

Sample Number	Curatorial Description	Strip Color (Visual)	Microscopic Description	Elemental Composition of Strip			Strip/Thread Type
				Major	Minor	Trace	
cat. 112	French, ca. 1710						
#1 (weft)		gold	golden-colored strip	Ag	Au, Cu	Si, Ca, Mg	I or IV
#2 (weft)		gold	golden-colored strip—some corrosion product on surface	Ag	Au, Cu	Ca, Mg	I or IV
cat. 118	French, ca. 1730						
#1 (weft)		silver	bright silver-colored strip; some corrosion present	Ag	Au	Cu, Fe, Si, Ca, Mg	II
#2 (weft)		silver	narrow silver-colored strip	Ag	Au	Cu, Fe, Si, Ca, Mg	II
#3 (weft)		gold	bright golden-colored strip	Ag	Au	Cu, Fe, Si, Ca, Mg	I*
#4 (weft)		gold	golden-colored strip, corrosion underneath	Au, Ag	Cu	Si, Ca, Mg	I
#5 (trim)		gold	golden-colored strip	Ag	Au, Cu	Si, Ca, Mg	I or IV
#6 (trim)		gold	golden-colored strip	Ag	Au, Cu	Si, Ca, Mg	I or IV
#7 (trim)		gold	golden-colored strip, black corrosion underneath	Ag	Au, Cu	Si, Ca, Mg	I
#8 (trim)		gold	dark colored surface	Ag	Au, Cu	Si, Ca, Mg	I or IV
cat. 114	French, ca. 1735						
#1 (weft)		silver	silver-colored strip; some corrosion present	Ag	Au, Cu	Si, Ca, Mg	II
#2 (weft)		silver	possible silver-colored strips; extensively corroded	Ag	Au, Cu	Si, Ca, Mg	II
#3 (trim)		silver	entire strip surface corroded (black)	Ag	Au, Cu	Si, Ca, Mg	II
#4 (trim)		silver	strip surface corroded (black)	Ag	Au, Cu	Si, Ca, Mg	II
cat. 113	French, ca. 1735						
#1 (weft)		silver	black corroded strip w/few gold patches	Ag	Au, Cu	Si, Cu, Mg	II
#2 (weft)		silver	black strip surface—no gold visible	Ag	Au, Cu	Si, Al, Fe, Ca, Mg	II
cat. 127 (embroidery)	French, ca. 1780	gray-silver	one very thin fiber loosely wrapped around core which appeared to have resin-like coating on bundle of fibers. Crystalline (Ag?) substance in spots on resin layer	Ag	—	Si, Mg	VII

*Assignment also based on SEM analysis for these samples.

Sample Number	Curatorial Description	Strip Color (Visual)	Microscopic Description	Elemental Composition of Strip			Strip/Thread Type
				Major	Minor	Trace	
cat. 151	French, ca. 1925						
#1 (embroidery)		gray-copper	darkened strip (golden?), interior and exterior of strip same color; highly corroded	Cu	—	—	IV
#2 (embroidery)		gold	black (corroded) surface, golden-colored in places; also some blue corrosion product	Cu	Ag	—	IV
#3 (embroidery)		gold	golden-colored strip; darkened in patches, with small spots of light blue or green corrosion product	Cu, Au	Ag	Si, Mg	IV
cat. 94 (weft)	Italian, ca. 1475	—	golden-colored strip surface with black corrosion underneath	Ag	Au, Cu	Si, Pb, Ca, Mg	I*
cat. 96	Italian, velvet— ca. 1475 orphrey— 1500-1550						
#1 (weft)		gold	golden-colored surface layer-corrosion underneath	Au, Ag	Cu	Si, Pb, Mg	I*
#2 (embroidery)		gold	golden-colored strip	Au, Ag	Cu	Si, Ca, Mg	I or IV
#3 (embroidery)		gold	corroded (black) strip surface with few golden patches	Au, Ag	Cu	Mg	I
#4 (trim)		gold	golden-colored strip surface, reverse side silver-colored	Au, Ag	Cu	Si, Mg	I
cat. 98 (weft)	Italian, ca. 1550	gold	golden-colored surface, strip largely intact	Ag	Au, Cu	Si, Pb, Sn, Ca, Mg	I or IV
cat. 105	Italian, ca. 1700						
#1 (embroidery)		gold	dark golden-colored strip	Ag	Au, Cu	Si, Ca, Mg	I or IV
#2 (embroidery)		silver	black-colored strip w/few golden patches (tarnish?)	Ag	Au, Cu	Si, Mg	II
#3 (embroidery)		silver	silver-colored strip w/some golden-colored patches (tarnish?)	Ag	Au, Cu	Si, Ca, Mg	II
#4 (embroidery)		silver	blackened strip surface w/ very few golden-colored patches (tarnish?)	Ag, Au	Cu	Si, Mg	II
cat. 119	Italian or French, ca. 1735						
#2 (trim)		gold	golden-colored strip	Au, Ag	Cu	Si, Pb, Al, Ca, Mg	I or IV
#3		gold	0.055 mm diameter silver-colored wire, slightly tarnished	Ag	Au, Cu	Pb, Mg	III
#4 (embroidery)		gold	golden-colored strip, darkened in spots	Ag	Au, Cu	Pb, Ca, Mg	I or IV

*Assignment also based on SEM analysis for these samples.

Sample Number	Curatorial Description	Strip Color (Visual)	Microscopic Description	Major	Minor	Trace	Strip/Thread Type
				Elemental Composition of Strip			
cat. 120	Italian or French, ca. 1740						
#1 (trim)		gold	golden-colored surface layer over black corrosion	Au, Ag	Cu	Si, Ca, Mg	I
#2 (trim)		gold	golden-colored strip	Au, Ag	Cu	Si, Ca, Mg	I or IV
cat. 97	Spanish, ca. 1500						
#1 (weft)		gold	0.060 mm diameter black-colored wire	Ag	Au, Cu	Si	III
#2 (weft)		gold	golden-colored surface w/ very few corrosion spots	Ag	Au, Cu	Si, Pb, Al, Ni, Ca	I or IV
#3 (weft)		gold	golden-colored strip; surface intact	Ag	Au, Cu	Si, Pb	I or IV
#4 (weft)		gold	bright golden-colored strip with corrosion underneath	Ag	Au, Cu	Si, Pb	I
#5 (weft)		silver	silver-colored strip w/some black corrosion	Ag	Au, Cu	Si, Pb, Mg	II
#6 (trim)		silver	uncorroded silver-colored strip on both sides	Ag	Cu	Au, Si, Pb, Ca, Mg	II
cat. 115	Spanish, ca. 1700						
#1 (weft)		gold	golden-colored strip; surface intact but "lumpy"	Au, Ag	Cu	Si, Ca, Mg	I or IV
#2 (weft)		gold	intact golden-colored strip; lumpy surface	Au, Ag	Cu	Si, Al, Mg	I or IV
cat. 123	German(?), ca. 1760						
#1 (embroidery)		gold	golden-colored intact strip	Au, Ag	Cu	Si, Pb, Ca, Mg	I or IV
#2 (embroidery)		silver	golden surface layer with corrosion underneath	Ag	Au, Cu	Si, Ca, Mg	I or II
#3 (embroidery)		silver	black corroded strip surface	Ag	Cu	Au, Si, Pb, Ca, Mg	II
#4 (embroidery)		silver	silver-colored strip	Ag	Cu	Au, Si, Mg	II
cat. 100	Swiss, ca. 1520						
#1 (embroidery)		gray	0.325 mm diameter copper-colored wire	Cu	Fe, Zn	Ag, Si, Pb, Mn, Sn, Ni, Ca, Mg	III
#2 (embroidery)		gold	golden-coppery strip; black corrosion in some spots	Cu	—	Ag, Pb, Mn, Sn, Fe, Ni, Mg	IV
cat. 152 (embroidery)	American, ca. 1925	copper	blue corrosion product over reddish-golden surface— strip badly deteriorated	Cu	—	Ag, Zn, Ca, Mg	IV
cat. 44 (weft)	Japanese, 17th century fabric— 16th century	gold	golden-colored surface layer over strip of fibrous backing—no red underlayer	Au	Ag	Cu, Si, Ca, Mg	V(a)*
cat. 45 (weft)	Japanese, 17th-18th century	gold	golden-colored surface layer (w/gray-green corrosion) on fragmentary fibrous backing	Ag	Au, Cu	Si, Ca, Mg	V(a) or V(b)
cat. 46 (embroidery)	Japanese, 1675-1700	gold	golden-colored surface layer on fibrous backing	Au	—	Ag, Cu, Ca, Mg	V(a)*

*Assignment also based on SEM analysis for these samples.

Sample Number	Curatorial Description	Strip Color (Visual)	Microscopic Description	Major	Minor	Trace	Strip/Thread Type
cat. 43 (weft)	Japanese, ca. 1775	—	red-golden surface layer on red underlayer on fibrous backing	sample too small			VI (—)
cat. 49 (embroidery)	Japanese, 1775-1800	gold	shiny red-golden surface layer on fibrous backing	Au	Ag	Cu, Ca, Mg	V(a)
cat. 47 (embroidery)	Japanese, 1775-1850	gold	red-golden surface layer on fibrous backing	Au	Ag	—	V(a)
cat. 48 (embroidery)	Japanese, 1800-1850	gold	golden-colored surface layer on fibrous backing	Au	Ag	—	V(a)
cat. 34 (weft)	Chinese, 1775-1825	gold	golden-colored surface layer, cracked in spots exposing red-colored underlayer on top of fibrous (paper?) backing	Au	Si	Ag, Cu, Ca, Mg	VI(a)*
cat. 38	Chinese, ca. 1820						
#1 (embroidery)		copper	yellowish-colored surface layer over red underlayer on fibrous backing; green core thread	Cu	—	Ag, Si	VI(c)
#2 (embroidery)		gold	golden surface layer over red underlayer—fibrous backing fragmentary	Ag	Cu, Si	—	VI(b)
cat. 35 (weft, seat)	Chinese, ca. 1820	gold	golden-colored surface over brick red underlayer over fibrous backing; red tinted core thread	Cu	Au, Ag	Si	VI(c)
cat. 35 (weft, back)	Chinese, ca. 1820	gold	golden-colored layer over red underlayer over fibrous backing	Au	—	Ag, Cu, Fe, Al, Si, Ca, Mg	VI(a)
cat. 33	Chinese, ca. 1870						
#1 (embroidery)		copper	gold-red strip, corroded; underlayer present (yellow?) fibrous backing	Ag	Cu	—	VI(b)
#2 (embroidery)		gold	golden surface, red underlayer, fibrous backing	Ag	Cu	—	VI(b)
cat. 36	Chinese, ca. 1880						
#1 (embroidery)		gold	golden-colored layer over brick-red underlayer over fibrous backing—reddish core thread	Au	Ag, Cu	Si, Ca, Mg	VI(a)
#2 (embroidery)		gold	golden-colored strip, jagged around edges; no fibrous backing—some black corrosion	Ag	Au, Cu	Si, Ca, Mg	I or IV
#3 (embroidery)		silver	silvery-colored strip, black corrosion underneath; no fibrous backing	Ag	—	Si, Ca, Mg	II
#4 (embroidery)		gray-silver	black corrosion product over yellow underlayer over fibrous backing	Ag	Cu	Au, Si, Ca, Mg	VI(b)

*Assignment also based on SEM analysis for these samples.

Sample Number	Curatorial Description	Strip Color (Visual)	Microscopic Description	Elemental Composition of Strip			Strip/Thread Type
				Major	**Minor**	**Trace**	
cat. 32	Chinese, ca. 1900						
#1 (embroidery)		gold	bright golden-colored surface layer over red underlayer over fibrous backing	Cu	Au	Ag, Si, Mg	VI(c)
#2 (embroidery)		copper	reddish-golden-colored surface layer over red underlayer over fibrous backing and surface intact	Cu	Ag	—	VI(c)
cat. 81	Moroccan, 19th century						
#1 & 2 (embroidery)		gold	golden-colored surface with black corrosion underneath	Au, Ag, Cu	—	Si, Pb, Ca, Mg	I
#3 & 4 (embroidery)		gold	golden-colored strip; black corrosion underneath	Au, Ag, Cu	—	Si, Pb, Ca, Mg	I
cat. 85 (embroidery)	Moroccan, 19th century	gold	golden-colored strip with some corrosion	Cu	Au, Ag	Zn, Fe	IV
cat. 80 (weft)	Moroccan, 19th century	gold	golden-colored surface with black corrosion underneath	Au, Ag	Cu	Si, Pb, Ca, Mg	I
cat. 78	Tunisian, 19th century						
#1 (embroidery)		gold	silver-colored strip	Ag	Au, Cu	Fe, Ni	I or IV
#2 (embroidery)		silver	silver-colored strip, some corrosion	Ag	Cu	Si, Al, Ca, Mg	II
cat. 61 (weft)	Turkish, 16th century	dark gray	black (corroded) strip	Au, Ag	Cu, Mg	Si, Al, Pb, Mn, Fe, Ca	I*
cat. 62	Turkish, ca. 1600						
#1 (weft)		gold	golden-colored strip; uneven edges	Au, Ag	Cu	Si, Ca, Mg	I or IV
#2 (embroidery)		silver	silver-colored surface	Ag	Cu	Si, Al, Ca, Mg	II
#3 (embroidery)		silver	golden-colored strip	Au, Ag	Cu	Si, Ca, Mg	I or II or IV
cat. 64 (embroidery)	Turkish, 19th century	gold	brass-colored strip	Au, Ag	Cu	Al, Mg	I or IV
cat. 63	Turkish, 19th century						
#1 (embroidery)		gray-silver	silver-colored strip	Au, Ag	Cu	Si, Mg	II
#2 (embroidery)		gold	golden-colored strip, black on reverse side	Au, Ag	Cu	Si, Pb, Mg	I
#3 (trim)		gold	light golden-colored strip	Au, Ag	Cu	Si, Ca, Mg	I or IV
cat. 56 (embroidery)	Iranian, ca. 1875	—	black strip, badly corroded	Ag	Cu	Si	II
cat. 57	Iranian, 19th century(?)						
#1 (embroidery)		gold	golden-colored surface layer on dark corrosion underneath	Ag, Au	Cu	Si, Ca, Mg	I
#2 (embroidery)		silver	tarnished silver-strip surface	Ag, Au	Cu	Si, Ca, Mg	II

*Assignment also based on SEM analysis for these samples.

Sample Number	Curatorial Description	Strip Color (Visual)	Microscopic Description	Elemental Composition of Strip			Strip/Thread Type
				Major	Minor	Trace	
cat. 52 (weft)	Iranian, 18th or 19th century	gold	golden-colored strip; surface intact	Ag	Cu	Au, Si, Ca, Mg	I or IV
cat. 5 (weft)	Sumatran, 19th century	silver	silver-colored layer over yellow resin-like layer on fibrous backing	Ag	Si	Ca, Mg	VII
cat. 7	Sumatran, ca. 1900						
#1 (weft)		gold	silver-colored strip; scoring of surface observed	Ag, Cu	Au	Si, Ca, Mg	I or IV
#2 (trim)		gold	black surface with some golden-colored patches	Cu	Ag	Au, Fe, Si, Ca, Mg	IV
#3 (fringe)		gold	black surface on flat strip; some reddish-golden spots seen	Cu	—	Au, Ag, Zn, Si, Ca, Mg	IV
cat. 8 (weft)	Sumatran, ca. 1900	gold	golden-colored layer over brick red layer over fibrous backing, specimen badly deteriorated	Au, Ag	Cu, Si	Pb, Al, Fe, Ca, Mg	VI(a) or VI(b)
cat. 2 (gold leaf)	Javanese, 19th century	gold	golden-layer over cracked *bright* yellow layer (crevasses present)	Au	—	Cu, Ag	VII
cat. 28 (embroidery)	Indian, ca. 1775	gray	three small diameter threads wound together (not braided); each thread wrapped with dark metallic strip	Ag	—	Au, Cu, Fe, Si, Ca, Mg	II
cat. 26 (weft)	Indian, ca. 1900	gold	silver-colored strip with slight reddish-gold hue	Au, Ag, Cu	Ca	Pb, Fe, Si, Mg	IV
cat. 22	Indian, ca. 1900						
#1 (embroidery)		gold	golden-colored strip, slightly damaged	Ag	Au	Cu, Pb	I or IV
#2 (embroidery)		silver	silvery gold strip, slightly damaged	Ag	—	Au, Cu, Pb	II
cat. 23	Indian, ca. 1900						
#1 (embroidery)		gold	golden-colored strip; red-colored core thread	Ag	Au, Cu	Si, Ca, Mg	I or IV
#2 (embroidery)		silver	silver-colored strip—some surface corrosion; small tears on strip edges	Ag	Cu	Si, Ca, Mg	II
#3 (hem trim)		gold	golden-colored strip with black corrosion—torn edges in some places	Ag	Cu	Si, Mg	IV
#4 (hem trim)		silver	silver-colored strip with black corrosion	Ag	—	Fe, Si, Mg	II
#5 (seam trim)		gold	steel-blue colored strip with black corrosion products	Ag	Cu, Pb	Si, Cr, Ca, Mg	II or IV
#6 (seam trim)		silver	silvery-colored strip; tarnished	Ag	Cu, Pb	Si, Ca, Mg	II or IV
#7 (seam trim)		gold	golden-colored strip; corrosion on surface	Au, Ag	Cu	Si, Fe, Mg	I or IV

*Assignment also based on SEM analysis for these samples.

Bibliography

Abegg, Margaret. *Apropos Patterns for Embroidery, Lace and Woven Textiles.* Bern: Stämpfli and Cie, 1978.

Abun-Nasr, Jamil M. *A History of the Maghrib.* 2nd Ed. Cambridge, Mass.: Cambridge University Press, 1975.

Adam, André. *Bibliographique critique de sociologie, d'ethnologie et de géographie humaine du Maroc.* Memoires du Centre de Recherches Anthropologiques Préhistoriques et Ethnographiques, XX. Algiers: Imprimerie Louis-Jean, 1972.

——————. "Le costume dans quelques tribus de l'Anti Atlas." *Hespéris,* XXXIX, 3-4, 1952, pp. 459-85.

Adams, Marie Jean. *Leven en Doop op Sumba.* [Life and death on Sumba] Rotterdam: Museum voor Land-en Volkenkunde, 1965.

——————. *System and Meaning in East Sumba Textile Design: A Study in Traditional Indonesian Art.* Southeast Asia Studies Cultural Report Series, no. 16. New Haven: Yale University, 1969.

——————. "Symbolic Scenes in Javanese Batik." *Textile Museum Journal,* III, 1, 1970, pp. 25-40.

Akurgal, Ekrem; Mango, Cyril; Ettinghausen, Richard. *Treasures of Turkey.* Geneva: Skira, 1966.

Alport, E. A. "The Mzab." *Arabs and Berbers: From Tribe to Nation in North Africa.* Edited by Ernest Gellner and Charles Micaud. Lexington, Mass.: D. C. Heath and Co., 1972.

Amicis, Edmondo de, *Morocco: Its People and Places.* 2nd Ed. Translated by C. Rollin-Tilton. New York: Putnam, 1893.

Arseven, Celal Esad. *Les arts décoratifs Turcs.* Istanbul: Milli Egitim Basimevi, n.d.

Arts du Maghreb fin XVIIe-debut XXe [siècle]. Paris: Musée National des Arts Africains et Oceaniens, Département des Arts Maghrebins Musulmans, 1973.

The Arts of Islam. [London]: The Arts Council of Great Britain, 1976.

van Asperen de Boer, J. R. J. "An Introduction to Scientific Examination of Paintings." *Scientific Examinations of Early Netherlandish Paintings, Applications in Art History,* pp. 1-40. Netherlands Yearbook for History of Art, 26, Bussum: Fibula-Van Disoeck, 1976.

Atil, Esin, ed. *Turkish Art.* Washington, D.C.: Smithsonian Institution Press, 1980.

Bacon, Lenice Ingram. *American Patchwork Quilts.* New York: William Morrow and Co., 1973.

Baldoui, Jean. "Les arts indigènes." *Encyclopédie de l'Afrique française.* Edited by Eugène Guernier. Volume III: *Maroc.* Paris: Éditions de l'Empire Français, 1948.

Barbour, Nevill. *Morocco.* New York: Walker and Company, 1966.

Basehart, Harry W. "Transhumance." *A Dictionary of the Social Sciences.* New York: The Free Press of Glencoe for U.N.E.S.C.O., 1964.

Basset, Henri. "Les rites du travail de la laine à Rabat." *Hespéris,* II, 1-2, 1923, pp. 139-60.

Batchelor, Elisabeth. *Art Conservation: the Race Against Destruction.* Cincinnati: Cincinnati Art Museum, 1978.

Beer, Alice Baldwin. *Trade Goods: A Study of Indian Chintz.* Washington, D.C.: Smithsonian Institution Press, 1970.

Bel, Alfred. "La population musulmane de Tlemcen." *Revue des Études Ethnographies et Sociologiques,* I, 1908, pp. 200-24, 417-47.

——————. *Les industries de la céramique à Fès.* Algiers: Carbonel, 1918.

Bel, Alfred, and Ricard, Prosper. *Le travail de la laine à Tlemcen.* Algiers: Jourdan, 1913.

Bel, Marguerite A. *Les arts indigènes féminins en Algérie.* Algiers: Gouvernement Général de l'Algérie, 1939.

Bernès, J. P. *Arts et objets du Maroc: le costume marocain, etc.* Paris: C.P.I.P., 1974.

Bernès, J. P., and Jacob, Alain. *Arts et objets du Maroc: meubles, zellidjs, tapis.* Paris: C.P.I.P., 1974.

Berque, Jacques. "Remarques sur le tapis Magrebin." *Études Maghrébines: Mélanges Charles-André Julien.* Série "Études et Methods," II. Publications de la Faculté des Lettres et Sciences Humaines de Paris. Paris: Presses Universitaires Françaises, 1964.

——————. "The Rural System of the Maghrib." *State and Society in Independent North Africa.* Edited by Leon Carl Brown. Washington, D.C.: The Middle East Institute, 1966.

——————. *Structures sociales du Haut Atlas.* 2nd Ed. Paris: Presses Universitaires de France, 1975.

Berr de Turique, Marcelle. *Raoul Dufy.* Paris: Librairie Floury, 1930.

Bertrand, A., and Bertrand, R. *Tribus Berbères du Haut Atlas.* Lausanne: Edita S.A., 1977.

Blum, Stella. *Victorian Fashion and Costumes from Harper's Bazar: 1867-1898.* New York: Dover Publications, 1974.

Bokhara. Jerusalem: Israel Museum, 1967.

Bond, David. *The Guinness Guide to Twentieth Century Fashion.* London: Guinness Superlatives Ltd., 1981.

Bonete, Yves. "Note sur la teinture dans le territoire de Ghardaia." *Cahiers des arts et techniques d'Afrique du Nord,* V, 1959, pp. 120-28.

Boser-Sarivaxévanis, Renée. *Recherche sur l'Histoire des Textiles Traditionels Tissús e Teints de l'Afrique Occidentale.* Basle: n.p., 1975.

Bourrilly, Joseph. *Éléments d'ethnographie Marocaine.* Paris: Librarie Coloniale et Orientaliste Larose, 1932.

Bridier, Marcelle. "Tissage nomade Algérien." *Cahiers des art et techniques d'Afrique du Nord,* II, 1953, pp. 40-51.

Brignon, Jean, et al. *Histoire du Maroc.* Paris: Hatier, 1967.

Brown, Kenneth. *People of Salé: Tradition and Change in a Moroccan City 1830-1930.* Manchester, England: Manchester University Press, 1976.

——————. "An Urban View of Moroccan History: Salé, 1000-1800." *Hespéris-Tamuda,* XII, 1971, pp. 5-106.

Brunot, L. "La cordonniere indigène à Rabat." *Hespéries,* XXXIII, 3-4, 1946, pp. 227-321.

Bryans, Robin. *Morocco, Land of the Farthest West.* London: Faber and Faber, 1965.

Buck, Anne. *Dress in Eighteenth Century England.* New York: Holmes and Meier, Inc., 1979.

Bullock, Alice May. *Lace and Lacemaking.* New York: Larousse and Co., 1981.

Bunt, Cyril G. E. *The Silks of Lyon.* Leigh-on-Sea, England: F. Lewis Publishers, Ltd., 1960.

——————. *Hispano-Mooresque Fabrics.* Leigh-on-Sea, England: F. Lewis Publishers, Ltd., 1966.

Burke, Edmund, III. "The Image of the Moroccan State in French Ethnological Literature: A New Look at the Origin of Lyautey's Berber Policy." *Arabs and Berbers: From Tribe to Nation in North Africa.* Edited by Ernest Gellner and Charles Micaud. Lexington, Mass.: D. C. Heath and Company, 1972.

Burnham, Dorothy K. *Warp and Weft: A Textile Terminology.* Toronto: Royal Ontario Museum, 1980.

Bühler, Alfred. "The Geographic Extent of the Use of Bark Fabrics." *Ciba Review,* XXXIII, 1940, pp. 1170-79.

——————. "Geographical Distribution and Patterns of Plangi Technique." *Ciba Review,* CIV, 1954, pp. 3734-41.

——————. "Ikats." *Ciba Review,* LXIV, August 1942, p. 1586.

——————. "The Origin and Extent of the Ikat Technique." *Ciba Review,* LXIV, August 1942, pp. 1604-11.

——————. "Origins of the Plangi Technique." *Ciba Review,* CIV, 1954, pp. 3743-48.

——————. "Turkey Red Dyeing in South and Southeast Asia." *Ciba Review,* XXXIX, 1941, pp. 1423-26.

Bühler, Alfred, and Fischer, Eberhard. *The Patola of Gujarat.* 2 vols. Basel: Krebs A G, 1979.

Bühler, Alfred; Fischer, Eberhard; and Nabholz, Marie-Louise. *Historic Textiles of India at the Calico Museum.* Volume IV: *Indian Tie-Dyed Fabrics.* Ahmedabad, India: Calico Museum of Textiles, 1980.

Camman, Schuyler. "Embroidery Techniques in Old China." *Archives of the Chinese Art Society in America,* XVI, 1962, pp. 16-40.

Casal, Father Gabriel; Jose, Jr., Regalado Tiota; Casino, Eric S.; Ellis, George R.; and Sondheim II, Wilhelm G. *The People and Art of the Philippines.* Los Angeles: Museum of Cultural History, University of California at Los Angeles, 1981.

Catalogue of a Retrospective Exhibition of Painted and Printed Fabrics. New York: Metropolitan Museum of Art, 1927.

Chantréaux, Germaine. "Les tissages décorés chez les Beni-Mguild." *Hespéris,* XXXII, 1, 1945, pp. 19-33.

──────────. "Le tissage sur métier de haute lisse à Aït-Hichem et dans le Haut Sebaou." *Revue Africaine,* LXXXV, 1941, pp. 78-116; LXXXVI, 1942, pp. 261-313.

Chatinières, Paul. *Dans le Grand Atlas Marocain, 1912-1916.* Paris: Plon-Nourrit et Cie, 1919.

Chénier, Louis de. *The Present State of the Empire of Morocco.* London: G. G. J. and J. Robinson, 1788.

Clark, Fiona. *William Morris: Wallpapers and Chintzes.* New York: St. Martin's Press, 1973.

Clarke, Bryan. *Berber Village: the Story of the Oxford University Expedition to the High Atlas Mountains of Morocco.* London: Longmans, 1959.

Clouzot, Henri. *Painted and Printed Fabrics.* New York: Metropolitan Museum of Art, 1927.

Cohen, Mark I., and Hahn, Lorna. *Morocco: Old Land, New Nation.* New York: Frederick A. Praeger, 1966.

Coon, Carleton Stevens. *Tribes of the Rif.* Harvard African Studies, no. 9. Cambridge, Mass.: Peabody Museum of Harvard University, 1931.

Cootner, Cathryn. *Flat Woven Textiles: The Arthur D. Jenkins Collection.* Washington, D.C.: The Textile Museum, 1981.

Les Costumes Traditionnels Féminins de Tunisie. Tunisia: Centre des Arts et Traditions Populaires, Maison Tunisienne de l'Edition, 1978.

Coustillac, L. "Note sur la rénovation des tissus traditionnels de la région de Gabès." *Cahiers des arts et techniques d'Afrique du Nord,* III, 1954, pp. 64-73.

Cox, Ian, ed. *The Scallop.* London: Shell Transport and Trading Co., Ltd., 1957.

Creekmore, Anna, and Pokornowski, Ila M. *Textile History.* Washington, D.C.: University Press of America, 1982.

Cunninghame-Graham, Robert Bontine. *Mogreb-el-Acksa.* [A journey in Morocco] n.p., 1898; reprint ed., New York: Viking Press, 1930.

Cunnington, C. Willet, and Cunnington, Phyllis. *Handbook of English Costume in the Eighteenth Century.* Boston: Plays, Inc., 1972.

──────────. *Handbook of English Costume in the Nineteenth Century.* Boston: Plays, Inc., 1970.

Dapper, Olfert. *Description de l'Afrique, contenant les noms, la situation et les confins de toutes ses parties. . . .* Amsterdam: Wolfgang, Waesberge, Boom & van Someren, 1686.

Davison, Mildred, and Mayer-Thurman, Christa C. *Coverlets.* Chicago: Art Institute of Chicago, 1973.

Delpy, A. "Note sur le tissage dans les Zemmour." *Cahiers des arts et techniques d'Afrique du Nord,* III, 1954, pp. 9-48.

Denny, Walter B. *Oriental Rugs.* Washington, D.C.: Smithsonian Institution, Cooper-Hewitt Museum, 1979.

Dhamija, Jasleen. *Living Tradition of Iran's Carpets.* New Delhi: Vikas Publishing House PVT, Ltd., 1979.

Digby, George Wingfield. *Elizabethan Embroidery.* London: Faber and Faber, 1963.

de Dillmont, Thérèse. *Encyclopedia of Needlework.* Mulhouse, France: Editions Th. de Dillmont, n.d.

──────────. *The Complete Encyclopedia of Needlework.* Philadelphia: Running Press, 1972.

──────────. *Morocco Embroideries.* Mulhouse, France: Editions Th. de Dillmont, 1955.

Dimand, M. S. *Oriental Rugs in the Metropolitan Museum of Art.* New York: Metropolitan Museum of Art, 1973.

Douette, Edmond. *En tribu: Missions au Maroc.* Paris: P. Geuthner, 1914.

Dozy, Reinhart Pieter Anne. *Dictionnaire détaillé des noms des vêtements chez les Arabes.* Amsterdam: Jean Müller, 1845.

Dunn, Ross E. "Berber Imperialism: the Ait Atta Expansion in Southeast Morocco." *Arabs and Berbers: From Tribe to Nation in North Africa.* Edited by Ernest Gellner and Charles Micaud. Lexington, Mass.: D. C. Heath and Company, 1972.

Dwyer, Jane Powell. "Chronology and Iconography of Late Paracas and Early Nazca Textile Designs." Ph.D. dissertation, University of California at Berkeley, 1971.

──────────. *Paracas and Nazca Textiles, 500-200 B.C.* Boston: Museum of Fine Arts Gallery Guide, 1973.

Earnshaw, Pat. *The Identification of Lace.* Bucks, England: Shire Publications Ltd., 1980.

Eiland, Emmett, and Shockly, Maureen. *Tent Bands of the Steppes.* Berkeley: University of California Press, 1976.

Eiland, Murry L. *Oriental Rugs.* Boston: New York Graphic Society, 1973.

Ellson, Vickie. *Dowries from Kutch.* Los Angeles: Museum of Cultural History, University of California at Los Angeles, 1979.

Embroidered Flowers from Thrace to Tartary. London: David Black Oriental Carpets, 1981.

Emery, Irene. *The Primary Structures of Fabrics: An Illustrated Classification.* Washington, D.C.: The Textile Museum, 1966.

English Chintz. London: The Victoria and Albert Museum, 1960.

Erdmann, Kurt. *Seven Hundred Years of Oriental Carpets.* Berkeley: University of California Press, 1970.

Fabulous Fashion: 1907-67. Australia: International Cultural Corporation of Australia, Ltd., n.d.

Fiske, Patricia; Pickering, W. Russell, and Yohe, Ralph S., eds. *From the Far West: Carpets and Textiles of Morocco.* Washington, D.C.: The Textile Museum, 1980.

Flint, Bert. *Tapis, Tissages.* Volume II: *Formes et symboles dans les arts Maghrébins.* Tangiers: Imprimerie E.M.I., 1974.

Floud, Peter. *English Chintz.* London: The Victoria and Albert Museum, 1955.

Forelli, Sally, and Harries, Jeanette. "Domestic Weaving in Central Morocco: Three Contemporary Examples." *From the Far West: Carpets and Textiles of Morocco.* Edited by Patricia Fiske, W. Russell Pickering, and Ralph S. Yohe. Washington, D.C.: The Textile Museum, 1980.

──────────. "Traditional Berber Weaving in Central Morocco." *Textile Museum Journal,* IV, 4, 1977.

Fox, James J. "Figure Shark and Pattern Crocodile: The Foundations of the Textile Traditions of Roti and Ndao." *Indonesian Textiles: Irene Emery Roundtable on Museum Textiles 1979 Proceedings.* Washington, D.C.: The Textile Museum, 1980, pp. 39-55.

Frank, Barbara E. "Woven Traditions of Rural Morocco." Master's thesis, Indiana University, 1982.

Franses, Michael, and Penner, Robert. "Large Medallion Suzani from Southwest Uzbekistan." *Hali,* I, 2, Summer 1978, pp. 128-33.

Fry, Gladys Windsor. *Embroidery and Needlework.* London: Sir Isaac Pitman and Sons, Ltd., 1944.

Gabus, Jean. *Au Sahara: Arts et Symboles.* Neuchâtel: Éditions de la Baconniére, 1958.

Gallagher, Charles F. "Language and Identity." *State and Society in Independent North Africa.* Edited by Leon Carl Brown. Washington, D.C.: The Middle East Institute, 1966.

Galloti, Jean. "Weaving and Dyeing in North Africa." *Ciba Review,* XXI, May 1939, pp. 738-60.

Galloy-Jorelle, Suzanne. "Les tissages ras de Djebala." *Cahiers des arts et techniques d'Afrique du Nord,* VI, 1960-61, pp. 103-15.

Garner, W. *Textile Laboratory Manual.* London: Heywood Books, 1967.

Gary, Dorothy. *Morocco.* New York: The Viking Press, 1971.

Geertz, Clifford. *Islam Observed: Religious Development in Morocco and Indonesia.* New Haven: Yale University Press, 1968.

──────────. "Suq: the Bazaar Economy in Sefrou." *Meaning and Order in Moroccan Society: Three Essays in Cultural Analysis.* Cambridge, England: Cambridge University Press, 1979.

Geertz, Hildred. "The Meaning of Family Ties." *Meaning and Order in Moroccan Society: Three Essays in Cultural Analysis.* Cambridge, England: Cambridge University Press, 1979.

Gellner, Ernest, and Micaud, Charles, eds. *Arabs and Berbers: From Tribe to Nation in North Africa.* Lexington, Mass.: D. C. Heath and Company, 1972.

Gernsheim, Allison. *Victorian and Edwardian Fashion: A Photographic Survey.* New York: Dover Publications, 1981.

Gervers, Veronika, ed. *Studies in Textile History.* Toronto: Royal Ontario Museum, 1977.

Giacobetti, R. P. *Les tapis et tissages du Djebel-Amour.* Paris: Librarie Ernest Leroux, 1932.

Gilfoy, Peggy S. "Textiles in Africa and Indonesia: A Connection." *Indonesian Textiles: Irene Emery Roundtable on Museum Textiles 1979 Proceedings.* Washington, D.C.: The Textile Museum, 1980, pp. 357-64.

Gilfoy, Peggy S., and Vollmer, John E. "Oriental Textiles." *Arts of Asia,* XI, 2, March-April 1981, pp. 126-37.

Ginestous, P. "Tissage d'un 'hamel' à Gafsa." *Cahiers des arts et techniques d'Afrique du Nord,* II, 1953, pp. 52-62.

Gittinger, Mattiebelle. "An Introduction to the Body Tension Looms and Simple Frame Looms of Southeast Asia." *Looms and Their Products: Irene Emery Roundtable on Museum Textiles 1977 Proceedings.* Washington, D.C.: The Textile Museum, 1979 (a), pp. 54-68.

——————. *Master Dyers to the World: Technique and Trade in Early Indian Dyed Cotton Textiles.* Washington, D.C.: The Textile Museum, 1982.

——————. "Selected Batak Textiles: Technique and Function." *Textile Museum Journal,* IV, 2, 1975, p. 13.

——————. *Splendid Symbols: Textiles and Tradition in Indonesia.* Washington, D.C.: The Textile Museum, 1979 (b).

Gluck, Jay, and Gluck, Sumi Hiramoto, eds. *A Survey of Persian Handicraft.* Tehran: The Bank Melli, 1977.

Goichon, Amelie Marie. *La vie féminine au Mzab, étude de sociologie musulmane.* 2 vols. Paris: Librarie Orientaliste Paul Geuthner, 1927.

Golvin, Lucien. *Aspects de l'artisanat en Afrique du Nord.* Paris: Presses Universitaires de France, 1957.

——————. "Le 'métier' à la tire' des fabricants de brocarts de Fès." *Hespéris,* XXXVII, 1-2, 1950, pp. 21-52.

——————. "Les tapis et tissages principaux de l'Algérie." *Cahier des arts et techniques d'Afrique du Nord,* II, 1953, pp. 36-9.

Gönül, Macide. *Turkish Embroideries, XVI-XIX Centuries.* Turkey: Touring and Automobile Club of Turkey, n.d.

Goudard, J. "Tapis berbères des Beni Alaham (Moyen Atlas Marocain)." *Hespéris,* VI, 1, 1926, pp. 83-9.

de Groot, H. *The Religious Systems of China.* Vol. VI, Book II. Leiden: Brill, 1910.

Gross, Edith Loew. "Halston: Style . . . and Something More." *Vogue,* CLXX, June 1980, pp. 161-238.

Groussin, Pierre. "Note sur la teinture au Maroc." *Cahiers des arts et techniques d'Afrique du Nord,* V, 1959, pp. 111-13.

Grube, Ernst J. *The World of Islam.* New York: McGraw-Hill Book Co., 1966.

Guérard, Martha. "Contribution à l'Étude de l'Art de la Broderie au Maroc: Part I." *Hespéris-Tamuda,* VIII, 1967, pp. 5-23.

——————. "Contribution à l'Étude de l'Art de la Broderie au Maroc: Part III." *Hespéris-Tamuda,* X, 1969, pp. 191-217.

——————. "Contribution à l'Étude de l'Art de la Broderie au Maroc: Part IV." *Hespéris-Tamuda,* XV, 1974, pp. 225-50.

Guyot, R.; Le Tourneau, R., and Paye, L. "Les cordonniers des Fès." *Hespéris,* XXIII, 1, 1939, pp. 9-54.

Harris, Walter B. *Tafilet: The Narrative of a Journey of Information in the Atlas Mountains and the Oasis of the North West Sahara.* London: W. Blackwood & Sons, 1895.

Harrison, Marguerite. "Design in Old Moroccan Embroidery." *International Studio: Associated with the Connoisseur,* n.p., June 1928, pp. 28-32.

Hart, David Montgomery. *The Aith Waryaghar of the Moroccan Rif: An Ethnography and History.* Wenner-Gren Foundation for Anthropological Research, Viking Fund Publications in Anthropology, no. 55. Tucson, Arizona: University of Arizona Press, 1976.

——————. "The Tribe in Northern Morocco: Two Case Studies." *Arabs and Berbers: From Tribe to Nation in North Africa.* Edited by Ernest Gellner and Charles Micaud. Lexington, Mass.: D. C. Heath and Company, 1972.

Heine-Geldern, Robert von. *Indonesian Art: A Loan Exhibition from the Royal Indies Institute, Amsterdam, the Netherlands.* Buffalo, New York: Albright-Knox Gallery, 1949.

Hofenk-de Graaff, Judith. "Dyestuff Analysis of the Buyid Silk Fabrics of the Abegg Foundation." *Bulletin de Liaison du Centre International d'Étude des Textiles Anciens,* XXXVII, 1973, pp. 120-34.

Hoffman, Bernard G. *The Structure of Traditional Moroccan Rural Society.* The Hague: Mouton and Co., 1967.

Hoke, E., and Petrascheck-Heim, I., "Microprobe Analysis of Gilded Silver Threads from Medieval Textiles," *Studies in Conservation,* XXII, 1977, pp. 49-62.

Holmgren, Robert J., and Spertus, Anita E., "Tampan Pasisir: Pictorial Documents of an Ancient Indonesian Coastal Culture." *Indonesian Textiles: Irene Emery Roundtable on Museum Textiles 1979 Proceedings.* Washington, D.C.: The Textile Museum, 1980, pp. 157-98.

Holstein, Jonathan. *The Pieced Quilt: An American Design Tradition.* Greenwich, Conn.: New York Graphic Society, 1973.

Hours, Madeleine. *Conservation and Scientific Analysis of Painting.* New York: Van Nostrand Reinhold Co., 1976.

Hyōbu, Nishimura; Mailey, Jean; and Hayes, Jr., Joseph. *Tagasode Whose Sleeves . . . Kimono from the Kanebo Collection.* New York: Japan Society, Inc., 1976.

Identification of Textile Fibers. 7th Ed. Manchester: The Textile Institute, 1975.

Impey, Oliver. *Chinoiserie: The Impact of Oriental Styles on Western Art and Decoration.* New York: Charles Scribner's Sons, 1977.

Inventive Paris Clothes: 1909-1939. New York: A Studio Book, The Viking Press, 1977.

Irwin, John. "Bizarre Designs in Silks: *Trade and Tradition* by Vilhelm Slomann." *The Burlington Magazine,* XCVII, 1955, pp. 153-4.

——————. *The Kashmir Shawl.* London: Her Majesty's Stationery Office, 1973.

——————. *Shawls: A Study in Indo-European Influences.* London: Her Majesty's Stationery Office, 1955.

Irwin, John, and Brett, Katherine B. *Origins of Chintz.* London: Her Majesty's Stationery Office, 1970.

Irwin, John, and Hall, Margaret. *Historic Textiles of India at the Calico Museum.* Volume II: *Indian Embroideries.* Ahmedabad, India: Calico Museum of Textiles, 1973.

——————. *Historic Textiles of India at the Calico Museum.* Volume I: *Indian Painted and Printed Fabrics.* Ahmedabad, India: Calico Museum of Textiles, 1971.

Irwin, John, and Schwartz, P. R. *Studies in Indo-European Textile History.* Ahmedabad, India: Calico Museum of Textiles, 1966.

Islemeler: Ottoman Domestic Embroideries. London: David Black Oriental Carpets, 1978.

Johnstone, Pauline. *Greek Island Embroidery.* London: Alec Tiranti, 1961.

——————. *A Guide to Greek Island Embroidery.* London: The Victoria and Albert Museum, 1972.

Jones, Stella M. *Hawaiian Quilts.* Honolulu: Honolulu Academy of Arts and Mission Houses Museum, 1973.

Jouin, Jeanne. "Les Thèmes Décoratifs des Broderies Marocaines: Leur Caractère et leurs Origines, Part I." *Hespéris,* XV, 1931-32, pp. 11-52.

——————. "Les Thèmes Décoratifs des Broderies Marocaines: Leur Caractère et leurs Origines, Part II." *Hespéris,* XX, 1935-36, pp. 149-62.

Julien, Charles-André. *History of North Africa: Tunisia, Algeria, Morocco from the Arab Conquest to 1830.* Translated by John Petrie. Edited and revised by R. le Tourneau. New York: Praeger Publishers, 1970.

Kahlenberg, Mary Hunt. *Rites of Passage: Textiles of the Indonesian Archipelago from the Collection of Mary Hunt Kahlenberg.* Introduction by Bronwen and Garrett Solyom. San Diego: Mingei International Museum of World Folk Art, 1979.

——————. *Textile Traditions of Indonesia.* Los Angeles: Los Angeles County Museum of Art, 1977.

Kajitani, Nabuko. "The Physical Characteristics of Silk Generally Classified as Buyid." *Archeological Textiles: Irene Emery Roundtable on Museum Textiles 1974 Proceedings.* Washington, D.C.: The Textile Museum, 1975, pp. 191-204.

Karpinski, Caroline. "Kashmir to Paisley." *Metropolitan Museum of Art Bulletin.* New York: Metropolitan Museum of Art, November 1963, pp. 116-24.

Kartiwa, Suwati. "The Social Functions of the Kain Songket Minangkabau." *Indonesian Textiles: Irene Emery Roundtable on Museum Textiles 1979 Proceedings.* Washington, D.C.: The Textile Museum, 1980 pp. 56-80.

Katzenberg, Dena. *Blue Traditions: Indigo Dyed Textiles and Related Cobalt Glazed Ceramics from the 17th through the 19th Century.* Baltimore: The Baltimore Museum of Art, 1973.

Keck, Sheldon. *The Technical Examination of Paintings.* Brooklyn: Brooklyn Museum Journal, 1942.

Kemper, Rachael. *A History of Costume.* New York: Newsweek Books, 1977.

Kent, Kate Peck. *Introduction to West African Cloth.* Denver: Denver Museum of Natural History, 1971.

King, Donald, and Goedhuis, Michael. *Imperial Ottoman Textiles.* London: Colnaghi, n.d.

Knapp, Wilfrid. *Tunisia.* New York: Walker & Co., 1970.

Koller, P. Angelus. *Essai sur l'esprit du Berbère marocain.* 2nd Ed. Fribourg: Editions Franciscaines, 1949.

Kooijman, Simon. *Ornamented Bark Cloth in Indonesia.* Leiden: Rijksmuseum voor Volkerkunde, 1963.

——————. *Tapa in Polynesia.* Bernice P. Bishop Museum Bulletin no. 234. Honolulu: Bishop Museum Press, 1972.

Kramer, Hilton. *Richard Lindner.* Boston: Paul Bianchini, 1975.

Landreau, Anthony N. *From the Bosporus to the Samarkand: Flat-Woven Rugs.* Washington, D.C.: The Textile Museum, 1969.

——————, ed. *Yörük: The Nomadic Weaving Tradition of the Middle East.* Pittsburgh: Museum of Art, Carnegie Institute, 1978.

La Nézière, J. de. *La Décoration Marocaine.* Paris: Librarie des Arts Décoratifs, 1923.

Langewis, Laurens, and Wagner, Frits. *Decorative Art in Indonesian Textiles.* Amsterdam: C. P. J. Van der Peet, 1964.

Lantz, Elizabeth. *Moroccan Embroideries.* Unpublished research paper, 1982.

Laoust, Émile. "L'habitation chez les transhumants du Maroc central: I, La tente et le douar." *Hespéris,* X, 2, 1930, pp. 151-253.

——————. *Mots et choses berbères.* Paris: Augustin Challamel, 1920.

Lapanne-Joinville, J. "Les métiers à tisser de Fès." *Hespéris,* XXVII, 1, 1940, pp. 21-92.

Larsen, Jack Lenor. *The Dyers Art: Ikat, Batik, Plangi.* New York: Van Nostrand Reinhold, 1976.

Leared, Arthur. *Morocco and the Moors: An Account of Travels, with a General Description of the Country and its People.* 2nd Ed. Revised and edited by Sir Richard Burton. New York: Scribner and Welford, 1891.

Lee, Sarah Tomerlin, ed. *American Fashion: Fashion Institute of Technology.* New York: Quadrangle/New York Times Book Co., 1975.

Lee-Whitman, Leanna. "The Silk Trade: Chinese Silks and the British East India Co." *Winterthur Portfolio,* XVII, 1, Spring 1982, pp. 21-41.

Legey, Françoise. *The Folklore of Morocco.* Translated by Lucy Hotz. London: George Allen & Unwin Ltd., 1935.

Legeza, Laszlo. "Chinese Taoist Art." *Arts of Asia,* VII, 6, December 1977, pp. 32-7.

Lemberg, Mechthild. "The Buyid Silks of the Abegg Foundation, Berne." *Bulletin de Liaison du Centre International d'Étude des Textiles Anciens,* 37, 1973, pp. 28-54.

Leonard, Anne, and Terrell, John. *Patterns of Paradise.* Chicago: Field Museum of Natural History, 1980.

Levey, Santina. "Lace and Lace Patterned Silks: Some Comparative Illustrations." *Studies in Textile History.* Edited by V. Gervers. Toronto: The Royal Ontario Museum, 1977, pp. 184-201.

Lévi-Provençal, Évariste. *Textes Arabes de L'Ouargha: Dialect des Jbala (Maroc Septentrional).* Publications de l'Institut des Hautes Études Marocaines, no. 9. Paris: Éditions Ernest Leroux, 1922.

Link, Howard A. *Exquisite Visions: Rimpa Paintings from Japan.* Honolulu: Honolulu Academy of Arts, 1980.

Liu, Robert K., and Wataghani, Liza. "Moroccan Folk Jewelry." *African Arts,* VIII, 2, 1975, pp. 28-35, 80.

Lombard, Maurice. "Les Textiles dans le Monde Musulman du VIIe au XIIe Siècle." *Études d'Économie Médiévale.* 3 vols. Paris: Mouton Éditeur, 1978.

Lubell, Cecil, ed. *Textile Collections of the World.* 3 vols. New York: Van Nostrand Reinhold, 1976, 1976, 1977.

Mackie, Louise W. *The Splendor of Turkish Weaving.* Washington, D.C.: The Textile Museum, 1973.

Mackie, Louise, and Thompson, Jon, eds. *Turkmen: Tribal Carpets and Traditions.* Washington, D.C.: The Textile Museum, 1980.

McClellan, Elizabeth. *History of American Costume, 1607-1870.* New York: Tudor Pub. Co., 1969.

McCreary, Carol Fillips. *The Traditional Moroccan Loom: Its Construction and Use.* Santa Rosa, Cal.: Tresh Publications, 1975.

McMorris, Penny. *Crazy Quilts.* New York: E. P. Dutton, 1983.

MacMillan, Susan L. *Greek Island Embroideries.* Boston: Museum of Fine Arts, n.d.

Maeder, Edward, ed. *An Elegant Art: Fashion and Fantasy in the 18th Century.* Los Angeles: Los Angeles County Museum of Art, 1983.

Maher, Vanessa. *Women and Property in Morocco.* London: Cambridge University Press, 1974.

Marçais, Georges. *Le costume musulman d'Algér.* Paris: Librarie Plon, 1930.

Marçais, W. "Djellāb." *Encyclopedia of Islam,* Vol. I. Leyden: Brill, 1913.

——————. *Textes Arabes de Tanger.* Paris: Leroux, 1911.

de Mármol, Carvajal Luis. *L'Afrique de Marmol.* 3 vols. Translated by Nicolas Perrot sieur d'Ablancourt. Paris: Louis Billame, 1667.

Mauersberger, Herbert R., ed. *Matthews' Textile Fibers: Their Physical, Microscopical and Chemical Properties.* 5th Ed. New York: John Wiley & Sons, 1947.

Maxwell, John R., and Maxwell, Robyn J. *Textiles of Indonesia: An Introductory Handbook.* Victoria, Australia: Indonesian Arts Society, National Gallery of Victoria, 1976.

Maxwell, Robyn J. "Textile and Ethnic Configurations in Flores and the Solor Archipelago." *Indonesian Textiles: Irene Emery Roundtable on Museum Textiles 1979 Proceedings.* Washington, D.C.: The Textile Museum 1980, pp. 141-55.

May, Florence Lewis. *Silk Textiles of Spain: Eighth–Fifteenth Centuries.* New York: The Hispanic Society of America, 1957.

Mayer-Thurman, Christa C. *Raiment for the Lord's Service: A Thousand Years of Western Vestments.* Chicago: The Art Institute of Chicago, 1975.

Meakin, Budgett. *Life in Morocco and Glimpses Beyond.* London: Chatto and Windus, 1905.

——————. *The Moors: A Comprehensive Description.* London: S. Sonnenschein & Co., 1902.

Menzel, Dorothy. *The Archeology of Ancient Peru and the Work of Max Uhle.* Berkeley: Lowie Museum of Anthropology, University of California at Berkeley, 1977.

Meyer-Heisig, Erich. *Weberei Nadelwerk Zeugdruck.* Munich: Prestel Verlag, n.d.

Micaud, Ellen. "The Craft Tradition in North Africa." *African Arts,* III, 2, Winter 1970, pp. 38-43, 81, 90-91.

Mikesell, Marvin W. *Northern Morocco: A Cultural Geography.* University of California Publications in Geography, no. 14. Berkeley and Los Angeles: University of California Press, 1961.

Miller, David. "Conservation Laboratory Examination Techniques and Conservator's Report." *Perceptions,* Indianapolis Museum of Art, vol. 1, 1981, pp. 23-33.

Minnich, Helen Benton. *Japanese Costume and the Makers of its Elegant Tradition.* Tokyo: Charles E. Tuttle Co., 1963.

Montagne, Robert. *Les Berbères et le makhzen dans le sud du Maroc.* Paris: F. Alcan, 1930.

——————. *The Berbers: Their Social and Political Organisation.* Translated by David Seddon. London: Frank Cass & Co., Ltd., 1973.

Montbard, Georges. *Among the Moors: Sketches of Oriental Life.* London: S. Low, Marston and Co., 1894.

Montgomery, Florence M. *Printed Textiles: English and American Cottons and Linens, 1700-1850.* New York: Viking Press, 1970.

Montgomery, Pauline. *Indiana Weavers and Their Coverlets.* Indianapolis: Hoosier Heritage Press, 1974.

Morris and Company, 1861-1940. London: The Arts Council, 1961.

Murdock, George Peter. *Africa, Its People and Their Culture History.* New York: McGraw-Hill Book Co., 1959.

da Mota, A. Teixera. *Some Aspects of Portuguese Colonisation and Sea Trade in West Africa in the 15th and 16th Centuries.* Hans Wolff Memorial Lecture, no. 7. Bloomington, Indiana: Indiana University African Studies Program, 1978.

Nanavati, J. M. *The Embroidery and Beadwork of Kutch and Saurashtra.* Gujarat State, India: Department of Archaeology, 1966.

Naval Intelligence Division, Government of Great Britain, Foreign Office. *Morocco.* 2 vols. Geographical Handbook Series, B. R. 506A. London: Her Majesty's Stationery Office, 1941/42.

Naylor, Gillian. *The Arts and Crafts Movement.* Cambridge, Mass.: The M.I.T. Press, 1980.

Noma, Seiroku. *Japanese Costume and Textile Arts.* Tokyo: Weatherhill/Heibonsha, 1974.

O'Conner, Francis V. *WPA: Art for the Millions.* [Greenwich, Conn.]: New York Graphic Society, 1973.

Olson, Eleanor. *Catalogue of the Tibetan Collection and Other Lamaist Articles.* Newark: The Newark Museum, 1951.

Orlofsky, Patsy, and Orlofsky, Myron. *Quilts in America.* New York: McGraw-Hill Book Co., 1974.

Osma, Guillermo de. *Mariano Fortuny: His Life and Work.* New York: Rizzoli, 1980.

Pantzer, Kurt F. "The Provenance of the Tapestries." *Art Association of Indianapolis Bulletin,* LIII, 1, March 1966, pp. 11-24.

Paul, Anne Cheryl. *Paracas Ritual Attire: Symbols of Authority in Ancient Peru.* Ph.D. dissertation, University of Texas at Austin, 1980.

——————. *Paracas Textiles Selected from the Museum's Collection.* Göteborg: n.p., 1979.

Peebles, Merrily. *Court and Village: India's Textile Traditions.* Santa Barbara: Santa Barbara Museum of Art, 1981.

Pereira, Duarte Pacheco. *Esmeraldo de Situ Orbis.* Translated and edited by George H. T. Kimble. Hakluyt Society Works, no. LXXIX. London: The Hakluyt Society, 1937.

Pertegato, Francesco, ed. *Conservazione E Restauro Dei Tessili: Convegno Internazionale, Como, 1980.* Milan: Centro Italiano per lo Studio della Storia del Tessuto, 1982.

Petsopoulos, Yanni, ed. *Tulips, Arabesques and Turbans: Decorative Art from the Ottoman Empire.* New York: Abbeville Press, 1982.

Pettit, Florence H. *America's Indigo Blues.* New York: Hastings House, 1974.

——————. "The Printed Textiles of 18th-Century America." *Imported and Domestic Textiles in 18th-Century America: Irene Emery Roundtable on Museum Textiles 1975 Proceedings.* Washington, D.C.: The Textile Museum, 1975, pp. 33-57.

Picton, John, and Mack, John. *African Textiles.* London: British Museum Publications, Ltd., 1979.

Plummer, Cheryl. *African Textiles.* East Lansing: Michigan State University, 1971.

Poinssot, L., and Revault, Jacques. *Tapis Tunisiens.* 3 vols. Paris: Horizons de France, 1950, 1953, 1955.

Pommerol, Jean. *Among the Women of the Sahara.* Translated by Mrs. Arthur Bell. London: Hurst and Blackett, Ltd., 1900.

Pope, Arthur Upham, and Ackerman, Phyllis, eds. *A Survey of Persian Art,* Vol. 5. Tehran: Soroush Press, 1977.

Priest, Alan, and Simmons, Pauline. *Chinese Textiles.* New York: Metropolitan Museum of Art, 1934.

Rackow, Ernst. *Beiträge zur Kenntnis der Materiellen Kultur Nordwest-Marokkos: Wohnraum, Hausrat, Kostüm.* Wiesbaden: Otto Harrassonwitz, 1958.

Reath, Nancy A., and Sachs, Eleanor B. *Persian Textiles and their Technique from the Sixth to the Eighteenth Centuries, including a System for General Textile Classification.* New Haven: Yale University Press, 1937.

Reswick, Irmtraud. "Traditional Textiles of Tunisia." *African Arts,* XIV, 3, 1981, pp. 56-65, 92.

Revault, Jacques. "Broderies Tunisiennes." *Les Cahiers de Tunisie,* VIII, 1960.

——————. *Designs and Patterns from North African Carpets and Textiles.* New York: Dover Publications, Inc., 1973.

——————. "Note sur la rénovation des tapis à haute laine et à poil ras en Tunisie." *Cahiers des arts et techniques d'Afrique du Nord,* IV, 1955, pp. 81-95.

Ricard, Prosper. *Arts Marocains: Broderies.* Alger: Editions J. Carbonel, 1918.

——————. "Le batik berbère." *Hespéris,* IV, 4, 1925, pp. 411-26.

——————. *Corpus des Tapis Marocains,* 3 vols. Paris: Librarie Orientaliste Paul Geuthner, 1923, 1926, 1927.

——————. "Les métiers manuels à Fès." *Hespéris,* IV, 2, 1924, pp. 205-24.

——————. *Moroccan Carpets.* Paris: Office Marocain du Tourisme et Office Cherifien de Controle et d'Exportation, 1952.

——————. "Note annexe sur les 'hanbels' nord-africains." *Annales de l'Institut d'Études Orientales,* II. Paris: Librarie Larose, 1936.

——————. *Pour Comprendre l'Art Musulman dans l'Afrique du Nord et en Espagne.* Paris: Hachette, 1924.

——————. "Technique et rites du travail de la laine en Algérie." *Mémorial Henri Basset: Nouvelles études nord-africaines et orientales.* Publications de l'Institut des Hautes Études Marocaines, XVIII. Paris: Librarie Orientaliste Paul Geuthner, 1928.

Ricard, Robert. "Le commerce de Berbérie et l'organisation economique d l'Empire Portugais aux XVe et XVIe siècles." *Annales de l'Institut d'Études Orientales,* II. Paris: Librarie Larose, 1936.

Risselin-Steenebrugen, M. *Trois Siècles de Dentelles.* Brussels: Musèe Royaux d'Art et d'Histoire, 1980.

Rohlfs, Gerhard. *Adventures in Morocco and Journeys through the Oases of Draa and Tafilet.* London: S. Low, Marston & Searle, 1874.

Rosen, Lawrence. "Social Identity and Points of Attachment: Approaches to Social Organization." *Meaning and Order in Moroccan Society: Three Essays in Cultural Analysis.* Cambridge, England: Cambridge University Press, 1979.

——————. "The Social and Conceptual Framework of Arab-Berber Relations in Central Morocco." *Arabs and Berbers: From Tribe to Nation in North Africa.* Edited by Ernest Gellner and Charles Micaud. Lexington, Mass.: D. C. Heath and Co., 1972.

Rosenblum, Robert. *Transformations in Late Eighteenth Century Art.* Princeton, N.J.: Princeton University Press, 1967.

Ross, Denman W. "Some Textiles from Morocco." *Bulletin of the Boston Museum of Fine Arts,* XX, 1922, pp. 36-9.

Rossbach, Ed. *The Art of Paisley.* New York: Van Nostrand Reinhold, 1980.

Roth, H. Ling. *Studies in Primitive Looms.* Halifax: Bankfield Museum, 1918.

Rothstein, Natalie. "Ornements d'Église." *Bulletin de Liaison du Centre International d'Étude des Textiles Anciens,* III, p. 85.

Rousseau, Gabriel. *L'Art Décoratif Musulman.* Paris: Marcel Rivière, Éditeur, 1934.

——————. *Le costume au Maroc.* Paris: Boccard, 1938.

Rowe, Ann Pollard. *A Century of Change in Guatemalan Textiles.* New York: The Center for Inter-American Relations, 1981.

——————. *Warp-Patterned Weaves of the Andes.* Washington, D.C.: The Textile Museum, 1977.

Sammlung Leopold Ikle, St. Gallen Textilien. Katalogband, I (teil), II (tafeln), n.p., 1923.

Samte, Velvets, Velours. Krefeld: Das Textilmuseum Krefeld, 1979.

Sandler, R. "Islamic Art: Variations on Themes of Arabesque." *Islamic Civilization.* Edited by R. M. Savory. Cambridge, England: Cambridge University Press, 1976.

Santangelo, Antonio. *A Treasury of Great Italian Textiles.* New York: Harry N. Abrams, Inc., 1964.

Schacht, Joseph, and Basworth, C. E., eds. *The Legacy of Islam.* Oxford: Clarendon Press, 1974.

Schoelwer, Susan Prendergast. *A Rustle of Silk: Costumes from the Caroline Burford Danner Estate.* Indianapolis: Indianapolis Museum of Art, 1979.

Secret Splendors of the Chinese Court: Qing Dynasty Costume from the Charlotte Hill Grant Collection. Denver: Denver Art Museum, 1981.

Seddon, J. David. "Local Politics and State Intervention: Northeast Morocco from 1870 to 1970." *Arabs and Berbers: From Tribe to Nation in North Africa.* Edited by Ernest Gellner and Charles Micaud. Lexington, Mass.: D. C. Heath and Co., 1972.

Seni, Nihon, and Sentā, Ishō. *Textile Designs of Japan.* 2 vols. Osaka: Japan Textile Color Design Center, 1962.

Serjeant, Robert B. *Islamic Textiles: Material for a History up to the Mongol Conquest.* Beirut: Librarie du Liban, 1972.

Sethom, Samira. "La Tunique de Mariage en Tunisie." *Cahiers des Arts et Traditions Populaires,* III, 1969, pp. 5-20.

Shepherd, Dorothy G. "Medieval Persian Silks in Fact and Fancy (A Refutation of the Riggisberg Report)." *Bulletin de Liaison du Centre International d'Étude des Textiles Anciens,* XXXIX/XL, 1974.

——————. "The Archeology of the Buyid Textiles." *Archeological Textiles: Irene Emery Roundtable on Museum Textiles 1974 Proceedings.* Washington, D.C.: The Textile Museum, 1975, pp. 175-90.

Sieber, Roy. *African Textiles and Decorative Arts.* New York: Museum of Modern Art, 1972.

Sijelmassi, Mohamed. *Les Arts Traditionnels au Maroc.* Paris: l'Avenir Graphique, 1974.

Sill, Gertrude Grace. *A Handbook of Symbols in Christian Art.* New York: MacMillan, 1975.

Singh, Chandramani. *Textiles and Costumes from the Maharaja Sawai Man Singh II Museum.* Jaipur: n.p., 1979.

Simeon, Margaret. *The History of Lace.* London: Stainer and Bell, 1979.

Simmons, Pauline. *Chinese Patterned Silks*. New York: Metropolitan Museum of Art, 1948.

Slomann, Vilhelm. *Bizarre Designs in Silks, Trade and Traditions*. Copenhagen: Ejnar Munksgaard, 1953.

Slouschz, Nahum. *Travels in North Africa*. Philadelphia: The Jewish Publication Society of America, 1927.

Snook, Barbara. *Embroidery Stitches*. London: B. T. Batsford Ltd., 1963.

Solyom, Bronwen, and Solyom, Garrett. "Cosmic Symbolism in Semen and Alasalasan Patterns in Javanese Textiles." *Indonesian Textiles: Irene Emery Roundtable on Museum Textiles 1979 Proceedings*. Washington, D.C.: The Textile Museum, 1980, pp. 248-74.

Sonday, Milton. *Lace in the Collection of the Cooper-Hewitt Museum*. Washington: Smithsonian Institution Press, 1982.

Sonday, Milton, and Moss, Gillian. *Western European Embroidery in the Collection of the Cooper-Hewitt Museum*. New York: Cooper-Hewitt Museum, 1978.

Spanish Textile Tradition of New Mexico and Colorado. Santa Fe, New Mexico: Museum of International Folk Art, 1979.

Spencer, William. *Historical Dictionary of Morocco*. Metuchen, N.J.: The Scarecrow Press, 1980.

——————. *The Land and People of Tunisia*. New York: J. B. Lippincott Co., 1967.

Stapley, Mildred. *Popular Weaving and Embroidery in Spain*. New York: William Helburn, Inc., 1924.

Steinman, Alfred. *Batik: A Survey of Batik Design*. Leigh-on-Sea: F. Lewis Publishers, Ltd., 1958.

——————. "Batiks." *Ciba Review*, LVIII, 1947, pp. 2090-2125.

——————. "The Patterning of Ikats." *Ciba Review*, XLIV, 1942, pp. 1612-18.

Stillman, Yedida K. "The Evil Eye in Morocco." *Folklore Research Center Studies*, Vol. I. Edited by Dov Noy and Issachar Ben-Ami. Jerusalem: The Magus Press, 1970.

Symbols of Faith. Washington, D.C.: National Committee, Islam Centennial Fourteen, 1981.

Terrasse, Henri, and Hainaut, Jean. *Les Arts Décoratifs au Maroc*. Paris: Henri Laurens Éditeur, 1925.

Textiles and Ornaments of India. New York: Museum of Modern Art, 1972.

Thomson, Joseph. *Travels in the Atlas and Southern Morocco: A Narrative of Exploration*. New York: Longmans, Green and Co., 1889.

Thornton, Peter. *Baroque and Rococo Silks*. New York: Taplinger Pub. Co., Inc., 1965.

Tirtaamidjaja, N. *Penerbit Djambatan*. Translated by B. R. O. G. Anderson. Djakarta: n.p., 1966.

Tokugawa, Yoshinobu. *The Tokugawa Collection: Nō Robes and Masks*. Translated by Louise Allison Cort and Monica Bethe. New York: Japan Society, 1977.

Torrens, Deborah. *Fashion Illustrated*. New York: Hawthorn Book, Inc., 1975.

Le Tourneau, Roger. *Fez in the Age of the Marinids*. Translated by Besse Alberta Clement. Norman: University of Oklahoma Press, 1961.

——————. *La vie quotidienne à Fès en 1900*. Paris: Hachette, 1965.

Treasures of Indian Textiles, Calico Museum, Ahmedabad. Bombay: Marg Publications, 1980.

Trudel, Verena. "Swiss Linen Embroidery." *Ciba Review*, LXXIX, April 1950, pp. 2870-94.

Tschebull, Raoul. *Kazak: Carpets of the Caucasus*. New York: New York Rug Society, Inc., 1971.

Tuchscherer, Jean-Michel, and Vial, Gabriel. *Le Musée Historique des Tissus de Lyon*. Lyon: Albert Guillot, 1977.

d'Ucel, Jeanne. *Berber Art: An Introduction*. Norman: University of Oklahoma Press, 1932.

Uzbek: The Textiles and Life of the Nomadic and Sedentary Uzbek Tribes of Central Asia. Basel: n.p., 1975.

Vaclavir, Antonin, and Orel, Jaroslav. *Textile Folk Art*. London: Spring Books, n.d.

Vial, Gabriel. "Technical Study of the Buyid Silk Fabrics of the Abegg Foundation." *Bulletin de Liaison du Centre International d'Étude des Textiles Anciens*, XXXVII, 1973, pp. 70-103.

Vial, Gabriel, and Gruber, Alain. *Ceintures Marocaines*. Berne: Fondation Abegg, 1980.

Vicaire, Marcel. "La fabrication des Taritat Ahel Telt." *Quatrième Congrès de la Fédération des Sociétés Savantes de l'Afrique du Nord, Rabat 18-20, Avril, 1938*, Volume II. Algiers: Société Historique Algérienne, 1939.

Vicaire, Marcel; Le Tourneau, R.; and Noyelle, I. "La technique du tissage à Fès et les moyens propres à l'améliorer." *Quatrième Congrès de la Fédération des Sociétés Savants de l'Afrique du Nord, Rabat 18-20, Avril, 1938*, Volume II. Algiers: Société Historique Algérienne, 1939.

Vinogradov, Amal R. "The Socio-Political Organization of a Berber 'Taraf' Tribe: Pre-Protectorate Morocco." *Arabs and Berbers: From Tribe to Nation in North Africa*. Edited by Ernest Gellner and Charles Micaud. Lexington, Mass.: D. C. Heath and Co., 1972.

Voe, J. "Textile Patterns and the 'Evil Eye.'" *Ciba Review*, XXI, May 1939, p. 763.

Vogelsanger, Cornelia. "A Sight for the Gods: Notes on the Social and Religious Meaning of Iban Ritual Fabrics." *Indonesian Textiles: Irene Emery Roundtable on Museum Textiles 1979 Proceedings*. Washington, D.C.: The Textile Museum, 1980, pp. 115-26.

Vogt, John. "Notes on the Portuguese Cloth Trade in West Africa, 1480-1540." *International Journal of African Historical Studies*, VIII, 4, 1975, pp. 623-51.

Vollmer, John E. "Archaeological Evidence for Looms from Yunnan." *Looms and Their Products: Irene Emery Roundtable on Museum Textiles 1977 Proceedings*. Washington, D.C.: The Textile Museum, 1979, pp. 78-89.

——————. "Chinese Tapestry Weaving: K'o-ssu." *Hali*, V, 1, 1982, pp. 36-43.

——————. "Costume as Symbol in Traditional China." *Arts of Asia*, VIII, 5, October 1978, pp. 42-53.

——————. *Decoding Dragons*. Eugene: University of Oregon, 1983.

——————. *Five Colours of the Universe: Symbolism in Clothes and Fabrics of the Ch'ing Dynasty (1644-1911)*. Edmonton: Edmonton Art Gallery, 1980.

——————. *In the Presence of the Dragon Throne: Ch'ing Dynasty Costume (1644-1911) in the Royal Ontario Museum*. Toronto: Royal Ontario Museum, 1977.

Vollmer, John E. and Webb, Glenn T. *Japanese Art*. Victoria: The Art Gallery of Greater Victoria, 1972.

Wace, A. J. B. *Catalogue of Algerian Embroideries*. London: The Victoria and Albert Museum, 1935.

——————. *Mediterranean and Near Eastern Embroideries: From the Collection of Mrs. F. H. Cook*. London: Halton and Co., Ltd., 1935.

Walz, Barbara and Morris, Bernadine. *The Fashion Makers*. New York: Random House, 1978.

Wardle, Patricia. *Victorian Lace*. New York: Frederick A. Praeger, 1968.

Wardwell, Anne, "The Holy Kinship: A Sixteenth Century Immaculist Embroidery." *Bulletin of the Cleveland Museum of Art*, November 1980.

Wasserman, Tamara E., and Hill, Johnathan S. *Bolivian Indian Textiles: Traditional Designs and Costumes*. New York: Dover Publications, 1981.

Waugh, Nora. *The Cut of Women's Clothes, 1600-1930*. New York: Theatre Arts Books, 1968.

Weibel, Adele. *2000 Years of Silk Weaving*. Los Angeles: Los Angeles County Museum of Art, 1944.

——————. *2000 Years of Textiles*. New York: Hacker Art Books, 1972.

Weinhardt, Jr., Carl J. "A Splendid Gift of Tapestries." *Art Association of Indianapolis Bulletin*, LIII, 1, March 1966, pp. 5-10.

Westermarck, Edward. "The Magic Origin of Moorish Design." *Journal of the Royal Anthropological Society*, XXIV, 1904, pp. 212-22.

——————. *Ritual and Belief in Morocco*. 2 vols. London: MacMillan and Co., Ltd., 1926.

William Morris. London: The Victoria and Albert Museum, 1958.

Wilson, Kax. *A History of Textiles*. Boulder, Colo.: Westview Press, 1979.

Woven Treasures of Persian Art. Los Angeles: Los Angeles County Museum of Art, 1959.

Wulff, Hans E. *The Traditional Crafts of Persia*. Cambridge, Mass.: The M.I.T. Press, 1966.

Index

A

B

P

painted, *30*, 90, 93, 124, 126, 131, 136, 138, 144, 146, 148, 150

paisley, *300*, 301, 302

pakiri mbala, 83

palampore, 108, 111, 112

palang posh, 108

Palembang, 75, 76

palepai, 70

pallav, 106

palmette (see pomegranate)

pants, 159, 284

paper mulberry, *25*, 90, 92, 93

Paracas, 349

Paris, 221, 223, 257, 338

Patan, 106

patania quilts, 104

patchwork (see pieced work)

patola, 65, 66, 77, 78, 80, 83, 97, *106*

patolu sari, 106

pattern books, 236, 255

pattern drawers, 180, 202, 208, 239, 257, 262, 278, 280, 282, 290, 292, 294, 298, 330, 332, 336

pattern warp (also see supplementary warp, pattern), *30*

pattern weft (also see supplementary weft, pattern), *30*

pawlonia, *141*, 142, 148

Pazaryk, 152

Pekalongan, 69

Periplus of the Erythrian Sea, 288

Persepolis, 152

Persia (see Iran)

Persian (also see Iranian), 56

Peru, 349, 350

peşkir, *172*

petono, 90

petticoat, 112, 222, 280

phanung, *114*

Philippines, 89, 106, 134

Phoenician, 191

phoenix, 68, 121, 129, 139, 142, 143, 148

picots, *252*, 253

pieced work, *30*, 115, 139, 141, 142, 163, 206, 300, 312, 318, 336

pile-on-pile velvet, *30*, 224, 228, 229

Pine, Plum, and Bamboo (see Three Wintry Comrades)

plaid, *300*

plain and twill weaves (damask), 121

plain weave, balanced, *30*, 67, 68, 69, 71, 77, 83, 106, 110, 112, 114, 136, 144, 157, 159, 160, 161, 172, 173, 174, 175, 180, 202, 204, 205, 206, 207, 208, 234, 236, 237, 246, 254, 255, 280, 288, 290, 292, 294, 296, 298, 308, 309, 314, 315, 316, 328, 330, 334, 342, 349, 350, 358

plain weave, warp-faced or warp-dominant, *30*, 72, 79, 80, 82, 84, 88, 89, 134, 176, 178, 179, 278, 279, 284, 320, 322, 338, 351, 358

plain weave, weft-faced or weft-dominant, *30*, 76, 111, 148, 150, 159, 160, 194, 209, 214, 216

plain weave with discontinuous weft (also see kilim, k'o-ssu, tapestry weave), *30*, 124, 126, 133, 164, 184, 210, 211, 212, 240, 354

plaiting, *30*

plangi, *30*, 80, 98, 138, 143, 144, 146, 209

platyphylla, *175*

point de gaz, *304*

point de Paris, *256*

point de rose, *256*

point plat, *252*

points rentrès, *262*

polonaise, *280*, 320

Polynesia, 90, 92, 93

pomegranate, 171, 192, 224, 226, 230, 232

pomme de pin (see pomegranate)

"poor man's tapestry," 228

Portugal, 65, 96, 138, 212, 233, 251

pounced, *108*, *112*, 115

pouter pigeon, 223

prada, *30*, *68*, 76

prayer rug, 188

pre-Columbian, 349, 350

printed (also see copper plate printed, copper roller printed, block printed), 93, 159, 288, 290, 292, 294, 296, 298, 329, 330, 332, 334

printing technique, 222, 290, 332

Prologomenes, 196

prophylactic patterns, 181, 194, 206, 218

pua, 65, *86*, 88

puns (see rebus)

pusher machine, 303

putti, 306

Q

qmajja, *192*

quercitron, 296

quilted, *30*, 108, 168, 176, 255, 314, 316, *318*

quilters, 314, 316

quilting bee, 314

R

Rabat, 214

radigup, *72*

raffia, *25*, 358

rafugar, *115*

ramie, *25*, 119, 142, 211

rangara, *98*

rayon (see synthetic fiber)

Rayy, 154, 191

ready-to-wear, 338

rebus, 118, 121, 124, 126, 129, 131, 132

religious garments (see ceremonial cloth)

Renaissance Europe, 207, 221, 224, 226, 228, 230, 232, 239, 300